An Introductory English Grammar

FIFTH EDITION

An Introductory English Grammar

FIFTH EDITION

NORMAN C. STAGEBERG
Late of the University of Northern Iowa

DALLIN D. OAKS
Brigham Young University

THOMSON

™

WADSWORTH

Australia Canada Mexico Singapore Spain United Kingdom United States

An Introductory English Grammar
Fifth Edition
Norman C. Stageberg and Dallin D. Oaks

Publisher: *Earl McPeek*
Market Strategist: *John Meyers*
Project Editor: *Kathryn M. Stewart*
Art Director: *Sue Hart*
Production Manager: *Cindy Young*

Cover Image: *Courtesy of Cluzi Design*

Printed in the United States of America
5 6 7 8 — 08 07 06 05 04

For more information contact Thomson Wadsworth, 25 Thomson Place, Boston, MA 02210 US, or you can visit our Internet site at http://www.thomson.com

Some material in this work previously appeared in AN INTRODUCTORY ENGLISH GRAMMAR copyright © 1981, 1977, 1971, 1965 Wadsworth. All rights reserved.

Copyrights and Acknowledgements appear on page C-1, which constitutes a continuation of the copyright page.

ISBN: 0-0301-8384-7

Library of Congress Catalog Card Number: 99-67364

Preface

It has been a number of years since the previous edition of *An Introductory English Grammar* first appeared. As some may have guessed, the delay in the appearance of a new edition stems from the death of Norman C. Stageberg. The enduring popularity of his textbook, however, has suggested that many teachers of grammar and introductory linguistics courses prefer his approach over those of newer books. But even a popular and effective textbook needs to be updated every few years, and it has been my privilege to prepare this latest edition. I have tried to preserve those features most appreciated by teachers and students, such as the largely structuralist orientation, the incremental approach to teaching about the structure of the English language, and the large number of exercises.

The book maintains its basic structuralist approach to language, but it is perhaps a little more eclectic in some places than earlier editions. A close examination of this new edition will reveal some places where transformational grammar has influenced a particular discussion or treatment of a grammatical issue; for example, questions are handled as transformations of statements, and where the previous edition might refer to a "noun," acknowledging that other modifiers might also be present, this edition uses the term "noun phrase" (which in transformational grammar can consist of a single word).

This latest edition has a number of features that distinguish it from the previous edition. One of these features is the inclusion of an applications section after each chapter, indicating how some of the content of the chapter can be applied in different fields or tasks. In addition, each chapter is now preceded by an observation, joke, or quotation that relates to something in the chapter and which is intended to help draw students into that chapter.

Two new chapters have been added. One of these, Chapter 18, treats usage, and the other, Chapter 19, outlines some matters of dialects and historical linguistics. Because the focus of this text is on the structure of language rather than an attempt to survey the field of linguistics, these two chapters are not intended to be thorough treatments of their subject areas but rather illustrative of phonological, morphological, and syntactic concepts and information that appear in previous chapters.

Another difference between the two editions occurs in the use of tree diagrams rather than bracketing to show morphemic constituent structure. An appendix briefly introduces students to tree diagrams of sentence structures. Also included is a new appendix that introduces students to transformational grammar. Although there are newer grammatical models than the transformational one, none of the newer grammatical models has been as influential. The model remains an important one for students to study.

In his previous edition, Stageberg acknowledged the importance of many individuals in helping him prepare his book, and he singled out several individuals whose academic treatments of particular subjects were formative in his shaping of several chapters in the text. Those chapters remain in this text, even as some changes have been introduced, so it seems fitting once again to acknowledge those individuals. In Stageberg's words from the 4th edition: "For particular works I owe an especially heavy debt of gratitude to three linguists. Ilse Lehiste's *An Acoustic-Phonetic Study of Internal Open Juncture* furnished the information for my pages on internal open juncture. Archibald A. Hill's chapter on phonotactics in his *Introduction to Linguistic Structures* is the source of my treatment of the distribution of phonemes. James Sledd's *A Short Introduction to English Grammar* suggested the pattern for the double-track system of parts of speech that I have adopted."

On my part, I would like to acknowledge the useful suggestions that I have received from the following reviewers: William Lutz, Rutgers University at Camden; George K. Monroe, Kutztown University; Gordon Loberger, Murray State University; and Janet Baker, National University. In addition to the reviewers, I am grateful to my colleagues Paul Baltes and Don Norton. Besides providing some helpful direction, Paul Baltes authored the appendix material introducing transformational grammar, and Don Norton co-authored the chapter on usage. I also wish to thank my acquisitions editor, Claire Brantley, and my development editor, Kim Allison, as well as others who served in the production work of this book. Special thanks also goes to June Stageberg and Michael A. Rosenberg for their encouragement and support in getting this project underway, and to my wife, Marleen, for her enduring support and patience with my project. Last of all, I pay tribute to Norman C. Stageberg, a great teacher and scholar, who wrote a book that was worth updating.

Dallin D. Oaks

Contents

Part Two

Part Three

THE SYNTAX OF ENGLISH   201

Part Four

FURTHER PERSPECTIVES 315

18. Usage 317

19. Language Variation: Historical, Regional, and Social 347

Appendix A: A Basic Introduction to Tree Diagramming 369

Introduction

As the title of this book indicates, the subject matter that you will be studying is the grammar of English. For many students the term *grammar* is associated with prescriptivism, that is, an approach that prescribes sets of rules to be followed, such as not using the contraction *ain't*. And to the degree that spoken or written forms comply with these rules, prescriptivists label them as "correct" or "incorrect." In contrast to the prescriptive approach, the focus of this book is descriptive. In other words we will describe patterns and forms as they are used by native speakers of our language. An example of a descriptive rule would be that speakers of English form the past tense of most verbs by adding the suffix -*ed*, or that questions requiring a yes or no answer usually begin with an auxiliary verb.

The term *grammar* as it is used in this book thus refers to the systems and patterns of our language as well as their description. In addition to syntax, that is, word ordering, our discussion of these systems and patterns includes some attention to sounds and minimal units of meaning. Thus we will be looking at not only syntax, but phonology and morphology as well.

Although the grammatical information in this book is known by native speakers, much of it is known only on an unconscious level. For example, most native speakers, unless they have had some training in linguistics, would be unable to explain how they form the different sounds of their language and how these sounds are transformed as they combine with other sounds. But this lack of a conscious understanding of the sound system has not interfered with the ability of native speakers to communicate. We might therefore ask why there is any point in learning about language patterns that we intuitively know anyway and can follow without any conscious training.

One answer to this may be that, like art and music, the study of language provides important insights into our own humanity. One well-known linguist has remarked, "To acquire insight into the workings of a language, and to recognize the infinitely delicate system of relationship, balance, and interplay that constitutes its grammar, is to become closely acquainted with one of man's most miraculous creations, not unworthy to be set beside the equally beautiful organization of the physical universe."[1]

---

[1]"Revolution in Grammar" by W. Nelson Francis as it appears in *Linguistics for Teachers,* ed. Linda Miller Cleary and Michael D. Linn. New York: McGraw-Hill, 1993, p. 439.

1

But perhaps a more powerful argument for the value of grammar study is a pragmatic one. Grammar study equips people to make more informed decisions in a variety of tasks and settings. In short it helps people to be more resourceful in problem solving. Why would this be the case? A solid theoretical understanding of a subject matter is often a precondition of creative application, which can include diagnosing problems and resolving them. It is common for people not to pay much attention to how something works until a problem develops or a new task appears. This is generally true whether we are speaking of our cars, our physical bodies, or even the language we speak. But once confronted with a new problem or situation, people often become very interested in principles and theories they once took for granted. Someone with an understanding of the theory behind how things work is much more likely to be able not only to resolve an existing problem but to be more resourceful in adjusting to changing circumstances.

Most of the chapters in this book contain an application section that briefly illustrates applications of the material presented in the chapter. These sections are not intended to be exhaustive, presenting the only ways in which the material in the chapter is relevant or applicable. Rather, they are meant only to give an idea of some of the ways in which the material you have studied could be useful. Other applications will perhaps occur to you as you work through this book. And some applications no doubt await a future circumstance that might make a person's knowledge of how language works vital to the successful completion of a project. For example, the advent and continued development of computers has certainly required a greater conscious awareness of linguistic issues from programmers who have sought to equip computers with language capabilities.

Throughout most of this book we will employ a synchronic approach. A synchronic approach is one in which we limit our consideration to a particular point in time. More specifically, we will be examining American English as it exists now, and the rules we express apply to how the language is put together in our time. Naturally, if we were to discuss how sentences were formed one thousand years ago, our descriptions would be very different. One chapter in this text, however, does address some diachronic analysis, that is, a consideration across time. Because some knowledge about the history of the English language is useful, and because so much of that history illustrates and exemplifies the kinds of materials that are presented throughout this text, we have included a brief discussion of the history of the English language in chapter 19. The same is true of dialectal differences in English, which are also briefly treated in the same chapter.

Although the focus of this book is descriptive as it outlines the structural patterns of the language, we realize that one of the reasons that some students have for studying grammar is the greater understanding it can provide about the prescriptive rules (the rules about the so-called "proper" forms) that traditional grammarians have advocated and which students are expected to know. We have therefore included a chapter on usage, which discusses some of the prescriptive rules of the language in the light of the grammatical information you will have studied in this text. In addition, some of the application sections throughout the book draw connections between grammatical material presented in a particular chapter and prescriptive usage rules. Such usage information has practical application for the kinds of choices that students will need to make in the editing they do in their writing not only in their college coursework but also throughout their lives.

Finally, appendix B of this book provides a brief discussion of Transformational-Generative grammar. Most of the grammatical discussion within this book is grounded in structuralism, but it is important for students to realize that there are other approaches to grammar than the one followed here. Because Transformational-Generative grammar has been enormously influential, with some of its concepts having informed even our own discussion within this text, it is appropriate for students to have at least a basic familiarity with it.

Part One

The Phonology of English

The Production and Inventory of English Phonemes

In all likelihood you have already wondered about issues involved in articulatory phonetics. If, for example, you have ever watched a ventriloquist and wondered how he or she is able to produce particular sounds without any lip movement, then you have considered that aspect of articulatory phonetics known as the "place of articulation." Later in the chapter we will briefly examine an important strategy used by ventriloquists, but first you will need to understand something about how speech sounds are produced.

A descriptive structural grammar of English progresses upward through three levels of structure. The first or lowest level deals with the system of speech sounds employed by native speakers of English. The study of this level is called *phonology*. The next higher level is concerned with the meaningful forms made from the individual speech sounds. Generally speaking, we may say that it deals with words and their meaningful parts. This is the realm of *morphology*. The top level pertains to the ways in which words are arranged to form phrases and sentences, and here we are in the area of *syntax*. Hence we begin our study of English grammar at the first level, with a consideration of the speech sounds of English.

At the outset, as we approach our study of English phonology, we must bear in mind two important facts.

First, language itself is ORAL—it lives on the lips and in the ears of its users—and writing is a visual symbolization of language itself. To realize that language is independent of writing, we have only to recall the many tribes, nations, and ethnic groups whose members possess no form of writing but whose LANGUAGES are being avidly studied today by linguistic scientists and anthropologists. When we study the grammar of a language through the medium of writing, as we will do in this book, we must often supplement the writing with special marks to indicate the stresses, pitches, and breaks of oral speech; and sometimes we must replace writing with a different set of symbols to represent the sounds of the living voice.

Second, the English language as spoken in the United States is not uniform. It is made up of numerous dialects and subdialects, about which our knowledge is yet far from complete. In addition, each person has individual modes of expression that are unique. These modes comprise what we call an *idiolect*. Thus every person speaks an idiolect that is not quite the same as the speech of any other individual. We have chosen to present here the phonology of what could be called the Rocky Mountain dialect of English.

The lack of uniformity of spoken English will soon become apparent as you do the exercises in which you represent your own pronunciation; for your pronunciation will differ in some respects from that of your classmates and from the Rocky Mountain dialect, which is the form given in the answers. Do not be concerned about "correct" and "incorrect" pronunciation. Any pronunciation that is in normal use among the educated speakers in YOUR community is "correct."

A. The Speech-Producing Mechanism

Speech sounds are sound waves created in a moving stream of air. They are disturbances of the medium such as you would observe if you were to drop a stone on the quiet surface of a pool. The air is expelled from the lungs, passes between the two vocal cords in the larynx (Adam's apple), and proceeds upward. As you will note in diagram 1, this moving stream of air has two possible outlets. It can pass through the nasal cavity and emerge through the nose, or it can pass through the oral cavity and come out through the mouth. But why doesn't it go through both passages, which are shown to be open on the diagram? Because in speech one of them is ordinarily closed.

How does this happen? Let us consider the oral sounds first. In diagram 1 you will notice the velum, marked *V.* This is a movable curtain of flesh. If you run your finger back along the roof of your mouth, you will feel at first the bony structure of the hard palate, marked *P.* Just behind this hard palate you will feel the soft flesh of the velum. It ends in a pear-shaped pendant, called the uvula, which you can see

Diagram 1   Speech-producing mechanism.

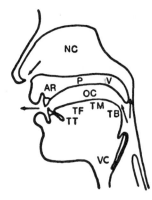

AR	Alveolar ridge
NC	Nasal cavity
OC	Oral cavity
P	Hard palate
V	Velum, or soft palate
TT	Tongue tip
TF	Tongue front
TM	Tongue middle
TB	Tongue back
VC	Vocal cords

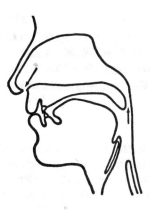

Diagram 2
Air passing through oral cavity.
Tongue position for /a/.

Diagram 3
Air passing through nasal cavity.
Lip position for /m/.

hanging in your throat if you look in the mirror. Now, when you produce any oral sound, one that goes through the mouth—for example, *a-a-a-a-a-a-a*—you at the same time raise the velum until it touches the back of the throat, closing the nasal cavity. You can actually see this raising of the velum if you will open your mouth wide, flash a light into your mouth, look in the mirror, and say *a-a-a-a-a-a* several times in succession. The process is illustrated in diagram 2.

Now let us turn from the oral sounds to the nasals, those that pass through the nasal cavity. To make the three nasal sounds of English, you leave the velum in the position shown in diagram 1 and block off the oral cavity in one of three ways: with the lips (diagram 3), with the tongue tip (diagram 4), or with the tongue back (diagram 5). Thus, with the oral cavity blocked off, the sound can emerge only through the nasal cavity. It is evident now that every speech sound we utter is either an oral or a nasal sound. For illustration try exercise 1–1.

Exercise 1–1

As you pronounce the following words, hold the final sound for some time. As you hold the final sound, stop your nose with your fingers. If this action stops the sound, the sound is obviously a nasal sound. But if the sound continues, close your lips. The sound will thereupon be cut off, demonstrating that it is an oral sound. After each word write "nasal" or "oral" to label the final sound.

1. rim _nasal_
2. saw _oral_
3. bin _nasal_

4. see _oral_
5. sing _nasal_
6. tall _oral_

7. trim _nasal_
8. pain _nasal_
9. wrong _nasal_

You may wonder about the "nasal twang" that you occasionally hear with some speakers. This is caused by the habit of slightly lowering the velum for sounds that are normally oral, thus permitting some of the air to go out through the nasal cavity.

You have now learned the three nasals of English, which we symbolize in a special notation as /m/, /n/, and /ŋ/. The /m/ is a bilabial nasal, made by closing the two lips. The /n/ is an alveolar nasal, made by stopping the flow of air with the tongue tip against the alveolar ridge. The /ŋ/ is a velar nasal, made by stopping the flow of air with the back of the tongue against the velum. In all three the air moves through the nasal cavity. They are illustrated in diagrams 3, 4, and 5.

But one element is missing from our description of the three nasals. Where does the sound come from? To answer this question we must examine the vocal cords.

Inside the larynx (Adam's apple) are two short bands of flesh and muscle stretching from front to rear. In breathing and during the production of some speech sounds, such as /f/ and /s/, these bands are held open, allowing free ingress and egress of air. But with many sounds they are pressed together, and the air passing between them causes them to vibrate. These vibrations are given resonance by the cavities of the mouth and nose, and the result is the phenomenon called voicing. In the making of every speech sound, then, these vocal cords are either vibrating or not vibrating. If they are vibrating, the sound is called voiced. If they are not vibrating, the sound is called voiceless. An exercise will illustrate.

Exercise 1–2

Hold your hands tightly over your ears and pronounce the last sound in each of the following words. Write "voiced" after those during the pronunciation of which you hear the vibration of your vocal cords, which will sound like a strong hum. Write "voiceless" after those during the pronunciation of which such vibration is absent.

1. less   voiceless
2. hum   voiced

3. if   voiceless

4. pin   voiced
5. sheath   voiceless
   (noun)
6. among   voiced

7. mush   voiceless
8. fin   voiced

9. song   voiced

Diagram 4
Air passing through nasal cavity.
Tongue position for /n/.

Diagram 5
Air passing through nasal cavity.
Tongue position for /ŋ/.

We see now that to our description of the three nasals we must add the fact that each one is voiced, that their sound comes from the vibration of the vocal cords.

Let us now turn for a moment to examine the voicing or voicelessness of speech sounds other than the nasals. As we pointed out above, every speech sound is either voiceless or voiced. The next two exercises will give you practice in distinguishing these two kinds.

Exercise 1–3

Pronounce the first sound in the following words with your hands over your ears. Write "voiced" after each word in which you hear the hum of your vocal cords during the pronunciation of this first sound. Write "voiceless" after those that are pronounced without the hum.

1. fine *voiceless*
2. vine *voiced*
3. thin *voiceless*

4. then *voiced*
5. seal *voiceless*
6. zeal *voiced*

7. shock *voiceless*
8. late *voiced*
9. rate *voiced*

Exercise 1–4

This is a little harder. Do the same as you did in exercise 1–3, but be very careful to keep the first sound in each word separate from the one that follows in the same word.

1. pin *voiceless*
2. bin *voiced*

3. time *voiceless*
4. dime *voiced*

5. coop *voiceless*
6. goop *voiced*

By this point, from the foregoing discussion of nasals, orals, and voicing, you should have acquired a working knowledge of these parts of the speech-producing mechanisms: nasal cavity, oral cavity, lips, alveolar ridge, hard palate, velum, tongue tip, tongue back, and the vocal cords. Test yourself by writing these terms in the appropriate places on diagram 6. Verify your answers by consulting diagram 1, and correct any errors.

B. The Phoneme

Before continuing with an inventory of English speech sounds and the ways of producing them, we must clearly understand one basic concept—the phoneme.

The phoneme is a speech sound that signals a difference in meaning. Consider, for example, the words *dime* and *dine*. They sound exactly alike except for the /m/ and the /n/, yet their meanings are different. Therefore it must be the /m/ and /n/ that made the difference in meaning, and these two nasals are thereby established as English phonemes. Likewise, if we compare the sounds of *sin* and *sing*, we find only

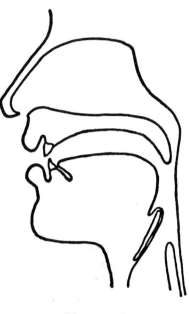

Diagram 6

one difference between them: *sin* ends in the alveolar nasal /n/ and *sing* in the velar nasal /ŋ/. (Don't be deceived by the spelling of *sing;* the letters *ng* represent a single sound /ŋ/, one that you can prolong as long as your breath holds out.) This contrast is evidence that /n/ and /ŋ/ are both phonemes. Pairs of words like those above that demonstrate a single phonemic contrast are called minimal pairs.

Exercise 1–5

After each minimal pair write the phonemes that are established by the sound contrast between them. Be sure to contrast pronunciations, not letters. Because you have not yet learned most of the phonemic symbols, use letters to represent the phonemes.

1. pin __p__		6. rattle __r__		11. sad __d__	
bin __b__		tattle __t__		sat __t__	
2. big __b__		7. fine __f__		12. made __d__	
dig __d__		vine __v__		make __k__	
3. late __l__		8. zoo __z__		13. tool __l__	
rate __r__		too __t__		tomb __m__	
4. pill __p__		9. hot __h__		14. fate __t__	
kill __k__		got __g__		feign __n__	
5. go __g__		10. sick __s__		15. thin __n__	
so __s__		wick __w__		thing __ŋ__	

A phoneme may be pronounced in different ways, depending on its position in the utterance, and still remain the same phoneme. As an example, let us take /l/. If you pronounce *lit* and *well* slowly and distinctly, you will hear two different [l]s. The second one seems to be preceded by an "uh" sound. With a little practice you can place your tongue tip on the alveolar ridge and change from the first to the second [l] without moving the tongue tip. Now, if you pronounce *well* with the [l] of *lit,* the word will sound different, a little unEnglish, but the meaning will not be changed. The use of one or the other of these two [l]s never makes a difference in meaning; hence they are not two phonemes but merely variants of the /l/ phoneme. You will sometimes hear still another [l] in words such as *play* and *sled.* Here there may be a voiceless [l̥], whereas the [l]s of both *well* and *lit* were voiced. But whether you pronounce *play* and certain other words with a voiced or a voiceless [l], the meaning remains unchanged; so this third [l̥] is another variant of the /l/ phoneme.

Such variants of a phoneme are called allophones. (Allophones are enclosed in brackets with the occasional addition of diacritical marks to indicate the exact pronunciation. Phonemes are enclosed in slants.) Thus we may say that the /l/ phoneme has three allophones: [l] as in *lit,* [ɫ] as in *well,* and [l̥] as in *play.* A phoneme then is not an individual sound but a small family or class of similar sounds.

Let us consider one more case to illustrate the concept of phoneme and allophones. Pronounce *how* and *huge* slowly, prolonging the initial *h* in each word. You will probably discover that the *h* of *how* is breathy, whereas the *h* of *huge* has a scraping, frictional, almost hissing sound.[1] But though these two *h*'s do not sound the same, the difference in sound never makes a difference in meaning. Each is heard as an *h,* and the difference in sound goes unnoticed. This is to say they are allophones of the /h/ phoneme.

In contrast let us look at two Dutch words, *heel,* meaning very, and *geel,* meaning yellow. The *h* of the Dutch *heel* is pronounced the same as the breathy *h* of the English *how;* the *g* of the Dutch *geel* is pronounced the same as the scraping *h* of the English *huge.* It is this difference in pronunciation between these two Dutch *h*'s that distinguishes between the two words of the minimal pair *heel–geel.*[2] Thus these two *h* sounds that were allophones in English are phonemes in Dutch.

With this introduction to the concept of the phoneme, we are now ready to examine the inventory of English phonemes.

C. The English Phonemic System: Vowels

The classification of English vowels is a complex and controversial matter; it is even difficult to define a vowel with precision. But we can make four statements about vowels that will help to show their nature:

1. Vowels are oral sounds. In some dialects and in certain contexts vowels may become partially nasal, but normally they are orals, not nasals.
2. Vowels are voiced.

---

[1]This scraping *h* is the same as the last sound in German *ich.* It is possible that you may use the breathy *h* in both words, but many persons make the difference described here.

[2]These two Dutch words rhyme with the English *sale.*

3. Vowels are characterized by a free flow of air through the oral cavity.
4. The distinguishing features of the different vowels are determined largely by tongue position.

English may be said to have eleven vowels, though one could argue a larger inventory, depending on how detailed and precise a particular consideration of the vowel system needs to be. For our purposes here, we will distinguish eleven vowels—five front, four back, and two central vowels—which we will now take up systematically.

Front Vowels

If you pronounce the final sound of *be,* symbolized by /i/, and hold the /i/, you will find that the tongue front and middle are humped high in the mouth, leaving a narrow passage for the flow of air between the hard palate and the surface of the tongue. The tongue position of /i/ is the top one on diagram 7.

Next, say the same vowel /i/, holding your jaw in your hand, and then say the first sound of *add,* symbolized by /æ/. You will observe a considerable drop of the jaw and some flattening of the tongue. The tongue position of the vowel /æ/ is the bottom one on diagram 7. To fix these differences of position in your mind, hold your jaw and say /i/, /æ/ rapidly a number of times in succession.

Between the two extremes /i/ and /æ/ are three other vowels. To hear them in order from the top tongue position to the bottom one, pronounce the following words, noting the middle sound: *beat, bit, bait, bet, bat.* Now say just the vowels in the same order, holding your jaw, and observe how the jaw drops a little as each one is uttered. These five vowels are called the FRONT VOWELS, because they are formed in the front of the mouth by the position of the tongue front. For each front vowel the lips are spread, or unrounded. The tongue positions and the symbols for them are indicated on diagram 7.

English spelling cannot be used to represent accurately the speech sounds of English because of its inconsistencies. How, for example, would you symbolize the vowel of *bait* in English spelling? By *ai* as in *wait, eig* as in *reign, ey* as in *they, ay*

Diagram 7   Front vowels.

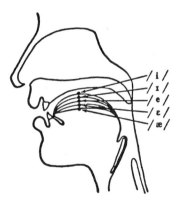

as in *say, a* as in *late, ei* as in *vein, au* as in *gauge, ea* as in *steak*? So, to represent the sounds of words, we will use a special alphabet in which one symbol always represents one and the same phoneme, and each phoneme is always represented by only one symbol. In this alphabet the five illustrative words in the preceding paragraph are written as follows:

beat = /bit/.
bit = /bɪt/
bait = /bet/
bet = /bɛt/
bat = /bæt/

The symbols and words written in these symbols are enclosed in slants, such as /bæt/.

In exercise 1–6 you are given transcription practice employing the five front vowels and six consonants. The phonemic symbols for these eleven sounds are written as follows:

/i/	*meet*	/p/	*pie*
/ɪ/	*mitt*	/b/	*by*
/e/	*mate*	/t/	*ten*
/ɛ/	*met*	/d/	*den*
/æ/	*mat*	/k/	*cob*
		/g/	*gob*

Exercise 1–6

In the second column transcribe the words in the first column as you normally pronounce them. The first two are done to show you how.

1.	pack	pæk	11.	beak	bik	21.	get	gɛt
2.	cape	kep	12.	big	bɪg	22.	gate	get
3.	Pete	pit	13.	date	det	23.	gat	gæt
4.	pit	pɪt	14.	debt	dɛt	24.	back	bæk
5.	pate	pet	15.	kick	kɪk	25.	bake	bek
6.	pet	pɛt	16.	cap	kæp	26.	tap	tæp
7.	pat	pæt	17.	peck	pɛk	27.	tape	tep
8.	keep	kip	18.	pick	pɪk	28.	tip	tɪp
9.	kid	kɪd	19.	peek	bik			
10.	cat	kæt	20.	gad	gæd			

Back Vowels

Pronounce the final sound of *too,* symbolized by /u/. For this vowel, /u/, the lips are rounded and the back of the tongue is raised to a place near the velum, leaving a little space for the air to flow. The tongue position is the top one on diagram 8.

As the back of the tongue is lowered from the /u/ position, it reaches in turn the positions for the three other back vowels: /ʊ/ as in *hood,* /o/ as in *note,* and /ɔ/ (written

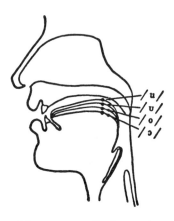

Diagram 8   Back vowels.

like a backwards *c*).[3] The /ɔ/ is the vowel sound that some American English speakers pronounce in *ought, law,* and *ball.* You might, however, use a different vowel sound in these words. If you have trouble determining what the sound /ɔ/ represents, consider whether you have heard speakers who distinguish between the vowel sounds in the words *cot* and *caught.* Among those speakers who make such a distinction, the vowel being used in *caught* is typically /ɔ/.

The tongue position for /ɔ/ is the bottom one represented in diagram 8. If you utter the vowels /u/ and /ɔ/ in rapid succession, with your hand on your jaw, this will show you the upper and lower extremes of the range of the four back vowels. If you will look in the mirror while uttering the successive /u/s and /ɔ/s, you will see the close rounding of the lips for /u/ and the open rounding for /ɔ/. If you move through the back vowels from /u/ to /ɔ/ and watch this progression in the mirror, you can observe the successive opening of the lip rounding. The four back vowels, from top to bottom, can be illustrated by this series:

    cooed = /kud/
    could = /kʊd/
    code   = /kod/
    cawed = /kɔd/[4]

In exercise 1–7 you are given transcription practice in the four back vowels and are introduced to nine new consonants. The phonemic symbols for these thirteen sounds are written as follows:

/u/ as in b*oo*m	/f/ as in *f*ine	/z/ as in *z*eal
/ʊ/ as in b*oo*k	/v/ as in *v*ine	/š/ as in *sh*un
/o/ as in n*o*te	/θ/ as in *th*in	/ž/ as in a*z*ure
/ɔ/ as in *a*we[4]	/ð/ as in *th*en	/h/ as in *h*ow
	/s/ as in *s*eal	

---

[3]This vowel /ɔ/ is not present in some American dialects except as part of a diphthong and prior to /r/ as we will discuss later.

[4]Some dialects use /a/ in this word.

Exercise 1-7

Transcribe the following words.

1. food   _fud_
2. foot   _fʊt_
3. foe   _fo_
4. fought   _fɔt_
5. shoe   _ʃu_
6. show   _ʃo_
7. though   _ðo_
8. thaw   _θɔ_
9. soup   _sup_
10. ought   _ɔt_

11. voodoo   _vudu_
12. shook   _ʃʊk_
13. who   _hu_
14. hoe   _ho_
15. zone   _zon_
16. zoo   _zu_
17. thought   _θɔt_
18. those   _ðoz_
19. oath   _oθ_
20. vision   _vɪʒən_

(Use /ə/ for the second vowel sound.)

Central Vowels

The first central vowel we will examine is the mid central vowel. This vowel is the first sound of *up* and *upon*. It is written /ə/, like an upside-down *e,* and its position is shown in diagram 9. It is heard as the pronunciation of the italicized vowels in the following words:

Stressed: s*u*n, d*o*ne, fl*oo*d
Unstressed: sof*a,* *a*lone, kingd*o*m, c*o*nnect, s*u*ppose, hunt*e*d, ros*e*s, garb*a*ge.

The /ə/ is a commonly used vowel in English, especially in unstressed syllables, and is technically called *schwa*. Sometimes it approaches an /ɪ/ in pronunciation.

In addition to the kinds of linguistic environments that have been shown above, you also commonly pronounce the schwa immediately preceding the /r/ in a word such as *her* /hər/—that is, unless you belong to the minority of Americans who "drop their r's." Thus we will use the pair of symbols /ər/ to represent the final sounds of such words as *fur, sir,* and *her.* We could be even more precise and distinguish between those pronunciations of *her* that use /ər/ and those that actually contain an r-colored vowel /ɚ/ instead. But making such a distinction is unnecessary in an introductory course, and we will therefore represent both pronunciations with the /ər/ combination.

Another central vowel is the sound you make when the doctor says, "Open your mouth and say *a-a-a-a*." For most Americans this is the vowel of *not* and the first vowel of *father.* It is symbolized by /a/. In sounding this vowel you will note that the mouth is widely opened and that the tongue is nearly flat. The tongue position is the lower one in diagram 9. The central vowels, as well as the schwa plus /r/, are illustrated below:

nurse = /nərs/
nut   = /nət/
not   = /nat/

In exercise 1–8 two new consonant symbols in addition to /r/ are added to your repertoire. The phonemic symbols for these six sounds or combinations are written as follows:

/ər/ bird   /č/ churn /čərn/
/ə/ up   /ǰ/ judge /ǰəǰ/
/a/ pot   /r/ rap   /ræp/

Transcribe in phonemic symbols the following words as you normally pronounce them.

1. purr   pər
2. murder   mərdər
3. children   čIldrən
4. gopher   gofər
5. churches čərčəž
6. rubs   rəbz

7. wooded   wᵘdəd
8. folded   foldəd
9. return   ritərn
10. herd   hərd
11. hurt   hart
12. hut   hət

Transcribe in phonemic symbols the following words as you normally pronounce them.

1. urge   ərǰ
2. stop   stap
3. cut   kət
4. sofa   sofæ
5. rug   rəg
6. above
7. bird   bərd
8. rust
9. run
10. birch   bərč

11. leisure   liǰər
12. urban   ərbIn
13. odd   ɔd
14. afféct (verb) əfɛkt
15. efféct (noun)
16. pocket   pɔkIt
17. today
18. cupboard
19. journey ǰərni
20. hot   hɔt

Diagram 9   Central vowels.

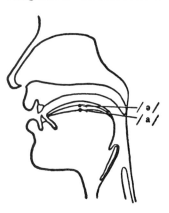

/ə/
/a/

The eleven vowel phonemes of English can be seen in relation to one another on the vowel chart in diagram 10, a two-dimensional grid of tongue positions, the mouth being at the left and the throat at the right. You will note that the chart below provides an additional feature of vowels as it labels some of them according to whether they are tense or lax. This feature refers to the relative constriction of the tongue muscle. Using this chart we can easily give to the eleven vowels descriptive names that will be useful in discussing them:

/i/ High-front tense	/ə/ Mid-central	/u/ High-back rounded tense
/ɪ/ High-front lax	/a/ Low-central	/ʊ/ High-back rounded lax
/e/ Mid-front tense		/o/ Mid-back rounded (tense)
/ɛ/ Mid-front lax		/ɔ/ Low-back rounded
/æ/ Low-front		

This classification of vowels by tongue position is imprecise and generalized. Their relative positions, however, are correct. Also, there are further classifications—close, open; narrow, wide; long, short—that we are bypassing in the interest of a stringent simplicity. But by and large the above description and classification of vowel phonemes—though limited—will serve our purpose.

Before leaving our discussion of vowels, it will be useful to consider further the vowel environment that occurs before an /r/ in the same syllable. We previously noted that the schwa vowel sometimes precedes /r/, as in the word *learn* /lərn/. Some other vowels that occur in this same environment are evident in words such as *farm*/farm/; *tore*/tɔr/; *tour*/tur/; *fair*/fɛr/; and *fear*/fɪr/. The exercise below will provide some practice with the schwa as well as these additional vowels in this environment.

Exercise 1-10

Transcribe the following words into phonemic symbols, following your own natural pronunciation.

1. we're	_____	10. morning	_____	19. pair	_____
2. gear	_____	11. mourning	_____	20. payer	peyər
3. they're	_____	12. north	_____	21. stair	_____
4. there	_____	13. northern	_____	22. stayer	_____
5. care	_____	14. floor	_____	23. mare	_____
6. merry	mɛrri	15. here	_____	24. mayor	_____
7. Mary	M ___	16. lure	_____	25. park	p___
8. marry	_____	17. horse	_____	26. purr	pər
9. barge	_____	18. hoarse	_____		

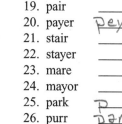

The Syllable

Before moving ahead to the next group of phonemes, the diphthongs, it is necessary to examine the nature of the syllable.

	Front	**Central**	**Back**
High	i (*kee*p)		u (*coo*p)
	ɪ (d*i*p)		ʊ (f*oo*t)
Mid	e (c*a*pe)	ə (c*u*t)	o (t*o*ne)
	ɛ (w*e*t)		
Low	æ (c*a*t)	a (c*o*t)	ɔ (c*au*ght)*

Diagram 10   Chart of vowel phonemes in English.

---

*Only some speakers use /ɔ/ rather than /a/ in *caught*. For many speakers *caught* and *cot* are pronounced the same way.

When we speak, we can observe that certain sounds have a greater sonority or carry-ing power than others. For example, in *soap* /sop/, the /o/ has greater sonority than the /s/ or the /p/, even though all are spoken with equal force. If /sop/ is spoken at some dis-tance, the listener may hear distinctly only the /o/. In *potato* /pəteto/, the /e/ and /o/ are more sonorous, more audible, than the /p/ and the /t/s. The sounds that have this greater inherent sonority or carrying power are mostly the vowels. Thus, as we utter connected discourse, we become aware of a peak-and-valley effect of sonority or audibility. The peaks of sonority are the vowels; the valleys of less distinctness are the consonants, as in *echo* /ɛko/, or the slight diminution of loudness, as in *create* /kri-et/. This brings us to the syllable. A syllable is a sound or a short sequence of sounds that contains one peak of sonority. This peak is usually a vowel, and the vowel is said to be the nucleus of the syllable. A segment of speech, then, contains as many syllables as there are peaks. Here are some examples of words with the peaks, or syllabic nuclei, italicized.

One syllable:	be	/b*i*/
	string	/str*ɪ*ŋ/
Two syllables:	believe	/bəl*i*v/
	being	/b*i*ɪŋ/
	stirring	/st*ə*r*ɪ*ŋ/
Three syllables:	believing	/bəl*i*v*ɪ*ŋ/
Four syllables:	unbelieving	/*ə*nbəl*i*v*ɪ*ŋ/
Five syllables:	unbelievingly	/*ə*nbəl*i*v*ɪ*ŋl*i*/

Exercise 1–11

Transcribe the following words in phonemic symbols, underline the peaks, and indi-cate how many syllables each word has.

	Word	*Transcription*	*No. of Syllables*
Example:	spoonful	/sp<u>u</u>nf<u>ə</u>l/	2
	1. seat	_____	_____
	2. infect	_____	_____
	3. paper	_____	_____
	4. disenchant	_____	_____
	5. unostentatious	_____	_____

We have seen that vowels are peaks of sonority and are therefore syllabic nuclei. But there are five consonants—/m/, /n/, /ŋ/, /l/, and /r/ —that also have considerable sonority and that can be syllabic nuclei.

As our first example, let us take the two-syllable expression *stop 'em*. This can be uttered in two ways. The first is /stap əm/. After the lips are closed to make the /p/, they are opened for the /ə/ and closed again for the /m/. But there is a second way. Here the lips are closed for the /p/ and remain closed for the /m/. Try it and see for yourself. While you are making the /p/, no air can escape from the mouth. The closed lips shut off the mouth exit and the raised velum shuts off the nasal exit. Now, holding the lips closed, you open the velum by lowering it, and what happens? The air escapes with a slight explosion through the nasal cavity, producing an /m/. Here the /m/ is a peak of sonority and by itself constitutes a syllable. This /m/ is called a syllabic /m/.

Oral Exercise 1–A

Practice saying these expressions, using for the last syllable both (1) a schwa plus /m/ and (2) a syllabic /m/.

1. leap 'em
2. rob 'em
3. open 'em

The syllabic /n/ is formed similarly. Consider, for example, *button.* You may pronounce it /bətən/ by dropping the tongue from the /t/ position on the alveolar ridge, uttering the /ə/, and then replacing the tongue for the /n/. But you can also pronounce *button* without removing the tongue. At the /t/ position the air is prevented from escaping by the tongue against the alveolar ridge and by the closed velum, which shuts off the nasal cavity. If you hold the tongue in the /t/ position and open the velum, you will get an /n/ as the air escapes through the nasal cavity. This is a syllabic /n/.

Oral Exercise 1–B

Practice saying these expressions, using for the last syllable both (1) a schwa plus an /n/ and (2) a syllabic /n/.

1. beaten
2. cotton
3. sudden

The syllabic /ŋ/, which is less frequent, is heard in expressions like *Jack and Jill,* /ǰækŋǰɪl/. At the /k/ position the air is held in by the back of the tongue against the velum and by the velum, which has been raised to cut off the nasal cavity. With a lowering of the velum, the nasal cavity is opened and the syllabic /ŋ/ is heard.

Oral Exercise 1–C

Practice saying these expressions in two ways. After the /k/ or /g/ position, use first the schwa plus an /n/, and then the syllabic /ŋ/.

1. back and forth
2. bag and baggage
3. rack and ruin

The syllabic /l/ is somewhat differently articulated. To make the common /l/, you place the tongue on the alveolar ridge, vibrate the vocal cords, and let the air flow over and off the tongue on one or both sides and escape through the mouth. To make the syllabic /l/, as in *rattle,* you first have the air completely closed off by the tongue in the /t/ position on the alveolar ridge and by a raised velum cutting off the nasal cavity. Then you open one or both sides of the tongue, without removing the tip from the alveolar ridge, activate the vocal cords, and let the air go around the tongue and out the mouth.

Oral Exercise 1–D

Pronounce the following words in two ways, using for the last syllable both (1) a schwa plus /l/ and (2) a syllabic /l/.

1. cattle
2. saddle
3. beetle

One other consonant sound that may be syllabic is /r/. Just as /l/ may be preceded by the schwa or occur as its own syllable without a vowel, so also the /r/ in a word like *batter* may occur without a preceding vowel and yet function syllabically.

You will have noticed that the preceding exercises dealing with syllabic consonants have been oral exercises. In this text you will not need to learn to transcribe syllabic consonants, though you should be aware of them. For the purposes of this text, if you transcribe a word such as *cotton* or *batter,* use the schwa vowel with the appropriate consonant symbol rather than try to represent a syllabic consonant as part of your transcription.

Although it is easy to locate the peaks of sonority that indicate syllabic nuclei, the vowels and syllabic consonants, it is sometimes impossible to find the boundary between syllables—that is, the point of minimum sonority. In the two-syllable *hushing* /həšɪŋ/, for example, where is the syllable boundary? After the /ə/? Before the /ɪ/? Or in the middle of /š/? It is like trying to establish in a valley the exact line separating the two hills on either side. For our purpose here we need not be much concerned with syllable division, and where the boundary is not audible, we can resort to an arbitrarily selected break.

Diphthongs

A diphthong consists of a vowel plus a glide that occur in the same syllable, the tongue moving smoothly from one position to the other without hiatus, as in *sigh* /say/, *sow* (female pig) /saw/, and *soy* /sɔy/. The two sounds together represent the peak of sonority, though one always has greater prominence than the other. Many of our vowels are diphthongized in various subareas of English, and four of them are normally diphthongized in Standard English: /i/, /e/, /u/, and /o/. For these, however, we will use the symbols just given, because there is no phonemic difference between the pure vowels and the diphthongized vowels.[5] According to the system we are using, the diphthongs are only three: /ay/ as in *by*, /aw/ as in *bough*, and /ɔy/ as in *boy*. All three are subject to considerable dialectal variation. For example, /ɔy/ is pronounced /oy/ by many speakers of Northern; /aw/ becomes /æw/ in the South and South Midland; /ay/ becomes /əy/, and /aw/ becomes /əw/, in parts of Canada.

Exercise 1–12

Transcribe the following words into phonemic symbols, using your own natural pronunciation.

1. my	may	6. joy	jɔy	11. high	____	16. try	tray
2. toy	tɔy	7. chives	c____	12. ouch	____	17. stripe	____
3. how	h____	8. thou	____	13. mighty	____	18. rowdy	____
4. tie	____	9. shy	šay	14. roil	rɔl	19. Kilroy	kɪlrɔy
5. cow	____	10. rye	ray	15. coy	kɔy	20. destroy	d____

D. The English Phonemic System: Consonants

Vowels, you have learned, are characterized by a free flow of air. Consonants, on the other hand, except for the three nasals, are produced by stopping or obstructing this flow of air.

When we examine the articulation of consonants, three main features must be considered: voicing, place of articulation, and manner of articulation. We have discussed **voicing,** which refers to whether or not the vocal cords are vibrating. **Place of articulation** refers to the location where obstruction of the airstream occurs. You have gained some familiarity with important regions of the oral cavity, which include places of articulation. In the material that follows, we will focus on the **manner of articulation,** that is, what kind of obstruction occurs. As we examine the

---

[5]You may think that you are uttering single vowels in words such as *cease* /sis/, *maim* /mem/, *noon* /nun/, *moan* /mon/. But the vowel sounds you are actually making are diphthongized vowels something like these: 1. [ɪy], 2. [ey], 3. [ʊw], and 4. [ow].

manner of articulation of the various consonants, we will also identify the voicing and place of articulation of each.

We will now consider consonants with regard to the six manners of articulation: stops, fricatives, affricates, nasals, liquids, and glides. First we will begin by looking at six stop consonants, those produced by a stoppage of air: /p b t d k g/.

Stops: /p/, /b/. If you hold your velum and lips closed and exert outward air pressure, nothing will happen except that your cheeks may puff out. Now if you suddenly open your lips, the air explodes outward and you have made a /p/. This consonant is called a voiceless bilabial stop because (1) the vocal cords do not vibrate, (2) two lips are used, and (3) a complete stop of the air flow is made. If during the same process you vibrate your vocal cords, you will produce a /b/, a voiced bilabial stop.

Stops: /t/, /d/. Instead of using the lips, you can stop the air flow by holding the tongue against the alveolar ridge, with the velum closed, and exerting outward air pressure. A sudden removal of the tongue will then produce a /t/, a voiceless alveolar stop. But if the vocal cords vibrate during the process, you will produce a /d/, a voiced alveolar stop.

Stops: /k/, /g/. The third pair of stops is produced by raising the tongue back against the velum, which is also raised to cut off the nasal cavity. When the tongue back is released, the outrushing air results in a /k/, a voiceless velar stop, or a /g/, a voiced velar stop, depending on whether or not the vocal cords are vibrating.

Oral Exercise 1–E

To increase your awareness of the three stop positions, pronounce slowly and in succession /p/, /t/, and /k/, and try to feel, tactually and kinesthetically, what is going on inside your mouth. Do this six times, and then repeat the process in reverse.

Exercise 1–13

Transcribe the following words into phonemic symbols.

1. pip	pɪp	8. stopgap	stapgæp	15. hands	hænz
2. bib	bɪb	9. hiccough	hɪkkəf	16. flicker	flɪkər
3. tot	tat	10. subpoint	sabpɔynt	17. six	sɪks
4. deed	did	11. fast	fæst	18. guest	gɛst
5. coat	kot	12. fasten	fæsɪn	19. keep	kip
6. gag	gæg	13. oozed	uzd	20. coop	kup
7. stopped	stapt	14. hand	hænd		

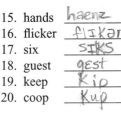

Exercise 1–14

In *keep* and *coop* there are two different [k]s, which are allophones of /k/. In what way are they different? To answer this, try whispering the [k] of *keep* and that of *coop* alternately and note your tongue position and lip rounding. Furthermore, if you bear in mind the positions of the two vowels, you may be able to explain why the [k]s differ.

Fricatives

English contains nine consonants that are produced by an obstruction of the air stream causing audible friction. These nine fricatives are:

$$/f\ v\ \theta\ \eth\ s\ z\ \check{s}\ \check{z}\ h/$$

We will discuss these in pairs, beginning with those in the front of the mouth and moving to the back.

The first pair, /f/ and /v/, are heard in *fail* and *vale*. They are produced when the outgoing air is obstructed by the lower lip touching the upper teeth. The /f/ is called a voiceless labiodental fricative, and /v/ a voiced labiodental fricative. They differ only in the fact that /v/ is voiced. You can feel the vibration of the vocal cords for /v/ if you press your fingers around the top of the larynx, sound a continuous /f/, and then change, without stopping, to a /v/. The next three pairs of fricatives can be tested in the same way for voicelessness and voicing.

The second pair, /θ/ and /ð/, are heard in *ether* and *either*. They are made with the tongue between the upper and lower teeth, obstructing the air stream between its tip and the upper teeth. The /θ/ is a voiceless interdental fricative, and /ð/ a voiced interdental fricative.

The third pair is /s/ and /z/, as in *face* and *faze*. These are pronounced by the tongue permitting a small stream of air to hiss over its surface at the alveolar ridge. The /s/ is a voiceless alveolar fricative, and /z/ a voiced alveolar fricative.

The fourth pair of fricatives is /š/, the third consonant in *dilution,* and /ž/, the third consonant in *delusion*. These are made by the friction of moving air between the tongue front and the palatal region just behind the alveolar ridge. The /š/ is a voiceless alveopalatal fricative, and /ž/ a voiced alveopalatal fricative. To get the feel of the voiceless alveolar and alveopalatal fricatives, take a deep breath and on a continuous stream of air repeat /s/ and /š/ in alternation, noting the movements of the tongue and the lips.

The last fricative is /h/, as in *hat* contrasted with *at*. This is produced by the breath rushing through the vocal cords closing to a position for vibrating, and through the oral cavity. Its tongue and lip position is that of the following sound. You can see this easily by preparing your mouth to say *ha, he, who*. It is called the voiceless glottal fricative, the glottis being the space between the vocal cords.

Exercise 1-15

Transcribe the following words in phonemic symbols.

1. enough	ɪnəf	8. scent	sɛnt	15. luxury	___
2. wife	wayf	9. close (adjective)	klos	16. luxurious	___
3. wives	wɑyvz	10. clothes (noun)	kloz	17. measure	mɛš
4. fifth	fɪfθ	11. news	nuz	18. humble	___
5. south	sawθ	12. newspaper	nuzpepə	19. honest	___
6. southern	səðərn	13. house	___	20. homage	___
7. with	wɪθ	14. husband	___		

Exercise 1-16

For each word below, find a word that, with it, forms a minimal pair demonstrating the phonemic status of the fricative. Write this word in phonemic notation.

Example: *th*ick /kɪk/

1. *f*ind _____
2. *v*ase _____
3. bo*th* _____
4. *th*us _____
5. *s*eem _____
6. ja*zz* _____
7. *sh*irk _____
8. a*z*ure _____
9. *h*ang _____

Affricates

English has two affricates—the voiceless /č/, as in *chill,* and the voiced /ǰ/, as in *Jill.* The /č/ begins with the voiceless stop /t/, which is exploded as a voiceless fricative /š/. Thus it is sometimes written /tš/. It is known as the voiceless alveopalatal affricate. The /ǰ/ consists of a voiced stop /d/, which is exploded as a voiced fricative /ž/, and is sometimes written /dž/. It is called the voiced alveopalatal affricate.

Nasals

The three nasals—/m/, /n/, and /ŋ/—have already been described on pages 9–10.

Liquids

Liquids involve a very light constriction of the airstream and consist of the lateral /l/ and the retroflex /r/.

The lateral /l/, as in *louse,* is made by placing the tongue tip on the alveolar ridge and vibrating the vocal cords as the air passes out on one or both sides of the tongue. To feel the tongue position, hold the tongue firmly at the alveolar ridge and make a series of /l/s and /n/s, noting how the sides of the tongue open and close as you alternate sounds.

The retroflexive /r/ is a sound typically produced by curling the tip of the tongue near the alveolar ridge. The similar nature of the lateral /l/ and retroflex /r/ is apparent in the fact that some languages regard them as allophones of the same phoneme in the same way that we might not notice the different h's in the words *huge* and *how.*

Glides

The two glides—/y/ and /w/—are signaled by a moving, not a stationary, tongue position. They are both voiced.

For /y/, the high front glide, the tongue begins in the /i/ region and moves toward the position of whatever vowel follows. For /w/, the high back glide, the tongue takes an /u/ position and then moves into the following vowel. The vowel-like nature of these glides has prompted some linguists to refer to them as "semivowels."

These glides also follow vowels to form diphthongs, as in *my* /may/, *cow* /kaw/, and *coy* /kɔy/.

Exercise 1-17

Transcribe the following words into phonemic notation.

1. food   _____
2. feud   _____
3. eon   _____
4. yon   _____
5. judge   _____
6. solemn   _____
7. each   _____
8. singer   _____
9. linger   _____
10. strong   _____

11. stronger   _____
12. illusion   _____
13. folk   _____
14. milk   _____
15. use (verb)   _____
16. opinion   _____
17. try   _____
18. wear   _____
19. where   _____
20. berate   _____

We have now covered briefly the eleven vowels (and several diphthongs), as well as the twenty-four consonant phonemes of English. The vowel and consonant phonemes are charted on the diagrams on page 20 and below. You will find that memorizing these charts is an excellent way to keep in mind the basic facts about each sound.

Note that the consonant chart, like the vowel chart, is arranged from the front of the mouth at the left to the throat at the right.

Where the sound comes from [handwritten annotation]

Diagram 11 Chart of English consonant phonemes.

	Bilabial	Labio-dental	Inter-dental	Alveolar	Alveo-palatal	Velar	Glottal
Stops vl	p			t		k	
vd	b			d		g	
Fricatives vl		f	θ	s	š		h
vd		v	ð	z	ž		
Affricates vl					č		
vd					ǰ		
Nasals	m			n		ŋ	
Liquids Lateral				l			
Retroflex				r			
Glides						y	w

Exercise 1-18

As a review of the vowel, consonant, and diphthong symbols, write in phonemic notation one illustrative word for each phoneme given below.

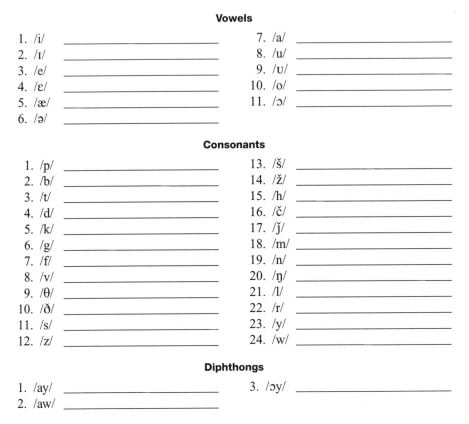

Vowels

1. /i/ _____
2. /ɪ/ _____
3. /e/ _____
4. /ɛ/ _____
5. /æ/ _____
6. /ə/ _____

7. /a/ _____
8. /u/ _____
9. /ʊ/ _____
10. /o/ _____
11. /ɔ/ _____

Consonants

1. /p/ _____
2. /b/ _____
3. /t/ _____
4. /d/ _____
5. /k/ _____
6. /g/ _____
7. /f/ _____
8. /v/ _____
9. /θ/ _____
10. /ð/ _____
11. /s/ _____
12. /z/ _____

13. /š/ _____
14. /ž/ _____
15. /h/ _____
16. /č/ _____
17. /ǰ/ _____
18. /m/ _____
19. /n/ _____
20. /ŋ/ _____
21. /l/ _____
22. /r/ _____
23. /y/ _____
24. /w/ _____

Diphthongs

1. /ay/ _____
2. /aw/ _____

3. /ɔy/ _____

Exercise 1-19

Read aloud the following words and word groups. Watch out for this danger: You may recognize a word and pronounce it as you ordinarily do instead of following the notation. A stress mark /ˊ/ has been added to show the syllable of greatest emphasis. In the blanks write out in ordinary spelling the word or word group. These are all real pronunciations made by native speakers of American English.

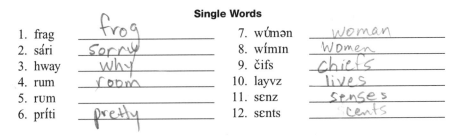

Single Words

1. fræg   _frog_
2. sári   _sorry_
3. hway   _why_
4. rum   _room_
5. rʊm   _____
6. príti   _pretty_

7. wúmən   _woman_
8. wímɪn   _women_
9. čifs   _chiefs_
10. layvz   _lives_
11. sɛnz   _senses_
12. sɛnts   _cents_

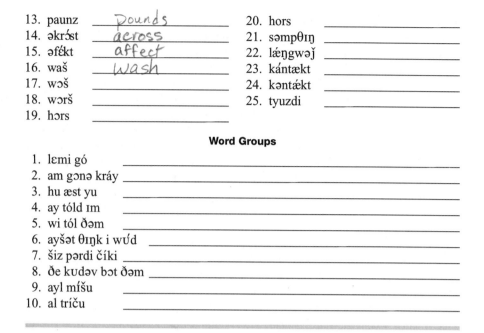

13. paunz   *Dounds*
14. əkrɔ́st   *across*
15. əfɛ́kt   *affect*
16. waš   *wash*
17. wɔš
18. wɔrš
19. hɔrs

20. hors
21. səmpθɪŋ
22. lǽŋgwəǰ
23. kántækt
24. kəntǽkt
25. tyuzdi

Word Groups

1. lɛmi gó
2. am gɔnə kráy
3. hu æst yu
4. ay tóld ɪm
5. wi tól ðəm
6. ayšət θɪŋk i wǔd
7. šiz pərdi číki
8. ðe kʊdəv bɔt ðəm
9. ayl mɪ́šu
10. al tríču

Some Observations and Applications

A knowledge of articulatory phonetics is relevant for the work of people in a variety of professions, including speech pathology, education, software design, marketing, and more. We'll briefly look at some articulatory issues. The first is an example from speech pathology.

Consider the problem known as a "lisp." A lisp is sometimes referred to as "tongue thrusting" because the tongue is brought further forward than it should be, and thus an interdental fricative /θ/ rather than an alveolar fricative /s/ is articulated. You can test out the similarity in the two sounds by producing /s/ and holding it while you slowly move your tongue forward. With very little movement you will begin to perceive an interdental sound. This is a simple illustration, but the problems that speech pathologists deal with can be quite complex. They must understand articulation and the relationship between sounds and groups of sounds in order to more effectively diagnose and treat particular speech problems.

Speech therapists are not the only ones who can benefit from an awareness of articulatory phonetics and phonology. Various educators can also benefit from insights gained through the study of how speech is produced and interpreted. This chapter has introduced you to the notion of the phoneme and how a phoneme may be manifested in varying allophones. You probably recall our example of how the phoneme /h/ is pronounced differently in the words *how* and *huge,* and yet because both pronunciations are allophones of /h/, they are still perceived as the "same" sound. The ability to perceive varying allophones as belonging to the same phoneme and to distinguish what constitutes separate phonemes is an important preliminary skill for beginning readers to have. But as Janet E. Spector shows, some young children entering school vary in their "phonemic awareness," and this can account for differences in the success that children have as they start learning to read. She illustrates the importance of one aspect of phonemic awareness as she points out that the sounds of /p/, /æ/ and /t/ in isolation are different from the way those phonemes are manifested when they are blended into a word. The phoneme /p/, for example, is always accompanied by a schwa ([ə]) when articulated in isolation. Spector further explains, "as anyone who has ever heard a beginning reader trying to blend knows, the sequence *puh-ah-tuh* yields a three-syllable word that is a far cry from *pat.*" Fortunately, as Spector shows, there are some ways in which teachers can help students develop phonemic awareness if they have begun school without this important ability.[6]

One of the challenges facing the public schools is how best to accommodate the needs of students who enter the schools speaking a nonstandard dialect of English. An important part of what distinguishes dialects from each other is in many cases their phonetics and phonology. Later in this text we will briefly consider social and regional dialects. But for right now it is important for you to know something about the sound system of English, which we are studying in the first few chapters of this text. A teacher who has studied the sound system of English and who is aware of the close relationship between the high front vowels /i/ and /ɪ/ is more prepared to understand the spelling and pronunciation struggles of a student whose native language is Spanish. Garcia has shown that although English has two separate phonemes that are high front vowels (/i/ and /ɪ/), Spanish has only one (/i/). This knowledge could be useful to a teacher who works with English-speaking students whose native language is Spanish.[7]

At the beginning of this chapter we referred to the art of ventriloquism. Now that you have studied the phonemes of English, you are better prepared to consider the following explanation about how ventriloquists perform their art. The two places of articulation that cause the most trouble for ventriloquists are the bilabial and labiodental. These places of articulation involve /p b m f v/ (and to a lesser extent /w/, which although it is a velar consonant, does involve lip rounding). To avoid moving their lips and still be able to use words such as *make* or *fat*, ventriloquists use some carefully selected substitutions. Instead of articulating the bilabial nasal /m/, for example, they may articulate the alveolar nasal /n/, or the velar nasal /ŋ/. And instead of articulating a voiceless labiodental fricative /f/, they may articulate a voiceless interdental fricative /θ/. With enough practice and the right kinds of semantic contexts, ventriloquists can make us think we are hearing sounds that really aren't being articulated.[8]

---

[6]"Phonemic Awareness Training: Application of Principles of Direct Instruction." From *Reading & Writing Quarterly* Vol. 11. (1995) pp. 37-51. The article has also been reprinted in *Linguistics at Work: A Reader of Applications.* ed. Dallin D. Oaks. Fort Worth: Harcourt Brace College Publishers, 1998. pp. 387-403.

[7]"A Linguistic Frame of Reference for Critiquing Chicano Compositions" by Ricardo L. Garcia in *College English* 37:2(1975): 184–188.

[8]The nature of ventriloquial substitutions and the role of semantic context in shaping what we think we are hearing is discussed in a forthcoming article by Renee M. Johnson and Dallin D. Oaks.

Assimilation and Other Phonetic Processes

Some authors have used what is known as an eye dialect to indicate something about the social level, educational status, or informality of a particular character in a literary work. When an author uses an eye dialect, he or she represents a character's speech through nonstandard spellings (not phonemic transcription). An example might be a character's dialogue containing such spellings as "gotcha" (got you) or "jokt" (joked). Ironically enough, eye dialects sometimes represent pronunciations that are in fact used even by speakers of the standard dialect, as the previous two examples illustrate, though the spelling of the words (for which the characters themselves should not be held responsible) are nonstandard. In this chapter you will learn about some natural phonological tendencies in the pronunciations we make of particular linguistic combinations.

A. Assimilation

Up to this point we have been dealing mainly with words in isolation. The pronunciation of such words is called the citation form. But the citation form of words is often not the pronunciation heard in everyday speech. For words are compounded with other words to make new ones; they take on prefixes and suffixes; and usually they are met as part of a continuous stream of speech. Thus the sounds with which a word begins and ends are frequently in contact with adjoining sounds. When two sounds occur cheek by jowl, a change is likely to occur in one (or both) of them: it becomes more like its neighbor in some respect. A few examples will make this tendency clear.

The citation form of *news* is /nuz/ or /nɪuz/. Let us take *news,* with its final /z/, and add *paper* to it. Now the voiced /z/ of *news* is juxtaposed to the voiceless /p/ of *paper.* Do the two sounds remain the same? In the speech of many persons the voiced /z/ changes to a voiceless /s/—/nuspepər/. The change can also work the other way, from voicelessness to voicing. The citation form of *north,* /nɔrθ/, ends in a voiceless /θ/, but when the voiced suffix -*ern* /ərn/ is added, the /θ/ becomes /ð/, thus *northern* /nɔrðərn/.

The process we have just illustrated is called assimilation. Assimilation may be defined as the phonetic process by which one speech sound comes to resemble or become identical with a neighboring sound between words or within a word. In the cases above we were concerned with voice assimilation, a very common kind. In many two-syllable words such as *matter, butter, dirty,* where the voiceless /t/ is surrounded by voiced sounds, there is a tendency to voice the /t/, making it a kind of /d/. In such cases as *sit down* /sɪdawn/ the /t/ becomes identical with the /d/; that is to say, it disappears.

Exercise 2-1

Transcribe the following. Use double underlining to show voice assimilation to neighboring sounds. Be able to explain each assimilation.

1. letter _____
   bottle _____
   forty _____
2. south _____
   southern _____
3. it _____
   it is _____
4. worth _____
   worthy _____
5. got _____
   I've got it _____
6. cup _____
   cupboard _____

7. shut _____
   shut up _____
8. have _____
   I have to fish _____
   I have two fish _____
9. How many guests will you have to feed?
   a. _____
   b. _____
10. used _____
    He used to dance _____
    He used two eggs _____

Voice assimilation plays a role in the formation of English s plurals. In spelling, the s plural consists of the addition of an *s* or *es* to the singular form of the noun. But in the spoken language, there are three s plurals. You can readily discover these by means of the next exercise.

Exercise 2-2

Transcribe the following words in both their singular and plural forms. When you have finished, compare the plural suffix you added with the final sound of the singular to see what relationship the two have. Then answer these two questions:

1. What are the three forms of the s plural?
2. What principle governs the choice of the plural suffix?

	Singular	Plural			Singular	Plural
1. stop	_____	_____		4. muff	_____	_____
2. right	_____	_____		5. breath	_____	_____
3. cake	_____	_____		6. mob	_____	_____

	Singular	Plural		Singular	Plural
7. ride	_____	_____	14. fear	_____	_____
8. frog	_____	_____	15. glass	_____	_____
9. wave	_____	_____	16. rose	_____	_____
10. sum	_____	_____	17. dish	_____	_____
11. son	_____	_____	18. mirage	_____	_____
12. song	_____	_____	19. ditch	_____	_____
13. doll	_____	_____	20. edge	_____	_____

There are apparent exceptions to the principle governing the choice of the s plural suffix—for example, pairs such as *life, lives* and *wreath, wreaths*—which can be explained historically. The principle is also operative with two other grammatical suffixes—the noun possessive, as in *Jack's, John's, George's,* and the *s* ending of the verb in the present tense, third person singular, as in *bakes, begs, itches.* All this we will take up later in the study of English morphology.

A case of assimilation similar to that of the s plural exists with the past-tense suffix *-ed.* Here again we will proceed inductively with an exercise.

Exercise 2-3

Transcribe each word both in the present-tense form given and in the past-tense form. Then study your results and answer two questions:

1. How many phonemic forms does the *-ed* suffix have?
2. What principle governs the choice of suffix?

	Present	Past		Present	Past
1. pass	_____	_____	11. hug	_____	_____
2. laugh	_____	_____	12. rave	_____	_____
3. mop	_____	_____	13. mill	_____	_____
4. back	_____	_____	14. stir	_____	_____
5. rush	_____	_____	15. rot	_____	_____
6. wrench	_____	_____	16. load	_____	_____
7. rob	_____	_____	17. seat	_____	_____
8. seem	_____	_____	18. sod	_____	_____
9. loan	_____	_____	19. need	_____	_____
10. wrong	_____	_____	20. repeat	_____	_____

Assimilation may stem not only from the action or inaction of the vocal cords, but also from the action of other parts of the speech-producing apparatus. As two adjoining speech sounds are uttered, the set of movements producing one of these sounds may accommodate itself to the movements that produce the other sound. In brief, the production of the two sounds is short-cut, resulting in economy of effort and a change in the sounds themselves. An example will clarify this point. Consider the last two sounds of *length* /lɛŋθ/. This is sometimes heard in the assimilated form of /lɛnθ/, in which the velar nasal /ŋ/ has become the alveolar nasal /n/. In the first form, /lɛŋθ/, the tongue back is raised to the velum for /ŋ/; then the tongue tip is placed at the bottom of the upper teeth for /θ/. Two tongue movements are needed. But in /lɛnθ/ the two tongue movements are reduced to one. The tongue tip goes immediately to the bottom of the upper teeth to produce a dental instead of an alveolar /n/, and then remains in exactly the same position for /θ/. Thus production is short-cut with a consequent alteration of sound. The phonetician describes this by saying that the /ŋ/ has been assimilated to (= made like) the /θ/, becoming /n/. This kind of assimilation is called place assimilation.

In the preceding example of *length,* one sound was made to resemble another: the /n/ became partially like the dental /θ/ in that it changed from an alveolar to a dental. In the next example of place assimilation, one sound becomes identical with the second. If we utter *horse* and *shoe* individually, we find that *horse* ends in /s/ and *shoe* begins with /š/. But if we utter them as one word, *horseshoe,* the final /s/ of *horse* is assimilated to the initial /š/ of *shoe,* becoming identical with it in /hɔršu/. In short, the /s/ disappears. The assimilative disappearance of sounds in spoken discourse is not uncommon. When /t/, for instance, becomes part of a consonant cluster, usually enclosed by consonants, as in *softness,* it tends to disappear.

Exercise 2-4

Transcribe the following expressions and be able to explain in class, in terms of the vocal apparatus, just what assimilation is likely to occur at the places in boldface type.

1. stre**ngth** _____
2. thi**s s**ugar _____
3. gran**dp**a _____
4. gran**dm**a _____
5. han**dk**erchief _____

6. co**nqu**er _____
   (cf. contact)
7. He le**ft th**e town. _____
8. Just **th**ink. _____

Before leaving our discussion of assimilation, we should note the very common type of assimilation known as palatalization. Palatalization occurs when the alveopalatal glide /y/ (or sometimes even the high front vowel /i/) influences the preceding consonant, making it palatal. As an example, consider a word such as *issue.* In British English many speakers pronounce this as /ɪsyu/. American English speakers, on the other hand, palatalize the /s/, making it a /š/ because of the following alveopalatal glide and thus pronounce the word like /ɪšyu/ or even just /ɪšu/. Palatalization is also involved in words such as *gradual, education,* or *cordial* in which the alveolar /d/ is palatalized to /ǰ/ because of the following alveopalatal glide or high front vowel. This process of palatalization occurs not only in English but in many other languages as well. For example, the word for *today* in Italian is *oggi,* pronounced /oǰi/ and apparently resulted from palatalizing a form of the Latin *hodie.*

The examples of palatalization up to this point have been within words, but the process can occur across word boundaries and frequently does in the more rapid speech of individuals. Notice how the pronunciation of "did you" or "want you" changes when these words are pronounced more rapidly. Sometimes we contract our speech so substantially that an alveopalatal glide or high front vowel occurs next to a consonant that it would not otherwise occur next to and thus be able to affect. In the utterance "what are you doing?" or even the contracted "what're you doing?" the alveopalatal is sufficiently separated from the consonant /t/ to prevent palatalization. But if the auxiliary verb *are* or its contracted form - *'re* is removed, the conditions are ripe for palatalization, and the first part of the utterance is likely to come out as /wəčə/ (or as it is sometimes casually spelled, "Whatcha").

Exercise 2-5

For each of the words or expressions below, underline the consonant sound that would be palatalized or is likely to be palatalized, even if only in rapid speech.

1. arduous	4. impetuous	7. Please wait your turn.
2. glacier	5. fracture	8. What was your idea?
3. Parisian	6. congratulate	9. Did you come?

Exercise 2-6

Answer the following questions.

1. In the sixteenth century the two forms *unpossible* and *impossible* existed side by side. Why do you think *impossible* survived as the standard form?
2. In *Webster's Third New International Dictionary* we find the variant verb forms *enplane* and *emplane*. Which do you believe will survive? Why?
3. The Latin *cum,* meaning "with," became *con-* in many words. The *n* of *con-* represents either /n/ or /ŋ/. Which is it in these words: *condemn, congress.* Why?
4. A sentence like "She was writing this morning" is sometimes misunderstood as "She was riding this morning." Explain.
5. Chinese *san pan,* meaning "three planks," appears in English as *sampan.* Explain the *m.*
6. Explain the assimilations in the following historical cases:
   a. Vulgar Latin **patre* (= father) developed into Italian *padre.*
   b. Vulgar Latin **domna* (= mistress of household) developed into *donna* in Italy and into *damme,* later *dame,* in France.
   c. Vulgar Latin **debta* (= sum owed) developed into French *dette.*
   d. Vulgar Latin **armata* (= armed, army) developed into Spanish *armada* (= armed fleet).
   e. Vulgar Latin **amta* (= father's sister) developed into Old French *ante* (= aunt).
   f. Vulgar Latin **salata* (= salted) developed into Portuguese *salada* (= salad).
   g. Vulgar Latin **securo* (= secure, safe) developed into Portuguese *seguro* (= secure).
   h. Old English *hæfde* (= had) developed into Middle English *hadde.*
   i. The altered form of *Acadian* is now commonly pronounced with a medial /ǰ/ and spelled as *Cajun.*

B. Metathesis

Metathesis is the transposition of speech sounds. The person who says *tradegy* for *tragedy* or *revelant* for *relevant* is metathesizing. The dialect form *axe* /æks/ for *ask* /æsk/ is another case, going back a thousand years to Old English. Small children sometimes metathesize when they pronounce *spaghetti* as "pusghetti." And even some adults struggle with a word like *aluminum*. The most commonly heard metatheses occur in the phonetic situation of /r/ plus a vowel. Take *pretty* for example. In the sentence "She's a pretty girl," we are likely to say /prɪti/. But when *pretty* is given minimal stress, as in "That's pretty good," the word tends to become /pərti/. If you listen carefully to the pronunciation of *hundred, apron, pronounce,* and similar words with /r/ plus vowel in an unstressed position, you will notice many metathesized /ər/s in the speech of educated people.

Exercise 2-7

In word history, metathesis has been occasionally responsible for changing pronunciations and spellings. As examples, look up the etymology of these words and write the early unmetathesized forms in the blanks.

      1. bird   _____
      2. third   _____
      3. grass   _____
      4. dirt   _____

C. Epenthesis

Epenthesis is the insertion of an extra consonant within a word, such as the /p/ you may hear in *something* or the /t/ in *sense*. The extra sound is termed excrescent. Of the various epenthetic situations we will discuss one that is rather common.

After an /m/ an excrescent /p/ may occur before these voiceless consonants: /t/, /k/, /f/, /θ/, /s/, and /š/. The /p/ occurs because of a slight lack of coordination in the speech-making mechanism, which can be illustrated with *something*. To pronounce *something* as /səmθɪŋ/ requires a precise functioning of the speech apparatus at the critical point of /-mθ-/. For /m/ the lips are closed, the velum is lowered, and the vocal cords vibrate as the /m/ hums through the nose. Now, in shifting to the /θ/, four actions must take place at exactly the same time: the vocal cords must cease vibrating, the tongue tip take an interdental position, the velum rise to close off the nasal passage, and the lips open. However, if the velum closes off the nasal passage a fraction of a second before the lips open, then air pressure builds up behind the lips, and when they are opened, the air bursts out in a /p/.

In other words in which /m/ is followed by a voiceless consonant, the reason for the excrescent /p/ is fundamentally the same: the velum closes the nasal passage before the lips open.

Answer the following questions.

1. Is the *p* in *glimpse* and *empty* the result of epenthesis? To find out, look up etymologies of these words.
2. What variant spellings do *Samson* and *Thomson* have? Explain.
3. Which of these words may be heard with an excrescent /p/: *comfort, combat, warmth, warmly, Tomkins, Tomlin, dreamt.*

D. Epithesis

Epithesis is the addition of an extra consonant to the end of a word. It occurs after a final /n/ or /s/. Consider the word *sound*. In Middle English this was *soun* /sun/. First, we must note that /n/ and /d/ are homorganic; this means that both are made at the same position of the speech organs—the tongue tip at the alveolar ridge. If, when /n/ is being sounded, the vocal cords stop vibrating as the tongue is released from the alveolar ridge, the /n/ merely ceases. But if the velum should be raised, closing off the nasal passage, before the tongue is lowered, air pressure builds up behind the tongue. Upon release of the tongue a /d/ is produced. It was doubtless the latter set of articulatory movements, made by many people in early England, that gave *sound* its /d/, which later appeared in the spelling. The same /d/ can be heard today in /draund/, a nonstandard pronunciation of *drown*.

After final /s/ an epithetic /t/ occasionally appears. It is caused by the fact that the tongue, instead of being lowered to end the /s/ sound, is pressed against the alveolar ridge while the breath is moving outward; then, when the tongue is lowered, the release of air pressure produces a /t/. You will now and then hear this /t/ at the end of *once, across,* and *wish.*

Look up the etymology of the following words to determine the source of the final sound: *lend, bound* (adjective), *against, midst, amongst.*

E. Syncope and Apocope

Syncope and apocope involve the loss of a sound or sounds at the middle or end of a word, respectively. Often, though not always, the loss of a sound or sounds from a word occurs in syllables that are unstressed, and frequently involves a vowel next to /r/. This can be seen in the word *different* in which the vowel sound, constituting the middle and unstressed syllable is dropped from the pronunciation of the word, though it remains in the spelling. We must be cautious, however, not to assume that the presence of any letter found in the spelling of a word, though not pronounced, necessarily represents a case of deletion. Some English words, for example, contain spellings that do not correspond to pronunciations that have ever characterized the language. The word *island* never did contain the -s sound in its pronunciation. The -s was added in the spelling on analogy with the comparable word in Latin (*insula*).

Exercise 2-10

Consider the words below with regard to how you usually hear them pronounced. Identify whether their pronunciation displays syncope or apocope.

1. interest   *Syncope*
2. corporal   *Syncope*
3. mus(t)   *apocope* (Consider the pronunciation of this word by dialect speakers who avoid a word-final consonant cluster)
4. government *Syncope*
5. laboratory   *Syncope*

Some Observations and Applications

A knowledge of articulatory phonetics and the kinds of phonetic processes that affect our pronunciation of sounds in particular environments can be helpful to those who teach a language to nonnative speakers of that language. Such knowledge could certainly help those teachers to be more resourceful and aware of potentially important material not addressed in their textbook. As one brief example, consider what you have learned about assimilation and how that process can work across word boundaries. A textbook may show how the word *did* can begin questions, and students may learn to pronounce the word as /dɪd/. But it might be helpful for a teacher to also acquaint students with the fact that *did* is frequently pronounced differently when it occurs immediately before a word like *you*. Otherwise with an utterance like "Did you come?", students might not recognize that the sequence /dɪǰə kəm/ is just a variant of /dɪd yu kəm/. Teachers with some familiarity of linguistics will be more aware of such variations than teachers who have never consciously considered the sound systems of their language.

In a similar way, those engaged in projects that prepare computers to mimic or interpret human speech must be knowledgeable about phonemes, allophones, and such phonetic processes as assimilation. Otherwise, the computer would be very limited in its ability to produce or interpret speech, because human speakers naturally utilize, display, and interpret such distinctions.

3

Spelling and Pronunciation

In commenting on the problematic spelling of English, George Bernard Shaw claimed that the word *fish* could be spelled as *ghoti.* This spelling would be possible because *gh* could represent the /f/ sound as in *enough;* the *o* could represent the vowel sound /ɪ/ as in *women;* and the *ti* could represent the /š/ sound as in *nation.* Shaw's example makes an important point about some of the variability that exists in possible English spellings. But it ignores some of the regularities that do exist in English spelling. For example, contrary to what his example implies, although *gh* can represent an /f/ at the end of words, it never does so at the beginning of them.

A. Relations Between Spelling and Pronunciation

Languages are reduced to writing by means of three kinds of writing systems. Some systems, such as Cherokee, use one symbol for each syllable. Others, such as Chinese, use one symbol for each morpheme, the smallest segment of an utterance that carries meaning. But most languages, including English, use an alphabetic, that is to say, a phonemic system. This means that the letters stand for phonemes. An ideal alphabetic writing system would be one in which each letter always stood for the same phoneme and each phoneme was always represented by the same letter. Such a two-way one-for-one correspondence between letters and phonemes does not exist in any standard alphabet now in general use. Of course you have been using such a phonemic system in this book, but systems like this are used only by the relatively few who are students of language.

English is far from the ideal writing system, as anyone with spelling difficulties is well aware. In fact, English does not contain a single instance of a two-way one-to-one correspondence—letter to sound and sound to letter. Small wonder. Our language has eleven vowel phonemes and twenty-four consonant phonemes—thirty-five in all. And to represent these thirty-five it has only twenty-six letters, of which three are superfluous. A few illustrations will reveal this inadequacy of letter-sound and sound-letter correspondences. The first letter of the alphabet, *a,* can represent at least seven phonemes, as shown by this series: *dame* /e/, *any* /ɛ/, *pan* /æ/, *father* /a/, *ball* /ɔ/ (as pronounced in some dialects), *pillage* /ɪ/, *opera* /ə/. If we go the other way, from sound to letter, we find that nearly all phonemes have from two to over a dozen spellings. In this respect the vowel phonemes are worse offenders than the consonants. Here are some ways in which the phoneme /i/ is spelled: *ee,* feet; *e,* me; *ae,* Caesar; *eo,* people; *ea,* beat; *ei,* deceive; *oe,* amoeba; *ie,* relieve; *i,* ravine; *ey,* key; *ay,* quay.

Exercise 3-1 (from letter to sound)

Write in each blank the phonemic symbol for the boldface letter.

a. 1. such _____s_____   8. delicious _____š_____
   2. devise _____z_____   9. cello _____č_____
   3. sure _____š_____   c. 10. be _____i_____
   4. treasure _____ž_____   11. met _____ɛ_____
   5. aisle _____   12. English _____ɪ_____
b. 6. cite _____s_____   13. silent _____ə_____
   7. copper _____k_____   14. sergeant _____a_____

Exercise 3-2 (from sound to letter)

a. Write one word illustrating each of the spellings of the phoneme /š/ listed below.

   1. sh _____shop_____   8. se _____
   2. ch _____machine_____   9. si _____
   3. ce _____ocean_____   10. ti _____
   4. ci _____   11. ss _____
   5. sch _____   12. ssi _____
   6. sci _____   13. xi _____
   7. s _____   14. x _____luxury_____

b. Write one word illustrating each of the spellings of the phoneme /o/ listed below.

   1. o _____dote_____   7. eo _____
   2. oh _____oh_____   8. au _____
   3. oa _____boot_____   9. ew _____sew_____
   4. oe _____toe_____   10. eau _____
   5. ou _____soul_____   11. ough _____
   6. ow _____row_____   12. ot _____rote_____

Illustrations like the foregoing, which could be multiplied, suggest that English spelling is unpredictably capricious. But remember that we have been selective, choosing examples that demonstrate this one aspect of spelling, its irregularity. If all English spelling were like this, it would be virtually useless as a writing system. Yet we do succeed in representing the spoken language with our spelling; witness the fact that most persons can read aloud with little trouble. Furthermore, when we meet new words in our reading, we seldom have trouble in pronouncing them. An exercise in nonsense words will illustrate this point.

Exercise 3-3

a. *Spelling to sound.* Write the following nonsense words in phonemic notation to show your pronunciation of them.

1. lete ___/lit/___
2. vake ___/vek/___
3. zite ___/zayt/___
4. noke ___/nak/___
5. fube ___/fub/___

6. theet ___/θit/___
7. noot ___/nut/___
8. deat ___/dit/___
9. poat ___/pot/___
10. boe ___/bo/___

b. *Sound to spelling.* The following words are given in phonemic notation. Write them out in conventional spelling.

1. /dɪt/ ___dit___
2. /tɛt/ ___tet___
3. /jæt/ ___jat___
4. /zat/ ___zot___
5. /čət/ ___chut___

6. /zel/ ___zale___
7. /pabi/ ___pobby___
8. /bæmθəm/ ___bamthum___
9. /sayl/ ___sile___
10. /θut/ ___thoot___

Up to this point we have seen that English spelling contains both regularities and irregularities. Professor Robert A. Hall, Jr., in his excellent *Sound and Spelling in English,* divides English spellings into three groups—the regular, the semiregular, and the downright irregular. He offers a list of forty-seven phonemes and combinations of phonemes that have regular letter equivalents and concludes, "English orthography does afford to each phoneme of the language at least one regular, clear and consistent alphabetic representation." The semiregular spellings, he points out, are irregular only in the way they symbolize one or two phonemes of a word; furthermore, these spellings fall into subsets that are consistent within themselves. The downright irregular are relatively few. As examples of the last, Hall lists such words as *quay, busy, schism, who, debt, choir.*

Here is an exercise that will give you instances of some of the simpler regularities in English spelling.

Exercise 3-4

Begin with the syllable /ɪn/. Go through the chart of English consonant phonemes, diagram 11, and list all the words you can make by placing single consonants at the beginning of /ɪn/. Write each word in both phonemic notation and conventional spelling. Then do the same for /æt/. What correspondence do you find between the consonant phonemes and the letters representing them?

/ɪn/		/æt/	
Phon. Not.	*Spelling*	*Phon. Not.*	*Spelling*
1. pɪn	pin	1. tæt	tat
2. bɪn	bin	2.	
3. tɪn	tin	3.	
4. dɪn	din	4.	
5. sɪn	sin	5.	
6. kɪn	kin	6.	
7. fɪn	fin	7.	
8. ɣɪn	gin	8.	
9. wɪn	win	9.	
10. θɪN	thin	10.	
11. šɪn	shin	11.	
12. čɪn	chin	12.	
		13.	
		14.	

Exercise 3-4 suggests, within its limited data, that English consonant phonemes have one spelling that may be considered regular and stable. In addition to one regular spelling nearly all consonant phonemes have others. The number of spellings varies considerably. At one end of the scale is /θ/, which is always spelled *th*. At the other end are /k/, which has eleven spellings, and /š/, which has fourteen. Within all this irregularity, however, are subsets of words that tend to be regular and consistent within each set. The phoneme /f/ will serve to illustrate these subsets. In initial position its regular spelling is *f*, as thousands of words will attest. But a large subset spell this initial /f/ as *ph*, words such as *physics, phenomenon, philosophy, pheasant, pharmacy.* In final position the /f/ phoneme has its regular spelling in words such as *if, loaf, serf, spoof, beef.* But the subsets give us more possibilities.

> *ff* as in *biff, miff, off, scoff, buff*
> *gh* as in *laugh, cough, tough, rough, enough*

And there are the less frequent final spellings of *fe* as in *knife, ph* as in *epitaph,* and *ffe* as in *giraffe.*

Subsets like these are manifold. They are the basis of the spelling "rules" that you learned in school—for example, "*i* before *e* except after *c*"—which were often accompanied by lists of exceptions. The presence of such subsets, which lead a random existence in our minds, both aids and misleads us in our spelling. They aid us in that they limit spelling choices. If a word begins with the phoneme /f/, we know automatically that it begins with *f* or *ph* and that it does not begin with *ff* or *gh*. Or if we wish to spell a word containing the sounds /ayt/, we are reasonably sure that the spelling will be either *-ight,* following the subset *might, night, light, right, sight, fight, delight*—or *-ite,* following *mite, kite, site, recite, bite.* But such dual sets mislead us, too, for the sounds do not tell exactly which spelling to choose; and also there are exceptions to harass us, such as *height* and *indict.*

Exercise 3-5

English has numerous subsets involving the addition of a suffix. In subsets *a* and *b* below state the principle that governs the spelling of a word when the suffix *-ed, -ing,* or *-er* is added.

a.			b.		
1.	hope	hoped	1.	hop	hopped
		hoping			hopping
2.	dine	diner	2.	din	dinned
		dining			dinning
		dined			
3.	ride	rider	3.	rid	ridder
		riding			ridding
4.	cite	cited	4.	sit	sitter
		citing			sitting
5.	dote	doting	5.	dot	dotting
		doted			dotted

a. _____

_____

b. _____

_____

Exercise 3-6

This is a continuation of exercise 3-5. Study the words below ending in silent *e* and state the spelling principle governing the addition of suffixes.

1.	care	+ ed	= cared	+ ful	= careful
2.	love	+ ing	= loving	+ ly	= lovely
3.	blame	+ able	= blamable	+ less	= blameless
4.	fine	+ ed	= fined	+ ness	= fineness
5.	disgrace	+ er	= disgracer	+ ful	= disgraceful

_____

_____

_____

We may conclude that English spelling is far removed from an ideal phonemic system with a two-way one-to-one correspondence between sounds and letters, but despite the uncertain and insecure relations between spelling and pronunciation, it does have many regularities that are available to the alert writer.

B. Spelling Pronunciation

In the act of reading we sometimes meet words that we have never heard sounded, that are familiar to our eyes but not to our ears. In such cases we do the natural thing—we give them the most plausible pronunciation suggested by the spelling. If, for instance, a plains dweller, in reading a sea story, comes across the words *boatswain* and *gunwale,* he or she is likely to pronounce them /botswen/ and /gənwel/; whereas one reared in a boating environment would have learned by ear the traditional pronunciations of /bosən/ and /gənəl/. This contrast affords an illustration of spelling pronunciation, which is simply a pronunciation that departs from the traditional pronunciation and conforms closely to the spelling.

The words we acquire in childhood, before learning to read, are those that are resistant to spelling pronunciation. The word *cupboard* is a good example. This is normally spoken as /kəbərd/, and few persons notice how far this traditional pronunciation has moved away, by assimilation and weakening of stress on the last syllable, from an aural combination of *cup* and *board.* Now let us compare *cupboard* with *clapboard,* which has gone through exactly the same processes of change and has the traditional pronunciation of /klæbərd/. Many Americans have never heard this word, certainly not in childhood, and others have seen it only in print. Thus it is only to be expected that it should be given the spelling pronunciation of /klæpbɔrd/.

Place names, which may endure for centuries, tend to develop vagaries of pronunciation known only to those in intimate association with the places. It is not surprising that strangers to these places, with only the spelling to guide them, will mispronounce the names. Countless Americans pronounce *Edinburgh* as /ɛdɪnbərg/, not realizing that in Scotland the city is known as /ɛdɪnbəro/. Personal names too tend to change through the influence of spelling. A well-known instance is *Theobald.* When Pope slandered "piddling Theobald" some two centuries ago, he created in the word combination an especially effective collocation of sounds, for *Theobald* still had at that time its traditional pronunciation of /tɪbəld/. Today it is generally known by the spelling pronunciation of /θiəbald/.

It is not uncommon for spelling pronunciations to be generally adopted by all speakers of English, thus becoming the standard pronunciation. A special class of such words deserves mention. English contains hundreds of words borrowed from Latin and French with a *th* spelling. In these words the *th* was pronounced /t/ in Latin and French, and it was with this voiceless stop /t/ that they came into English. Two examples are *theme* and *theater,* both first recorded in English in the fourteenth century. In that century they were spelled in English with either *th* or *t,* the latter reflecting the actual pronunciation. The spelling *th* eventually prevailed, and with it came the spelling pronunciation /θ/ that we use today. In personal first names with *th* an interesting situation exists that can be made clear by an exercise.

Exercise 3-7

After each name in the first column write in phonemic notation your pronunciation
of it. In the second column spell out your nickname for each personal name. In the
third column write in phonemic notation your pronunciation of the nickname.

1. Anthony _ænθəni_ _Tony_ _toni_
2. Theodore _θiədər_ _Teddy_ _tɛdi_
3. Dorothy _dɔrθi_ _Dottie_ _dadi_
4. Arthur _arθər_ _Art_ _ert_
5. Elizabeth _əlɪzəbeθ_ _Betty_ _bɛdi_
6. Matthew _mæθyu_ _Matt_ _mæt_
7. Nathaniel _naθæniəl_ _Nate_ _net_

Explain the /θ/–/t/ disparity in these names. Note that two Biblical names with *th*
have resisted spelling pronunciation and are still pronounced with a /t/. These names
are *Thomas* and *Esther.*

Exercise 3-8

After each word write in phonemic notation your pronunciation of it. Then look it
up in your desk dictionary to see whether you have used a spelling pronunciation. If
your dictionary records two or more pronunciations, try to decide whether one is a
spelling pronunciation that has become acceptable. Sometimes the Middle English
form of the word will give you a clue to the traditional pronunciation. After your notation write SP (spelling pronunciation) or TP (traditional pronunciation) to show
which pronunciation you used.

1. breeches _brĭčɪz_ _____
2. blackguard _____ _____
3. comptroller _K_____ _____
4. alms _almz_ _____
5. victual _vittle_ _____
6. coxswain _____ _____
7. Greenwich _____ _____
8. falcon _____ _____
9. grindstone _____ _____
10. forehead _____ _____

That the spelling of words has at times wrought changes in their pronunciation
does not at all mean that spelling is an infallible guide to pronunciation. Yet you will
frequently hear people justify a pronunciation by an appeal to spelling. They may
insist, for example, that *often* should be pronounced /aftɪn/, because it is spelled
with a /t/, though they do not remember to apply this argument to *soften.* Or they
may wish to pronounce the *h* in *vehicle,* the *b* in *subtle,* or the *l* in *calm* or *salmon*
because their eyes have seen these letters in the printed word. Such a principle is
rendered impossible of application by the irregularities of English spelling, as we

have already seen. The answer to those who appeal to spelling to justify pronunciation is to ask them to apply this principle to words like those in the next exercise.

Exercise 3-9

Write in phonemic notation your pronunciation of the following words.

1. come   Kəm
   home   hom
2. move   muv
   shove   šəv
3. friend _____
   fiend   _____
   sieve   _____
4. swore _____
   sword _____
5. hornet _____
   hour   _____

6. house
   (noun) _____
   carouse _____
   famous _____
7. corps   _____
   island _____
   debt   _____
   sovereign _____
   pneumatic _____
8. colonel _____

Some Observations and Applications

An awareness of the patterns and subpatterns within the spelling system of our language can have useful applications for the teaching of both reading and spelling. Regardless of the approach used in teaching students to read and spell, a teacher will be more effective if he or she is consciously aware about not only the regular patterns within the spelling system, but also the less common patterns, and even the irregularities. This awareness will guide both the teaching methodology as well as the selection of reading materials or spelling exercises that the students will complete.

Another area of application involves deliberate violations of expectations that people have about particular spellings or pronunciations. Such violations are commonly found in advertising and marketing in which it is important to devise product names that are memorable and which are distinctive enough that they can be legally protected from being copied or used by other competitors. Thus one can see spellings such as *nite* and *lite,* which violate spelling conventions but which have a predictable pronunciation based on their form, which parallels another available, though less common pattern found within the language. The selection of an unusual spelling for a product name thus involves more than just coming up with a misspelling. It requires some sensitivity and attention to the spelling system of the language. But even a departure from the expected pronunciation rather than the spelling can perhaps be used for advantage. Two linguists have commented on the unusual pronunciation [nayki] for the brand name *Nike.* As they point out, "In no other word in English do the letters *ike* signal the pronunciation that they do in this word, and yet most American English speakers pronounce the name as it is shown here."[1]

_____

[1]"*MC*–: Meaning in the Marketplace" by Genine Lentine and Roger W. Shuy. In *American Speech* Vol. 65. no. 4. (1990). pp. 349–366.

4

Stress

The joke below involves two different interpretations of *bar tender.* Notice that each interpretation uses a very different stress pattern from the other.

"Then there was the termite who sauntered into the saloon and asked, 'Is the bar tender here?'"[1]

A. Stress Phonemes

In our discussion of phonemes up to now we have been concerned with the thirty-five phonemes of English. These are called segmental phonemes because each is a segment of the continuous flow of speech. But this is only part of the phonemic story. We utter phonemes with varying degrees of prominence or stress; we sound voiced phonemes on different pitch levels; and we employ breaks or disjunctures to break up the whole utterance into groupings. The consequence of these three oral practices is that three more language elements require scrutiny—stress, pitch, and juncture (the common term for disjuncture). All three are phonemic, and as they accompany, and are said to be superposed on, the segmental phonemes, they are called suprasegmental phonemes. In this chapter we shall investigate the first of these three suprasegmental phonemes, that of stress.

Stress refers to the degree of prominence a syllable has. In *agree,* for example, the *gree* sounds more prominent than the *a.* In any utterance there may be as many degrees of stress as there are syllables, but many of the differences will be slight and even imperceptible. We are concerned here only with those differences of stress that have the power to distinguish meanings, namely, the stress phonemes. Of these there are three, when we limit our analysis to individual words. Going from the most prominent to the weakest, we distinguish them by the following diacritics and names:

´ Primary stress
` Mid stress
˘ Weak stress (usually not indicated)

They are all illustrated in the word *légĕndàrў.*

[1]From *1,001 Great Jokes* by Jeff Rovin. New York: Signet, 1987. p. 203.

To demonstrate that stress is phonemic in words we will again employ a minimal pair. If we contrast /pərmít/ with /pə́rmìt/, we see that the segmental phonemes are identical and that the two words differ only in the position of their primary and mid stresses. So it must be these stresses that distinguish them as signifying a verb and a noun, respectively, and the stresses must therefore be phonemic.

Because some students have difficulty in differentiating various degrees of stress, a few graduated exercises may be useful.

Exercise 4-1

Place a primary stress mark over the syllable that has the greatest prominence.

1. defér
2. díffer
3. pervért (verb)
4. pérvert (noun)
5. conflíct (verb)
6. cónflict (noun)
7. évil
8. supérb
9. rómance
10. detáil
11. résearch
12. defénse

Exercise 4-2

Place a mid-stress mark over the syllable that has the next-to-the-greatest prominence. The primary stress marks are supplied.

1. díctionàry
2. sécretàry
3. sèparátion
4. íntellèct
5. fùndaméntal
6. àviátion
7. pèrpendícular
8. àcadémic
9. ùnivérsity
10. àbsolútely

Exercise 4-3

Mark the primary and mid stresses on the following words.

1. accent (noun)
2. austere
3. ambush
4. humane
5. blackbird
6. forgive
7. irate
8. pathos
9. diphthong
10. phoneme

Exercise 4-4

Mark all three degrees of stresses that you hear in the following words.

1. intellectual
2. designate
3. education
4. busybody
5. interruption
6. humanitarian
7. socialized
8. ceremony
9. military
10. uninspired

In the preceding exercises you have been putting stress marks of three degrees on isolated words, the citation forms. When we turn our attention to word groups and sentences, we shall need four degrees of stress. These are indicated as follows:

  ´ Primary stress
  ^ Secondary stress
  ` Third stress (same as mid stress on words)
  ˘ Weak stress

The word *intelléctual* has all three degrees of word stress; but when it occurs in a phrase, *intellêctual cùriósity,* its primary stress is demoted to second, as the markings show, and four degrees of stress are needed to describe the stress patterning. An exercise will furnish more illustrations.

Exercise 4-5

Place a primary stress mark on the single words, and both the primary and the secondary stress marks, /´/ and /^/, on the longer expressions. Omit the third and the weak stress marks.

1. remárkable
2. remârkable invéntion
3. tíresome
4. tîresome jób
5. cóntract (noun)
6. côntract brídge

7. praiseworthy
8. praisewôrthy remárk
9. académic
10. acadêmic procéssion
11. blóoming
12. blôoming plánt

Note, however, that the secondary stress, as in *remârkable invéntion,* is still the strongest stress in the individual word, even though it has been demoted.

    The reason for the demotion of stress we saw in exercise 4-5 lies in the nature of English phrase stress. Only one primary stress can occur in a phrase, and the strongest stress in a phrase (construction or word group) is normally near or at the end, as in these examples: *a tall búilding, an iron tóol, in the pántry, very háppy, delightfully ígnorant, way óut, often wálks, goes for the góld, the day before yésterday, joyful as a lárk, get up éarly, wants to léave, ladies and géntlemen, up and dówn, walk or ríde.* Exceptions to this principle occur, especially with phrases containing personal pronouns.

Exercise 4-6

Place a primary stress mark on the most strongly stressed syllable in each phrase.

1. a wooden gáte
2. a gate of wóod
3. completely góne
4. gone complétely
5. run for the práctice
6. practice for the rún

7. Jack and Jíll
8. bread or wáter
9. not at áll
10. all at ónce
11. call the thief a líar
12. call the liar a thíef

The phonemic status of stress in individual words has been mentioned above, just before exercise 4-1. But stress can also be phonemic in word groups. As an illustration let us look at a minimal pair, *Òld Glóry* (= the flag) and *òld glóry* (= a glory that is old). The difference between the two lies in the secondary and third stresses. A newspaper story telling of the discovery of a very old American flag juxtaposed these two *old*'s in a way that highlights the difference in stress: *ôld Òld Glóry.*

B. Shifting Stress

Many words in English have what is called shifting stress; the position of stress may shift with a change of context. In isolation, before a pause, or before weakly stressed syllables, these words have a primary stress on the last syllable, such as *unknówn* and *downtówn.* But when the primary stress in such a word occurs directly before another syllable with primary stress, two things happen, as is illustrated in *an ûnknòwn thíef* and *the dôwntòwn bákery.* First, the stronger stress is shifted toward the front of the word, because English tends to avoid consecutive primary stresses. English is an iambic language and favors an alternation of weaker with stronger stresses. Second, the primary stress is demoted to secondary, because an English phrase can have only one primary stress, and that is near or at the end, as we learned above in exercise 4-6.

Exercise 4-7

Place primary /′/, secondary /^/, and third /ˋ/ stress marks on the words in italics.

1. His job was *inside.*
2. He had an *inside job.*
3. Our *overnight guests* did not stay *overnight.*
4. The *cut-glass bowl* was not really *cut-glass.*
5. *Inlaid tiles* are always *inlaid.*
6. Wasn't he *almost killed? Almost.*
7. She went *overseas* for her *overseas job.*
8. The soldiers are *Chinese* in the *Chinese army.*
9. He waited to be *fourteen* for *fourteen years.*
10. A *left-handed pitcher* doesn't always bat *left-handed.*

C. Grammatical Stress Patterns

Grammatical patterns are accompanied by regular stress patterns. Sometimes such stress patterns are the sole means of differentiating one grammatical pattern, with its concomitant meaning, from another. At other times the stress patterns just ride along. Of those in English we will take up only four.

Pattern 1. A compound noun is usually accompanied by the stress pattern of ´`. It is exemplified by *blúebìrd, hígh schòol, díning ròom.* A compound may be spelled as two words, as one, or as a hyphenated word. Both *sidewalk* and *shoe store* are compounds, because of their stress pattern, regardless of the fact that one is written as a single word and the other as two.

Exercise 4-8

Place the compound noun stresses over the following words.

1. bláckboàrd
2. hótbèd
3. blúeberrỳ
4. máilmàn
5. shórtcàke

6. róundhòuse
7. páperbàck
8. rócking chàir
9. spínning whèel
10. flýing tèacher

Pattern 2. The modifier + noun pattern is signaled by the stress pattern of ˆ´, as in *sîck núrse, pôor hóuse, wôrking mán.*

Exercise 4-9

Some of the word combinations below could be interpreted as compound nouns or as modifiers + nouns. For the exercise below, consider all to be modifiers + nouns and place the stress marks accordingly.

1. hôt hóuse
2. dârk róom
3. blâck bírd
4. tênder fóot
5. hândy mán

6. swêet potáto
7. fûnny bóne
8. dâncing téacher
9. shôrt stóry
10. môving ván

Exercise 4-10

Here are twelve pairs of compound nouns and modified nouns distinguished by stress. The items in column 1 have modifier + noun stress; those in column 2 have compound-noun stress. Write a brief statement of the meaning of each.

1a. hîgh cháir
   a chair this is high

1b. hígh chàir
   a chair for babies

2a. snôw jób
   a job involving snow

2b. snów jòb
   a deception

3a. blûe bóok
   a book that is blue

3b. blúebòok
   an exam book

4a. grêen hóuse
   a house that is green

4b. gréenhòuse
   a place where flowers are grown

5a. dôuble ú
   two u's

5b. dóuble ù
   w

6a. râcing hórse
a horse that is racing

6b. rácing hòrse
a horse that is used to race

7a. smôking róom
a room that is smoking

7b. smóking ròom
a room that is for smoking

8a. hîgh júmp
a jump that is high

8b. hígh jùmp
an athletic event

9a. dâncing gírl
a girl that is dancing

9b. dáncing gìrl
a girl whose profession is dance

10a. côoling lótion
a lotion that is cooling

10b. cóoling lòtion
a lotion for cooling

11a. Frênch téacher
a teacher that is French

11b. Frénch tèacher
a teacher that teaches French

12a. lông hánd
a hand that is long

12b. lónghànd²
writing by hand instead of typing

Pattern 3. The verb + noun-object grammatical pattern has a stress pattern of ˆ´, as in *They lôve bírds* and *They are bâking ápples*. This pattern occasionally contrasts with the compound-noun stresses ´ˋ, as you will see in the next exercise.

Exercise 4-11

Restate the following sentences so as to explain the meaning of the word combinations that have stress marks.

1. They are râcing hórses. _____

_____

2. They are rácing hòrses. _____

_____

3. Rûnning gréyhounds is his favorite sport. _____

_____

---

²The distinction between compound noun {´ˋ} and modifier-plus-noun {ˆ´} cannot be consistently maintained in English. Here are a few of the complications:

1. Compare *his pêrsonal ínterests* with *his párty ìnterests*. By our rules the first is a modifier-plus-noun and the second a compound noun. Now let's make a sentence out of them:

   He has both *pêrsonal* and *párty* interests.

   Here *personal* and *party* are coordinated by *and*, so that *party* must be a modifier and not part of a compound noun. You can repeat this coordination test with pairs such as *mîlitary clóthes—búsiness clòthes*.

2. Apart from the stress patterns, there seems to be no structural difference between *Fîrst Strèet* and *Fîrst Ávenue*, *páperbàck* and *pâper dóll*, *bóy frìend* and *bôy scíentist*, *flýing machìne* and *flŷing sáucer*, and similar pairs. Thus it does not appear sensible to call the first member of each pair a compound noun and the second a modifier-plus-noun.

3. English contains such expressions as *grêat grándfather*, *sprîng féver*, and *grând júry*, which have modifier-plus-noun stress but whose meanings are certainly not the additive total of those of their components. Furthermore, when the first member is an adjective, we cannot add a second modifier after the first without destroying the meaning, e.g., *great old grandfather*. Hence these seem to be compound nouns with a secondary-primary stress pattern.

   Despite such limitations we will maintain the distinction because it is so widely operative.

4. He raises rúnning grèyhounds. _____

5. They are côoking ápples. _____

6. They are cóoking àpples. _____

7. Sally has a drîving ambítion: she wants to become a doctor. _____

8. Sally has a dríving ambìtion: she wants to use the family car as soon as she can get a driving license. _____

We have seen that the stress pattern ˆ′ is used for both a modifier plus a noun and for a verb plus a noun-object. This situation results in ambiguity when we do not know which of the two grammatical patterns is intended by the ˆ′. For example, in *Flŷing plánes can be dangerous,* the first two words can mean either "planes that are flying" or "the act of piloting planes."

Exercise 4-12

State briefly the two meanings of the italicized phrases.

1. She abhors *scrâtching dógs.*

_____

_____

2. *Môving bóoks* always disturbed him.

_____

_____

3. We enjoy *entertâining vísitors.*

_____

_____

4. They are *encôuraging repórts.*

_____

_____

5. *Bûrning óil* frightened him.

_____

_____

Exercise 4-13

Place stress marks over the words to indicate the verb + noun-object and the compound-noun patterns.

1. Júmp rópes are used by boxers.
2. They *jûmp ròpes* for exercise.
3. He has to *wâsh rágs* after cleaning his gun.
4. *Wáshràgs* are hard to get.

5. She likes to *máp roútes* for travel.
6. We never follow *máp ròutes.*
7. The guards *flásh líghts* into the dark corners.
8. They all carry *fláshlìghts.*
9. We *wátch dógs* with great interest during hunting season.
10. There are three *wátchdògs* on their farm.

Pattern 4. The verb + adverbial grammatical pattern also has a ˆ´ stress pattern, as in *You must lôok óut* and *The tent had been pûshed óver.* The compound noun derived from such verb + adverbial combinations has the usual ´ˋ pattern, as in *The lóokòut had a long vigil* and *This problem is no púshòver.*

Exercise 4-14

Place stress marks over the italicized words to indicate the verb-adverbial and the compound-noun combinations.

1. George is always *cùtting úp.*
2. He is an inveterate *cutúp.*
3. This information is not to be *hânded óut.*
4. These *hándòuts* will give you the necessary information.
5. The movie was *hêld óver.*
6. This movie is a *hóldòver* from last week.
7. She doesn't want to *côme dówn.*
8. What a *cómedòwn* she had.

D. Gradation

Let us approach gradation through examples. The vowel of the word *and* is pronounced /æ/ when it is uttered with any of the three upper degrees of stress, as in

Not Tom ór I but Tom ánd /ænd/ I.

But when *and* is spoken with weak stress, as is customary, its vowel is likely to change to schwa /ə/, as in

Tom ănd /ən/ I have been appointed.

Or consider *to.* With primary, secondary, or third stress the vowel is /u/, as in

The party he cáme tò. /tu/

But under weak stress the vowel will probably become a schwa, that is, the mid-central vowel /ə/, as in

He came tŏ /tə/the party.

As a third example let us take -*ate*. Here the vowel is /e/ when it has one of the stronger stresses, as in

to graduate /grǽǰuèt/

Now if the stress is reduced to the weakest, the vowel tends to change to the mid-central vowel /ə/, as in

a graduate /grǽǰuə̆t/

A final example will complete our case. Some words with a vowel plus /r/, such as *for* and *are,* also have a change of vowel quality under weak stress. The vowel of *for* is /ɔ/ under strong stress, as in

What is it fór? /fɔr/

Under weak stress, however, the combination /ɔr/ may use the mid-central vowel, resulting in /ər/, sometimes spelled "fer" in dialect stories and comic strips. You will hear this frequently in expressions such as

This is fŏr /fər/ you.

With these examples in mind we are ready to define gradation. Gradation is a change in vowel quality, when stress is reduced to weak stress, to the central vowel /ə/. As spoken discourse contains many weakly stressed syllables, it is obvious that occurrences of this vowel are very frequent in daily speech. This frequency is disguised by the fact that there are many spellings for this vowel.

Exercise 4-15

Write the following items in phonemic notation as you say them in natural speech. Don't bother indicating stress marks other than the ones already provided.

1. instáll   /Instȧl/
2. instăllátion
3. áre   /ȧr/
4. They ăre góne.   ðe ĕr gȧn
5. depóse   dipóz
6. depŏsítion
7. háve
8. He must hăve léft.
9. ór
10. Will it be wind ŏr ráin?
11. He cán but he wón't.
12. Hé can do it.
13. Âs you sée
14. Just ăs góod
15. mán
16. póstmăn

Some Observations and Applications

Written texts (whether in print or electronic form) have some powerful advantages over spoken ones. Thus in many situations, when an accurate report of what has been said is needed, we often work with a written report. But written reports also have some drawbacks, one of which is that they often inadequately convey some important phonemic information that is contained within suprasegmental features such as stress, pitch, and juncture. This chapter has briefly acquainted you with some examples of how stress can serve to distinguish meaning. In the chapters that follow you will learn something of the other suprasegmental features. At this point, however, you should already begin to understand how such information can relate to a profession such as law, which sometimes relies heavily on written transcripts of material that was originally spoken. More specifically, you can understand why in some cases an alert lawyer should choose to examine a video or audiotape recording of the actual speech rather than depend on the written transcript version when a determination of the guilt or innocence of an individual relies on a particular utterance. Even as the words may have been transcribed accurately, some important meaning may have been lost.

5

Pitch Levels and Terminals

In the situation described below, notice how intonation would completely change whether a question is to be interpreted as requiring a yes-or-no answer or the selection of a choice.

"An applicant for a job with the federal government was filling out the application form. He came to this question: 'Do you favor the overthrow of the United States government by force, subversion, or violence?' Thinking it was a multiple-choice question, he checked 'violence.'"[1]

A. Intonation Contours

Because vowels and many consonants are voiced, they possess the tonal quality of pitch, for pitch is a necessary concomitant of the vibration of the vocal cords. In English we make use of this pitch as a part of our signaling system. Although we employ many degrees of pitch in speaking, we use only four levels of relative pitch as phonemes, that is, to make distinctions in meaning. These four are as follows:

4. extra-high
3. high
2. normal
1. low

This is to say, the normal pitch of your speaking voice, whatever its actual height, is called level 2; and from this you make departures upward and downward. Take these two sentences:

---

[1]From *A Treasury of Humor: An Indexed Collection of Anecdotes,* by Eric W. Johnson. New York: Ivy Books, 1989. p. 173.

```
2        3   1
```
I'm going hóme.

```
2                                    3   1
```
Her dog found the bone there in the back yárd.

You begin on level 2, your natural and normal level, and remain there until you reach the last primary stress. Here your voice rises one level and then drops to level 1. This 2 3 1 pattern is the pitch signal for statements. The extra-high level, 4, is reserved as a substitute for level 3 when you wish to express special emphasis or excitement. It is rather sparingly used.

Pitches combine into patterns to make meaningful melodies over the whole phrase or sentence—like the 2 3 1, meaning that a statement or proposition is being uttered. These melodies have three methods of closure, which are called terminal junctures or merely terminals.

The first terminal, which occurs at the end of a sentence, is the fading terminal. It is characterized by a rapid fadeaway of the voice into silence and by a considerable prolongation of the preceding word with pitch level 3. It is symbolized by /↓/. This symbol should be used to indicate the closure of our last example sentence:

```
2        3   1
```
I'm going hóme ↓

To sense the prolongation of *home,* the pitch 3 word, compare it with the length of *home* in the next sentence:

```
2                    3     1
```
I'm going home Thúrsday ↓

The second terminal is the rising terminal. It is a short, slight rise in pitch from the last level heard, but it does not go all the way up to the next level. The preceding pitch 3 word is somewhat prolonged, but less so than for the fading terminal. It is symbolized by /↑/ and commonly occurs at the end of yes-or-no questions:

```
2     3   3
```
Are you thére ↑

The third terminal is the sustained terminal. One recognizes this terminal by a slight lengthening of the preceding pitch 3 word, less than before the second terminal, and by a sustaining of the last-heard pitch. The following word, however, may be at a different pitch level. Its symbol is /→/, and it may be heard at the end of a long sentence-subject:

```
2                        3 2  2                3   1
```
All the occupants of the cár → seemed dazed by the shóck ↓

To hear this terminal more sharply, compare what happens at *car* with what you hear in this sentence:

```
2        3   1
```
The car is réady ↓

Patterns of pitch, with their accompanying terminals, like the three above—2 3 1 ↓, 2 3 3 ↑, and 2 3 2 →—are called intonation contours. Note that of the two preceding sentence examples the first has two intonation contours and the second only one.

All sentences, as well as some grammatical word-group units within a sentence, have an intonation contour. In symbolizing contours you should indicate the pitch levels at three places: the beginning of the grammatical unit, the beginning of the syllable bearing the primary stress, and the end of the unit before the terminal. There will be a primary stress somewhere between every two terminals. Primary stress usually accompanies pitch level 3.

There are two exceptions to this requirement of three pitch indications for every contour, as you will note in the pages to follow. First, the initial syllable of a contour may be given primary stress for emphasis, as in

3   1
Jósephine got the reward ↓ (not Harry)

In such cases a beginning 2 pitch need not be shown. Second, a single word may take an intonation contour, as in

2   3   1 1   2
Come hóme ↓ Tómmy ↑

In these cases only the beginning and end pitches are shown.

We are now ready to examine some of the more commonly used intonation contours in American English and the kinds of grammatical units they accompany. But first a word of caution. The contours described below are widely employed, but not to the total exclusion of variant ones. For instance, instead of the 2 3 1 pattern for "I'm going home," some speakers will use a 2 2 1 pattern. So, when you do the exercises, don't try to slavishly follow the contours described in the text; just put down exactly what you hear yourself say.

1. 2 3 1 ↓ (or 2 2 1 ↓). These contours occur in three kinds of sentences.

a. Statement or declarative sentence:

2   3   1
We drove to the láke ↓

b. Command:

2   3   1
Go to your róom ↓

c. QW question (this means a question that begins with a question word, such as *who, what, which, when, where, why, how*):

2   3   1
Who is your fríend ↓

The ordinary statement contour can be used for this kind of question because the sentence already contains a sure signal that a question is coming: the question word at the beginning.

Although the 2 3 1 ↓ contour accompanies the three types of sentences just described, it also is used randomly, especially in long sentences. If you listen carefully to serious TV speeches, you may hear it in unexpected places.

2. 2 3 3 ↑ (or 2 2 3 ↑). This contour is used in three common situations.

  a. Yes-or-no question in statement form:

> 2   3 3
> He's góne ↑

  Here a special contour is needed to signal a question, for without it the sentence would be a statement.

  b. Yes-or-no question in question form:

> 2   3   3
> Are you thére ↑

  c. Initial grammatical unit (phrase or clause or sentence segment)

> 2 3   3
> In shórt ↑
> 2   3 3
> If you'll wáit ↑

Exercise 5–1

For each sentence or grammatical unit supply the marks of the intonation contour—the pitch levels and terminal junctures. It will help you to put in the primary stress first.

1. He walked to the lab.
2. Get out of my sight!
3. Where is my necktie?
4. She won't be home till twelve?
5. Are you going to the game early?
6. To tell the truth, I haven't learned to dance.
7. Unless you take the car, I won't go.

---

3. 2 3 2 →. This contour signals incompleteness. In the first situation below it is an alternate for the 2 3 3 ↑ of 2c.

  a. Initial grammatical unit (phrase or clause):

> 2 3   2
> In shórt →
> 2   3 2
> If you'll wáit →

b. Statement, to indicate that the speaker has more to say; often the word following this contour is *but:*

2　　　　3 2
She's a nice gírl →

4. 3 2 ↓ (or 2 2 3 ↑). This is a call, such as you hear from neighborhood parents. The handful of English names that are stressed on the last syllable—for example, *Marie, Eugene, Bernice, Monroe*—may take the 2 2 3 ↑ intonation pattern:

2　23
Maríe ↑　　　　　　　　　　　　　　　　　，

Others take either pattern:

3　2　　2　3
Hárry ↓ or Hárry ↑

If neither of these patterns brings results, a parent may change to the threatening

3　1
Hárry ↓

which is more likely to bring the culprit scampering home.

5. 2 3 ↑. On an individual question word this contour signals a request for repetition of some part of the preceding message:

2　　　　　　3　　1　2　3
Jane has a new piáno teacher ↓ Whó ↑

6. 3 1 ↓. On an individual question word this contour constitutes a request for further information:

2　　　　　　3　　1　3　1
Jane has a new piáno teacher ↓ Whó ↓

Exercise 5-2

For each sentence or grammatical unit supply the primary stress and the marks of the intonation contour—the pitch levels and terminal junctures.

1. When do we eat?
2. If you'll come,
3. For the most part,
4. He's very handsome, (but)
5. George, (come home at once).
6. We're going to eat in Chicago. Where? (= In what city did you say?)
7. We're going to eat in Chicago. Where? (= In which restaurant?)

7. 2 2 3 ↑ (or 2 3 ↑). This contour is used on a stressed word, phrase, or clause in a series, with the exception of the last item. Note that in each example there are three contours because there are three primary stresses:

2   2   3 2 3 2 3   1
She prefers óranges ↑ ápples ↑ and chérries ↓

2   2 3 2   2   3 2   3 1
She looked under the béd ↑ in the dráwers ↑ and in the clóset ↓

8. Repetition of Previous Pitch. This is used for a quoted clause of the "he said" kind in medial or final position:

2   3   3 3 3   3
Are you góing ↑ he ásked ↑
2   3   1   1 1   1
I'm thróugh ↓ he sáid ↓

9. 1 2 ↑ (or 3 3 ↑). The name of the person whom you are addressing is accompanied by various contours, of which these are quite common:

2   3   1   1 2
Why are you wáshing → Jóhn ↑
2   3 1   1 2
What did you put on the táble ↓ Sálly ↑
2   3   3   3
Are you cóming ↑ Géorge ↑

10. 2 3 3 ↑ 2 3 1 ↓. In this and the following section two contours combine to make a distinction in meaning. This one signals a choice of two possibilities:

2   3 3 2 3 1
Do you want júice ↑ or sóda ↓

This means, "Which of the two do you want, juice or soda?"

11. 2 3 3 ↑ 2 3 3 ↑. This contour proposes a yes-or-no question:

2   3 3 2 3 3
Do you want júice ↑ or sóda ↑

The meaning is "Do you want juice or soda in preference to something else?"

Exercise 5–3

For each sentence or grammatical unit, supply primary stress, pitches, and terminals.

1. Will you have hot chocolate or milk? (one or the other)
2. Will you have hot chocolate or milk? (or something different)
3. I'm taking physics, chemistry, German, and American history.
4. "When are you driving home?" she asked.
5. Give me a lift, Gertrude.

B. Variations for Emphasis

The contours described above are modified when we single out certain words for emphasis. One way to get special emphasis is to give primary stress and a higher pitch level to the word we wish to emphasize.

                2   3 1
Normal: He wants to eat all the tíme ↓
                2   3 2 2   3 1
Emphatic: He wants to éat → all the tíme ↓

Such a primary stress on the emphasized word abrogates the primary stress that would normally come later in the same contour:

                2   3 1
Normal: He fell into the pónd ↓
                2 3   1
Emphatic: He féll into the pond ↓ (He didn't jump.)

In sentences like the foregoing the pitch slopes gradually down from level 3 to level 1. If the emphasized word has more than one syllable, it is the syllable with the highest word-stress that is given the primary stress and the higher pitch level.

                2   3 1
Normal: Spike does not enjoy intellectual gámes ↓
                2   3   1
Emphatic: Spike does not enjoy intelléctual games ↓
                (He prefers other kinds.)

Another mode of emphasis is found in yes-or-no questions. The word to be emphasized takes a primary stress and higher pitch level, just as in the previous examples, but the pitch remains at this higher level for the duration of the question. The next illustrative sentences show the contours used when the emphasis is placed on different words.

                2   3   3
Normal: Are you walking to the párty this evening ↑
                2   3   3
Emphatic: Are yóu walking to the party this evening ↑
                2   3   3
Emphatic: Are you wálking to the party this evening ↑
                2   3   3
Emphatic: Are you walking to the party this évening ↑

Exercise 5–4

You are given below two groups of sentences. For the first sentence in each group indicate the normal intonation contour and primary stress. For the others indicate the contours and primary stresses that take into account the emphasized (italicized) word.

1a. Did his sister make him a cake?
 b. Did his *sister* make him a cake? (not his mother)
 c. Did his sister *make* him a cake? (not buy)
 d. Did his sister make *him* a cake? (not his brother)
2a. Is the library in your college quite large?
 b. Is the *library* in your college quite large? (not the gym)
 c. Is the library in *your* college quite large? (not Jim's)

C. Some Additional Exercises on Stress, Pitch Levels, and Terminals

Exercise 5–5

On each expression place the stress marks that will result in the meaning stated.

1a. fair crowd	a. a medium-sized crowd
b. fair crowd	b. a crowd at the fair
2a. wet suit	a. a special suit for divers and surfers
b. wet suit	b. a suit that is wet
3a. a record sale	a. a sale of records
b. a record sale	b. a sale that breaks the record
4a. a secondary road program	a. a program for secondary roads
b. a secondary road program	b. a road program that is secondary
5a. They're running programs	a. They are programs for running
b. They're running programs	b. They are running some programs

Oral Exercise 5–A

Practice reading these sentences aloud, following the signs of stress, pitch, and juncture. Be prepared to restate the meaning of each.

```
        2                        3    1
 1. What are you going to find óut there ↓
        2                    3  3  2    1
 2. What are you going to find → out thére ↓
        2                        3    1
 3. We have ladies ready-to-wear clóthes ↓
        2        3    2  2        3   1
 4. We have ládies → ready to wear clóthes ↓
        2                    3    1
 5. Give poor food instead of tíckets ↓ (headline)
        2    3   2   3                1
 6. Give póor → fóod instead of tickets ↓
```

```
    2      32   2   3      1
```
7. I had to gó → on Súnday ↓
```
    2           32   3      1
```
8. I had to go ón → Súnday ↓
```
    2                       3   1
```
9. Hope you are both wêll and wárm ↓
```
    2              3   3   2      3   1
```
10. Hope you are bóth → wêll and wárm ↓
```
    2           3      1
```
11. Harris is a black cóunselor ↓
```
    2        3            1
```
12. Harris is a bláck counselor ↓
```
    2           3   3   2   3   1
```
13. They work oút → in the fíeld ↓
```
    2      3   3   2       3   1
```
14. They wórk → out in the fíeld ↓
```
    2                  2   3   2      2   3   2      3      1
```
15. He lives with his wífe ↑ a former módel ↑ and his dáughter ↓
```
    2                  3   2   2      3   2   2      3      1
```
16. He lives with his wífe → a former módel → and his dáughter ↓
```
    2                  3   1
```
17. Some teenagers are home léss ↓
```
    2              3      1
```
18. Some teenagers are hómeless ↓
```
    2  3  3   3            1
```
19. Adúlt → bóokstore owner ↓
```
    2      3   3   3         1
```
20. Adult bóok → stóre owner ↓
```
    2    3    2   2      3              1
```
21. Austrálian → Language Résearch Center ↓
```
    2         3      2   3              1
```
22. Australian Lánguage → Résearch Center ↓
```
    2                                3   2   3  1
```
23. Listeners have said they do Brahms Sécond → bést ↓
```
    2                        3   2   2      3   1
```
24. Listeners have said they do Bráhms → second bést ↓
```
    2                3   2   2      3   1
```
25. The chauffeur will dúst → or wash and polish the cár ↓
```
    2                     3   2   2              3   1
```
26. The chauffeur will dust or wásh → and polish the cár ↓
```
    2              3      1
```
27. Mỳ fâvorite fârmer's dáughter ↓
```
    2              3           1
```
28. Mỳ fâvorite fármer's daughter ↓

Exercise 5-6

Supply sustained junctures /→/ where needed to make, or help make, the differentiation in meaning. Some of the stresses are supplied. Remember that sustained juncture is a matter of the lengthening of the preceding pitch 3 word.

1a. Every dáy passengers enjoy a meal like thís.
   = Passengers enjoy the meal every day.
 b. Everyday pássengers enjoy a meal like thís.
   = Ordinary passengers enjoy a meal like this.
2a. The blue dréss particularly ínterested her.
   = interested her particularly.
 b. The blue dress partícularly ínterested her.
   = particularly the blue dress.
3a. French pláne with twenty-four cráshes
   = the plane that has had twenty-four crashes
 b. French plane with twenty-fóur cráshes
   = Plane crashes with twenty-four aboard.
4a. I consider thése érrors.
   = I consider these things to be errors.
 b. I consider these érrors.
   = I think about these errors.
5a. The sóns raise méat.
 b. The sun's ráys méet.

Exercise 5-7

In these pairs of sentences the segmental phonemes are identical, but the intonation contours and the positions of the primary stresses are different. Explain briefly the difference of meaning in each pair.

```
      2                                3            1
1a. He took pictures of the Salvation Army cóoking students ↓
```

```
      2                           3   2   2     3      1
 b. He took pictures of the Salvation Ármy → côoking stúdents ↓
```

```
      2          3   1
2a. I called Bill a dóctor ↓
```

```
      2      3  1  2 3    1
 b. I called Bíll ↓ a dóctor ↓
```

```
      2                     3  1
3a. Why are you scratching Béss ↓
```

    2   3   1 1 2
b. Why are you scrátching ↓ Béss ↑

---

    2   3   1
4a. Have some hóney ↓

---

    3   1 1   2
b. Háve some ↓ hóney ↑

---

    2   3 1   1   2
5a. What are we having for a snáck → Cándy ↑

---

    2   3 1   2   3
b. What are we having for a snáck ↓ Cándy ↑

---

    2   3   1
6a. I have instrúctions to leave ↓

---

    2   3 1
b. I have instructions to léave ↓

---

    2   3 1
7a. I suspect that you were right thére ↓

---

    2   3   1
b. I suspect that you were ríght there ↓

---

    2   3 2   2   3   1
8a. People who eat Irish potátoes → don't knów any better ↓

---

    2   3 2   2   3 1
b. People who eat Irish potátoes → don't know âny bétter ↓

---

    2   3 1
9a. I believe thăt man is idealístic ↓

---

    2   3   2   3 1
b. I believe thât mân is idealístic ↓

---

    2   3   1
10a. Gêorge's bódy wòrks ↓

---

    2   3 1
b. Gêorge's bôdy wórks ↓

```
     2         3          1
11a. Hè gâve the líbrary bòoks ↓
```

```
     2               3   1
  b. Hè gâve the lîbrary bóoks ↓
```

```
     2                     3         1
12a. More and more doctors are spécializing ↓
```

```
     2       3  2   2       3         1
  b. More and móre → doctors are spécializing ↓
```

Some Observations and Applications

In this chapter and the previous one you have learned something about the role of suprasegmental features such as stress and pitch patterns in the interpretation of utterances, whether in questions such as "Do you want to sing or play the guitar," statements such as "I gave the library books," or mere noun phrases such as "French teacher." You saw that suprasegmentals are phonemic, that is, they can make a difference in meaning. An awareness of the phonemic nature of suprasegmentals is important for careful writing. Many less-experienced writers, even those who are conscientious enough to proofread their writing, whether silently or out loud, fail to notice that the intonation or stress patterns they are vocalizing or hearing in their head may not be the only possible ones that others would attribute to a particular written expression. Thus one important step in improving the clarity of one's writing is to recognize the possible alternative intonation or stress patterns that exist and the need to consider how what one has written may be read with different intonation and stress patterns by someone else. Such an awareness could help someone in making revisions to his or her own writing.

6

Internal Open Juncture

"A famous teacher of literature was sick. He received a get-well card which began, 'Dear ill literate . . .'"[1]

In the preceding chapter we studied the three terminal junctures and noted that they occur at the end of grammatical units or sentences. The fourth juncture of English differs from the others in that it occurs within grammatical units or sentences. It is found between words and between parts of words and is called *internal open juncture.* Like the other three it is phonemic, as this minimal pair will show:

> keep sticking
> keeps ticking

Internal open juncture is indicated by a plus sign /+/ and is sometimes called plus juncture. Here it is with a complete phonemic notation of the pair above:

> 2   3   1
> kîp + stíkɪŋ ↓
> 2   3 1
> kîps + tíkɪŋ ↓

By means of internal open juncture we are able to make distinctions between pairs such as these: *an itch, a niche; its praise, it sprays; Grade A, gray day; see Mabel, seem able.* But although most native speakers have little difficulty in perceiving internal juncture, they have trouble explaining just what gives them a sense of break or separation at the junctural point. It is only through the combined efforts of sharp-eared linguists and spectrograph analysts that we have been able to learn the conditions under which internal juncture occurs. In general, it is the nature of the sounds surrounding the juncture that serves to locate it. The details are numerous and complex and vary with the kinds and positions of the sounds involved. All we

---

[1]From *1,000 Howlers for Kids,* by Joel Rothman. New York: Ballantine Books, 1986. p. 117.

can do here is to examine a few examples of the sound characteristics that define internal open junctures. You will find it good ear training to try to detect for yourself the differences in sounds between the members of each pair before you read the explanation that follows each.

> 1a. kêep stícking
> b. kêeps tícking

There are three differences here between *a* and *b* in the sounds around the junctures. First, the /p/ of *keep* is longer than the /p/ of *keeps;* that is to say, the lips remain closed for a longer time. Second, the /s/ of *sticking* is longer than the /s/ of *keeps.* Initial (postjunctural) consonants are usually longer than those in other positions. Third, the /t/ of *ticking* has more aspiration than that of *sticking.* This means merely that there is more air following the explosion. See for yourself. Hold the palm of your hand an inch from your mouth, say *stick* and *tick,* and notice which /t/ is followed by the stronger blast of air. The same difference is true of all three voiceless stops /p t k/. In initial position before a stressed vowel they have heavy aspiration, but after an /s/ (with no juncture intervening), only slight aspiration. Such are the differences in sound that cue the listener to differentiate between *keep sticking* and *keeps ticking.*

> 2a. a + níce màn (with emphatic stress).
> b. an + íce màn

In *2a* the /n/ of *nice* is about twice as long as the /n/ of *an.* This is the clue that it belongs in initial position with *nice.*

> 3a. it + swings
> b. its + wings

Here we find two sound differences that determine internal juncture. The first you already know—the initial /s/ of *swings* is longer than the final /s/ of *its.* The second is a kind of assimilation. In *wings* the /w/ is voiced, as it normally is in initial position, but in *swings* the /w/ is wholly or partly devoiced because of the preceding voiceless /s/. This kind of devoicing is common; a voiceless consonant tends to make voiceless a following /w/, /l/, /r/, /m/, /n/. A few examples of this devoicing are *twist, flee, cream, smoke, snow.*

> 4a. why + choose
> b. white + shoes

In this pair the /ay/ is longer in *why* than it is in *white.* In general, final (prejunctural) vowels and diphthongs are longer than those in other positions. The /š/ of *shoes,* being initial, is longer than the /š/ that is the second component of /č/ in *choose.* (Remember that /č/ consists of /t/ plus /š/ uttered as a single speech sound.)

The foregoing examples illustrate a few of our speech habits that enable us to distinguish internal open junctures between words. Now let us recapitulate those that you will find helpful in doing exercise 6–1.

> 1. Initial (postjunctural) consonants are longer than those in other positions. For example, the /m/ in *may* is longer than the /m/ in *seam.*

2. Final (prejunctural) consonants are longer than internal consonants. The /p/ in *keep* is longer than that in *keeps*.
3. Initial voiceless stops /p t k/ are strongly aspirated. Examples are *pot, tot, cot.* If, however, these are preceded by /s/, the aspiration is greatly reduced. Compare the aspiration of these pairs: *pan, span; top, stop; kill, skill.* But when there is a juncture between the /s/ and the /p/, /t/, or /k/, there is no reduction of aspiration. For example, you can feel on your hand the aspiration after the /p/ in *this + pot* but not in *this + spot.*
4. In initial position the consonants /w l r m n/ are voiced, as in *way, led, ray, might,* and *nag.* But after a voiceless consonant they tend to become devoiced, as in *sway, fled, pray, smite,* and *snag.*
5. Final (prejunctural) vowels and diphthongs are longer than those in other positions. For example, the /u/ is longer in *new* /nu/ than in *nude* /nud/, and the /a/ is longer in *I saw + Ted* than in *I sought + Ed.*

Exercise 6-1

Write the following expressions in phonemic notation with segmental phonemes and internal junctures. After each pair, explain what characteristics of the surrounding sounds identify the position of the internal junctures. All the information you need for these cases has been included in the foregoing discussion.

1a. I scream _____
 b. ice cream _____

2a. night-rate _____
 b. nitrate _____

3a. that stuff _____
 b. that's tough _____

4a. seem able _____
 b. see Mabel _____

5a. its lid _____
 b. it slid _____

6a. new dart _____
 b. nude art _____

7a. it sprays _____

  b. its praise _____

_____

_____

Can you distinguish by ear between *a name* and *an aim?* Many persons find this difficult because there may be no internal juncture between a weakly stressed and a strongly stressed syllable. In the history of English such difficulty has led to some changes in spelling, as this exercise will reveal.

Look up the etymology of each of the following words in your desk dictionary, write down its ME (Middle English) original, and show how each received a new spelling through incorrect division.

	Present Form	ME Form	Process
Example:	newt	an ewte	became "a newt"
	1. adder	_____	_____
	2. apron	_____	_____
	3. auger	_____	_____
	4. nickname	_____	_____
	5. umpire	_____	_____

An accurate and exceptionless statement about the distribution of internal junctures cannot be made because the habits of speakers vary too much. It can be said that in running discourse many words are separated from one another by /+/. But also, there are cases in which words run together in close transition without the /+/, like the unstressed *tŏ thĕ abóve.* Contrariwise, internal juncture may occur within words, as in *sly + ness* compared with *minus.* We can at best offer just a few principles that will help guide your ear to the presence of internal junctures, with the warning that they are not inviolable.

1. If two vowels in successive syllables carry primary or secondary stresses, there will be a /+/ somewhere between them.

   lîkes + méat   blûe + dréss

   But if two such vowels carry primary and third stresses, there may or may not be a /+/ between them.

   bóathòuse   bóot + blàck

2. Two adjoining vowels are usually separated by /+/.

   ăn ópĕră + of   thĕ + ĭdéă + ămúses

3. A vowel with weak stress followed by a consonant is often in close transition with the consonant, and there is no /+/.

   ăbóve   ă bág   thĕ bést

4. A consonant followed by a vowel with weak stress is in close transition, with no intervening /+/.

   móst ŏf   fóund ĭn

5. Between successive syllables with weak stress there is no /+/.

   ŏf thĕ wáter

Exercise 6–3

Put in internal junctures where they belong, following the five principles given above. Then read these expressions aloud, following the markings, and try to hear the difference between internal juncture and close transition.

1. fîne   jób
2. môst   of   the   tíme
3. the   párty
4. thât   párty
5. tâlk   wísely
6. sòme   of   the   inspîred   ártists
7. Jâne   lôves   cándy
8. stône   fénce
9. bîrd   in   the   búsh

Some Observations and Applications

A consideration and awareness of internal open juncture can be of great importance to those involved in advertising and marketing internationally. Consider, for example, the much publicized problem that Chevrolet had when it named one of its cars the *Nova* and tried to market it in Spanish-speaking countries. In the same way that an English speaker without a proper context could sometimes have trouble differentiating *ice cream* and *I scream* in a spoken situation, despite the phonological cues that exist, some Spanish speakers reportedly misinterpreted the car name *Nova* to be "No va." Unfortunately, this latter interpretation in Spanish means "It doesn't work" or "It doesn't go." Failing to consider the possibilities of internal open juncture in a major target language could lead to disastrous consequences in sales. On the other hand, one business that has exploited the potential for word-boundary ambiguity is the pet store called PetSmart. In this case, both interpretations "Pets mart" and "Pet Smart" carry desirable meanings that the business wants to convey.

Internal open juncture is the last phoneme in our enumeration of the suprasegmentals. Now we will revert to the segmental phonemes and see how they pattern in English words.

7

Phonotactics

The phoneme /ŋ/ does not begin syllables in English. But Curly, the pudgy member of the comic team The Three Stooges, cracked up audiences with his violation of this phonotactic constraint as he frequently uttered his self-satisfied /ŋa ŋa ŋa/.

The English language, as we have seen, has thirty-five segmental phonemes. These phonemes are peculiar to English in that no other language has exactly the same inventory. The *th* phonemes that seem so natural to us, /θ/ and /ð/, are not found in most European languages; and the high front rounded vowel of French, German, and Chinese does not exist in English.

When phonemes are joined together in syllables and words, it becomes apparent that there are limitations to the positions they may occupy and to the ways in which they may be arranged in sequences. For example, an English word never begins with /ŋ/ or ends with /h/. An English word may begin with /st/ but not with /ts/. Spanish words, on the other hand, do not begin with /st/ and German words do begin with /ts/. Thus languages vary not only in their stock of phonemes, but also in the ways they permit these phonemes to associate together. The totality of the positions in which any language element may occur is called its distribution, and it will now be our task to examine in part the distribution of English phonemes, known as phonotactics. We will begin with the consonants.

First, however, we must be clear about the meaning of two terms that will be used frequently in this chapter—*initial position* and *final position*. Initial position means a position that begins a syllable. Thus a group of consonants in initial position, such as /str/, will occur not only at the beginning of words but also within a word, at the beginning of a syllable, as in *restress* /ri + strɛs/. The second term, final position, means a position that follows a vowel and ends a syllable. It ordinarily means the position at the end of words.

English consonant phonemes occur singly or in groups, and in the word, they occupy three positions—initial, medial, and final. This descriptive statement is not as trite as it appears, for it is not necessarily true of other languages. In Japanese, for instance, consonants occur only singly, not in groups, and in Mandarin Chinese consonants do not appear in final position, except for nasals. Our immediate concern now will be with consonants in groups in the initial positions. A group of two or more consonants that adjoin each other in the same syllable is called a consonant cluster; and a cluster after a juncture is called an initial consonant cluster.

A preliminary exercise with nonsense words will perhaps reveal that you, as a native speaker, are already aware of which initial consonant clusters are permitted and which are not permitted in English, even though you have given the matter no thought.

Exercise 7–1

Write E after each nonsense word that sounds English to you, and NE after each one that sounds non-English.

1. /ŋwa/   NE
2. /spro/   E
3. /pfunt/   NE
4. /glɪŋ/   E
5. /šči/   NE

6. /frun/   E
7. /kpadi/   NE
8. /twab/   E
9. /psalmist/   NE
10. /plon/   E

It is the odd-numbered words above that contain the non-English initial consonant clusters. They are real words taken from these languages: 1. ancient Chinese, 3. German, 5. Russian, 7. Loma (Liberian), and 9. French.

In English initial consonant clusters, the maximum number of phonemes is three. These clusters of three have the following positional characteristics:

1. Only /s/ can occupy first position.
2. Only the voiceless stops /p t k/ appear in second position.
3. Only /l r y w/ appear in third position.

But all possible combinations do not occur, and we actually have only the nine of the following exercise.

Exercise 7–2

Give in conventional writing one word beginning with each of the following three-consonant clusters. Note carefully here and in the following exercises that /y/ at the end of a cluster is always followed by /u/. In such words as *student, duty, tune, suit, chew, juice,* and *lute* the pronunciation may vary between /u/ and /yu/.

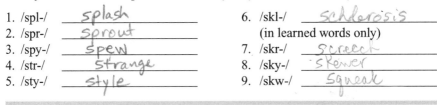

1. /spl-/   splash
2. /spr-/   sprout
3. /spy-/   spew
4. /str-/   strange
5. /sty-/   style

6. /skl-/   sclerosis
    (in learned words only)
7. /skr-/   screech
8. /sky-/   skewer
9. /skw-/   squeak

From the three-consonant initial clusters we derive four classes of two-consonant clusters. Each class has one consonant position vacant, and the two remaining consonants retain the same order as that of the three-consonant cluster. All clusters in these derived classes are listed in the next exercise.

Exercise 7–3

Give in conventional writing one word beginning with each of the following two-consonant clusters. (Numbers refer to the three positions listed above exercise 7–2). Remember that some answers will vary according to your dialect.

a. Derived 1–2 class
    1. /sp-/   *space*
    2. /st-/   *state*
    3. /sk-/   *skate*
b. Derived 2–3 class
    1. /pl-/   *place*
    2. /pr-/   *pray*
    3. /py-/   *pew*
    4. /tr-/   *try*
    5. /tw-/   *twist*
    6. /ty-/   *Tuesday*
    7. /kl-/   *clean*
    8. /kr-/   *cry*
    9. /ky-/   *cute*
    10. /kw-/   *quiet*
c. Derived 1–3 class
    1. /sl-/   *slate*
    2. /sw-/   *swing*
    3. /sy-/   *suit*
d. Derived 3–3 class (first two positions vacant)
    1. /ly-/   *loot*

In addition to the three-consonant and the two-consonant derived clusters in initial position there is also a sizable group of nonderived two-consonant clusters. Each of these contains only one consonant found in the three-consonant clusters. Therefore it is not a derived but a nonderived cluster.

Exercise 7–4

Give in conventional writing one word to exemplify each of the following non-derived two-consonant initial clusters. Some answers will vary according to your dialect, particularly when /y/ is in the second position.

1. /sn-/   *snail*   5. /by-/   *beautiful*
2. /sm-/   *smile*   6. /dr-/   *dream*
3. /bl-/   *blue*   7. /dy-/   *duty*
4. /br-/   *brute*   8. /dw-/   *dwell*

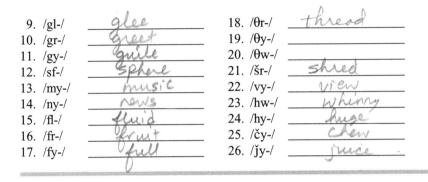

9. /gl-/	*glee*	18. /θr-/	*thread*
10. /gr-/	*greet*	19. /θy-/	
11. /gy-/	*guile*	20. /θw-/	
12. /sf-/	*sphere*	21. /šr-/	*shred*
13. /my-/	*music*	22. /vy-/	*view*
14. /ny-/	*news*	23. /hw-/	*whinny*
15. /fl-/	*fluid*	24. /hy-/	*huge*
16. /fr-/	*fruit*	25. /čy-/	*chew*
17. /fy-/	*full*	26. /ǰy-/	*juice*

A useful generalization can be made about the initial two-consonant clusters. It is the principle that the louder of the two consonants occurs next to the vowel. **Obstruents** (stops, fricatives, and affricates) are softer than **sonorants** (nasals, liquids, and glides). Thus we can say that initial two-consonant clusters follow the order of O–S before a vowel. Here are a few examples, employing all the sonorants except /ŋ/, which does not follow another consonant: *shriek* /šrik/, *play* /ple/, *beauty* /byuti/, *quite* /kwayt/, *smoke* /smok/, and *snake* /snek/.

In two-consonant clusters after the vowel, the sonorant occurs next to the vowel and is followed by the obstruent. Some examples are *hand* /hænd/, *self* /sɛlf/, *ramp* /ræmp/, and *fort* /fɔrt/. Thus the formula for two-consonant clusters before and after the vowel can be expressed as OSVSO.

Exercise 7–5

Classify the first three sounds of each word by writing over each the abbreviation V (vowel), O (obstruent), or S (sonorant).

1. tree
2. class
3. swig
4. cute (second consonant is not shown)
5. smell
6. sneeze

Exercise 7–6

Classify the last three sounds of each word by the abbreviations V, O, or S.

1. clump
2. hint
3. help
4. hard
5. sink
6. porch

The two-consonant clusters you have seen in exercises 7–5 and 7–6 are thoroughly English. Besides these there are some that exist in a sort of twilight zone. They belong to foreign words that have come into English retaining something of their foreign pronunciation, such as *moire* and *pueblo,* and especially to foreign personal and place names, such as *Buena Vista, Schmidt,* and *Vladivostok.* Whether such consonant clusters belong in the inventory of initial English consonant clusters is difficult to say. If you'd like to try your hand at them, do the next exercise.

Exercise 7–7

Give in conventional writing one word exemplifying each of the following two-consonant clusters. For some you may have to resort to names of persons or places. An unabridged dictionary will help you with the more resistant ones. If some baffle you, don't waste time but look at the answers.

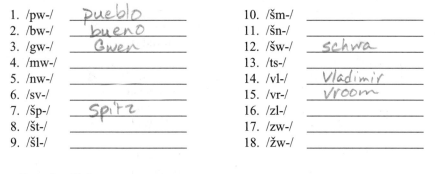

1. /pw-/ _Pueblo_
2. /bw-/ _bueno_
3. /gw-/ _Gwen_
4. /mw-/ _____
5. /nw-/ _____
6. /sv-/ _____
7. /šp-/ _Spitz_
8. /št-/ _____
9. /šl-/ _____
10. /šm-/ _____
11. /šn-/ _____
12. /šw-/ _schwa_
13. /ts-/ _____
14. /vl-/ _Vladimir_
15. /vr-/ _vroom_
16. /zl-/ _____
17. /zw-/ _____
18. /žw-/ _____

Exercise 7–8

When we turn to the single-consonant phonemes that may occupy initial position, we find that all but two may begin a word. Go through the chart of English consonant phonemes, diagram 11 (page 27), find these two, and list them.

1. _ŋ_   2. _ž_

So much for initial consonants and consonant clusters. The clusters that remain, those in medial and final positions, are numerous. We will deal with them scantly, however, because our look at initial clusters will be sufficient to illustrate this area of language patterning known as phonotactics.

In final position—that is, after a vowel and ending a syllable—the maximum number of consonants that can cluster together is five, though it is doubtful whether clusters of five are ever sounded in normal speech.

Exercise 7–9

In the first column write in phonemic notation your pronunciation of the final consonant or consonant clusters in each of the following words. In the second column write down the number of consonantal phonemes sounded in the final clusters.

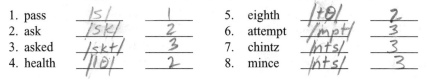

1. pass /s/ 1
2. ask /sk/ 2
3. asked /skt/ 3
4. health /lθ/ 2
5. eighth /tθ/ 2
6. attempt /mpt/ 3
7. chintz /nts/ 3
8. mince /nts/ 3

9. strength	_____	_____	13. twelfth	/f+θ/	3
10. text	_____	_____	14. texts	_____	_____
11. first	_____	_____	15. sixths	_____	_____
12. sixth	_____	_____	16. twelfths	_____	_____

The answer-key to this exercise will give the greatest number of consonants that might possibly be heard in deliberate speech. But you will probably, like many speakers, assimilate and take shortcuts through the prickly maze of consonant sounds. For instance, in number 3 one can easily say /æskt/, but more often the /k/ is assimilated to the /t/, giving /æst/. And in *twelfth,* instead of the full /twɛlftθ/, one is likely to produce a shortened form, such as /twɛlθ/ or /twelfθ/.

Vowels do not cluster. When two or more of them occur successively, one of two things happens: (1) one glides effortlessly into the other, as in /tray/ and /kɔy/, producing a diphthong; or (2) they are separated by juncture, as in *naïve* /na + iv/. So, in the distribution of English vowels, one has only position to consider.

Now we will examine three propositions in regard to vowel positions.

1. Every vowel can begin an English word.

Exercise 7–10

To see whether every English vowel can be used at the beginnings of words, write in phonemic notation one word beginning with each of the eleven vowels.

1. /i/	it	7. /a/	ar
2. /ɪ/	It	8. /u/	uz
3. /e/	et	9. /ʊ/	umlaut
4. /ɛ/	ɛvri	10. /o/	ozon
5. /æ/	æt	11. /ɔ/	ɔtəl
6. /ə/	əp		

Exercise 7–11

The vowels /u/ and /ʊ/ have a low frequency in initial position. List in phonemic notation all the words you can think of in ten minutes that begin with /u/ and /ʊ/.

/u/	/ʊ/
_____	_____
_____	_____
_____	_____
_____	_____
_____	_____
_____	_____

2. Every vowel can be preceded and followed by a single consonant, as in /bɛd/ and /sup/.

Exercise 7–12

To test this proposition, give one example for each vowel of the pattern CVC, that is, consonant-vowel-consonant.

1. /i/   _sit_   7. /a/ _____
2. /ɪ/   _tɪp_   8. /u/ _____
3. /e/ _____   9. /ʊ/ _____
4. /ɛ/ _____   10. /o/ _____
5. /æ/ _____   11. /ɔ/ _____
6. /ə/ _____

3a. Not all vowels can end a word or morpheme. Here we must make a distinction between checked vowels and free vowels. Checked vowels are those that cannot end a morpheme or word. The checked vowels are /ɪ/, /ɛ/, /æ/, and /ʊ/.

3b. Free vowels are those that can occur at the end of morphemes and words. The free vowels are /i/, /e/, /ə/, /a/, /u/, /o/, and /ɔ/.

Exercise 7–13

Give an example of each free vowel occuring at the end of a word. Use phonemic notation.

1. /i/ _____   5. /u/ _____
2. /e/ _____   6. /o/ _____
3. /ə/ _____   7. /ɔ/ _/fɛnəmɪnɔ/_
4. /a/ _____

The phonotactic patterns of a language have a compulsive effect upon its speakers in that these speakers find it hard to break the patterns of their native tongue and habituate themselves to the use of new ones. If, for example, you try to teach a Spaniard to pronounce *student,* he is likely to persist in saying /ɛstudɛnt/ for some time because /st-/ is not an initial consonant cluster in Spanish, whereas /ɛst-/ is common. Likewise, an American in India has great difficulty in pronouncing the native term for washerman, *dhobi* /dʰobi/, because /dʰ-/, an aspirated /d/, does not occur initially in English. Instead, he will say /dobi/. Yet this same American can say *Toby* /tʰobi/ with perfect ease because initial /tʰ-/, an aspirated /t/, is a normal word-beginning in English.

The general tendency is for a speaker to pronounce words borrowed from another tongue with the phonotactic patterns of his own language, even when he can utter the foreign clusters. For instance, it is easy for us to say /šn-/ at the beginning of a word, as in the German *Schnorchel,* but we normally change the word to /snɔrkəl/ to conform to our own English initial cluster /sn-/.

Here are eleven words, each beginning with a consonant or consonant cluster that is not native to English in initial position. Assume that you see each one in print and wish to pronounce it. Write down in phonemic symbols your probable pronunciation. Some will be easy; others may be difficult and require the substitution of English initial sounds.

1. German *Pfund* /pfunt/, pound   _____
2. German *Zeit* /tsait/, time   _____
3. French *Psyché* /psiše/, Psyche   _____
4. Mazahua (an unwritten Mexican
   language) /ndišu/, woman   _____
5. African *Mboya* /mbɔya/, = a proper name _____
6. Norwegian *sving* /sviŋ/, curve   _____
7. Chamorro *nganga* /ŋanga/, duck   _____
8. Dutch *wrak* /vrak/, wreck   _____

The next three are not transliterated but are given only in phonemic symbols. Can you pronounce them as given or would you make substitutions?

9. Modern Greek /dzikas/, grasshopper   _____
10. Modern Greek /ksilo/, wood   _____
11. Russian /ščɛpka/, sliver   _____

Some Observations and Applications

In the previous chapter we showed that failure to consider a potential problem in the internal open juncture of a product name that will be marketed in a foreign country can result in a problem. In this chapter we have examined the issue of phonotactics and could appropriately issue a similar caution in relation to this subject matter. Indeed, international marketers involved in product naming should be aware of the phonotactics in the languages of those areas that will be targeted for marketing. Some sounds and sound combinations are clearly easier than others for speakers of particular languages. The name *Kodak* was reportedly chosen quite deliberately for its ease of articulation for speakers in many languages.

If a company is considering the option of not accommodating or adapting a product name for a given speech community that might have trouble with the sound sequence, then that company should at least examine one other phonotactic issue: What word will likely result in the target community's language if the speakers of the language adapt the pronunciation of the product name to fit their own phonotactics? Depending on the nature of the resulting word meaning, the company may decide it is in fact worth the effort to change the name.

A knowledge of phonotactics can also be useful in a language classroom, especially when the teacher is a native speaker of a language that differs from what is spoken by his or her students. This can happen, for example, in an ESL (English as a Second Language) classroom. If teachers are aware of the potential areas of articulatory difficulty, before classroom teaching even begins, they can be better prepared to address those problems. At the very least, teachers should understand the issue of phonotactics so that they do not automatically attribute certain mispronunciations to other factors.

With this chapter on phonotactics we conclude the description of basic English phonology, that is, of that phonological information that you will need in the later sections on morphology and syntax.

Part Two

The Morphology of English

8

Morphemes

We now turn our attention to the study of the internal structure of words, which is known as morphology. We will use the term *word* loosely, in its familiar sense, because a strict definition will not be necessary till later.

A. Definition of Morpheme

Before we can examine the structure of words, we must become acquainted with an entity known as the morpheme. A morpheme is a short segment of language that meets three criteria:

1. It is a word or a part of a word that has meaning.
2. It cannot be divided into smaller meaningful parts without violation of its meaning or without meaningless remainders.
3. It recurs in differing verbal environments with a relatively stable meaning.

Let us examine the word *straight* /stret/ in the light of these criteria. First, we recognize it as a word and can find it listed as such in any dictionary. Second, it cannot be divided without violation of meaning. For example, we can, by dividing straight /stret/, get the smaller meaningful forms of *trait* /tret/, *rate* /ret/, and *ate* /et/, but the meanings of these violate the meaning of *straight*. Furthermore, when we divide it in these ways we get the meaningless remainders of /s-/, /st-/, and /str-/. Third, *straight* recurs with a relatively stable meaning in such environments as *straightedge, straighten,* and *a straight line.* Thus *straight* meets all of the criteria of a morpheme.

As a second example let us compare the morpheme bright (= light) with the word *brighten* (= make light). In sound the only difference between the two words is the added /-ən/ of *brighten,* and in meaning the difference is the added sense of "make" in *brighten.* This leads us to conclude that /-ən/ means "make." Thus we

---

[1]From Alva Johnston's *The Great Goldwyn* as quoted in *Familiar Quotations,* 15th edition, by John Bartlett, ed. by Emily Morison Beck. Boston: Little, Brown and Company, 1980, p. 777.

see that /-ən/ is a part of a word that has meaning. We also know that it cannot be divided into smaller meaningful units and that it recurs with a stable meaning in words such as *cheapen, darken, deepen, soften,* and *stiffen.* It is therefore obvious that /-ən/ must be considered a morpheme. So *brighten* contains two morphemes: *bright* and *-en.*

Exercise 8-1

After each word write a number showing how many morphemes it contains.

1. play	1		11. keeper	2	
2. replay	2		12. able	1	
3. date	1		13. unable	2	
4. antedate	2		14. miniskirt	2	
5. hygiene	1		15. rain	1	
6. weak	1		16. rainy	2	
7. weaken	2		17. cheap	1	
8. man	1		18. cheaply	2	
9. manly	2		19. cheaper	2	
10. keep	1		20. cover	1	

Exercise 8-2

Write the meaning of the italicized morphemes.

1. *ante*date   before
2. *re*play   again
3. man*ly*   like
4. keep*er*   doing something
5. *un*able   not
6. rain*y*
7. cheap*est*   perlative (most)
8. *in*active   not
9. *im*possible   not
10. *mal*function (noun)   evil or bad

B. Free and Bound Morphemes

Morphemes are of two kinds, free and bound. A free morpheme is one that can be uttered alone with meaning, such as the words *straight* or *bright* that we saw earlier. A bound morpheme, unlike the free, cannot be uttered alone with meaning. It is always annexed to one or more morphemes to form a word. The italicized morphemes in exercise 8–2 are all bound, for one would not utter in isolation such forms as *ante-, re-, -ly, -er,* and *un-.* Here are a few more examples: *pre*view, play*ed,* activ*ity,* su*pervise, inter-, -vene.*

Exercise 8–3

Underline the bound morphemes. It is possible for a word to consist entirely of bound morphemes.

1. speaker
2. kingdom
3. petrodollar
4. idolize
5. selective

6. biomass
7. intervene
8. remake
9. dreamed
10. undo

C. Bases

Another classification of morphemes puts them into two classes: bases and affixes (such as prefixes and suffixes). A base morpheme is the part of a word that has the principal meaning.[2] The italicized morphemes in these words are bases: *denial, lovable, annoyance, re-enter.* Bases are very numerous, and most of them in English are free morphemes; but some are bound, such as *-sent* in *consent, dissent* and *assent.* A word may contain one base and one or more affixes. *Readability,* for example, contains the free base *read* and the two suffixes *-abil-* and *-ity;* and *unmistakable* has the free base *take* and the prefixes *un-* and *mis-,* as well as the suffix *-able.*

Exercise 8–4

Underline the bases in these words.

1. womanly
2. endear
3. failure
4. famous
5. infamous

6. lighten
7. enlighten
8. friendship
9. befriend
10. Bostonian

11. unlikely
12. prewar
13. subway
14. falsify
15. unenlivened

All the bases in the preceding exercise are free bases. Now we will look at bound bases, to which it is sometimes hard to attach a precise meaning. A good number of bound bases in English come from Latin and Greek, such as the *-sent-* in *sentiment, sentient, consent, assent, dissent, resent.* The standard way to pin

---

[2]This *ad hoc* definition will do for our present purpose. A more exact definition, which requires terms that you will not meet until later, would go something like this: A base is a linguistic form that meets one or more of these requirements:

1. It can occur as an immediate constituent of a word whose only other immediate constituent is a prefix or suffix.

   Examples: re*act, act*ive, *fertil*ize

2. It is an allomorph of a morpheme which has another allomorph that is a free form.

   Examples: *dep*th (*deep*), *wolv*es (*wolf*)

3. It is a borrowing from another language in which it is a free form or a base.

   Examples: *bio*metrics, *micro*cosm, phrase*ology*

The third point is open to the theoretical objection that it imports diachronic lore to clarify a synchronic description.

down the meaning is to search for the meaning common to all the words that contain the base (in these words, *-sent-* means "feel"). A base may have more than one phonemic form. In the above list it has these forms: /sɛntɪ-/, /sɛnš-/, /-sɛnt/, and /-zɛnt/. Here is an exercise in this method.

Exercise 8–5

Write in the blanks the meaning of the italicized bound bases. To be exact, we should write these words below in phonemic script to show the various forms of the base, but this would involve a complication that will be explained later. So here we must be content to indicate the base in a loose way with spelling.

1. *aud*ience, *aud*ible, *aud*ition, *aud*itory ____to hear____
2. sui*cide,* patri*cide,* matri*cide,* infanti*cide* _____
3. *or*al, *or*ation, *or*acle, *or*atory _____
4. *aqua*plane, *aqua*tic, *aqua*rium, *aqua*naut _____
5. photo*graphy,* bio*graphy,* calli*graphy* ____to write____
6. *corps, corpse, corpor*ation, *corpor*eal _____
7. *mono*chrome, *mono*logue, *mono*rail, *mono*gamy _____
8. *pend*ulum, *pend*ant, sus*pend*ers, im*pend*ing _____
9. *manu*al, *mani*cure, *manu*script, *mana*cle _____
10. e*ject,* in*ject,* pro*ject,* re*ject* _____

This method can be difficult and baffling. An easier way that often works is to look up in your dictionary the word in question, like *consent,* and in the etymology find out the Latin or Greek meaning of the base. Under *consent* you will find that *-sent* means "feel" in Latin, and this area of meaning seems to have been retained for the base of all the words in the *-sent* list. Also, you will find some of the more common base morphemes listed as separate entries. The following, for example, are all separately entered in *The American Heritage Dictionary of the English Language: phot-, photo-* (light); *xer-, xero-* (dry); *bi-, bio-* (life); *mis-, miso-* (hatred); *ge-, geo-* (earth); *biblio-* (book); *-meter* (measuring device); *tele-, tel-* (distance; distant).

Exercise 8–6

Look up in your desk dictionary the meanings of the bound bases italicized in the words below. Write the meanings of these bound bases in the first column. In the second column write another English word that contains the same base.

1. *geo* graphy ____writing____ ____geology____
2. *bio* logy _____ ____biography____
3. *biblio* phile _____ _____
4. inter*vene* _____ _____
5. com*prehend* _____ _____
6. re*cur* _____ _____
7. in*spect* _____ _____
8. op*pose* _____ _____

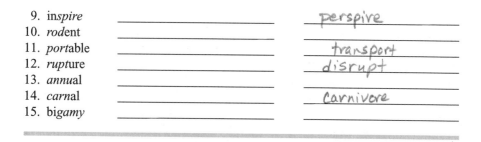

9. in*spire*　＿＿＿＿＿＿＿＿＿　*perspire*
10. *rod*ent　＿＿＿＿＿＿＿＿＿　＿＿＿＿＿＿＿＿
11. *port*able　＿＿＿＿＿＿＿＿＿　*transport*
12. *rupt*ure　＿＿＿＿＿＿＿＿＿　*disrupt*
13. *annu*al　＿＿＿＿＿＿＿＿＿　＿＿＿＿＿＿＿＿
14. *carn*al　＿＿＿＿＿＿＿＿＿　*carnivore*
15. big*amy*　＿＿＿＿＿＿＿＿＿　＿＿＿＿＿＿＿＿

D. Difficulties in Morphemic Analysis

Let us now digress long enough to point out that the identification of morphemes is not as tidy a business as may appear in these exercises and that there are serious, perhaps insoluble, difficulties in morphemic analysis.

The first difficulty is that you have your own individual stock of morphemes just as you have a vocabulary that is peculiarly your own. An example will make this clear. Tom may think of *automobile* as one morpheme meaning "car," whereas Dick may know the morphemes *auto-* (self) and *mobile* (moving), and recognize them in other such words as *autograph* and *mobilize.* Dick, on the other hand, may consider *chronometer* to be a single morpheme, a fancy term for "watch," but Harry sees in this word two morphemes, *chrono-* (time) and *meter* (measure), which he also finds in *chronology* and *photometer,* and Sadie finds a third morpheme *-er* in it, as in *heater;* thus, *mete* (verb) to measure, + – *er,* one who, or that which.

The second difficulty is that persons may know a given morpheme but differ in the degree to which they are aware of its presence in various words. It is likely, for instance, that most speakers of English know the agentive suffix /-ər/ (spelled *-er, -or, -ar*) meaning "one who, that which," and recognize it in countless words such as *singer* and *actor.* But many may only dimly sense this morpheme in *professor* and completely overlook it in *voucher, cracker,* and *tumbler.* Thus, can we say that *sweater* has enough pulse in its *-er* to be considered a two-morpheme word? This will vary with the awareness of different individuals. A less simple case is seen in this group: *nose, noseful, nosey, nasal, nuzzle, nozzle, nostril, nasturtium.* Only a linguistically knowledgeable person would see the morpheme *nose* in each of these words. Others will show considerable differences in awareness.

Thus, we conclude that one individual's morphemes are not those of another. This is no cause for deep concern, though it may be a source of controversy in the classroom, for we are dealing with the morphemes of the ENGLISH LANGUAGE, not merely with the individual morpheme inventories of Tom, Dick, Harry, and Sadie.

But in the language itself there are problems of morphemic analysis because the language is constantly changing. One problem is that of obsolescence.

Morphemes may slowly fade away into disuse as the decades and centuries roll by, affecting our view of their morphemehood. For instance, we can be sure that *troublesome, burdensome, lonesome,* and *cuddlesome* are two-morpheme words consisting of a base morpheme plus the suffixal morpheme *-some. Winsome,* however, has an obsolete base (Old English *wynn,* pleasure, joy), so that the word is now monomorphemic. Between these two extremes are words like *ungainly.* This means of course "not gainly," but what does *gainly* mean? Certainly it is not in common use. In current dictionaries it is called "rare" or "obsolete" or "dialectal," or is unlabeled. Then should we call *ungainly* a word of one or two or even three morphemes?

Another problem results from the fact that metaphors die as language changes. Let us take the morpheme *-prehend-* (seize) as an example. In *apprehend* (= to arrest or seize) and *prehensile* it clearly retains its meaning, but in *comprehend* the metaphor (seize mentally) seems to be dead, and the meaning of the word today is merely "understand." Does it then still contain the morpheme *-prehend-?* Another case is seen in *bankrupt* (bench broken). The morpheme *bank,* in the sense of a bench, may be obsolete, but *-rupt* is alive today in *rupture* and *interrupt.* The original metaphor is dead, however, and the meaning of these two morphemes does not add up at all to the current meaning of *bankrupt.* Is the word then a single morpheme?

This last matter, additive meanings, is a problem in itself. Meaning is very elusive, and when morphemes combine in a word, their meanings tend to be unstable and evanescent; they may even disappear altogether. Consider, for example, the morpheme *pose* (place). In "pose a question" the meaning is clear, and it is probably retained in *interpose* (place between). But in *suppose* and *repose* the meaning appears to have evaporated. Between these extremes are words like *compose, depose, impose, propose,* and *transpose,* in which the sense of *pose* seems to acquire special nuances in combination. Which of all these words, then, may be said to contain the morpheme *pose* (place)? Such are some of the problems in morphemic analysis that have plagued linguists.

Optional Exercise 8–7

This exercise is an excursus into dead metaphor, simply to show you a fascinating aspect of words that many people are unaware of. Look up the etymology of the following words in your desk dictionary and note the original meaning that underlies the words. A little thought will show you the connection between the original meaning and the present sense.

1. daisy	_____	6. hazard	_____
2. muscle	_____	7. calculate	_____
3. supercilious	_____	8. spurn	_____
4. window	_____	9. stimulate	_____
5. easel	_____	10. stagnate	_____

As a practical measure, when we perform morphological analysis, we will work synchronically rather than diachronically. In other words, we will identify morphemes on the basis of what they mean and how they function within our language now, rather than identifying them on the basis of earlier meanings or functions. The reason for a synchronic approach to morphological analysis, especially in an introductory course, becomes apparent if we consider the complications that might arise from a diachronic consideration. The examples in Exercise 8–7 make this quite clear. For example, in the case of the word *daisy,* it would be unreasonable to expect most people to spot the three morphemes whose historical presence in that word are now barely discernible in its current form and whose historical meanings are no longer a factor in our current perception about the word's meaning.

E. Affixes

An affix is a bound morpheme that occurs before or within or after a base. There are three kinds: prefixes, infixes, and suffixes, two of which you have already met in passing. Now we will deal with them in greater detail.

Prefixes are those bound morphemes that occur before a base, as in *im*port, *pre*fix, *re*consider. Prefixes in English are a small class of morphemes, numbering about seventy-five. Their meanings are often those of English prepositions and adverbials.

Exercise 8–8

Look up in your desk dictionary each italicized prefix. (Be careful here. If you are looking up the prefix *in-* in a dictionary, you will find various entries for *in,* including the word *in* itself, which you don't want. Prefixes will be indicated as such by a hyphen after the morpheme; thus, *in-.*) Sometimes, when you have located the exact entry you want, you will find several meanings for it. From the meanings given for the prefix, choose the one that fits the word and write it in the first column. In the second column write another word containing the same prefix with the same meaning. Numbers 3, 7, 8, and 11 contain variants of a prefixal morpheme.

1. *anti*freeze   _____   _____
2. *circum*vent   _____   _____
3. *co*pilot   _____   _____
   *col*lapse   _____   _____
   *com*pact   _____   _____
   *con*vene   _____   _____
   *cor*rode   _____   _____
4. *contra*dict   _____   _____
5. *de*vitalize   _____   _____
6. *dis*agreeable   _____   _____
7. *in*secure   _____   _____
   *im*perfect   _____   _____
   *il*legible   _____   _____
   *ir*reverent   _____   _____
8. *in*spire   _____   _____
   *im*bibe   _____   _____
9. *inter*vene   _____   _____
10. *intra*mural   _____   _____

11. *ob*struct _____ _____
    *op*pose _____ _____
12. *pre*war _____ _____
13. *post*war _____ _____
14. *pro*ceed _____ _____
15. *retro*active _____ _____
16. *semi*professional _____ _____
17. *sub*way _____ _____
18. *super*abundant _____ _____
19. *un*likely _____ _____
20. *un*dress _____ _____

Infixes are bound morphemes that have been inserted within a word. As a general rule, English does not have infixes, though we should acknowledge a few exceptional cases. Consider, for example, what we find in *un get at able,* where the preposition *at* of *get at* is kept as an infix in the *-able* adjective, though the preposition is usually dropped in similar words, like *reliable* (from *rely on*) and *accountable* (from *account for*). It might be tempting to consider as infixes the replacive vowels that occur in a few noun plurals, like the *-ee-* in *geese,* replacing the *-oo-* of *goose,* or those that occur in the past tense and past participles of some verbs, like the *-o-* of *chose* and *chosen* replacing the *-oo-* of *choose.* But these are more precisely "replacive allomorphs" and will not be considered to be infixes. These allomorphs will be examined later.

Suffixes are bound morphemes that occur after a base, such as shrink*age,* fail*ure,* nois*y,* real*ize,* nail*s,* dream*ed.* Suffixes may pile up to the number of three or four, whereas prefixes are commonly single, except for the negative *un-* before another prefix. In *normalizers* we perhaps reach the limit with four suffixes[3]: the base *norm* plus the four suffixes *-al, -ize, -er, -s.* When suffixes multiply like this, their order is fixed: there is one and only one order in which they occur.

Exercise 8–9

In these words the base is italicized. After each word write the number of suffixes it contains.

1. *organ*ists _____2_____
2. *person*alities _____3_____
3. *flirt*atiously _____2_____
4. *atom*izers _____3_____
5. *friend*liest _____2_____ *Superlative*

6. *contradict*orily _____3_____
7. *trust*eeship _____2_____
8. *greas*ier _____2_____ *comparitive*
9. *countr*ified _____2_____
10. *respons*ibilities _____3_____

for make it into try country

_____

[3] There is, however, the widely noted though highly contrived example of the word antidisestablish*ment ari an ism s,* which contains five suffixes and two prefixes.

Exercise 8–10

Each group contains a base and suffixes. Make each into a word. In each case see if more than one order of suffixes is possible.

1. -ed, live, -en — *livened*
2. -ing, -ate, termin — *terminating*
3. -er, -s, mor, -al, -ize — *moralizers*
4. provinc, -s, -ism, -ial — *provincialisms*
5. -ly, -some, grue — *gruesomely*
6. -ity, work, -able — *workability*
7. in, -most, -er — *innermost*
8. marry, -age, -ity, -abil — *marriageability*
9. -dom, -ster, gang — *gangsterdom*
10. -ly, -ion, -ate, affect — *affectionately*

F. Inflectional Suffixes

The inflectional suffixes can be schematized as follows:

Inflectional Suffix	Examples	Name
1. {-s pl}	dog*s*, bush*es*	noun plural
2. {-s sg ps}	boy'*s*	noun singular possessive
3. {-s pl ps}	boy*s*', men'*s*	noun plural possessive
4. {-s 3d}	run*s*, catch*es*	present third-person singular
5. {-ING vb}	discuss*ing*	present participle
6. {-D pt}	chew*ed*	past tense
7. {-D pp}	chew*ed*, eat*en*	past participle
8. {-ER cp}	bold*er*, soon*er*, near*er*	comparative
9. {-EST sp}	bold*est*, soon*est*, near*est*	superlative

The words to which these suffixes are attached are called stems. The stem includes the base or bases and all the derivational affixes. Thus, the stem of *cowboys* is *cowboy* and that of *beautified* is *beautify*.

The above chart should be accompanied by a few observations. The chart does not contain alternate forms that are sometimes used for the plural, past tense, or past participle. Thus although the plural inflection -*s* as in *dogs* is listed, there are some exceptional plural forms such as the -*en* of *oxen* (once a common inflection in English) and the non-inflectional inner vowel change of *mice,* which are not included in the chart. Similarly, although most past tense and past participle forms end in the inflectional -*ed*, there are some non-inflected forms that alter the vowel of the verb base, as happens in the forms *sang* and *sung*. Rather than list the kinds of exceptional forms that occur in addition to the typical inflectional forms that characterize such notions as plural or past, we have listed only the inflectional suffixes that typically characterize such notions and noted here that there are alternate forms that sometimes occur.

The overlapping form *-ed* for both the past tense and past participle does not normally cause a problem for interpretation, because the grammatical context of the two is different. For example, compare the difference between the past tense usage in "Jane composed the song" and the past participle usage in "Jane has composed the song" or "The music was composed (by Jane)." Furthermore, although *-ed* is the inflectional past participle form with regular verbs, the suffix *-en* occurs in the past participle with a number of irregular verbs such as *driven, written, eaten.* Because of this and because the inflectional *-en* can in some cases serve to distinguish the past participle from the past tense, we will list it as an alternate inflectional suffix form for the past participle. But we caution the reader to remember that past participles come in a variety of forms, some of which do not even utilize the *-ed* or *-en* suffixes.

Inflectional suffixes are not the only kind of suffix. English also has derivational suffixes such as the *-ish* in the word *childish.* Before looking at derivational suffixes in greater detail, we will first consider those ways in which the inflectional suffixes are different from derivational suffixes.

The inflectional suffixes differ from the derivational suffixes in the following ways, to which there are few exceptions.

1. They do not change the part of speech.
   Examples: sled, sled*s* (both nouns)
   cough, cough*ed* (both verbs)
   cold, cold*er* (both adjectives)

2. They come last in a word when they are present.
   Examples: wait*ed*, villaini*es*, industrializ*ing*

3. They go with all stems of a given part of speech.
   Examples: He eat*s*, drink*s*, dream*s*, entertain*s*, motivate*s*.

4. They do not pile up; only one ends a word.
   Examples: flake*s*, work*ing*, high*er*, writt*en*

An exception here is {s pl ps}, the plural possessive of the noun, as in "the student*s'* worries."

Exercise 8–11

Write the morphemic symbol and name for each italicized inflectional suffix below.

1. The flagpole remain*ed* in front of Main Hall. ~~Past tense~~ _____
2. Four pledge*s* were initiated. _____
3. Shirley pledge*s* to do her best. _____
4. The pledge*'s* shirt was torn. _____
5. The pledge*s'* shirts were torn. _____
6. We were discuss*ing* the editorial. _____
7. The novel was short*er* than I had expected. _____

8. They wait*ed* at the dock.
9. Which is the long*est* route?
10. Have you tak*en* calculus yet?
11. Chris play*ed* well in the second set.
12. The dealer weigh*ed* the poultry.
13. Would you mind repeat*ing* the question?
14. The sheet*s* were soon ironed.
15. He never lock*s* the door.

G. Derivational Suffixes

As has been noted, in addition to the short list of inflectional suffixes, English has a large supply of another kind of suffix, called derivational suffixes. These consist of all the suffixes that are not inflectional. Among the characteristics of derivational suffixes there are three that will be our immediate concern.

1. The words with which derivational suffixes combine is an arbitrary matter. To make a noun from the verb *adorn* we must add *-ment*—no other suffix will do—whereas the verb *fail* combines only with *-ure* to make a noun, *failure*.

Exercise 8–12

The left-hand column contains ten words. The right-hand column contains thirteen derivational suffixes used to make nouns and having the general meanings of "state, condition, quality, or act of." By combining these suffixes with the words listed, make as many nouns as you can.

1. happy
2. friend
3. boy
4. compose
5. shrink
6. active
7. supreme
8. true
9. pagan
10. discover

1. -hood   11. -ance
2. -acy   12. -th
3. -ism   13. -ure
4. -ness
5. -ment
6. -age
7. -y
8. -ation
9. -ship
10. -ity

Nouns: _happiness_ _composure_ _truance_
friendship _supremacy_ _activism_
boyhood _trueness_ _activation_
shrinkage _paganism_ _truth_
activity _discovery_ _truism_

2. In many cases, but not all, a derivational suffix changes the part of speech of the word to which it is added. The noun *act* becomes an adjective by the addition of *-ive,* and to the adjective *active* we can add *-ate,* making it a verb, *activate.* Although we have not yet taken up the parts of speech, you probably know enough about them to distinguish between nouns, verbs, adjectives, and adverbs, as you are asked to do in the next exercise.

Exercise 8–13

The words in the second column are formed by the addition of a derivational suffix to those in the first column. After every word in both columns indicate its part-of-speech classification by N (noun), V (verb), Aj (adjective), or Av (adverb). Some of the words may belong to more than one part of speech.

1. break	_____	breakage	_____
2. desire	_____	desirable	_____
3. conspire	_____	conspiracy	_____
4. rehearse	_____	rehearsal	_____
5. ideal	_____	idealize	_____
6. false	_____	falsify	_____
7. sweet	_____	sweetly	_____
8. doubt	_____	doubtful	_____
9. mouth	_N_	mouthful	_____
10. sing	_____	singer	_N_
11. familiarize	_____	familiarization	_____
12. passion	_____	passionate	_____
13. host	_N_	hostess	_N_
14. gloom	_____	gloomy	_____
15. martyr	_N_	martyrdom	_____
16. novel	_____	novelist	_N_
17. day	_____	daily	_____
18. prohibit	_____	prohibitory	_____
19. excel	_____	excellent	_____
20. create	_____	creative	_____
21. vision	_____	visionary	_____
22. cube	_____	cubic	_____
23. ripe	_____	ripen	_____
24. real	_____	realism	_____
25. accept	_____	acceptance	_____

3. Derivational suffixes usually do not close off a word; that is, after a derivational suffix one can sometimes add another derivational suffix and can frequently add an inflectional suffix. For example, to the word *fertilize,* which ends in a derivational suffix, one can add another one, *-er,* and to *fertilizer* one can add the inflectional suffix *-s,* closing off the word.

Exercise 8–14

Add a derivational suffix to each of these words, which already end in a derivational suffix.

1. reasonable ___reasonably___
2. formal ___formalize, formally___
3. organize ___organizer, organization___
4. purify ___purifier___
5. realist ___realistic___

Exercise 8–15

Add an inflectional suffix, one of those listed on page 95, to each of these words, which end in derivational suffixes. In the third column put any words you can think of that are formed by a suffix following the inflectional suffix you added in the second column.

s, en
ed

1. kindness ___kindnesses___ _____
2. beautify ___beautified___ _____
3. quarterly _____ _____
4. popularize ___popularized___ _____
5. depth ___depths___ _____
6. pressure ___pressured___ _____
7. arrival ___arrivals___ _____
8. orientate ___orientated___ _____
9. friendly ___friendlier___ _____
10. funny ___funniest___ _____

A glance in the dictionary will reveal that many words have relatives, close and distant, and in grammatical study it is often necessary to examine families of related words. To label such families we employ the word *paradigm.* There are two kinds of paradigms, inflectional and derivational. The inflectional will be explained in greater detail later. The derivational paradigm is a set of related words composed of the same base morpheme and all the derivational affixes that can go with this base. Here is an example: *man, manly, mannish, manful, manhood, manikin, unman, manliness, manward, manfully, mannishly.*

Exercise 8–16

You are given here five bases, or words with their bases italicized. Give all the words in the derivational paradigm of each. Do not include words with two bases, like *manhunt* or *manpower.* (Use other paper for this exercise.)

1. sin
2. kind
3. live /layv/
4. trans*port* (-port = carry)
5. *aud*ible (aud- = hear)

H. Suffixal Homophones

Some suffixes, both inflectional and derivational, have homophonous forms.

The inflectional morpheme {-ER cp} has two homophones. The first is the derivational suffix {-ER n}, which is attached to verbs to form nouns. This is a highly productive suffix, that is, it is used to produce hundreds of English nouns, such as *hunter, fisher, camper, golfer, lover.* It is often called the agent *-er* and conveys a meaning of "that which performs the action of the verb stem," as in *thriller* and *teacher.* It may also be attached to nonverbal stems, such as *probationer, New Yorker, teenager, freighter.* The *-er* on such words could be said to convey a more general meaning of "that which is related to"; and because this meaning is inclusive of the previous one, both these *-er* suffixes can be considered to belong to {-ER n}.

The second derivational *-er* morpheme appears at the end of such words as *chatter, mutter, flicker, glitter, patter.* This {-ER rp} conveys the meaning of repetition. The acceptance of this {-ER rp}, however, is problematic and raises questions about the analysis of the remainders in words of this class. For example, if the *-er* in *glitter* is a morpheme meaning repetition, we are left with the remainder *glitt-,* whose morphemic status is dubious.

Exercise 8–17

Identify the italicized *-er* as

1. {-ER cp} inflectional suffix, as in *bigger*
2. {-ER n} derivational suffix, as in *singer*
3. {-ER rp} derivational suffix, as in *flutter*

1. This is a heavi*er* tennis racket than I want.
2. We watched the shimm*er* of the evening light on the waves.
3. The fight*er* weighed in at 180 pounds.
4. He was tough*er* than he looked.
5. The jabb*er* of voices came through the open door.

The verbal inflectional suffix {-ING vb} has two homophones in *-ing.* The first one is the nominal derivational suffix {-ING nm}, which is found in words such as *meetings, weddings, readings.* This nominal {-ING nm} is obviously derivational, because it permits the addition of an inflectional suffix to close it off, the noun plural {-s pl}. When such a word occurs alone without the inflectional suffix, e.g., *meeting,* the *-ing* is ambiguous, for it could be either {-ING vb}, as in "He was meet*ing* the train" or {-ING nm}, as in "He attended the meet*ing.*"

The second homophone of {-ING vb} is the adjectival morpheme {-ING aj}, as in *a charming woman.* There are two tests by which the verbal {-ING vb} can be distinguished from the adjectival {-ING aj}.

The verbal {-ING vb} can usually occur after as well as before the noun it modifies, for example,

I saw a burning house.
I saw a house burning.

The adjectival {-ING aj} can be preceded by a qualifier such as *very, rather, quite,* or by the comparative and superlative words *more* and *most,* as in

It is a very comforting thought.
This is a more exciting movie.

but not

*I saw a rather burning house.

Also, compare

that interesting snake
that crawling snake.

The adjectival {-ING aj} can occur after *seems:*

That snake seems interesting,

whereas the verbal {-ING vb} cannot:

*That snake seems crawling.

Here and throughout the next chapters treating morphology and syntax, we will follow the conventional practice of using an asterisk (*), as we have done in the examples above, to indicate that a following phrase or clause is "ungrammatical." In this context, the term "ungrammatical" means that a native speaker of the language would normally not produce such an utterance and would not consider it to be well-formed.

Exercise 8–18

Identify the *-ing*'s of the italicized words by these symbols:

V-al = verbal {-ING vb}
N-al = nominal {-ING nm}
Aj-al = adjectival -ING aj}

1. It was a *charming* spot.   *Aj-al*
2. Jim lost both *fillings* from his tooth.   *N-al*
3. She saw the *waiting* cab.   *V-al*
4. It was *exciting* to watch the flight.   *Aj-al*
5. Old *sayings* are often half-true.   *N-al*
6. From the bridge we watched the *running* water.   *V-al*
7. That *barking* dog keeps everyone awake.   *V-al*
8. He told a *convincing* tale.   *Aj-al*
9. The *shining* sun gilded the forest floor.   *V-al*
10. Matisse's *drawings* are magnificently simple.   *N-al*
11. A *refreshing* shower poured down.   *Aj-al*

12. The attorney made a *moving* appeal.   _____ *Aj-al*
13. A *moving* elephant is a picture of grace.   _____ *V-al*
14. What an *obliging* fellow he is!   _____ *Aj-al*
15. That was a *touching* scene.   _____ *Aj-al*

Oral Exercise 8–A

There is an old joke that plays off the verbal versus adjectival sense of a word using the inflectional suffix *-ing*. In the joke, a mother of a student asks a teacher whether the student is trying. The teacher responds, "Yes. Very!" In this joke the qualifier *very* plays a critical role in triggering the punchline and changing our interpretation of how the word *trying* is being used. Explain the two interpretations of *trying* and how the use of *very* triggers a punchline with a specific interpretation.

The verbal inflectional {-D pp} has a homophone in the adjectival derivational {-D aj}, as in

Helen was *excited* about her new job.
She was a *devoted* mother.[4]

The adjectival {-D aj} is characterized by its capacity for modification by qualifiers such as *very, rather, quite,* and by *more* and *most.*

Example: A *rather faded* tapestry hung over the fireplace.

The verbal {-D pp}, on the other hand, does not accept such modifiers. We would not, for example, say

*The *very departed* guests had forgotten their dog.

The *seems* test for adjectival {-ING aj} is applicable to adjectival {-D aj}; for example, "The tapestry seems faded" but not *"The guests seem departed."

Exercise 8–19

Identify the suffixes of the italicized words with these symbols: V-al = {-D pp}; Aj-al = {-D aj}.

1. You should read the *printed* statement.   _____ *V-al*
2. Merle was a *neglected* child.   _____ *Aj-al*
3. This is a *complicated* question.   _____ *Aj-al*
4. His *chosen* bride had lived in India.   _____ *V-al*
5. He bought a *stolen* picture.   _____ *V-al*
6. The *invited* guests all came.   _____ *V-al*
7. We had a *reserved* seat.   _____ *V-al*

---

[4] {-D aj} is considered derivational because it often can be followed by another suffix, e.g., *excitedly, devotedness.*

8. The skipper was a *reserved* (= quiet) man. _____ *Aj-al*
9. A *celebrated* painter visited the campus. _____ *Aj-al*
10. A *worried* look crossed his face. _____ *Aj-al*

Exercise 8–20

Ambiguity occurs when the *-ed* suffix can be interpreted as either {-D pp} or {-D aj}. This exercise will illustrate. For each sentence below write two meanings.

1. He had a finished table.
   a. _____
   b. _____
2. The animal was spotted.
   a. *The animal had spots.*
   b. *The animal was seen.*

The adverbial derivational suffix {-LY av} is added to most adjectives to form adverbs of manner, as in *rich, richly; kind, kindly; formal, formally; happy, happily.* A small group of adjectives does not take this {-LY av}, among them *big, small, little, tall, long, fast.*

This adverbial {-LY av} has as a homophone the derivational suffix {-LY aj}, an adjectival morpheme that is distributed as follows:

1. It is added to monosyllabic nouns to form adjectives that are inflected with *-er, -est.*
   Examples: love, lovely; friend, friendly; man, manly
2. It is added to nouns to form adjectives that are not inflected with *-er, -est.*
   Examples: king, kingly; beast, beastly; scholar, scholarly; mother, motherly; leisure, leisurely
3. It is added to a few adjectives, giving alternate adjectival forms that are also inflected with *-er, -est.*
   Examples: dead, deadly; live, lively; kind, kindly; sick, sickly
   Here the adjectives *kindly* and *lively* are homophonous with the adverbs *kindly* and *lively,* which end in {-LY av}. For example, we see the adverb in "She spoke kindly to the children," and the adjective in "She was a kindly woman; in fact, she was the kindliest woman in the village."
4. It is added to a short list of "time" nouns to form adjectives.
   Examples: day, daily; hour, hourly; month, monthly

These are not inflected with *-er, -est,* and some of them undergo functional shift to become nouns, e.g., "He subscribes to two dailies and three quarterlies."

Exercise 8–21

Identify the italicized *-ly* as either (1) {-LY av} adverbial derivational suffix, as in *glumly;* or (2) {-LY aj} adjectival derivational suffix, as in *fatherly.*

1. The witness testified false*ly*. _____ A̲d̲
2. Grace has a dead*ly* wit. _____ A̲j̲
3. Janet always behaved with a maiden*ly* demeanor. _____ A̲j̲
4. He tiptoes soft*ly* into the room. _____ A̲d̲
5. Jimmy receives a week*ly* allowance. _____ A̲j̲
6. The dear old lady has a heaven*ly* disposition. _____ A̲j̲
7. She spoke quiet*ly* to her grandson. _____ A̲d̲
8. What a time*ly* suggestion! _____ A̲j̲
9. What a manner*ly* child! _____ A̲j̲
10. It was a coward*ly* act. _____ A̲j̲

Exercise 8-22

This is an exercise reviewing the inflectional and derivational suffixes. Label the italicized suffixes as DS (derivational suffix), IS (inflectional suffix), or Amb (ambiguous between a derivational or inflectional suffix).

1. prince*s* _____ IS
2. princ*ess* _____ DS
3. find*ings* _____ DS
4. friendl*ier* _____ IS
5. show*s* _____ IS
6. weav*er* _____ DS
7. lean*er* _____ Amb
8. satir*ize* _____ DS
9. sputt*er* _____ DS
10. bright*en* _____ DS
11. quick*ly* _____ DS
12. rect*ify* _____ DS
13. brother*ly* _____ DS
14. respect*able* _____ DS
15. young*er* _____ IS
16. hear*ing* _____ Amb
17. dr*ier* _____ Amb
18. griev*ance* _____ DS
19. dropp*ings* _____ DS
20. sunn*y* _____ DS

I. Noun Feminine Forms

English has a small group of nouns with feminine derivational suffixes. All but one of these feminizing suffixes (*-ster*) are of foreign origin. They have been added to a masculine form or to a base morpheme. Here is a list of most of them, with examples of the feminine nouns to which they have been attached and the corresponding masculine forms.

Suffix	Masculine	Feminine
1. -e	fiancé	fiancée
2. -enne	comedian	comedienne
3. -ess	patron	patroness
4. -etta	Henry	Henrietta
5. -ette	usher	usherette[5]

---

[5] The suffix *-ette* is now more commonly used as a diminutive, as in *kitchenette*.

6. -euse	masseur	masseuse
7. -ina	George	Georgina
8. -ine	hero	heroine
9. -ster	spinner	spinster
10. -stress	seamster	seamstress (=-ster + -ess)
11. -ix	aviator	aviatrix

These suffixes vary in vitality from -*ess,* the most productive, to -*stress,* which as a feminine suffix is completely dead, that is to say, it is no longer used to form new words. Two of them, -*enne* and -*euse,* occur only in words borrowed from French. The -*e,* also from French, is merely orthographic and is not heard in the spoken word. The -*ster* is no longer a feminizing suffix; it now indicates any person, whether male or female: *gangster, youngster, prankster.*

The feminine suffixes listed above and the words they help form must be used judiciously. This caution applies not only to obviously offensive words such as *spinster,* but even to such seemingly harmless forms as *poetess.* Although some individuals are unconcerned about morphological forms that distinguish women from men, others see such distinctions as unnecessary and perhaps even demeaning to women. But because feminine endings are still in use and common in earlier texts, it is still important for us to be familiar with them.

In addition to what has been discussed the above, English also has about fifty pairs of words with separate forms for the masculine and the feminine, e.g., *bull, cow; uncle, aunt; gander, goose.* But these are a matter of lexicography rather than morphology, and we will pass them by.

Exercise 8–23

Consulting a dictionary and the suffix list above, write the feminine form (or erstwhile feminine form) of these words.

1. Paul	*Paula*	9. Carol	*Carolina*
2. chanteur	*Chanteureuse*	10. emperor	*empress*
3. protégé		11. launderer	*launderette*
4. czar		12. executor	*exucutrix*
5. songster	*songstress*	13. proprietor	*proprietress*
6. major	*majorette*	14. waiter	*waitress*
7. heir	*heiress*	15. tragedian	*tragedienne*
8. equestrian	*equestrienne*		

J. Noun Diminutive Forms

In English six diminutive suffixes can be found. There are morphemes that convey a meaning of smallness or endearment or both. They are the following:

1. -ie, -i, -y	as in *auntie, Betty, sweetie, Willy*
2. -ette	as in *dinette, towelette*
3. -kin, -ikin, -kins	as in *babykins*
4. -ling	as in *duckling, darling* (= little dear)
5. -et	as in *circlet*
6. -let	as in *booklet, starlet*

The vowels of these diminutive suffixes are three front vowels: /i/, /ɪ/, and /ɛ/.

The first suffix, pronounced /i/ and spelled *-ie, -i,* and *-y,* is highly productive. It is frequently attached to one-syllable first names to suggest endearment and intimacy, or smallness, as in *Johnny, Janey, Jackie,* and *Mikey.* Similarly, it is attached to common nouns, sometimes indicating a diminutive notion about a participant in a discourse more than about the person or thing being referred to, as in *doggie, sweetie, birdie,* or *mommy.*[6]

The second suffix is also in active use, generally to indicate smallness. Thus, a *dinette* is a small dining area, and a *roomette* is a small room.

The other four diminutive suffixes exist in the language as diminutives but are rarely if ever added to new nouns. In short, they are unproductive, inactive. Furthermore, in some words, such as *cabinet* and *toilet,* the meaning of the diminutive suffix has faded away to little or no significance.

Exercise 8-24

Consulting a dictionary and the suffix list above, give a noun diminutive form for each of the following words.

1. Bob	*Bobby*	6. lamb	*lambkins*	11. hatch	*hatchling*
2. goose	*goosey*	7. pack	*packette*	12. drop	*droplet*
3. statue	*statuette*	8. pup	*puppy*	13. lad	*laddie*
4. pig	*piglet*	9. eagle	*eaglet*	14. disk	*diskette*
5. dear	*dearie*	10. Ann	*Annie*	15. cigar	*cigarette*

In addition to these six diminutives, many others have come into English as a part of borrowed words. These were diminutives in their own or parent language but are nonmorphemic in English. For illustration, here is a handful of them.

mosqu*ito*	pan*el*	Venezu*ela*
bamb*ino*	mors*el*	quart*et*
armad*illo*	dams*el*	bull*etin* (two successive diminutives here)

---

[6]Warning to students: Some of these diminutive suffixes have homophones that can be a source of confusion. Here, for instance, are four of them:

1. *-y,* an adjective-forming suffix added to a noun, as in *cloudy.*

2. *-ie,* a noun-forming suffix added to an adjective, as in *smartie, toughie.*

3. *-ette,* a feminine suffix, as in *majorette.*

4. *-ling,* a noun suffix denoting a particular characteristic or affiliation, as in *weakling* or *earthling.*

peccad*illo*	scalp*el*	fals*etto*
flot*illa*	satch*el*	stil*etto*
Prisc*illa*	mus*cle*	Maur*een*
cook*ie*	part*icle*	loch*an*
colon*el*	pup*il*	form*ula*
citad*el*	viol*in*	caps*ule*
	violon*cello*	
nov*el* (noun)	pupp*et*	calc*ulus*

Most of these borrowed diminutive endings, you will observe, contain the vowels /i/, /ɪ/, and /ɛ/, though these vowels have often been reduced to /ə/ in English because of lack of stress. Only the last four do not have a front vowel or /ə/ in the diminutive suffix. Furthermore, nearly all these suffixes have lost the diminutive sense that was once alive in them.

K. Immediate Constituents

Up to this point we have scrutinized the four sorts of morphemes—bases, prefixes, infixes, and suffixes—of which words are composed. Now we will see how these are put together to build the structure that we call a word.

A word of one morpheme, like *blaze,* has, of course, just one unitary part. A word of two morphemes, like *cheerful,* is obviously composed of two parts, with the division between them:

cheer   ful

But a word of three or more morphemes is not made up of a string of individual parts; it is built with a hierarchy of twosomes. As an illustration let us examine the formation of *gentlemanly,* a word of three morphemes. We might say that *man* and *-ly* were combined to form *manly* and that *gentle* and *manly* were then put together to produce the form *gentlemanly.* But the total meaning of *gentlemanly* does not seem to be composed of the meanings of its two parts *gentle* and *manly,* so we reject this possibility. Let's try again. This time we'll say that *gentle* and *man* were put together to give *gentleman.* And if we remember that *gentle* has the meanings of "distinguished," "belonging to a high social station," we see that the meaning of *gentleman* is a composite of those of its two constituents. Now we add *-ly,* meaning "like," and get *gentlemanly,* like a gentleman. This manner of forming *gentlemanly* seems to make sense.

Now when we analyze a word we show this process but in reverse. We usually divide a word into two parts of which it seems to have been composed. Thus

gentleman   ly

We continue in this way, cutting every part into two more until we have reduced the word to its ultimate constituents, that is, to the unit morphemes of which it is composed. Our analysis of *gentlemanly* would look like this:

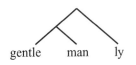

gentle   man   ly

Next, let us suppose that the word to be analyzed is *ungentlemanly.* If we make the same first cut as before, cutting off the *-ly,* we get *ungentleman* plus *-ly.* But as English contains no such word as *ungentleman,* our word could not be composed of the two parts *ungentleman* and *-ly,* Instead, let's cut after the *un-.* This gives *un-* plus *gentlemanly,* a common English negative prefix plus a recognizable English word. This seems to be the right way to begin, and as we continue we get this analysis.

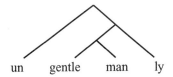

un   gentle   man   ly

We have now shown the layers of structure by which the word has been composed, down to the ultimate constituents—*un-, gentle, man,* and *-ly.*

In doing word diagrams like those above to show layers of structure, we make successive divisions into two parts, each of which is called an immediate constituent, abbreviated IC. The process is continued until all component morphemes of a word, the ultimate constituents, have been isolated.

Here are three recommendations on IC division that will assist you in the exercise to follow:

1. If a word ends in an inflectional suffix, the first cut is between this suffix and the rest of the word. So:

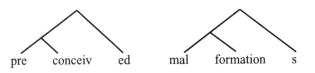

pre   conceiv   ed   mal   formation   s

2. One of the ICs should be, if possible, a free form. A free form is one that can be uttered alone with meaning, e.g., *enlarge, dependent, supportable.* Here are examples of wrong and right first cuts:

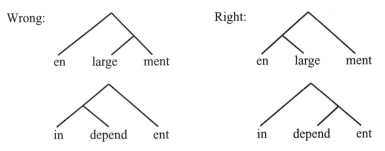

Wrong: Right:

en   large   ment   en   large   ment

in   depend   ent   in   depend   ent

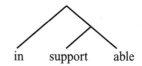

3. The meanings of the ICs should be related to the meaning of the word. It would be wrong to cut *restrain* like this:

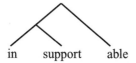

because neither *rest* nor *rain* has a semantic connection with *restrain*. Nor would a division of *starchy* as

be right because this would give an unrelated morpheme and a meaningless fragment. The two examples are properly cut in this way:

re   strain   starch   y

The ultimate constituents are the morphemes of which the word is composed.

Exercise 8–25

One of the following IC diagrams showing the layers of structure is wrong. Which one is it and why?

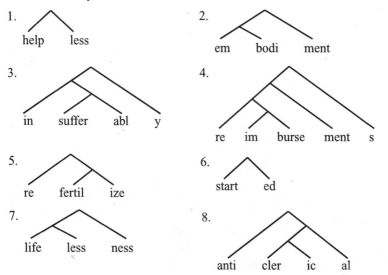

9.

favor   it   ism

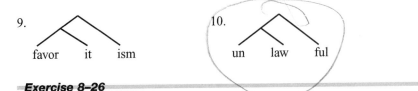

10.

un   law   ful

Exercise 8–26

Diagram these words to show the layers of structure.

1. item ize d

2. pre pro fess ion al

3. news paper dom

4. counter de clar ation

5. mal con struc tion

6. contra dict ory

7. dis en throne

8. mid after noon

9. Ice land ic

10. super natur al

11. un com fort able

12. fest iv al

13. en gag ing

14. ex press ion ism

15. mis judg ment

L. Allomorphs

It is now time to sharpen and extend our understanding of the morpheme. So far we have been treating the morpheme as if it were invariable in phonemic form, that is, in the way it is pronounced. But in the preceding exercises you may have noticed occasional variations in phonemic form. In a word such as *pressure,* the morpheme {press} ends in /š/, whereas the same morpheme standing alone as the word *press* ends in /s/. Likewise, the first morpheme in *depth* is pronounced /dɛp/, but the same morpheme occurring as the word *deep* has the phonemic form of /dip/. So we see that a morpheme may have more than one phonemic form.

Next we'll go back to the past-tense ending, the morpheme {-ᴅ pt}. We learned in exercise 2–3 of the phonology section that this morpheme has three phonemic forms, the choice depending on the preceding sound. After an alveolar stop, /t/ or /d/, the sound is /əd/, as in *parted* /partəd/ and *faded* /fedəd/. After a voiceless consonant other than /t/ it is /t/, as in *passed* /pæst/ and *laughed* /læft/. After a voiced sound other than /d/ it is /d/, as in *seemed* /simd/ and *begged* /bɛgd/. Furthermore, these three phonemic forms of {-ᴅ pt} are not interchangeable. The occurrence of one or another of them depends on its phonological environment, in this case, the preceding sound. This pattern of occurrence of related forms, according to which each form occupies its own territory and does not trespass on the domain of another, is called complementary distribution. When the related forms of a set, like the three forms of {-ᴅ pt}, have the same meaning and are in complementary distribution, they are called allomorphs, or positional variants, and belong to the same morpheme. So we say that the morpheme {-ᴅ pt} has three allomorphs: /-əd/, /-t/, and /-d/. This is expressed in the formula:

$$\{\text{-ᴅ pt}\} = /\text{-əd}/ \sim /\text{-t}/ \sim /\text{-d}/$$

Braces are used for morphemes and slants for allomorphs; a tilde (~) means "in alternation with." It must be emphasized that many morphemes in English have only one phonemic form, that is, one allomorph—for example, the morphemes {boy} and {-hood} each have one allomorph—/bɔy/ and /-hud/—as in *boyhood*.

Now we are in a position to refine our understanding of free and bound morphemes. It is really not the morpheme but the allomorph that is free or bound. Consider, for example, the morpheme {louse}. This has two allomorphs: the free allomorph /laws/ as a singular noun and the bound allomorph /lawz-/ in the adjective *lousy*.

Exercise 8–27

Each pair of words here contains one free and one bound allomorph of the same morpheme. Indicate the morpheme in braces and write each allomorph between slants in phonemic script.

	Morpheme	Free allomorph	Bound allomorph
Example: long, length	{long}	/laŋ/ (or /lɔŋ/)	/lɛŋ-/
1. strong, strength	_____	_____	_____
2. chaste, chastity	_____	_____	_____
3. courage, courageous	_____	_____	_____
4. Bible, Biblical	_____	_____	_____
5. wife, wives	_____	_____	_____

Exercise 8–28

Explain why *a/an* are allomorphs of one morpheme.

Exercise 8–29

Write the base morpheme and its allomorphs for each group. Supply primary stresses in answers that contain varying stress.

Examples: steal, stealth {steal} = /stil/ ~ /stɛl-/

1. wide, width   _____
2. broad, breadth   _____
3. wolf, wolves   _____
4. áble, abílity   _____
5. supreme, supremacy   _____
6. divine, divinity   _____
7. fame, fámous, ínfamy, ínfamous _____
8. vision, televise, revise   _____
9. sun, sunny, sunward   _____
10. átom, atómic   _____

Exercise 8–30

This exercise, related to exercise 2–2, concerns the plural morpheme {-s pl}, which (we'll say for the moment) has three allomorphs. Write out each plural word in phonemic script. Then, using these as evidence, list the allomorphs of {-s pl} and describe their complementary distribution.

1. sons _____
2. naps _____
3. passes _____
4. hogs _____
5. sacks _____

6. fizzes _____
7. dishes _____
8. garages _____
9. hoes _____
10. staffs _____

11. churches _____
12. gorges _____
13. sums _____
14. heaths _____
15. gongs _____

Allomorphs and complementary distribution:

_____
_____
_____
_____

M. Conditioning: Phonological and Morphological

In examining the past-tense morpheme {-D pt}, we saw that the three allomorphs /-əd ~ -d ~ -t/ were in complementary distribution and that this distribution was determined by the phonological environment, in this case by the preceding sound. The same was true of the plural morpheme {-s pl}, where the addition of /-əz/, /-z/, or /-s/ was also determined by the sound immediately preceding the suffix. In these and similar cases, when the phonological environment determines which allomorph is used, we say that the selection of allomorphs is phonologically conditioned.

But the plural morpheme {-s pl} has further allomorphs, as shown by the /-ən/ of *ox-oxen* and by the /Ø/ (zero) suffix of *sheep-sheep*. These two, /-ən/ and /Ø/, are in complementary distribution with all the others in that they stay in their own territory, associate only with specific words, and do not overlap in positions where /-əz/, /-z/, and /-s/ are found. But the positions in which they occur—that is, the words they attach themselves to—have nothing to do with their phonological environment. Instead the use of /-ən/ as the plural of *ox* is determined by the specific morpheme *ox;* in other words, *ox* simply takes /-ən/ and that's that. Likewise, the occurrence of the plural Ø allomorph in a few words—*swine, deer, sheep, trout, pike, quail, grouse,* and others—is determined by the fact that these special morphemes require a Ø plural. In such cases, when we can describe the environment that requires a certain allomorph only by identifying specific morphemes, we say that the selection of allomorphs is morphologically conditioned.

To describe by formula these five allomorphs of {-s pl} we write

{-s pl} = /-əz/ ~ /-z/ ~ /-s/ ∞ /-ən/ ∞ /Ø/

The ~ refers to a phonologically conditioned alternation and the ∞ to a morphologically conditioned alternation.

Exercise 8–31

Write the formula to express the fact that the past-tense morpheme {-D pt} has, in the verb *be,* the two morphologically conditioned allomorphs *was* and *were.*

N. Replacive Allomorphs

Most of the allomorphs we have been dealing with have been additive; that is, we have been forming words by adding prefixes and suffixes to bases. Now we must look at an allomorph of a different kind, the replacive, which can be illustrated by going back to the past-tense {-D pt}. We noted that this morpheme has three allomorphs, /-əd/ ~ -t ~ -d/. But if this is all, how do we account for forms like *sang*? It would appear to contain an allomorph of {-D pt}, because it is a parallel formation with regular past-tense forms:

Yesterday we *parted* /partəd/
Yesterday we *laughed* /læft/
Yesterday we *played* /pled/
Yesterday we *sang* /seŋ/ (or /sæŋ/)

What happens is that there is a replacement here instead of an additive. The /ɪ/ of *sing* is replaced by the /e/ (or /æ/) of *sang* to signal the past tense. This is symbolized as follows:

/seŋ/ = /sɪŋ/ + /ɪ > e/[7]

---

[7]The symbol > means "becomes."

Here the /ɪ > e/ is another allomorph of {-ᴅ pt}, and you can readily see how it is in complementary distribution with the others. Sometimes replacive allomorphs are called "infixes," because they are positioned *within* a word, as opposed to prefixes and suffixes, as in *sang* and *rode*. But we will refer to them as replacive allomorphs rather than infixes.

Exercise 8–32

Write the allomorphic formula for each of the following past-tense forms.

Examples: spin, *spun*   /spən/ = /spɪn/ + /ɪ > ə/

1. see, *saw* _____
2. begin, *began* _____
3. bite, *bit* _____
4. give, *gave* _____
5. grow, *grew* _____
6. ride, *rode* _____
7. grind, *ground* _____
8. take, *took* _____
9. tear, *tore* _____
10. speak, *spoke* _____

O. Homophones

You are acquainted with many pairs, trios, and even foursomes of words in English that sound alike but differ in meaning: *heir, air; pare, pair, pear.* Such words are called homophones. In morphology it must be remembered that words like these are different morphemes.

    Examples: Did you like the *meet*?   /mit/ (track meet)
                 Did you like the *meat*?   /mit/ (roast beef)

The same is true of bound forms. Compare

Verbal inflectional suffix:	It feels /-z/ good
Noun plural inflectional suffix:	Those frogs /-z/
Noun possessive inflectional suffix:	John's /-z/ book

These three homophonous /-z/s are three different morphemes.

Exercise 8–33

Write the morphemes to which each of these homophonous allomorphs belongs.

    Examples: /et/ = {ate}
                 /et/ = {eight}

(In a couple of the sets below, some homophones will be spelled the same.)

1. /mit/ _meet_
   /mit/ _meat_
   /mit/ _mete_
2. /mayt/ _might_
   /mayt/ _mite_
   /mayt/ _might_
3. /yu/ _you_
   /yu/ _ewe_
   /yu/ _yew_
4. /pɛr/ _pair_
   /pɛr/ _pear_
   /pɛr/ _pare_
5. /pel/ _pale_
   /pel/ _pail_
6. /tu/ _two_
   /tu/ _to_
   /tu/ _too_
   /tu/ _too_

P. Phonesthemes

Phonesthemes are speech sounds that in themselves express, elicit, or suggest meaning. For instance, let us consider a minimal pair, the Chinese words *ch'ing* /čɪŋ/ and *ch'ung* /čuŋ/. One of these means "heavy," the other "light." The question for you is "Which meaning goes with which word?" If you, like most respondents, say that *ch'ing* means "light" and *ch'ung* means "heavy," you are correct. And because the two words differ only in their vowels, it must be these vowels that elicit the two meanings. These vowels, then, are phonesthemes.

Two of the most common phonesthemes in English are the pair of high front vowels, /i/ and /ɪ/, suggesting smallness. These appear in many words that have smallness as a part of their meaning. Here are a few: *wee, peep, squeak, seep, bit, jiffy, clink, teeny, giggle, dwindle,* and *whimper.* They are also two of the three diminutive vowels in English, as exemplified in *birdie* and *lambkin.*

The presence of the "small" phonesthemes /i/ and /ɪ/ in English is not only known by language students but sensed by the average person. Witness two cases. One cartoon employed these two vowels to make its point. It showed an auto mechanic in a garage talking with an unhappy car owner whose engine had been malfunctioning. The mechanic pointed out, "In car language 'clunk, rattle, thump' means 'too bad you didn't listen when I said "ping, ping, squeak"'!" And a radio comedian presented a large public with this gag: "What do you call a large pipsqueak?" "A poopsquawk."

Another common English phonestheme is the vowel /ə/, as in *dung, drudgery, flunk.* Professor F. W. Householder, in a study of over six hundred English monosyllables, found that the vowel /ə/ has, in a large majority of cases, the general meaning of "undesirable"[8] These monosyllables will illustrate: *muck, gunk, dump, slum, grunt, dud, klutz, glum, grudge.* And in words of more than one syllable the meaning of "undesirable" seems to be present in such terms as these: *grumpy, grumble, blunder, clumsy, humdrum, muddle, slovenly, puddle, lunkhead.*

---

[8]"On the Problem of Sound Meaning, an English Phonestheme," *Word,* 2:83–84, 1946.

At the beginning of words, a number of consonant clusters appear to have phonesthematic value. Among them are these:

/gl-/ = light. Examples: *glow, glare, glint, gleam, glisten, glitter, glaze*
/fl-/ = moving light. Examples: *flame, flash, flare, flicker*
/sp-/ = point. Examples: *spire, spark, spot, spout, spade*
/sl-/ = movement. Examples: *slide, slink, slosh, slither, slouch, slump*

At the ends of one-syllable words, the voiceless stops /p/, /t/, and /k/ are expressive of an abrupt stoppage of movement. Examples of these are *slap, pat, flick, tap, hit, crack.* In contrast with these, a final voiceless fricative /š/ suggests an unabrupt stoppage of movement, as in *mash* and *squash.* The expressiveness of these sounds becomes especially noticeable when we observe contrasts like these: *clap* vs. *clash; bat* vs. *bash; smack* vs. *smash; crack* vs. *crash.*

At the ends of two-syllable words, we find the phonesthemes /-əl/ and /-ər/, each having the meaning of "repetition." The repetition may be of auditory or visual details. Examples:

/-ər/ *chatter, clatter, gibber, patter, sputter, mutter, jabber, twitter, litter, shatter, flutter, shimmer, stammer*
/-əl/ *babble, giggle, twinkle, waggle, freckle, dribble, juggle, crackle, chuckle, rattle, sparkle, stipple, prattle, wriggle, drizzle*

A speech sound is a phonestheme only when its imputed sense is related to the sense of the word of which it is a part. Thus, as the sense of /i/ and /ɪ/ is related to the sense of *wee* and *drizzle,* these two vowels are phonesthemes in these words. But in words whose meaning does not include smallness, the /i/ and /ɪ/ are merely meaningless vowels. Thus *seat* and *sit* and countless others with /i/ and /ɪ/ do not contain phonesthemes. Some words are doubtful cases. For example, does *whisper* really contain the phonesthemes /ɪ/ for smallness and /-ər/ for repetition?

The existence of phonesthemes is now generally accepted, and although they resemble morphemes in their behavior, they do not satisfy all of the conditions that we proposed at the beginning of this chapter for something to qualify as a morpheme. Therefore we will treat them as a different linguistic feature.

Exercise 8–34

The phonesthemes in the following words are underlined. Give the meaning of each.

1. spike	_____	11. glossy	_____
2. flicker	_____	12. spatter	_____
3. glimmer	_____	13. shrink	_____
4. nibble	_____	14. warble	_____
5. crud	_____	15. ugly	_____
6. sulky	_____	16. kid	_____
7. snap	_____	17. tack	_____
8. splash	_____	18. sniffle	_____
9. sip	_____	19. slit	_____
10. señorita	_____	20. jangle	_____

The eminent grammarian Otto Jespersen recounts this incident: "One summer, when there was a great drought in Fredriksstad (Norway), the following words were posted in a W.C. [= toilet]: 'Don't pull the string for bimmelin, only for bummelum.' This was immediately understood."[9]

With regard to phonesthemes, explain *why* this was immediately understood.

Some Observations and Applications

The reality of morphemes as a minimal unit of meaning is found in the attention that they receive from wordsmiths whose livelihood depends on careful attention to language. Some years ago 7UP had a highly successful advertising campaign that referred to its product as the "Uncola." The label or nickname was memorable at least in part because *un-* is normally combined with adjectives and verbs, not simple nouns. It is, of course, to an advertiser's advantage to use forms or expressions that will be memorable. The 7UP company coined a memorable nickname for its product through a creative use of morphology.

In an article published in *American Speech,* Genine Lentine and Roger Shuy describe their role in defending a business from a trademark infringement lawsuit lodged by McDonald's. The business had tried to use the morpheme *Mc-* in its business name. The McDonald's Corporation asserted ownership of the morpheme, explaining that McDonald's had promoted the morpheme in their advertising and marketing of such food items as McShakes and McFries. Lentine and Shuy, however, argued against McDonald's exclusive ownership of the morpheme, pointing out that *Mc-* has a number of different uses in contemporary American English. In this legal dispute it is clear that the importance of morphemes extends beyond mere academic considerations and can occasionally become an important issue in the legal and business communities.[10]

Morphological analysis can also be helpful in learning vocabulary for special purposes, such as for medical school. Whether you need to learn many specific terms for a class or for a graduate school entrance exam, your ability to learn vocabulary is greatly enhanced if you can intelligently recognize recurring morphemes in a variety of words, rather than approaching each new word as something entirely unrelated to others.

Teachers who are more aware of morphology might also help students who are struggling with spelling to make better choices about how to spell troublesome words. Elizabeth Grubgeld indicates that a student who might spell the word *major* like "majer" because of its pronunciation, would be less likely to misspell the vowel if he or she understood that *major* is part of the word *majority,* in which the pronunciation of the vowel before *r* more clearly reveals the appropriate spelling. Although

---

[9] "Symbolic Value of the Vowel I" (1922) in *Linguistica* (Copenhagen: Levin and Munksgard, 1933), p. 284.

[10] "*Mc-:* Meaning in the Marketplace" by Genine Lentine and Roger W. Shuy in *American Speech* 65:4 (1990): 349–366.

she acknowledges that students with a spelling problem may not be skilled in anticipating what other forms of a given word might be, she believes that "with practice and considerable drill on syllabification, compounding, and affixation, they may become more adept at the task."[11] Some teachers already spend time teaching morphology because of the insights it can bring to students as they learn to decode word meanings. But it could be argued that some morphological instruction, if carefully directed, might also have the additional application to spelling instruction.

This chapter has discussed phonesthemes such as *gl-* and even *p-*. The phenomenon of meaning associated with phonesthemes, sometimes known as "sound symbolism," has also proven to be useful in the business world. One entrepreneur has identified important aspects of sound symbolism and formed a business that helps companies to develop product names based on the meaning that people associate with particular sounds.[12]

---

[11] "Helping the Problem Speller Without Suppressing the Writer" by Elizabeth Grubgeld in *English Journal* (Feb. 1986) as reprinted in *Linguistics for Teachers,* eds. Linda Miller Cleary and Michael D. Linn. New York: McGraw-Hill, 1993.

[12] "There's More to a Name" by Bob Cohen in the *Stanford Business School Magazine* 63:3 (1995): 9.

Words

One of the interesting things about word compounds is that their meaning is not predictable through examining their individual word parts. We learn the meaning of compounds as a unit. Of course, if we already know the meaning of a compound, we can understand how the parts of the compound add up to its meaning. The problematic nature of compounds can be illustrated by the fact that although a redhead is a person with red hair, a blackhead is not a person with black hair.[1] Humor can, of course, be created around possible contrived meanings of compounds as the following joke illustrates:

> Cannibal Chief to Victim: What did you do for a living?
>
> Victim: I was an associate editor.
>
> Chief: Cheer up, after tonight you'll be editor-in-chief.[2]

A. Definition of "Word"

That the word is a genuine linguistic unit is scarcely questioned, and everyone seems to know what it is. Teachers have no difficulty in making up spelling lists, which consist of words. Lexicographers produce dictionaries, whose entries are mainly words. When we read, we recognize words by the white spaces between them. Occasionally, however, we are puzzled by printed forms of words that are inconsistent with one another. Here are several examples from one page of a scholarly desk dictionary, *Webster's Ninth New Collegiate Dictionary*. This book on the same page lists *woodchuck* and *woodcock* as one word and *wood duck* and *wood louse* each as two words. All four words have the same stress pattern, and no formal criteria are evident for differences in the printed form. Such moot cases apart, however, we commonly have no doubt about the identity of words.

---

[1] This example of contrasting meanings from words that appear similar on the surface is taken from *A Basic Grammar of Modern English,* 2nd ed., by Bruce L. Liles. Englewood Cliffs, NJ: Prentice-Hall, 1987, p. 91.

[2] *Jokes for Children* by Marguerite Kohl and Frederica Young. New York: Hill & Wang, 1963, p. 37.

But all these instances are concerned with written words, whereas in linguistic analysis our main interest is in the spoken word. Here again the isolation of the unit called a word appears easy. If one asks "What does _____ mean?" or "How do you pronounce _____?" the blank usually represents a word. And there is a high correlation between the written and the spoken forms of words. Yet the task of devising an exact definition of *word* is a prickly one that has engendered much controversy. In this book we will define a word as a free morpheme or a combination of morphemes that together form a basic segment of speech. The first part of this definition thus excludes single bound morphemes such as *pre-, -ceive,* or *-ful.* But it allows for a single free morpheme such as *bird* or a combination of morphemes such as *incredible.*

One way to identify words is through the way that they are treated in speech. When people are speaking, they often pause—formulating their thoughts, getting the sentence structure in order, and groping for the right word. Such pauses do not occur within words, but between words. This is our cue, and it leads us to another useful definition of *word,* that of Professor Charles F. Hockett: "A word is . . . any segment of a sentence bounded by successive points *at which pausing is possible.*"[3] This pausing can be either silent or vocalized by "u-u-u-h." The following sentence will illustrate:

 p p p   p p pp p p p   p[4]
 Since the streetlamp is out, I must call up our councilman.

In this sentence the positions of possible pauses are marked by *p*s, and every segment between two *p*s is a word. Note that *call up* is considered a word. *Call up* belongs to a special class of two-part verbs—such as *keep on* (continue), *take off* (depart), *butt in* (interrupt), and *show up* (appear)—that speakers of English seem to sense as single words. Hence there would normally be no pause between the two parts.

Exercise 9–1

In this exercise let us apply the foregoing description of pause behavior to ascertain the number of words in the following sentences. In the first blank write the numbered position or positions where a pause would NOT be possible, or likely. In the second blank write the number of words in the sentence.

     1 2 3 .4 5 6 7
Example: Cohen gave his brother a power-of-attorney.   <u> 6, 7 </u> <u> 6 </u>

    1 2 3 45 6 7
1. Little Jimmy plays with a big soft ball.   <u> 7 </u> <u> 7 </u>

    1 2   3 4 5 6 7
2. His older brother likes to play softball.   <u> 7 </u> <u> 7 </u>

    1 2 3 4 5
3. Will you look up the address?   <u> 3 </u> <u> 5 </u>

---

[3] *A Course in Modern Linguistics* (New York: Macmillan, 1958), p. 167.

[4] Each *p* marks not only a point where pausing is possible, but also positions where the insertion of other words is possible.

     1 2   3   4 5   6 7 8

4. He has always been a Johnny-on-the-spot.   *6,7,8*   *6*

    1   2   3 4   5 6

5. A dark room is conducive to sleep.   _____   _____

    1   2   3 4 5 6   7

6. He develops films in the darkroom upstairs.   _____   _____

B. Simple and Complex Words

English words may be classified on the basis of the kinds and combinations of morphemes of which they are composed. We will adopt a classification of three main classes: simple, complex, and compound words.

   1. Simple words consist of a single free morpheme.
       Examples: slay, flea, long, spirit

   2. Complex words contain, as their immediate constituents (ICs), either two bound forms or a bound and a free form.
       Examples of two bound forms as ICs:

       matri | cide   tele | vise
       ex | clude   cosmo | naut

       Examples of bound and free forms as ICs:
       dipso | mania   lion | ess
       tele | phone   eras | er

Exercise 9-2

Make the first IC cut in the words below that permit such cutting. Then classify each word, using S for simple and Cx for complex.

1. knave	*S*	8. purist	*Cx*	15. enable	*Cx*
2. knavish	*Cx*	9. oyster	*S*	16. mete	*S*
3. graph	*S*	10. misanthrope	*Cx*	17. meter	*Cx*
4. telegraph	*Cx*	11. philosophy	*Cx*	18. hydrometer	*Cx*
5. aquanaut	*Cx*	12. cannibal	*S*	19. discography	*Cx*
6. bicycle	*Cx*	13. refusal	*Cx*	20. shiny	*Cx*
7. pure	*S*	14. dental	*Cx*		

love of wisdom

C. Compound Words

The third class of words is compound words. These have free forms, usually two, as their immediate constituents.

Examples:

green | house	out | side	no | show
under | go	over | ripe	attorney | general

A small number of compound words have three or four free forms as coordinate ICs.

Examples:

happy \| -go \| -lucky   spic \| and \| span

Compound words resemble grammatical structures in that they imply, though they do not state, a grammatical relationship. Here are a few of the structures implied:

Implied Grammatical Structures	Examples
1. subject + verb	éarthquake (. . . earth quakes)
	crýbaby (. . . baby cries)
2. verb + object	kílljoy (. . . kills joy)
3. verb + adverbial	stópover (. . . stops over)
	dównpour (. . . pours down)
	stáy-at-home (. . . stays at home)
	underéstimate (. . . estimates under)
4. subject + *be* + adjectival	hígh chair (. . . chair is high)
5. subject + *be* + nominal	gírl friend (. . . friend is a girl)
6. subject + *be* + adverbial	íngroup (. . . group is in)
7. prepositional phrase	extrasénsory (beyond the senses)
8. adjective modified by	
prepositional phrase	cárefree (. . . free from care)
9. coordination	give-and-take

Exercise 9-3

Using the nine numbers given above, indicate the number of the grammatical structure implied by each compound word.

1. workman	_____	7. praiseworthy	_____
2. afternoon	_____	8. outgo	_____
3. pickpocket	_____	9. fly-by-night	_____
4. quicksand	_____	10. student teacher	_____
5. knockdown	_____	11. overheat	_____
6. airtight	_____	12. rough-and-ready	_____

Compound words can be distinguished from grammatical structures in three ways.

1. Compound words cannot be divided by the insertion of intervening material between the two parts, but grammatical structures can be so divided. As illustration, let us compare two sentences:

   a. She is a sweetheart.
   b. She has a sweet heart.

In the first the compound word *sweetheart* is indivisible: you cannot insert anything between *sweet* and *heart.* But in the second sentence you could say

> She has a swee*ter* heart than her sister.
> She has a sweet, *kind* heart.
> She has a sweet, *sweet* heart.

thereby dividing the components *sweet* and *heart.* Thus sentence *b* contains a grammatical structure, not a compound word. Following this principle of divisibility, we find that the next sentence is ambiguous:

> She loves sweet potatoes.

When *sweet potatoes* means the yellow kind, the expression cannot be divided and is therefore a compound word. But when the words refer to white potatoes that are sweet, then division is possible, as in

> She loves sweet, fresh potatoes.

and we have a grammatical structure.

2. A member of a compound word cannot participate in a grammatical structure. Compare *hârd báll* and *básebàll. Hârd báll* is a grammatical structure of modifier plus noun, and its first member, *hard,* can participate in the structure *very hard:*

> It was a very hard ball.

But one cannot say

> *It was a very baseball,

as *baseball* is a compound word. Ambiguous cases can occur in sentences like

> He is fond of sparkling water.

When *sparkling water* refers to ordinary water that sparkles, the first member, *sparkling,* can participate in a grammatical structure, e.g., *brightly sparkling water.* So *sparkling water* with this meaning is a grammatical structure. But when the expression refers to carbonated water, such participation cannot occur and we have a compound word.

3. Some compound nouns, you may recall, have the stress pattern { ˊ ˋ }, as in *blúe- bìrd,* that distinguishes them from a modifier plus a noun, as in *blùe bírd,* which structure carries the stress pattern { ˋ ˊ }. For the same reason, a *swímming tèacher* is different from a *swìmming téacher.* You should also remember that you cannot depend on the printed form of words to reveal this distinction. For example, the compound noun *hígh chàir* (a chair for children) and the modifier plus noun *hìgh cháir* (a chair that is high) are both written as two words.

---

*Remember that an asterisk *before* a sentence or a phrase means that the sentence or phrase is ungrammatical.

Exercise 9–4

Indicate whether each italicized expression is a compound word (Cd) or a grammatical structure (Gs). Pay no attention to spaces, for they can be deceptive.

1. Jim's new car is a *hardtop*. _____
2. This jar has a rather *hard top*. _____
3. It was a *jack-in-the-box*. _____
4. There was a *plant in the box*. _____
5. A *hót dòg* is not a *hòt dóg*. _____ _____
6. He has a *dog in the manger* attitude. _____
7. She has a *strong hold* on him. _____
8. She has a *stronghold* in the Women's Club. _____
9. George found his *father-in-law*. _____
10. George found his *father in trouble*. _____
11. They bought it on the *black market*. _____
12. The electricity went off, and we were caught in a *black, completely lightless, market.* G
13. Henry is a *desígning tèacher.* _____
14. Henry is a *desîgning téacher.* _____

Exercise 9–5

For a review of the three classes of words, identify the following items with these symbols:

    S   Simple word   Cd   Compound word
    Cx Complex word   Gs   Grammatical structure

Make the IC cuts for Cx and Cd.

1. shárpshòoter _____		12. rat-a-tat _____
2. shârp shóoter _____		13. beauty _____
3. act _____		14. beautify _____
4. react _____		15. geometry _____
5. rattlesnake _____		16. búll's èye
6. passbook _____		(of target) _____
7. apparatus _____		17. bûll's éye
8. glowworm _____		(of bull) _____
9. import _____		18. outlast _____
10. ripcord _____		19. biochemical _____
11. unearth _____		20. inaccessible _____

Some Observations and Applications

One of the skills you practiced in this chapter was the ability to distinguish between compound words such as a *sweet potato* and grammatical structures such as *sweet story.* This skill relates to the important usage issue of how to appropriately represent compound nouns in writing. Of course the first step is to recognize whether a construction is a compound word or a grammatical structure. If you determine that a word or set of words constitutes a compound word, then there are further decisions to make about how to represent that compound. *The Chicago Manual of Style,* which provides direction on a variety of matters for editors and writers, outlines the three forms that compound words may take. They may be an "open compound" such as *sweet potato,* a "hyphenated compound" such as *mother-in-law,* or a "closed compound" such as *airtight.* Determining which type of form should be used with a compound is often difficult without checking a dictionary, though *The Chicago Manual of Style* provides some useful guidelines.[5] If you write or edit others' writing, the ability to recognize compounds will help you make informed decisions about how to represent those compounds or will alert you to forms about which you should consult a dictionary or reliable style guide.

---

[5]*The Chicago Manual of Style,* 14th ed. Chicago: University of Chicago Press, 1993, pp. 202–203.

10

Processes of Word Formation

One of the best illustrations of multiple processes of word formation surrounds the word *hamburger*. The word originated from a name, the city of Hamburg, Germany. After establishing itself as the word for a type of sandwich, the word *hamburger* began to be falsely interpreted as a compound, with *burger* acquiring its own status as a morpheme. This reanalysis of *hamburger* as a compound then led to the development of a number of new words such as *baconburger, fishburger,* and *cheeseburger.*[1] The word *hamburger* thus illustrates processes that we will discuss in this chapter such as antonomasia, compounding, and folk etymology.

It has been estimated that the English language contains more than a million words, of which fewer than half are included in unabridged dictionaries. It is natural to wonder where all these words came from. The answer is not difficult to find.

First, our language contains a core of words that have been a part of it as far back as we can trace its history, 5,000-plus years. A few examples are these words: *sun, man, foot, father, eat, fire, I, he, with, of.*

Second, English has been a prodigious borrower of words from other languages throughout its history, and a vast number of borrowed words are now in our language. This has come about through invasions, immigration, exploration, trade, and other avenues of contact between English and some foreign language. Below are a few examples of these borrowings. In many cases a word may pass, by borrowing, through one or more languages before it enters English. A case in point is the Arabic plural noun *hashshashin,* hashish eaters, which entered French in the form *assassin,* and from French was borrowed into English.

---

[1]For a discussion of the development of *hamburger* and other related words, as well as further examples of words that have been developed from names, see *The Play of Words* by Richard Lederer. New York: Pocket Books, 1990, pp. 200–204, 216.

English Word	Source Language	Meaning in Source Language
1. chauffeur	French	stoker of train engine, driver
2. campus	Latin	field, plain
3. guru	Hindi	spiritual leader
4. sheikh	Arabic	old man, chief
5. alligator	Spanish	the lizard
6. window	Old Norse	wind eye
7. agnostic	Greek	unknowable
8. bazaar	Persian	market
9. chow mein	Chinese	fried noodles
10. sake	Japanese	rice wine
11. macho	Spanish	male

A look at the etymologies in your desk dictionary—they are the part of each entry enclosed in brackets—will give you an idea of the amount of borrowing that has taken place in English and of the many languages that have contributed to make the English word-stock rich and full.

Apart from borrowing, English gets new words by means of easily definable processes employed by users of English. It is to these that we will now turn our attention.

A. Compounding

Compounding is simply the joining of two or more words into a single word, as in *hang glider, airstrip, cornflakes, busybody, downpour, cutoff, skydive, alongside, breakfast, long-haired, devil-may-care, high school.* As the foregoing examples show, compounds may be written as one word, as a hyphenated word, or as two words. Occasionally it is hard to say whether or not a word is a compound; compare, for instance, *despite* with *in spite of* and *instead of* with *in place of.*

B. Derivation

Derivation is the forming of new words by combining derivational affixes or bound bases with existing words, as in *disadvise, emplane, deplane, teleplay, ecosystem, coachdom, counselorship, re-ask.* Words like these, some of which you have never heard before, are often formed in the heat of speaking or writing. You will note that they are immediately understandable because you know the meaning of the parts.

C. Invention

Now and then new words are totally invented such as *Kodak, nylon, dingbat, goof,* and *blurb,* but few of these find their way into the common vocabulary.

D. Echoism

Echoism is the formation of words whose sound suggests their meaning, such as *hiss* and *peewee*. The meaning is usually a sound, either natural such as the *roar* of a waterfall or artificial such as the *clang* of a bell. But the meaning may also be the creature that produces the sound, such as *bobwhite*. Examples: *moan, click, murmur, quack, thunder, whisper, lisp, chickadee, bobolink*. In literary studies, especially those related to poetry, you will probably see this process referred to as "onomatopoeia."

Exercise 10-1

For each of the words below, indicate which process of formation (compounding, derivation, invention, or echoism) is represented. Abbreviate your answers by using just the first letter of the formation process.

1. roughneck _____
2. codgerhood _____
3. clink (of glasses) _____
4. doodad _____
5. dacron _____

6. pop _____
7. cream puff _____
8. wheeze _____
9. weirdoism _____
10. exflux _____

E. Clipping

Clipping means cutting off the beginning or the end of a word, or both, leaving a part to stand for the whole. The resultant form is called a clipped word. The jargon of the campus is filled with clipped words: *lab, dorm, prof, exam, gym, prom, math, psych, mike,* and countless others. As these examples suggest, the clipping of the end of a word is the most common, and it is mostly nouns that undergo this process. Clipping results in new free forms in the language.

Exercise 10-2

Give the original words from which these clipped words were formed. Consult a dictionary as necessary.

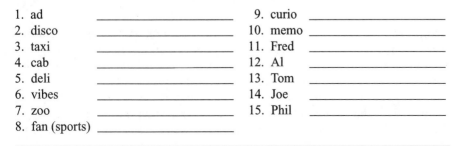

1. ad _____
2. disco _____
3. taxi _____
4. cab _____
5. deli _____
6. vibes _____
7. zoo _____
8. fan (sports) _____

9. curio _____
10. memo _____
11. Fred _____
12. Al _____
13. Tom _____
14. Joe _____
15. Phil _____

Less common than the back-clipped words, like the foregoing, are those words that lose their forepart, such as *plane* and *phone*.

Exercise 10–3

Give the original words from which these clipped words were formed. Consult a dictionary as needed.

1. gator	_____	6. wig	_____
2. pike (road)	_____	7. cute	_____
3. bus	_____	8. Gene	_____
4. van	_____	9. Beth	_____
5. chute	_____	10. Tony	_____

Only a very few words have been formed by both front and back clipping. Four common ones are *flu, Liz, still* (apparatus for distilling hard liquor), and *fridge*.

Clipped words are formed not only from individual words but also from grammatical units, such as modifier plus noun. *Paratrooper,* for example, is a clipped form of *parachutist trooper.* In cases like this it is often the first part that is shortened while the second part remains intact. Also, two successive words may be clipped to form one new word, as in *sitcom* (= situation comedy).

Exercise 10–4

Give the originals of these clipped words

1. Amerindian _____
2. maître d' /metər di/ _____
3. contrail _____
4. taxicab _____
5. moped _____
6. comsat _____
7. agribusiness _____

F. Acronymy

Acronymy is the process whereby a word is formed from the initials or beginning segments of a succession of words. In some cases the initials are pronounced, as in *MP* (military police, or Member of Parliament). In others the initials and/or beginning segments are pronounced as the spelled word would be. For example, *NATO* (North Atlantic Treaty Organization) is pronounced as /neto/ and *radar* (radio detecting and ranging) as /redar/. In the word *radar* we have an example of an acronym that has evolved to the point that it is written in lowercase letters and its acronymic origin is even unknown by most speakers.

Exercise 10–5

Pronounce these acronyms and give their originals.

1. RV   _____
2. NOW _____
3. MADD _____
4. OK   _____
5. scuba _____
6. OPEC _____
7. WASP _____
8. ICBM _____
9. laser _____
10. FDIC _____
11. IRS _____

During the latter part of the twentieth century there has been a great increase in the use of acronyms. They tend to abound in large organizations—for instance, in the army, in government, and in big business—where they offer neat ways of expressing long and cumbersome terms. The very names of some businesses have been acronymized, such as *Nabisco, Texaco,* and *Alcoa.* Many acronyms are used and understood only by initiates in a given field, like the medical terms *PRN, HR,* and *OR,* whereas others gain general currency, such as *CPR, IV,* and *AIDS.* It is likely that you employ some campus acronyms that would not be understood elsewhere.

G. Blending

Blending is the fusion of two words into one, usually the first part of one word with the last part of another, as in *gasohol,* from *gasoline* and *alcohol.* The resultant blend partakes of both original meanings. Many blends are nonce words, here today and gone tomorrow, and relatively few become part of the standard lexicon. The two classes, blends and clipped words, are not sharply separated, and some words may be put into either class.

Exercise 10–6

Give the originals of these blends.

1. brunch   _____
2. happenstance _____
3. stagflation _____
4. simulcast _____
5. motel   _____
6. smog   _____
7. dumbfound _____

8. telecast   _____
9. flustrated   _____
10. splatter   _____

Exercise 10–7

Give the blends that result from fusing these words.

1. transfer   + resistor   = _____
2. automobile   + omnibus   = _____
3. escalade   + elevator   = _____
4. blare or blow + spurt   = _____
5. squall   + squeak   = _____

H. Back-formation

If someone should ask you, "What does a *feeper* do?" you would probably answer, "He feeps, of course." You would answer thus because there exist in your mind such word-pairs as *tell-teller, reap-reaper, write-writer, sing-singer;* and you would reason, perhaps unconsciously, that on the analogy of these forms the word *feeper* must have a parallel verb *feep.* Likewise, in the past, with the introduction of the nouns *peddler, beggar, swindler,* and *editor* into our language, speakers followed the same analogy and created the previously nonexistent verbs *peddle, beg, swindle,* and *edit.* This process is just the reverse of our customary method of word formation, whereby we begin with a verb such as *speak* and, by adding the agent morpheme {ER n}, form the noun *speaker.* The process is called back-formation. It may be defined as the formation of a word from one that looks like its derivative. An example is *hedgehop,* from the noun *hedgehopper.* Back-formation is an active source of new words today.

Exercise 10–8

1. The noun *greed* is a back-formation from the adjective *greedy.* Write four pairs of words that constitute an analogy for the creation of *greed.*

2. The pairs *revise-revision* and *supervise-supervision* are in common use in English. From this analogy what verb is back-formed from *television?* _____

3. English has many pairs on the pattern of *create-creation, separate-separation,* and *deviate-deviation.* On this analogy what back-formations would you expect from *donation* and *oration?* _____ and _____

These verbs are back-formations. Write the words from which they are back-formed.

1. housekeep   _____
2. typewrite   _____
3. administrate   _____
4. resurrect   _____
5. baby-sit   _____
6. enthuse   _____
7. laze   _____
8. lase   _____

9. sidle   _____
10. escalate   _____
11. reminisce   _____
12. deficit-spend   _____
13. emote   _____
14. burgle   _____
15. party-poop   _____

I. Folk Etymology

The tennis term *let ball* affords a good illustration of our next process, folk etymology. In the term *let ball,* the word *let* has retained the obsolete meaning of "prevented," common in the language of Shakespeare.[2] A let ball is one that has been prevented from taking its true course by touching the top of the net. It is an entirely different word from the *let* that means "allow." But a neophyte, hearing the word on the tennis court, may understand it as *net,* because /l/ and /n/ are not far apart in sound and *net* makes sense to him whereas *let* does not. Thus he may use the term *net ball* until corrected by a more knowledgeable player.

Such a process—changing a word, in part or in whole, to make it more understandable and more like familiar words, though based on an inaccurate view of its origin—is known as folk etymology.

Look up in your desk dictionary the following examples of folk etymology and write the source of each in the blanks. Usually the reason for the change will be apparent.

1. female   _____
2. carryall   _____
3. cockroach   _____
4. hangnail   _____
5. Welsh rarebit   _____

6. coleslaw   _____
7. bridegroom   _____
8. helpmate   _____
9. woodchuck   _____

---

[2]In *Hamlet,* Act I, scene 4, Hamlet says to his two friends who are holding him back from following his father's ghost:
   "Unhand me, gentlemen.
   By heaven I'll make a ghost of him that lets me."
Here *lets* means "prevents." A modern reader, understanding *lets* as "allows," would get exactly the opposite meaning from that which Shakespeare intended.
   The obsolete meaning of *let* survives also in the legal phrase "without let or hindrance."

Some folk etymologies become established in the speech of particular individuals but are not widespread enough among speakers of a language to necessitate changes within a dictionary. Still, such forms are interesting for what they reveal about how some speakers perceive particular words. Consider, for example, the use of "Verging" instead of "Virgin" in the place name "The Virgin Islands," or those people who speak of "very close veins" instead of "varicose veins."

J. Antonomasia

Antonomasia means the formation of a common noun, a verb, or an adjective from the name of a person or place. For example, the word *frisbee* comes from the Frisbie Bakery in Bridgewater, Connecticut, whose pie tins were used for a throwing game. The term *vandal* derives from the Vandals, a Germanic people who overran southern Europe fifteen hundred years ago and sacked and looted Rome in the fifth century.

Names from history and literature have given us many common nouns. A lover, for instance, may be called a *romeo,* a *don juan,* or a *casanova.* If he is too *quixotic,* he may meet his *waterloo* at the hands of some *sheba* or *jezebel.*

Exercise 10-11

Look up in your desk dictionary the following instances of antonomasia and write the origin of each in the blanks.

1. sandwich _____   6. jeans _____
2. frankfurter _____   7. leotard _____
3. baloney, bologna _____   8. guy _____
4. denim _____   9. lynch _____
5. cashmere _____   10. boycott _____

K. Reduplication

Reduplication is the process of forming a new word by doubling a morpheme, usually with a change of vowel or initial consonant, as in *pooh-pooh, tiptop,* and *hanky-panky.* The basic, originating morpheme is most frequently the second half, like *dilly-dally,* but it may be the first half, like *ticktock,* or both halves, like *singsong,* or neither half, like *boogie-woogie.*

Because the word *reduplication* has three meanings relevant to our discussion—the process, the result of the process (that is, the new word), and the element repeated—let us avoid confusion by calling these words "twin-words."

Exercise 10-12

Underline the originating morpheme in each of these twin-words.

1. wiggle-waggle
2. pitter-patter
3. nitwit
4. super-duper
5. silly-willy
6. lovey-dovey

Twin-words can be divided into three classes, leaving only a small residue of irregular forms.

1. The base morpheme is repeated without change.
   Examples: clop-clop, tick-tick

   The twin-words in this group are often onomatopoetic—that is, they represent sounds, such as *gobble-gobble* and *chug-chug*. This class of morphemes is commonly used when speaking with small children, and it sometimes involves repetition of an already clipped form such as *dada* (dad) or *baba* (bottle).

2. The base morpheme is repeated with a change of initial consonant.
   Examples: fuddy-duddy, tootsie-wootsie, razzle-dazzle, roly-poly, teeny-weeny, heebie-jeebies, hootchy-kootchy

3. The base morpheme is repeated with a change of vowel.
   Examples: chitchat, tiptop, criss-cross

   The first vowel is usually the high front lax vowel /ɪ/, and the second is a low vowel /æ/, /a/, or /ɔ/.
   Examples: zigzag, ticktock, pingpong

Exercise 10-13

Identify the class of twin-word by one of these numbers:

1. Repetition without change
2. Repetition with change of initial consonant
3. Repetition with change of vowel

____ 1. knick-knack	____ 6. hotsy-totsy
____ 2. ding-dong	____ 7. hocus-pocus
____ 3. wishy-washy	____ 8. flipflop
____ 4. quack-quack	____ 9. humdrum
____ 5. rowdy-dowdy	____ 10. nitty-gritty

Some Observations and Applications

In an earlier chapter we mentioned a business that creates product names by taking into account the meanings that people associate with particular sounds. Here we will note the importance of morphological awareness in the generation of clever and effective product names. With the dramatic increase of inventions, new technologies, consumer products, and companies, it has become necessary to coin many new terms and names. Those who wish to market new products or services are very involved in creating new words and must use some of the processes of word formation that you have studied in this chapter. Consider, for example, such product or company names as *Papermate* (compounding), *Listerine* (antonomasia and derivation), *Coke* (clipping), *EPT* (acronymy—Early Pregnancy Test), *Nicorette* (blending of nicotine and cigarette), and *Fiddle-Faddle* (reduplication).

Let us consider another type of application of the word formation material that you have studied. A knowledge of back-formations and their development can help you to make more informed word choices in your writing. Back-formations require some time within a language before they achieve respectability in formal writing. Some back-formations that were once stigmatized are now completely acceptable in careful writing. But if you are doing careful writing that you wish others to regard as "correct," then you will certainly want to exercise caution in using words that seem to be relatively recent back-formations. Just being aware of what back-formations are and some of the kinds of forms they take will help you to be more suspicious of a word that you might otherwise want to use. For example, you have seen that a common type of back-formation results when someone assumes that a word ending in *-or, -ar,* or *-er* has a corresponding verb without that suffix. Your knowledge of back-formations should make you more cautious about assuming that a particular verb must exist based on a noun form that you are familiar with. If the verb you are thinking of using sounds a little strange to you (such as perhaps the word *burgle*), even if you have heard others use it, that might be a good indication that you are dealing with a relatively new back-formation. You can check on your suspicion by consulting a dictionary, particularly a usage dictionary.

11

Inflectional Paradigms

Paradimes

If the plural of *tooth* is *teeth,* shouldn't the plural of *booth* be *beeth*? One goose, two geese—so one moose, two meese? One index, two indices—one Kleenex, two Kleenices? If people ring a bell today and rang a bell yesterday, why don't we say that they flang a ball? If they wrote a letter, perhaps they also bote their tongue. If the teacher taught, why isn't it also true that the preacher praught? Why is it that the sun shone yesterday while I shined my shoes, that I treaded water and then trod on soil, and that I flew out to see a World Series game in which my favorite player flied out?[1]

A paradigm is a set of related forms having the same stem but different affixes. As a reminder, here is a derivational paradigm with the stem *head: ahead, behead, header, headlong, headship, heady, subhead.*

Paradigms are also formed by the words to which the inflectional affixes are attached. These are called inflectional paradigms. There are three of them, which are listed below.

NOUN PARADIGM

Forms:	Stem	Plural	Possessive	Plural+Possessive
Inflectional suffixes:		{s- pl}	{-s ps}	{-s pl ps}
Models:	doctor	doctors	doctor's	doctors'
	woman	women	woman's	women's

---

[1]Excerpt from "English Is a Crazy Language" in *Crazy English* by Richard Lederer. New York: Pocket Books, 1989, p. 13.

VERB PARADIGM

Forms:	Stem	Present Third-Person Singular	Present Participle	Past Tense	Past Participle
Inflectional suffixes:		{s 3d}	{-ING vb}	{-D pt}	{-D pp}
Models:	show	shows	showing	showed	showed (also shown)
	ring	rings	ringing	rang	rung
	cut	cuts	cutting	cut	cut

COMPARABLE PARADIGM

Forms:	Stem	Comparative	Superlative
Inflectional suffixes:		{-ER cp}	{-EST sp}
Models	sweet	sweeter	sweetest
	lively	livelier	liveliest
	friendly	friendlier	friendliest
	soon	sooner	soonest
	near	nearer	nearest

In addition, there is a pronoun paradigm which differs from the previous three in that it is not a stem-and-affix group but a small and closed set of words of fixed form. Such a closed set of words is called a structure class. We will take up the personal pronouns in chapter 13, together with the other structure classes.

In the paradigms above, the meaning of the stem remains constant; the suffixes produce the differences in meaning among the forms of each paradigm. Membership in one of these inflectional paradigms is one of the signals that enable us to group words into four of the major parts of speech—nouns, verbs, adjectives, and adverbs. We will take up this matter in chapter 12. Now we will examine the inflectional paradigms one by one.

A. The Noun Paradigm

The noun paradigm is as follows:

Forms:	Stem	Plural	Possessive	Plural + Possessive
Inflectional suffixes:		{s- pl}	{-s ps}	{-s pl ps}
Models:	doctor	doctors	doctor's	doctors'
	man	men	man's	men's

This four-form paradigm is maximal, and not all nouns have all the four forms. Many nouns do not take the possessive forms because an *of* structure often takes the place of the {-s ps} morpheme. For example, one is more likely to say "the ceiling of the room" than "the room's ceiling." In the spoken language we cannot always be sure which s morpheme we are hearing, because the possessive and the plural have identical forms—/-s/,/-z/, and /-əz/—except in the case of irregular plurals. If, for instance, you were to hear /ðə daktərz sɛmɪnar/, it could mean, "the doctor's seminar," "the doctors' seminar," or "the doctors seminar."

A few groups of so-called nouns have only one form of this paradigm. The words in one group—such as *tennis, courage,* and *haste*—have the form of the stem. Another group does not have a singular form but only that of the -s plural: *clothes, environs, trousers,* and others. These take *they/them* as a pronoun substitute and go with the plural form of the verb, e.g., "My clothes [they] are clean." Still another group ends in an -s, words such as *economics, linguistics, mathematics, physics,* but these take *it* as a pronoun substitute and go with a singular form of the verb, e.g., "*Linguistics* [it] is an exacting discipline." Words in a certain ill-defined group end in -s, such as *ethics, oats, pliers, suds, measles,* but may be either singular or plural, depending on the context in which they occur or on the meaning expressed.

Examples:

Singular:	*Measles* (= a malady) is a contagious disease.
Plural:	Have you ever had them, the *measles*? (= a malady)
Singular:	*Ethics* (= a philosophic discipline) is a challenging subject.
Plural:	His *ethics* are beyond reproach (-beliefs and actions).

Exercise 11–1

Write the paradigmatic forms of these nouns. For some slots you may have two forms or none.

	Stem	Plural	Possessive	Plural + Possessive
1.	carpenter	carpenters	carpenter's	carpenters'
2.	woman	women	woman's	women's
3.	brother	brothers	brother's	brothers'
4.	cloud	clouds	cloud's	clouds'
5.	cattle	cattle	—	cattle's
6.	duck	ducks	duck's	ducks'
7.	Japanese	Japanese		
8.	means	means	—	—
9.	athletics	athletics	athletics'	
10.	scissors	scissors	scissors'	scissors

Noun Plurals

At this point it is convenient to set forth the ways of distinguishing singular from plural nouns. For many nouns the long-used meaning test will do: a noun is singular if it means one and plural if it means more than one. But meaning does not always work as a test of number. Take for instance this sentence: "I like your *hair.*" Is *hair* singular or plural, assuming it means not a single strand but the coiffure or thatch on someone's head? Nor will form always do because some nouns ending in an -*s* seem to be singular, e.g., *physics,* and others without an -*s* plural seem to be plural, e.g., *several salmon.*

There remain three useful tests for number in the noun.

1. A noun is singular if it can take one of these substitutes: *he/him, she/her, it, this,* or *that.* It is plural if it can take as a substitute *they/them, these,* or *those.*
   Examples: The beach was covered with *white sand.* (= it)
   Have you studied *phonetics*? (= it)
   Where did you hang *my trousers*? (= them)

2. The number of a noun may be signaled by a modifier such as *several, many, this, that, these, those, fifteen,* or by a pronoun reference such as *his/her/its, their.*
   Examples: We saw *many fish* swimming under the bridge.
   In returning to the fold, the *sheep* changed *its* direction.
   In returning to the fold the *sheep* changed *their* direction.

   Be careful not to apply your test using a modifier such as *some,* which can be used with a singular or plural noun.
   Examples: He bought some cake.
   He bought some cakes.

3. When a noun functions as subject of a verb, its number is sometimes shown by the form of the verb. It is the singular noun that goes with the {-s 3d} form of the verb, as in

   Measles *is* a contagious disease.
   The fish *swims* in the pond.

   Contrast these with

   The goods *are* on the way.
   The fish *swim* in the pond.

   in which the verb form *are* or *swim* shows that *goods* and *fish* are plural.

   If the verb has a form that does not change for singular and plural (e.g., a past tense form other than *was* or *were*) one can usually substitute a present tense form, or the present or past tense of *be,* e.g.,

   The goods came (substitute present tense, *come*) late.
   The goods came (substitute present tense of *be, are*) late.
   The goods came (substitute past tense of *be,* namely, *were*) late.

Each of these substitutions shows that *goods* is plural.

Exercise 11–2

In the blanks of the first column provide *it, they,* or *them* as the appropriate pronoun substitute for the italicized word. In the blanks of the second column write Sg (singular) or Pl (plural) to show the number of the italicized noun.

1. Miss Shen is wearing panty *hose* today. _____them_____ _____
2. What did they do with the *molasses*? _____it_____ _____
3. The *summons* came in the mail. _____it_____ _____
4. Why doesn't she call the *police*? _____them_____ _____
5. Jack likes to fish for *pike*. _____them_____ _____
6. The firm transported the *goods* to Australia. _____them_____ _____
7. The jar is filled with *sugar*. _____it_____ _____
8. Have you ever had the *mumps*? _____them_____ _____
9. She became fond of *mathematics*. _____it_____ _____
10. Does your brother eat *soap*? _____it_____ _____
11. The *poor* among us needed assistance. _____they_____ _____

Exercise 11–3

Circle the noun modifier or pronoun reference that reveals the number of the italicized noun.

1. The hunting party saw (few) *deer* this season.
2. (That) *news* delighted her.
3. He studied *poetics* in all (its) complications. *antecedent*
4. My *scissors* lost (their) sharpness.
5. She shot both *quail* (on the wing.) *in flight*

Exercise 11–4

Circle the verb that reveals the number of the italicized noun.

1. The *Chinese* (was) preparing the dinner. S
2. The *Chinese* (were) preparing the dinner. Pl
3. *Oats* (is) his best crop. S
4. The *bass* (are) biting today. Pl
5. The *species* (has) become extinct. S

Some nouns, known as collective nouns, may be either singular or plural in meaning when they are singular in form. These are nouns that represent a collection or unit of individuals, such as *tribe, family, team, committee, faculty, choir.* Speakers are likely to use singular forms (verbs, pronouns, determiners) in connection with such nouns when thinking of the unit as a single whole, but they will use plural forms when intending the separate individuals within the unit.

Examples: Singular: The family (= it, the unit) *is* sitting at the dinner table.

Plural: The family (= they, the individuals) *have* gathered from many parts of the country.

Exercise 11–5

Indicate in the blanks by Sg or Pl whether the italicized collective nouns are singular or plural. Decide by using the tests for number that you have learned.

1. The *band* is playing well today. _____ Sg
2. The *band* are playing well today. _____ Pl
3. The *choir* became dissatisfied with their robes. _____ Pl
4. The *choir* became dissatisfied with its singing. _____ Sg
5. The *staff* of the college paper was a high-quality group. _____ Sg
6. The *staff* of the college paper were assembled to discuss their last edition. _____ Pl
7. The *tribe* were on the warpath. _____ Pl
8. The *tribe* was the owner of the river bottom. _____ Sg
9. The *congregation* rose to its feet. _____ Sg
10. The *congregation* have all helped with the fund-raising drive. _____ Pl

---

The plural form of the noun signals the meaning of more than one. The most frequently employed plural forms are the three allomorphs of {-s pl}, such as we hear in *hats* /-s/, *fads* /-z/, and *kisses* /-əz/. These -*s* plurals are customarily considered the regular forms, not only because of their numerical preponderance but also because new nouns, either from other languages (*pizzeria*) or composed from existing morphemes (*astronaut*), tend to follow the -*s* plural.

In addition to the regular -*s* plural there are several small groups of irregular plurals.

1. Three nouns still retain an -*en* plural—*oxen, children,* and *brethren*—the last two having in addition a replacive stem vowel and a suffixal -*r.*

2. Another group has a Ø (zero) suffixal plural. This is a convenient way of saying that the plural is the same as the singular. It is shown in this way:

   deer /dir/ (pl.) = /dir/ + /Ø/

   The Ø plural allomorph refers to a significant absence of suffix. The words in this group are the names of edible animals, game animals, fish, and birds. Among them are *deer, sheep, swine, antelope, bass, pike, carp, perch, pickerel, quail, grouse.* Beside these we may set similar words with a regular plural: *pigs, goats, suckers, muskies, bullheads, pheasants, ducks.* Some have both forms; a farmer, for example, who has *ducks* on his pond may go out hunting *duck.*

3. Seven common nouns form their plural by a replacive allomorph; for instance,

   /gis/ = /gus/ + /u > i/

   These are *man, woman, goose, tooth, foot, louse,* and *mouse.* In *women* there are two replacives:

   /wɪmɪn/ = /wumən/ + /u > ɪ/ + /ə > ɪ/

4. One set of nouns has as the stem of the plural an allomorph that is different from the stem of the singular. The morpheme {calf}, for example, has /kæf/ as the singular allomorph but /kæv-/ as the plural allomorph, and the plural suffix /-z/ conforms to the voiced sound /v/. Changes in the phonemic form of allomorphs as they are grouped into words, or as they appear in different forms of a word, are called morphophonemic changes. Among the morphophonemic changes we have already noted for the plural are these:

calf   >   calves   /kæf/   >   /kæv-/
child   >   children   /čayld/   >   /čɪld-/

Each of these changes in an allomorph is an example of a morphophonemic change. Nouns in this group end in /-f/ or /-θ/.[2] Here are two examples:

knife   >   knives   /nayvz/ = /naif/ + /f > v/ + /-z/
mouth   >   mouths   /mawðz/ = /mauθ/ + /θ > ð/ + /-z/

    Other examples include *half, loaf, self, wife, bath, path, oath.* Some nouns ending in /-f/ or /-θ/ do not make a morphophonemic change, such as *chiefs;* others may have two forms of the plural, such as /yuθs/ or /yuðz/.

Exercise 11–6

Write in phonemic script the allomorphic formula for the formation of the plural of these words.

    Example: brother   brethren
              /brɛðrən/ = /brəðər/ + /ə > ɛ/ + /ər > rən/

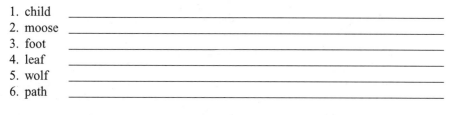

1. child   _____
2. moose _____
3. foot   _____
4. leaf   _____
5. wolf   _____
6. path   _____

Exercise 11–7

Divide these words into two groups: (1) those that undergo no change of the base allomorph in the plural, e.g., "those two coughs"; (2) those that have two forms of the plural, e.g., *hoofs, hooves.* The words are *grief, scarf, chief, truth, wharf, sheath, belief, wreath, waif, staff.* Respond according to pronunciation. The spelling does not vary in all cases.

One Allomorph		*Two Allomorphs*	
_____	_____	_____	_____
_____	_____	_____	_____
_____	_____	_____	_____

---

[2]Some speakers may add the consonant /-s/ to their list, because they change the final stem in *house* from /-s/ to /-z/ when adding the plural suffix. The resulting form of the word in this case is /hawzəz/.

Every language has its own ways of signaling plurality in nouns. In the Germanic tongues the suffixal consonants /-s/, /-n/, and /-r/ are common for this purpose. In Italian, on the other hand, the suffixal vowels /-i/ and /-e/ are employed. Chinese, an exception, does not signal plurality at all, except in the personal pronouns.

When foreign words are borrowed into English, their pronunciation becomes assimilated more or less to the phonemic system of English. This means that we follow our own native pronunciation habits as we utter these foreign words. Take, for example, the Italian noun *soprano* /soprano/. This is pronounced /səpræno/ by most Americans. We replace the first Italian /o/ by /ə/ because this accords with our way of pronouncing countless three-syllable words that have a primary stress on the medial syllable: /pəteto, bətænɪk/, /kənɛkšən/, /məlɪgnənt/. And the Italian /a/ becomes /æ/ because it is our habit to pronounce *an* as /æn/ in many words, such as *abandon, mechanic, outlandish, pedantic, titanic.*

Now, what happens to the pluralizing morpheme of foreign nouns that are imported into English? Frequently this pluralizer is completely abandoned, and the adopted noun is made to conform to the allomorphic pattern of the English plural {-s pl}. An instance is the Italian *soprano*, which has lost its native plural of /soprani/ and is pluralized like any English word ending in a vowel /səprænoz/. And this has been the fate of many such Italian imports in *-o: piano, cello, solo, rondo, casino, studio, canto.* Spanish plurals—/-s/ after a vowel and /-ɛs/ after a consonant—are so similar to the English that they seem to assimilate to the English plural pattern without exception. Witness such borrowings from Spanish as *patio, mosquito, barbecue, cafeteria, guitar, cigar, lariat, canyon, alligator, tornado.*

On other occasions the foreign spelling is retained but the pronunciation, with occasional exceptions, is modified. Thus the Latin singular and plural forms, *datum-data,* keep in English the original spelling, but the Latin plural /-a/ becomes /-ə/, whereas the Greek-Latin plural *phenomena*, with its classical /-a/ plural, may remain unchanged in English, though some speakers change it to /-ə/.

Many borrowed nouns have both plurals—their foreign ones, often modified, and the English plural, such as *concerti* and *concertos, curricula* and *curriculums, syllabi* and *syllabuses.* The tendency is for such words to adopt the English {-s pl}, but some have proved resistant to change, such as *alumni.*

Exercise 11–8

Look up the plurals of these words in your desk dictionary. Then write in phonemic script the pluralizing allomorph of each. If there are two pluralizers, write both.

Examples: criterion   1.   /-z/ or /-ən > -ə/
           thesis   /-ɪs/ > /-iz/

1. alumna   */-ə 7 -e/*
2. formula   */-ə 7- e/*
3. opus
4. appendix
5. stratum
6. hypothesis   */-ɪs/ 7 /-íz/*

7. kibbutz _____
8. apparatus _____
9. medium _____
10. stimulus _____
11. memorandum _____
12. graffito _____
13. nucleus _____
14. analysis /-ɪs/ 7/-ɪz/
15. fedayee _____

Noun Possessive

The noun possessive morpheme {-s ps} has the same phonologically conditioned allomorphs as the plural: /-s/, /-z/, and /-əz/, plus a zero allomorph as in *students'*. The term *possessive* is not a satisfactory label for this morpheme because a variety of different semantic relationships can exist between the possessive noun and the one that follows. The following cases will illustrate.

Relationship	Example
1. Possession or belongingness	John's hat
	Judy's home
2. Characterization or description	a cowboy's walk
	men's coats
3. Origin	Raphael's paintings
	Cary's novels
4. Measure (time, value, space)	an hour's wait
	a dollar's worth
	a stone's throw
5. Subject of act	John's flight (John flew)
	the judge's decision
	(the judge decided)
6. Object of act	Eliot's critics were many.
	(They criticized Eliot.)

Exercise 11–9

Using the numbers above, indicate the relation shown between the italicized possessive and its following noun.

1. We missed the other car by a *hair's breadth*. ___4___
2. A *wren's song* floated through the window. ___3___
3. They were playing *children's games*. ___2___
4. The police provided for *Richard's protection*. ___6___
5. The *boy's jump* saved his life. ___5___
6. The *moon's beams* were brilliant that night. ___3___

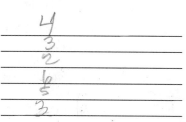

7. *Willard's arrival* was a surprise. _____ 7
8. He has never done a *day's work*. _____ 4
9. She met *Manuel's father*. _____ 1
10. He was happy about *Jane's winning*. _____ 5

A noun possessive is ambiguous when it expresses more than one of the above relationships at the same time. For example, "His son's loss grieved him" has two possible meanings: (1) He lost his son (object of underlying verb), and this grieved him; or (2) His son (subject of underlying verb) lost something, perhaps a family heirloom, and this grieved him.

Exercise 11–10

As in the previous exercise, use the numbers 1 to 6 to indicate the relationships expressed by each ambiguous possessive.

1. Dr. McCoy's examination was a long one. _____ 5
2. That is my father's photograph. _____ 1
3. He was carrying a woman's coat on his arm. _____ 2
4. We bought one of Rutherford's paintings. _____ 1
5. The case was about his wife's fatal shooting. _____ 6

In making a choice between the inflected possessive (*student's*) and the periphrastic *of* structure (*of the student*), there is no hard-and-fast guideline, and often the form chosen depends on personal taste. The tendency, however, is to use the inflected form with animate nouns and the *of* structure with inanimate nouns; thus, *the dog's leg,* but *the leg of the table.*

Exercise 11–11

This is an exercise to investigate the usage of the class in regard to the inflected possessive {-s ps} and the *of* structure. You will be given pairs of sentences like this:

a. The *garage's* cement floor is cracking.
b. The cement floor *of the garage* is cracking.

If you would use only one of these forms, put a check mark only after the sentence containing that one. If you would use either one of the two, put a check mark in both blanks. If you would give preference to one of the two, circle the check mark that corresponds to your preferred choice. For this exercise, there are no right or wrong answers.

1a. The *building's* roof was blown off by the wind. _____ ✓
 b. The roof *of the building* was blown off by the wind. _____
2a. The *soldier's* rifle had been thoroughly cleaned. _____ ✓
 b. The rifle *of the soldier* had been thoroughly cleaned. _____
3a. The *lawn's* color had become brown. _____ ✓
 b. The color *of the lawn* had become brown. _____

4a. We admired the *dog's* silky coat. _____ ✓ _____
 b. We admired the silky coat *of the dog.* _____
5a. The *hat's* brim was torn. _____ ✓ _____
 b. The brim *of the hat* was torn. _____

A quick tabulation on the board will show the extent to which the members of the class make a distinction between animate nouns (*soldier* and *dog*) and inanimate nouns (*building, lawn,* and *hat*) in their use of {-s ps} and the *of* structure.

The following exercise concludes our look at the forms of the noun paradigm. We will return to them again in our study of syntax. There our knowledge of the noun paradigm will help us to single out nouns in this simple way: If a word has two or more forms of the paradigm, we will label it a noun, e.g.,

daughter daughter's daughters daughters'

But if it has only one form, such as *bravery,* it is not a noun by this paradigmatic test, although it may be shown to be a noun by other tests.

Exercise 11–12

Write N after every word that is a noun *according to the paradigmatic test* described above.

1. player	N	6. nation	N	11. chess	
2. pray		7. uncle	N	12. field	N
3. sidewalk	N	8. discovery	N	13. pocket	N
4. chaos		9. together		14. game	N
				(in playground context)	
5. relax		10. bus	N	15. game	
				(in hunting context)	

B. The Verb Paradigm

The next set of forms we will examine is the verb paradigm. Verbs have three, four, or five forms. Those with four, such as *learn* below, are the most common. The verb paradigm goes as follows:

Forms:	Stem	Present Third-Person Singular	Present Participle	Past Tense	Past Participle
Inflectional suffixes:		{-s 3d}	{-ING vb}	{-D pt}	{-D pp}
Models:	learn	learns	learning	learned	learned
	choose	chooses	choosing	chose	chosen
	set	sets	setting	set	set

Each of these five forms has its own uses, which we will now run through.

1. The first form is the stem. This occurs after *to,* after auxiliaries such as *can* and *will,* and in the present tense, except for the third-person singular.

   Examples: to *sit,* can *go,* we *eat*

2. The present third-person singular is the form used with the pronouns *he, she it,* and with singular words or with word groups for which these pronouns will substitute.

   Examples: That *freshman* cuts his class every Wednesday.
   He cuts his class every Wednesday.
   Each is expected to do his duty.
   Somebody has left a note for you.
   Winning the championship cuts no ice with me.

   The morpheme {-s 3d} has the same allomorphs in the same distribution as the plural and possessive forms of the noun: /-s/, /-z/, and /-əz/, as in *cuts, begs,* and *buzzes.*

3. The present participle is the {-ING vb] form. Although it is called the "present participle," it isn't actually a present-tense form, so the name is a little misleading. But we will continue to use the term because it is the term most commonly used for this form. The present participle combines with seven of the eight forms of *be*—*am, is, are, was, were, be, been*—to make verb phrases.

   Examples: They *were writing* letters.
   She must have *been sleeping.*

   It is also used as a subjectless verbal, that is, when it is not the main verb and does not have a subject, as in

   His passion used to be *playing* golf.

   A few verbs—mostly referring to mental activities— are seldom heard in the {-ING vb} form as main verbs in the sentence. These verbs include *own, need, prefer, know, hear, like, remember,* and *understand.* The following sentences, for instance, are ungrammatical:

   *Jake is *owning* a cabin in the north woods.
   *She was not *knowing* what to say.

   But they are in common use as subjectless verbals, as in

   Owning a cabin in the north woods, Jake was very popular during the
   summer vacation period.
   Not *knowing* what to say, Marilyn maintained a discreet silence.

   This present-participle verbal {-ING vb} morpheme should not be confused with the nominal {-ING nm} morpheme or the adjectival {-ING aj} morpheme.

4. The past tense takes on numerous forms, e.g., *jumped, shrunk, kept, led, began, rode, built, found, knew, swore, shook.* The most usual ones end in the allomorphs /-t/, /-d/, and /-əd/, as in *passed, pleased,* and *parted.*

5. The term *past participle,* like the term *present participle,* is also a little misleading because it is not used to convey a past-tense notion. But once again, we will follow convention and continue to use this term. The past participle also has numerous forms. Those most frequently occurring end in the same three sounds mentioned above in connection with the past tense, but here they are allomorphs of {-D pp}. The past participle is used with *have, has, had, having* to form verbal phrases.

Examples: She *has selected* a stunning gown.
   He *had* never *flown* in a helicopter.

It is also used with the forms of *be* to form the passive.

Examples: The orchestra *was selected* by the committee.
   By night the missing lad *had been found.*

This past-participle verbal {-D pp} morpheme should not be confused with the adjectival {-D aj} morpheme, described earlier.

Exercise 11–13

Fill out the following verb paradigms. Then indicate by a 3, 4, or 5 whether the verbs are three-form, four-form, or five-form.

Stem	Pres. 3d Sg.	Pres. P.	Past T.	Past P.	Number
1. walk	walks	walking	walked	walked	4
2. bite	bites	biting	bit	bitten	5
3. keep	keeps	keeping	kept	kept	4
4. freeze	freezes	freezing	froze	frozen	5
5. set	sets	setting	set	set	3
6. sell	sells	selling	sold	sold	4
7. put	puts	putting	put	put	3
8. rise	rises	rising	rose	risen	5
9. tease	teases	teasing	teased	teased	4
10. sleep	sleeps	sleeping	slept	slept	4

Most verbs follow faithfully the first three forms—the stem, the present third-person singular, and the present participle—with occasional exceptions like *does* and *says,* which have replacive allomorphs in the stem:

/dəz/ = /du/ + /u > ə / + /-z/
/sɛz/ = /se/ + /e > ɛ / + /-z/

And in the past tense and past participle most verbs have identical forms, as in *learned, have learned; batted, have batted; cried, have cried.* Such are commonly known as regular verbs. It is because of the influence of this large number of verbs having this same pattern in the past tense and past participle that children utter such forms as *knowed, runned, drinked*. The child is simply following the pattern he knows best and in so doing he creates what we call an analogical form.[3] The process of analogy has operated historically in the language and has derived forms that are now used, even in the standard dialect. For example, the past tense of the verb *help* used to be formed very differently but has now been regularized and takes the past-tense suffix *-ed*.

There still remain, however, numerous verbs, many of them of high frequency, that form their past tense and past participle in various ways. If we should classify all English verbs according to the phonemic changes and patterns of change in the past tense and past participle, the total would amount to about fifty classes. This is hardly worth our time; an exercise in such classification will show you four of these classes as samples of the patterns of change in the past tense and past participle.

Exercise 11-14

Write in phonemic symbols the past tense and past participle of each verb. Then classify the verbs into four classes according to the phonemic forms they have in common.

		Past Tense	Past Participle
Examples:	1. blow	*blu*	*blon*
	2. freeze	*froz*	*frozən*
	3. grow	*gru*	*gron*
	4. speak	*spok*	*spokən*

Class 1:   *blow* and *grow.*   {-D pt} = /o > u/
              {-D pp} = /-n/

Class 2:   *freeze* and *speak.*   {-D pt} = /i > o/
              {-D pp} = /i > o/ + /ən/

1. sting   /stɔn/
2. creep   /krept/
3. drive   /drov/   /drɪvən/

---

[3]In language, analogy is the process by which a new form or pattern is created on the basis of existing forms or patterns. For example, the pattern *ring, rang* and *sing, sang* is the basis for *bring, brang*. And other nonstandard forms in the past tense are created analogically from other patterns. Pairs such as *fling, flung* and *sting, stung* are responsible for *bring, brung*, whereas the widespread use of the allomorph /-d/ following a voiced sound to signal past tense, as in *wing, winged, long, longed, seem, seemed, mow, mowed, rob, robbed*, results in *bring, bringed*, heard in children's speech. The suffixal morpheme /-ize/ added to adjectives to form such verbs as *legalize* and *rationalize* has brought about the analogical *finalize*. With nouns the child or foreign speaker who knows *years, fears*, and *peers* is likely to use the analogical plural *deers*. Both standard and nonstandard forms are brought into being by analogy.

New grammatical patterns as well as new forms are also created by analogy. The foreign learner of English who has heard "I want to tell you something" is likely to say "I want to explain you something." Among native speakers the high frequency of object pronouns like *me* after the verb, as in "The man saw me," "The man found me," and "The man met me," has produced the analogical pattern "The right man for the job is me" and "It is me."

Analogy is an important and widely operative process in language change.

4. sing _____ /seŋ/ _____ /seŋ/
5. ride _____ /rod/ _____ /ridən/
6. write _____ /rot/ _____ /ritən/
7. cling _____ /kleŋ/ _____
8. ring _____ /reŋ/ _____
9. keep _____ /kept/ _____
10. deal _____ /delt/ _____
11. swim _____ /swæm/ _____
12. spin _____ /span/ _____
13. win _____ /wən/ _____

Class 1: _____

Class 2: _____

Class 3: _____

Class 4: _____

Suppletion

As part of our discussion of verb forms, it would be useful to consider another process that has affected some of the forms within the paradigm of particular verbs. We previously noted the role of analogy. One other process is suppletion, which we will introduce through an example. Let's look at the five-part verb *go.*

> go   goes   going   went   gone

In this paradigm one form, *went,* seems out of place. It ought to be *goed,* or at least a word that begins with /g/. But the entire stem /go-/ has been replaced by a wholly different stem /wɛn-/. Such a total change within a paradigm is called suppletion, and the new form is a suppletive form. The suppletion here can be simply expressed by this diagram:

> /wɛnt/ = / go > wɛn/ + /t/

One English verb, *be,* is unique in that it has eight paradigmatic forms:

> be   am/is/are   being   was/were   been

The stem is obviously *be,* and the alien forms that have intruded themselves into the paradigm—*am, is, are, was, were*—are suppletive forms.

Despite some of the differences we have noted among verbs with regard to their paradigmatic forms, knowledge of the verb paradigm is helpful in determining whether or not a given word should be classified as a verb. If a word can fit into three or more slots of the paradigm, we comfortably classify it as a verb. The word *begin* fits into all five positions

> begin   begins   beginning   began   begun

and therefore is given the classification of verb.

With *cut,* however, the case is different. It does have three of the five possible forms:

cut   cuts   cutting   cut   cut

But it also fits partially into the noun paradigm

cut (singular)   cuts (plural)

So we are faced with two homophonous *cut*'s, one a verb and the other a noun, and we cannot classify the isolated word. When it occurs in context, however, the matter is simple: "She is *cutting* the bread." *Cutting* is one verb form, and we can make substitutions showing the other verb forms:

She *cuts* the bread.
She *cut* the bread yesterday.

Obviously *cut* in this context is a verb. Likewise, in "He has a cut on his finger," we can substitute a plural form

He has several *cuts* on his finger.

showing that *cut* here is a noun.

Exercise 11-15

Take a quick look again at the noun and verb paradigms. Then, using membership in a paradigm as a criterion, classify these words as N (noun), V (verb), or NV (both noun and verb).

1. driver	N		11. bird	N
2. compliment	NV		12. join	V
3. appear	V		13. end	NV
4. world	N		14. morning	N
5. agency	N		15. variety	N
6. agonize	V		16. mother	NV
7. truck	NV		17. grammar	N
8. decide	V		18. melt	NV
9. emotion	N		19. note	NV
10. book	NV		20. carve	V

Aspect in the Verb Phrase

As you consider verb phrases and their various forms, you should realize that they convey not only time but also aspect. Aspect is the expression of meanings concerned with the continuity or distribution of events in time. Here are a few such MEANINGS, expressed in various ways in English:

1. **Beginning of event**
   He began to sweat.
2. **End of event**
   He stopped sweating.
3. **Frequency of event**
   She sang often.
4. **Repetition of event**
   Jim pounded on the door.
5. **Habitual performance of event** (called habitual aspect)
   They used to eat dinner early.
6. **Single occurrence of event in time** (called indefinite aspect)
   I ate my lunch.
   He stepped down.
7. **Progression or duration of event in time** (called progressive or durative aspect)
   I was eating my lunch.
8. **Completion of event** (called perfective aspect)
   I have eaten my lunch.

In many languages such meanings are clearly signaled by the form of the verb itself rather than through a combination of verbs. In Russian, for example, if one adds to the verb /pisal/ (= wrote) the prefix /na/, the meaning becomes "has finished writing," the perfective aspect, number 8 above. In standard French, which has three past tenses, one can choose a form that signals both past time and either of two aspects simultaneously. An example is

Il travaillait.

Here the suffix -*ait* enables the verb to be translated in either of two ways:

He *was working.* (progressive aspect, number 7 above)
He *used to work.* (habitual aspect, number 5 above)

In English, aspectual meanings are expressed in many different ways. For instance, aspectual meaning may be implicit in the meaning of the verb itself. We can illustrate this by contrasting two verbs that both mean "hit" but differ in their aspectual meaning. Consider *strike* (single event in time, indefinite aspect, number 6) and *beat* (progressive aspect, number 7; or repetitive aspect, number 4). Aspectual meaning may also be determined by the context in which the verb is embedded. Often the aspectual meaning of a verb phrase is signaled by adverbials that answer the question of "when?" or "how long?" Examples:

He *wrote* a letter this morning. (single event, indefinite aspect, number 6)
She *wrote* in her diary every morning. (habitual aspect, number 5)
He *wrote* all morning to finish his report. (progressive aspect, number 7)

Although English expresses aspectual meanings in many various ways, English may be said to have only two aspects that are structurally signaled by a distinctive verb combination: progressive and perfective.

1. **Progressive** or durative **aspect,** as in

   She *was writing* a letter.

   The form of the progressive is *be* + verb + *ing*. The *be* may occur in any of its forms, for example:

   They may *be* sleeping.
   She *is* driving the car.
   She had *been* practicing law. *past perfect tense*

   In the progressive aspect the event is thought of as progressing, going on, without any indication of an end. This aspect may show something going on over a period in which other events happen, as in

   She was writing a letter when I entered.

   The progressive aspect is generally employed with verbs whose meaning is capable of noticeable extension in time; these are verbs of activity and process, such as *walk, throw, grow, change*. It tends not to be used with verbs of mental activity and feeling, such as *know, understand, remember, prefer, want, need, like*, or with verbs of nonaction such as *own, consist of,* and *seem*.

2. **Perfective aspect,** as in

   He *has written* a letter.

   The form is *have* (in any of its forms) + past participle. The perfective aspect presents us with two ways of interpreting the continuity of time. First, the event began in the past and has been completed, as in

   Jane has attended college.

   Second, the event continues up to the present, as in

   Jane has attended college since last September.

   In a sentence like this, with the present-tense *has* or *have* before the verb, the time adverbial is one of duration—*since last Sunday, for two months, the whole evening*—answering the question "How long?" But an adverbial of definite time (answering the question "When?") is not commonly used with the perfective aspect. For example, this sentence is ungrammatical:

   *Jane has attended college last year.

Exercise 11-16

Cross out the adverbials that are improperly used.

1. I have practiced my piano lesson yesterday afternoon.
2. I practiced my piano lesson yesterday afternoon.
3. Her roommate received an award last Wednesday.
4. Her roommate has received an award last Wednesday.

5. Two years ago I have visited Spain.
6. She stayed in the hospital fifteen days.
7. She has stayed in the hospital fifteen days.
8. It has rained since one o'clock.
9. She has played tennis last night.
10. I have worked in the garden for three days.

Thus far we have discussed the perfective aspect only in its *has/have* form (traditionally called the "present perfect tense"). It also has a past form ("past perfect")

They *had studied.*

and a seldom-heard future form ("future perfect")

They *will have studied.*

Each of these bears a sense of completion, as in

They *had studied* hard before the exam was canceled.
They *will have read* eleven novels by the end of the semester.

The perfective aspect combines with the progressive in verb phrases such as

George *has been working.*

This verb phrase is perfective for three reasons. First, it has the form of *have* + past participle—in this case, *been.* Second, it cannot take an adverbial of definite time, like *yesterday.* And finally, it can take an adverbial of duration, as in

George has been working all week.

On the other hand it is progressive because the form includes *be* + verb + *-ing, been working,* and in meaning it expresses the going-on of an event. So we can say that such verb phrases carry a compound aspect, perfective-progressive.

Exercise 11–17

Label the aspect of the underlined verb phrases according to whether they are progressive, perfective, or perfective-progressive.

_____ 1. Hans <u>was building</u> a doghouse.
_____ 2. Charlotte <u>had been</u> sick.
_____ 3. Miss Garcia <u>had been lecturing</u> on water pollution.
_____ 4. She <u>was preparing</u> for an exam.
_____ 5. They <u>have been practicing</u> the whole day.
_____ 6. <u>Have</u> you <u>done</u> your homework?
_____ 7. The student <u>is taking</u> a test.
_____ 8. We'<u>ve been preparing</u> for the worst.

Mood in the Verb Phrase

Sometimes the form of a verb does not tell us so much about the time of an event as it does about an attitude of the speaker in relation to what is being said. Such information corresponds to what has traditionally been called "mood." English has three moods: indicative, imperative, and subjunctive. Up to this point, we have considered verb forms in relation to the indicative mood. The indicative mood is primarily concerned with the exchange of factual information and is the mood we use in most of our daily communication. It is perhaps easier to understand what the indicative mood is by contrasting it with the imperative and subjunctive moods.

The imperative mood is used in conveying commands such as "Play outside!" or "Bring me the book." By its nature, the imperative is usually used in the second person, though the actual pronoun *you* is rarely used. The imperative mood uses the stem form of the verb paradigm. This is also frequently the same form as the second person present indicative. But, of course, this latter generalization does not apply to the *be* verb, which has a greater variety of forms. In an imperative involving the *be* verb, we don't use a form resembling the second person indicative form but rather the stem form *be* itself. Thus, although the verb form of a second person present indicative statement (e.g., "You work hard") is essentially the same as the second person imperative ("Work hard") with most verbs, we can see a difference when we use the *be* verb and compare the second person indicative ("You are quiet") with the imperative ("Be quiet").

The subjunctive mood with its distinctive forms is not as commonly used as it once was. In fact, we could say that it is one part of the language that is dying a slow death. But it is still an important part of the Standard dialect, especially in writing. There are two uses of the subjunctive that you should be familiar with.

First, it is sometimes used with particular verbs to express some kind of desired course or outcome. This use is common in a few fixed expressions such as "Long live the queen!" or "God bless America!" Let's look at how this is different from the indicative and imperative moods. When we say "Long live the queen," we are speaking of the queen in the third person. If we were in the indicative mood and merely making a statement to say that the queen lives a long time, then we would have inflected the verb *live* with the third person singular present-tense inflection *-s*. But as you can see, the verb form is not inflected with *-s*, because it is not making a statement about the queen but is rather an expression of a wish or hope. The subjunctive expression "Long live the queen" might initially appear like an imperative, especially because it uses the stem form of the verb. But you will recall that the imperative is used for the second person (telling someone what to do) rather than for the third person (speaking about someone or something).

Sometimes the expression of a desired course or outcome is found in clauses following such verbs as *request, ask,* and *insist,* or following such adjectives as *necessary* and *essential.* In the examples below you will notice that the subjunctive mood uses the stem form of the verb.

Examples: She suggested that I *be* the cook.
We request that you *be* appropriately dressed.

The boss insisted that Willard *arrive* at eight sharp.
It is necessary that she *go* at once.
It is imperative that they *be* on time.

The second major use of the subjunctive mood is to express something that is contrary to fact. For example, when I say something like "If I were you I would buy that," I am posing a situation that is contrary to fact because I am not you. This use of the subjunctive employs a form that appears to be past tense but in fact has nothing to do with past time.

Examples: I wish I *were* in Italy.
Betty looks as if she *were* exhausted.
If he *were* really my friend, he would get me a ticket.

Sometimes the subjunctive is replaced by other forms or structures.

Examples: It is necessary for *her to go* at once.
It is necessary that she *should go* at once.
If he *was* really my friend, he would get me a ticket. (informal usage)
I wish I *was* in Italy. (informal usage)

Exercise 11–18

Underline the subjunctive forms of the verb in these sentences.

1. If she (was   were) home, she would answer the phone.
2. I wish he (was   were) with me now.
3. God (save   saves) the King!
4. The director asked that Elizabeth (stands   stand) in the front row.
5. It is traditional that the table (is   be) decorated.
6. It is advisable that a lawyer (writes   write) the contract.
7. Rubinstein plays Chopin as though he (was   were) inspired.
8. The rules required that they (are   be) in uniform.
9. If I (was   were) the pilot, I'd avoid that thunderstorm.
10. The invitation requested that she (answers   answer) promptly.

Exercise 11–19

For each of the sentences below, indicate whether the italicized verb represents the indicative, imperative, or subjunctive mood.

1. *Tell* us what you want now.   Imp
2. We *spoke* to your friend yesterday.   Ind
3. *Don't* expect me to agree.   Imp
4. She insisted that he *meet* with her.   Sub
5. I don't know if he *is* coming.   Ind
6. If he *were* a good student, he could get a scholarship. Sub
7. *Be* a good example.   Imp
8. The athletes *were* not happy with the game.   Ind

9. *Walk* softly when you go past their dog.

10. I *walk* softly when I go past their dog.

                                                               Imp
                                                               Ind

---

C. The Comparable Paradigm

The comparable paradigm is as follows:

Forms:	Stem	Comparative	Superlative
Inflectional suffixes:		{-ER cp}	{-EST sp}
Models:	sweet	sweeter	sweetest
	deadly	deadlier	deadliest
	friendly	friendlier	friendliest
	soon	sooner	soonest

This paradigm furnishes the pattern for these groups:

1. Nearly all one-syllable adjectives, e.g., *hot, small, proud.*
2. Some two-syllable adjectives, especially those ending in *-ly* and *-y,* such as *lovely, funny, polite.*
3. A few adverbials of one or two syllables, e.g., *fast, early.*
4. One preposition, *near,* as in "She sat nearest the door."

Other adjectives and adverbs usually take a preceding *more* or *most* in lieu of the inflectional *-er* and *-est* to indicate the comparative or superlative.

Exercise 11–20

Here is a list of two-syllable adjectives. Write the comparative and superlative forms, *-er* and *-est,* of those that you would inflect in this way.

1. angry	*angrier*	*angriest*	11. quiet	*quieter*	*quietest*
2. healthy	*healthier*	*healthiest*	12. remote	*remoter*	*remotest*
3. bitter	*more*	*bitterest*	13. severe		*severest*
4. common	*commoner*	*commonest*	14. solid	*solider*	*solidest*
5. cruel	*crueler*	*cruelest*	15. stupid	*stupider*	*stupidest*
6. foolish			16. noble	*nobler*	*noblest*
7. handsome		*handsomest*	17. dusty	*dustier*	*dustiest*
8. honest			18. dirty	*dirtier*	*dirtiest*
9. mellow	*mellower*	*mellowest*	19. lively	*livelier*	*liveliest*
10. pleasant			20. gentle	*gentler*	*gentlest*

Exercise 11-21

Here is a list of adverbials of one and two syllables. Write out the comparative and superlative forms of those that you might inflect with *-er* and *est*. Write *no* after the adverbials that you would not use with these inflectional endings.

1. often	*oftener*	*oftenest*	11. under	*NO*	
2. seldom	*NO*		12. near	*nearer*	*nearest*
3. already	*NO*		13. upward	*NO*	
4. gently	*NO*		14. far	*farther*	*farthest*
5. late	*later*	*latest*	15. quick	*quicker*	*quickest*
6. ahead	*NO*		16. above	*NO*	
7. weekly	*NO*		17. loud	*louder*	*loudest*
8. perhaps	*NO*		18. quickly	*NO*	
9. sidewise	*NO*		19. high	*higher*	*highest*
10. slow	*slower*	*slowest*	20. low	*lower*	*lowest*

A few adjectives have suppletive and irregular forms in the comparative and superlative, such as *good*:

good   better   best

Thus the morpheme {good} has three allomorphs: /gʊd/, /bɛt-/, and /bɛ-/. The allomorphic diagrams of *better* and *best* go like this:

/bɛtər/ = /gʊd > bɛt-/ + /-ər/
/bɛst/ = /gʊd > bɛ-/ + /-st/

In the last one the /-st/ is an allomorph of {-est}, spelled *-est*.

Exercise 11-22

Write the forms of the comparative and superlative of these words.

1. well	*better*	*best*	4. little	*littler / less*	*littlest / least*
2. bad, ill, badly	*worse*	*worst*	5. much, many	*more*	*most*
3. old	*older*	*oldest*	6. few	*fewer*	*fewest*

The capacity to take the inflectional suffixes *-er* and *-est* is one of the signals that enables us to distinguish adjectives from nouns in the position of modifier preceding a noun. In the cluster *a stone fence* the *stone* is not an adjective because we would never say *a stoner fence* or *the stonest fence*. Thus, although the word *stone* may function like an adjective, it still retains its identity as a noun.

Exercise 11-23

In the blanks write Aj (adjective) or NA (nonadjective) to label the italicized words.

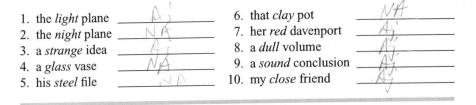

1. the *light* plane _____
2. the *night* plane _____
3. a *strange* idea _____
4. a *glass* vase _____
5. his *steel* file _____

6. that *clay* pot _____
7. her *red* davenport _____
8. a *dull* volume _____
9. a *sound* conclusion _____
10. my *close* friend _____

Even this inflectional test, however, must be applied judiciously because, as you have seen, some adjectives, particularly those with multiple syllables, may not take an inflectional ending.

Some Observations and Applications

One of the features that distinguishes nonstandard dialects from standard ones is the treatment of the inflectional paradigm. As a college student, you are not so likely to say or write something like "It don't matter that he seen the geeses." But in this chapter we have looked at linguistic items such as collective nouns and the plural forms of foreign borrowings, which might be useful information for you as you edit and proofread your writing to maintain grammatical number agreement between subjects and their verbs, or between pronouns and the nouns they refer to. We have also noted that the choice between using the inflectional possessive or the *of* possessive tends to correspond with whether a particular noun is animate or not. A conscious awareness of this stylistic tendency may help you in choices you make in your own writing.

All of this is not to say that usage and stylistic decisions must slavishly adhere to the prescriptive norms set down by traditional grammarians. With many usage issues, writers and editors must make informed choices that take into account the nature of the writing task and the audience. But writers who are better informed so that they can make conscious decisions will be more resourceful than writers who are not even aware that a particular usage is an issue. It is of course true that attention to a grammatical issue such as number agreement is not as important within a writing task as developing ideas and organizing information effectively, but it can help in proofreading and editing your own writing for forms that might otherwise distract some readers from seeing the value of your ideas.

In another application, those who teach non-native speakers of English to acquire the language must have a clear understanding of how the language is put together. And an important part of this is found not only in the inflectional paradigms, but also in the forms and uses of the verb aspects such as the perfective and progressive constructions that we examined in this chapter.

An understanding of the inflectional paradigm is not just a matter of interest for those seeking to monitor or teach written and spoken English. For example, some law enforcement agencies have consulted with linguists who examine features of discourse in the writing or speech produced by unknown or anonymous suspects. Among the important features that can be examined are characteristic patterns involving a person's handling of inflectional or paradigmatic forms. Because people have distinctive ways of expressing themselves, such linguistic analysis can help narrow down a list of suspects.[4]

---

[4]For an example of forensic linguistics, see "Forensic Analysis of Personal Written Texts: A Case Study" by Robert Eagleson in *Language and the Law,* ed. John Gibbons. London: Longman, 1994, pp. 362–73. This article has also been reprinted in *Linguistics at Work: A Reader of Applications.* ed. Dallin D. Oaks. Fort Worth: Harcourt Brace College Publishers, 1998, pp. 30–39.

12

Parts of Speech: Form Classes

Time flies like an arrow; fruit flies like a banana.
(Groucho Marx)

In the previous chapter we examined the inflectional paradigms of nouns, verbs, adjectives, and adverbs. In this chapter we will show how such inflectional morphology, as well as additional derivational morphology, can provide useful information for identifying words belonging to these four classes, or parts of speech. The paradigmatic forms of nouns, verbs, adjectives, and adverbs are so distinctive and useful in determining the class membership of a particular word that we will refer to these classes as "form classes." Now consider an illustration of how class membership may be assigned by form. If the form of a word can take the plural inflectional morpheme {-s ps}, or if the form ends in a noun-forming derivational suffix, such as *-ness* or *-ism,* it will be labeled a noun. Form classes are large and open; they readily admit new members, that is, new words coming into the language from other languages, as well as new words formed within English, such as *workaholic* and *minibus.*

In contrast to form classes there are also some words such as prepositions and pronouns whose class is not identifiable by distinctive morphology. The membership in these classes, which we will call "structure classes," is closed and relatively small. Thus, although the membership of these classes cannot be identified by form, it can readily be memorized. We will be examining the structure classes in the next chapter.

Before we examine some of the morphology that characterizes nouns, verbs, adjectives, and adverbs and how such morphological knowledge can be used to determine membership in a particular part of speech, some historical background would be appropriate. Many people who discuss grammatical classes in our language take for granted an inherited set of classes or part-of-speech classification into which all words must be fit. But the history of grammatical analysis and classification in English, particularly involving part-of-speech classification, reveals some interesting challenges and controversies relating to such classification.

Early in the 1500s a Renaissance Latinist, William Lyly, aided by Colet and Erasmus, prepared materials for the teaching of Latin at St. Paul's School, London. These materials were later published and became known as *Lyly's Grammar.* This was the first Latin grammar written in English. In 1540 it was "authorized" by Henry VIII, to the exclusion of competitors, and remained in wide use for three centuries. Most English schoolboys, as well as many in America, learned Latin from its pages. Its users included Shakespeare, Spenser, Jonson, Milton, Dryden, Pope, Samuel Johnson, and other famous men of letters. Because the explanation of Latin grammar was written in English, as the quotation below will show, this Latin grammar became a handy model for those writers who were later to write English grammars:

> A noune is the name of a thinge, that may be seene, felte, hearde, or understande: As the name of my hande in Latin is Manus: the name of an house is Domus: the name of goodnes is Bonitas.

The heading of the first section (in the 1567 edition) is of interest to anyone studying the parts of speech in English:

> An Introduction of the eyght parts of Latin speache. In Speache be these eight partes followinge:

Noune			Adverbe	
Pronoune	} declined		Coniunction	} undeclined
Verbe			Preposition	
Participle			Interiection	

In the text the adjective is a subclass of noun.

In 1640 Ben Jonson, who had cut his teeth on Lyly, brought out his little *English Grammar.* In this he wrote concerning the parts of speech:

> In our English speech we number the same parts with the Latines.

Noune,	Adverbe,
Pronoune,	Conjunction,
Verbe,	Præposition,
Participle,	Interjection.

> Only, we adde a ninth, which is the article. . . .

The English grammarians who followed Jonson continued to use the Latin parts of speech, but these writers varied in the number of parts of speech they employed, from two to nine. By the 1760s the participle had been dropped for the most part, and such eminent grammarians as the scientist Joseph Priestley and Bishop Robert Lowth chose these eight parts of speech: noun, adjective, pronoun, verb, adverb, preposition, conjunction, and interjection.

The question of which parts of speech would be used to classify English words was settled for many decades to come by Lindley Murray, whose *English Grammar* in 1795 was the first of a host of original grammars, revised grammars, and abridged grammars that appeared under his name. The estimated number of Murray grammars sold on both sides of the Atlantic is between 1,500,000 and 2,000,000, a world record. His influence was enormous, and he had many competitors. Murray espoused the eight parts of speech of Lowth, to which he added the article, and most of his competitors followed this lead.

In America about thirty English grammars appeared before 1800, and 265 more grammars came into print between 1800 and 1850. In general these adopted Murray's parts of speech. So the use of Latin-derived parts of speech to sort out our English vocabulary has had a long tradition, one that is still alive today. For you will find these same parts of speech—article, noun, adjective, pronoun, verb, adverb, preposition, conjunction, and interjection—in current dictionaries and grammars. These parts of speech can be satisfactorily employed to classify the words of English if we make some additions and refinements and if we define anew each part of speech. The latter condition is necessary because the conventional definitions are faulty. Let us test a few of them. For a starter try this sentence:

The motionless boy stared at the flames.

A verb, we are told in conventional grammars, is a word that shows action or state of being. In the sentence above we note that the only word showing action is *flames,* which, according to the definition above, must therefore be a verb. We also find a word showing state of being, namely *motionless,* so this too must be a verb, according to the definition. How much easier it would be for both student and teacher to conclude, with more exact definitions, that *flames* is a noun because it changes form to show plurality, that *motionless* is an adjective because it is composed of the noun *motion* plus the suffix *-less,* and that *stared* is the verb because it changes its form to show past time.

We are also told in conventional, or traditional, grammars that an adjective is a word that modifies a noun. This statement is true. But it obscures the fact that any, or almost any, part of speech can modify a noun.[1] Here are some instances where we should perhaps be unwilling to call the italicized words adjectives:

The *evening* train
The *waiting* train
The *stolen* box
Our friend
The *upstairs* room
The *in* group
The *above* statement
An *if* clause

Next, the adverb. This is traditionally defined as a word that modifies a verb, adjective, or another adverb. This definition produces these alleged adverbs:

It can't be *that* good.
Ice-cold lemonade

---

[1]That is to say, learners may turn it around mentally to "a word that modifies a noun is an adjective," which is false.

Boiling hot water
That tree is *fifty feet* high.

The italicized words above modify adjectives. Should they be called adverbs?
Now let us compare two sentences:

He ran swiftly.
She was very sick.

In the first sentence *swiftly* modifies the verb *ran,* and in the second *very* modifies the adjective *sick.* But can *very* modify verbs, as in "He ran *very*"? It seems as if words like *very, quite,* and *rather,* which do not modify verbs, ought to be distinguished from those that do.

Another difficulty with the definitions of the traditional parts of speech is that they are based on two different criteria. The definitions of noun and verb are based on meaning; the rest are based on function or their use in the sentence. The result of this double standard can be seen in a phrase such as

a red shirt.

The word *red* is the name of a particular color and hence is a noun. But *red* modifies the noun *shirt* and hence is an adjective. Likewise, in

the fighting dog

fighting means an action and is therefore a verb. But it modifies the noun *dog* and is therefore an adjective.

In view of complications like these it appears that the Latin-derived parts of speech, as traditionally defined, do not offer an effective instrument of language analysis. Instead of using them we will set up a more elaborate but more workable set of word classes (that is, parts of speech). We will now consider the various parts of speech, looking first at the form classes and then later, in the next chapter, examining the structure classes.

A. Nouns

Nouns are identified as nouns by two aspects of form, their inflectional morphemes and their derivational morphemes. The inflectional morphemes, you remember, are the noun plural {-s pl} and the noun possessive {-s ps}. Any word that has the possessive {-s ps} is a noun (except for nonstandard uses, like "the town I come from's mayor"). Any word that has the plural {-s pl} is also a noun. And if it does not have the {-s pl} but can take it in the same position, sometimes with a readjustment of context to allow for a plural form, it is a noun. Thus in

The author seems tired,

author is a noun because it can be changed to the plural in the same position, with the readjustment of *seems* to its plural form *seem:*

The *authors* seem tired.

But in the sentence

Her brother may author a new biography

author cannot be made plural in this position and in fact is not a noun.

Exercise 12-1

Underline the words that are nouns according to the inflectional criteria just above. After each, explain your choice with these numbers:

1. Has possessive morpheme.
2. Has plural morpheme.
3. Can take plural morpheme in same position, with or without a readjusted context to allow for a plural form.

The first column is for the first noun and the second column for the second noun, if there is one.

1. Our president has a new plan.   3   3
2. The janitors had not seen the umbrella.   2   3
3. The counselor may plan a different approach.   3   3
4. My aunt always mothers her youngest son.   3   3
5. Mother's cake never tasted so good.   1   3
6. The chef's sisters arrived.   1   2

In addition we will consider as nouns those words that have only a plural form, such as *clothes, goods, vitals, glasses* (spectacles), *oats, pants, pliers, scissors,* and *thanks*.

Nouns are identified not only by inflectional morphemes but also by noun-forming derivational suffixes added to verbs, adjectives, nouns, adverbs, and bound forms. Compare these sentences:

The quality is pure.
The quality is purity.

It is the form of *purity,* with its *-ity* added to an adjective, which signifies that it is a noun. In general the suffix itself, together with our consciousness of the part of speech to which it has been attached, provides the signal of nounness. Here is a partial list of word pairs, the second word in each containing one of the suffixes that enable us to classify a word as a noun.

Source Verb[2]	Derived Noun
accept	acceptance
achieve	achievement
advise /z/	advice /s/

---

[2]In this list and those to follow, the words labeled "source" usually provide the source in the sense that they take an affix to form the derived word. However, in a few cases—such as *bath* and *bathe, associate* /et/ and *associate* /ət/—we have significantly contrastive forms but with no discernible source-result relationship.

arrive	arrival
assist	assistant
block	blockade
break	breakage
complain	complaint
contemplate	contemplation
deceive	deceit
deceive	deception
decide	decision
defend	defense
deform	deformity
deform	deformation
deliver	delivery
depart	departure
draft	draftee
help	helper[3]
liberate	liberator[3]
lie	liar[3]
paint	painting
purify	purification
save	savior[3]

Source Adjective	**Derived Noun**
kind	kindness
brave	bravery
ideal	idealist
ideal	idealism
important	importance
pure	purity
supreme	supremacy
true	truth
violent	violence
wise	wisdom
wise	wizard

Source Noun	**Derived Noun**
advocate (or source verb)	advocacy
Asia	Asian (-n, -an)
book	booklet
cartoon	cartoonist
coward	cowardice

---

[3]The suffixes *-er, -or, -ar* are the same in spoken English.

dog	doggie
friend	friendship
gang	gangster
king	kingdom
Levi	Levite
lemon	lemonade
mathematics	mathematician
mile	mileage
monarch	monarchy
murder	murderess
novel	novelette
pagan	paganism
priest	priesthood
musket	musketeer
slave	slavery
Vietnam	Vietnamese

These same noun-forming suffixes are sometimes attached to bound stems, as in *dentist* and *tailor.*

Optional Exercise 12-2

You will find it rewarding to try to locate a matching set for each pair of words. This is an excellent way to become well acquainted with these noun-forming derivational suffixes.

Exercise 12-3

Underline each noun that can be identified by its derivational suffix. In the first blank write the source verb, adjective, or noun. In the second blank write the noun-forming suffix.

[handwritten annotations: unbound / free morpheme]

1. Jim was distressed by his underline{failure}. ✓ — fail — ure
2. The payment was not large. — pay — ment
3. What did the assistant say? — assist — ant
4. He was a clever sailor. — sail — or
5. The catcher missed the ball. ✓ — catch — er
6. A collision was narrowly averted. — collide — ion
7. There is a leakage under the sink. N *bound* — leak — age
8. The history class was studying the Reformation. — Reform — ation
9. Who made the discovery? ✓ — discover — y
10. The amusement proved dull. ✓ — amuse — ment
11. She is often troubled by sickness. *adj* — sick — ness
12. His refusal was polite. — refuse — al
13. He swam the width of the river. — wide — th
14. Can you doubt his sincerity? *adj* — sincere — ity
15. Who does not enjoy freedom from want? — free — dom

16. Childhood is an unhappy time.   *child*   *hood*
17. Jane became a lawyer.   *law*   *yer*
18. You might improve your scholarship.   *scholar*   *ship*
19. The fragrance was overwhelming.   *fragrant*   *ce*
20. The intimacy of the occasion was marred.   *intimate*   *cy*

During the discussion just above, one question may have occurred to you. Because inflectional endings follow derivational suffixes and are used to identify nouns, why should we bother at all about the derivational suffixes? The reason is that in practice some words with such suffixes are seldom or never inflected. Here are a few examples: *derision, drainage, fertility, iciness, manhood,* and *nourishment.* Thus it seems best not to short-cut this mode of noun recognition.

B. Verbs

Verbs have a maximum of five different forms, as you have already learned. All five are shown in the forms of *rise:*

Stem	Present Third-Person Singular	Present Participle	Past Tense	Past Participle
rise	rises	rising	rose	risen

Any word that has three or more of these forms is said to belong to the form class called the verb. For example, *cut* has the minimum of three forms—*cut, cuts, cutting.* One form, *cut,* does triple duty: the stem, which in most cases is the same as the present tense (except the third-person singular); the past tense; and the past participle. *Depart* has four forms, (*depart, departs, departing,* and *departed*), and *break* has five (*break, breaks, breaking, broke, broken*). Therefore, *cut, depart,* and *break* belong to the form class *verb.*

Exercise 12–4

In each of the sentences below, one verb is italicized. Indicate in the first column how many of the five forms it has. In the second column identify the form used in the sentence.

Example: Jim *lost* his slide rule.   4   past tense

1. The President *met* the leaders of the parade.   4   *past tense*
2. The mines had been *swept* away.   4   *past tense*
3. The bridge players would not *leave* the table.   4   *stem*
4. The water is *spreading* into the meadow.   3   *present participle*
5. The canary might have been *eaten* by the cat.   5   *past participle*
6. Theodore always *eats* between meals.   5   *present 3rd person sing.*
7. June *set* the table.   3   *past tense*

8. The ruler is *lying* on the table. <u>5</u> <u>present participle</u>
9. Have you *bought* the refreshments? <u>4</u> <u>past tense</u>
10. The ball *sank* into the pond. <u>5</u> <u>past tense</u>

The derivational suffixes by which a verb is identified are few. This list contains verbs with such suffixes and the source parts of speech from which the verbs are derived.

Source Noun	Derived Verb
bath	bathe
beauty	beautify
colony	colonize
length	lengthen
strife	strive

Source Adjective	Derived Verb
ripe	ripen
safe	save
solemn	solemnize
solid	solidify

These verb-forming suffixes are occasionally found combined with bound stems, as in *sanctify.*

Exercise 12–5

Underline each verb that can be identified by its derivational suffix. In the first blank write the source noun or adjective. In the second, write the verb-forming suffix. Do not include any inflectional suffixes in the second blank.

1. He <u>amplified</u> his statement. <u>ample</u> <u>ify</u>
2. The judge <u>personifies</u> justice itself. <u>person</u> <u>ify</u>
3. Can you <u>prove</u> your contention? <u>proof</u> <u>ve</u>
4. This paragraph will <u>weaken</u> your paper. <u>weak</u> <u>en</u>
5. Those dorm rules should be <u>liberalized</u>. <u>liberal</u> <u>ize</u>
6. Mann's novel may <u>strengthen</u> your intellectual life. <u>strength</u> <u>en</u>
7. Why do you <u>idolize</u> that actor? <u>idol</u> <u>ize</u>
8. That tale must have <u>terrorized</u> you. <u>terror</u> <u>ize</u>
9. I can't <u>soften</u> it. <u>soft</u> <u>en</u>
10. Dylan was <u>frightened</u> by the spectacle. <u>fright</u> <u>en</u>

C. Adjectives

You may recall from the previous chapter the comparable paradigm, with its compared words having the *-er* and *-est* inflectional suffixes. These suffixes enable us to set up a class of words called "comparables," but they do not permit us by themselves to separate into two classes the words traditionally called adjectives (e.g., *rich, kind*) and adverbs (e.g., *soon, often*). We can, however, dip into the reservoir of derivational suffixes and define adjectives by a combined test in this way: A word that is inflected with *-er* and *-est* and that is capable of forming adverbs with *-ly* and/or nouns with *-ness* is called an adjective. Although words passing this test are adjectives, there are some words that do not pass this test and are still adjectives.

Exercise 12–6

Fill in the blanks as follows: first column, *-er* form; second column, *-est* form; third column, *-ly* adverb form; fourth column, *-ness* noun form.

	-er	-est	-ly	-ness
1. close	closer	closest	closely	closeness
2. icy	icier	iciest	icily	iciness
3. sweet	sweeter	sweetest	sweetly	sweetness
4. sad	sadder	saddest	sadly	sadness
5. high	higher	highest	highly	highness
6. sunny	sunnier	sunniest	sunnily	sunniness
7. gentle	gentler	gentlest	gently	gentleness
8. small	smaller	smallest		smallness
9. little	littler	littlest		littleness
10. fast	faster	fastest		fastness
11. friendly	friendlier	friendliest	friendly	friendliness
12. natural			naturally	naturalness

Which one of the words above, though an adjective, does not pass the test that was outlined above? 12

In addition to the adjective test just described we can usually identify adjectives by derivational suffixes alone. With most of these words the degrees of comparison are expressed by *more* and *most* rather than by *-er* and *-est*. The adjective-forming suffixes are illustrated in this list.

Source Noun	Derived Adjective
age	agèd
child	childish
cloud	cloudy
consul	consular
crystal	crystalline
culture	cultural
economy	economic
economy	economical
fortune	fortunate
friend	friendly

moment	momentary
peace	peaceable
penny	penniless
picture	picturesque
pomp	pompous
power	powerful
science	scientific
sense	sensible
suburb	suburban
wood	wooden

Source Verb	**Derived Adjective**
associate /et/	associate /ət/ (also used as a noun)
collect	collective
continue	continual
exist	existent[4]
expect	expectant
prohibit	prohibitory
prosper	prosperous
read	readable[5]
restore	restorative
shake	shaky

Source Adjective	**Derived Adjective**
dead	deadly
red	reddish

These adjective-forming suffixes and others are frequently added to bound forms:

pens-	+ ive	> pensive
cred-	+ ible	> credible
loc-	+ al	> local
splend-	+ id	> splendid
frag-	+ ile	> fragile
cert-	+ ain	> certain
domest-	+ ic	> domestic
curi-	+ ous	> curious
terri-	+ fic	> terrific

Exercise 12–7

Here is a list of adjectives formed by derivational suffixes. In the first blank write the source noun, verb, adjective, or bound form. In the second write the adjective-forming suffix.

---

[4]Also *-ant,* as in *observant.*

[5]*-ible* is a variant spelling of *-able.* The source word is commonly a verb, as in *discernible* and *corruptible,* or a bound base, as in *visible* and *credible.*

1. golden	gold	en
2. helpless	help	less
3. lovely	love	ly
4. messy	mess	y
5. peaceful	peace	ful
6. insular	insul	ar
7. nervous	nerve	ous
8. fragmentary	fragment	ary
9. repentant	repent	ant
10. affectionate	affection	ate
11. foolish	fool	ish
12. rhythmic	rhythm	ic
13. regional	region	al
14. tired	tire	ed
15. separate /ət/	separate	/ət/
16. recurrent	recur	ent
17. instructive	instruct	ive
18. perishable	perish	able
19. meddlesome	meddle	some
20. congratulatory	congratulate	ory
21. pleasant	please	ant
22. goodly	good	y
23. lively	live	ly

D. Adverbs

The adverb has four suffixes to set it apart from other form classes—the derivational suffixes *-ly, -wise, -ward,* and *-s*—and the free form *like.*

1. Source Adjective	Derived Adverb
fortunate	fortunately

2. Source Noun	Derived Adverb
clock	clockwise

This *-wise* suffix, about five centuries old in English, has taken on renewed vitality in recent years and today may be heard attached to almost any noun to form an adverb. But this suffix must be used cautiously. A usage note in the *American Heritage Dictionary* (3rd ed.) indicates that although the use of *-wise* to mean "in the manner or direction of" is established, its "vaguer" usage to mean "with reference to" hasn't achieved the same level of respectability.

3. Source Noun	Derived Adverb
north	northward

Words consisting of a source noun + -*ward* are at home in the positions of both adjectives and adverbs, as in

1. The *earthward* drop of the parachutist was spectacular.
   (adjective position)
2. As she stepped out the plane door and parachuted *earthward,* she momentarily lost consciousness.
   (adverb position)
3. A population movement *cityward* has been observed.
   (adjective position)
4. He looked *cityward* for a sign of the train.
   (adverb position)

Here we will label such words as adverbs because -*ward* has a directional meaning that is usually considered adverbial (see entry "adverb" in *Webster's Third NID*). This applies to words like *shoreward, skyward, landward, churchward, deathward, manward, riverward,* and *heavenward.* It does not apply to words like *forward, inward, downward.* These are not formed on a source noun.

In examples 1 and 3 above, *earthward* and *cityward* are adverbs in form. Later you will learn that they are adjectivals in position and modifiers by function.

4. Source Noun	Derived Adverb
night	nights

This -*s* suffix is a remnant of the Old English genitive singular suffix -*es*. It is attached to words denoting a time period, such as

He works *days.*
He is busy *mealtimes.*
She plays golf *Saturdays.*

The italicized words here are classified as adverbs. They could, with equal justification, be considered plural nouns, adverbial in position. In addition, -*s* is suffixed to words in the -*ward* series, resulting in two forms of each word. For example,

Jeanne stepped *backward / backwards.*
They looked *toward / towards* the speaker.

Finally, this same -*s* closes some adverbs, such as *always, unawares,* and the adverb suffix -*wise* (formerly, the genitive of *way*). It is sometimes called the adverbial -*s*.

5. Source Noun	Derived Adverb
student	studentlike

6. Source Adjective	Derived Adverb
casual	casual-like

The free form *like* must be used selectively. Even though it easily combines with many words, some standard speakers object to it.

Exercise 12–8

Classify the italicized words according to the form class to which they belong: Av (adverb) or Aj (adjective).

1. Your ideas seem *sensible.* ___Aj___
2. They are playing *happily.* ___Av___
3. He turned the hands *clockwise.* ___Av___
4. Be *careful.* ___Aj___
5. Have you seen the paper *lately?* ___Av___
6. It's fragile. Lift it *easylike.* ___Av___
7. She walked *homeward.* ___Av___
8. *Luckily,* the brake was set. ___Av___
9. The student's reports were *creative.* ___Aj___
10. Her report was very *specific.* ___Aj___
11. You *richly* deserve the prize. ___Av___
12. Tharp is *professor-wise* pretty knowledgeable. ___Av___
13. Annie is a waitress *evenings.* ___Av___
14. A Gothic spire pointed *heavenward.* ___Av___
15. *Mondays* she sleeps late. ___Av___

There remains a number of words that do not have (or do not allow) an inflectional or derivational suffix that can be used to classify them in one of the four form classes—noun, verb, adjective, or adverb. We will refer to these words as "nonsuffixing forms." Here are examples:

1. Words that are traditionally called nouns:
   pathos, advice, tennis, evidence, botany, charisma.
2. Words traditionally called adverbs:
   often, seldom, also, never, perhaps.
3. Words traditionally known as adjectives:
   antic, menial, only.
4. Most of the words in the structure classes:
   the, must, quite, from, and, since, which, all.

Although these leftovers, and numerous others, do not contain suffixes that signal their inclusion in one of the form classes, this is no cause for concern. Grammarians frequently employ the dual criteria of form and position (often termed word order) to sort out the parts of speech, and so far we have employed only form for this purpose.

Later, in the section on syntax, we will classify words by the second criterion, position, using the parallel parts-of-speech classes of nominal, verbal, adjectival, and adverbial; and then many of the nonsuffixing words above will fall into place. However, some of the remaining words belong to structure classes and thus should not be expected to conform to characteristic patterns of the form classes. But even after classifying all of these, there may remain a few outcasts, for no part-of-speech system has ever been devised for English that neatly and fully classifies all the words of English.

Exercise 12–9

Classify the italicized words according to whether their suffix helps identify them as N (noun), V (verb), Aj (adjective), or Av (adverb). In the case of words allowing no suffix, label them as NS (nonsuffixing).

1. Sue likes to play *golf.* — *NS*
2. Only the *dregs* are left. — *N*
3. There will be a *meeting* at four tomorrow afternoon. — *N*
4. Which nation *colonized* Tierra del Fuego? — *V*
5. Every social class has its own *snobbery.* — *N*
6. May you be healthy and *prosperous.* — *Aj*
7. Be careful not to run *aground.* — *NS, AV*
8. She smiled *cheerfully.* — *AV*
9. The *quickest* way is to use your pocket calculator. — *Aj superlative*
10. We counted the tickets in *haste.* — *NS*
    V noun

Some Observations and Applications

Learning to identify nouns, verbs, adjectives, and adverbs by their form is an important skill because it prepares you for additional analysis and work with language. In a later chapter you will be learning to identify nominals, which occupy the same position as nouns, and you will be introduced to their functions, such as subject or direct object. You must have a clear idea of what a noun is before you can master the recognition of nominals and their functions. And being able to identify such grammatical elements is important in the work that you will do in revising and editing your own writing or in helping others to do the same. For example, being able to recognize and identify the grammatical subject of a sentence or clause is important in recognizing and removing such faulty constructions as fragments, comma splices, and subject-verb agreement errors. But beyond editing, grammatical knowledge about functional categories will also help you to study and learn a foreign language more efficiently or to help others to do so.

Recognizing the different part of speech categories is vital for those who program computers to process human language (natural language processing). These categories are important because they correspond to actual language behavior by native speakers. Nouns as a class behave differently from verbs. And verbs behave differently from adjectives and adverbs. Not only do the different parts of speech utilize different affixes, but they also appear in different slots within a sentence and combine with different kinds of structures. Because computers can only produce and interpret language that they have been adequately programmed to process, those who program computers must have a thorough understanding of the language, including the parts of speech and their characteristics.

13

Parts of Speech: Structure Classes

The story is told about Winston Churchill that on one occasion when he was corrected for ending a sentence with a preposition he responded with something like, "this is the sort of nonsense up with which I shall not put."

In this chapter we will continue our examination of the parts of speech. But our focus will be on those words such as *the, could, unless, him, of, very,* and *every,* which do not belong to classes that have affixes identifying their part of speech. These kinds of words belong to the parts of speech that we will call "structure classes." They have three characteristics:

1. Members of a given structure class are recognized mainly by position, as they have no characteristics of form in common and, excepting a few, do not change form.
2. A structure class is small, the largest one (prepositions) having only about fifty members.
3. A structure class has a stable membership and is a closed class, that is, it rarely admits new members.

Because structure classes are small, stable, and closed, we get to know their member words individually. For example, we are never in doubt about *could.* We know that it is an auxiliary and that its fellows are such words as *would, should, will,* and *can.* Thus, instead of defining these classes, it will be enough to describe their position and list the membership.

A. Qualifiers

The qualifier occurs in the position just before an adjectival or an adverbial as shown by the empty slots in these sentences.

The dinner was _very_ good.
She performed _very_ skillfully.

Thus it is evident that such words as *very* and *rather* are qualifiers. The function of a qualifier is to modify; and the word following the qualifier, such as *good* and *skillfully* (that is, the word modified), is called the head.

Exercise 13-1

Underline the qualifiers. In each blank indicate whether the qualifier modifies an Aj (adjective) or an Av (adverb).   *before adj or adv*

1. That is very kind of you.   *Aj*
2. It is too hot in this classroom.   *Aj*
3. You played quite acceptably in the second half.   *Av*
4. Marion was somewhat unhappy.   *Aj*
5. A rather shy boy was trying to dance.   *Aj*

Most qualifiers are uninflected words, like those in the preceding exercise. However, the qualifier position can accept any form class, as these examples show:

> Noun: The table was only *inches* wide.
> Verb: The water is *boiling* hot.
> Adjective: My dress seems *lighter* blue than yours.
> Adverb: You did *fairly* well.

Each of the italicized terms above is a qualifier by position. Its function is to modify.

Exercise 13-2

Indicate the form class of the italicized qualifiers, using the abbreviations N, V, Aj, or Av. If a qualifier cannot take a distinguishing suffix, then label it NS (nonsuffixing).

1. You are *too* kind.   *NS*
2. Are you *completely* happy with your courses?   *Av*
3. This water is *freezing* cold.   *Aj*
4. The bottle is *bone* dry.   *Aj*
5. He is *fighting* mad.   *Aj*
6. The novel proved *extremely* distasteful.   *Av*
7. I feel *quite* fine, thank you.   *NS Av*
8. Dorothy was *rather* gracious in her response.   *NS*
9. I prefer a *brighter* red tie.   *Aj*
10. Monty appears *enormously* wealthy.   *Av*
11. The baby is a *month* old.   *N*

A few qualifiers have the same form as adjectives—for instance, *pretty* good, *mighty* fine, *jolly* hot, *great* big, *full* well, *dead* right. In the qualifier position, however, these do not take *-er* and *-est*, so we will consider them as uninflected qualifiers that are homophones of adjectives.

Some qualifiers are not used before all adjectivals and adverbials but have a limited distribution. We will not take time to investigate the vagaries of such distributions, but a glance at a few examples might prove instructive.

stark naked	*much* alive	*about* exhausted
clean out	*just* under	*brand* new
fresh out	*almost* ready	*plumb* crazy
right along	*precious* little	*real* good
beastly cold	*that* good	

Sometimes noun phrases and idiomatic expressions are used in the position before adjectivals and adverbials and must therefore be regarded as qualifiers. Among the common ones are

a lot	kind of
a great deal	sort of
a little	a bit (of)

With qualifiers of adjectivals and adverbials in the comparative degree, the list is somewhat different. For example, look at these ungrammatical sentences:

*I feel *much* good.
*I feel *very* better.

As a native speaker you know at once that these are un-English. Now switch the qualifiers and the sentences will feel comfortable, like a well-tailored suit. The point is that the qualifiers used before a comparative are not quite the same ones as those before the positive degree. The first question of the following exercise will enable you to identify those qualifiers that are used with the comparative.

Exercise 13-3

You are given below a list of words and phrases that are qualifiers when in the qualifier slot. Following the list are questions to answer.

a bit	kind of	a whole lot
a good deal	least	enough
a great deal	less	even
almost	any	indeed
a lot	awful	just
lots	pretty	some
mighty	quite	somewhat
more	rather	sort of
most	real	still
much	right	too
no	so	very
plenty		

Remember that some words on this list have a homophone in another class, but looking at the position they occupy can help confirm their identity as qualifiers.

Adjectival: She was *pretty.*
Qualifier: We ran *pretty* fast.

Adverbial: She is coming *too.*
Qualifier: They are *too* picky.

Nominal: I've had *plenty.*
Qualifier: He was *plenty* angry. (dialectal)

Questions

1. Which qualifiers can occur in the slot before comparatives, as in one of these sentences?
   She is _____ happier.   _____ _____ _____
   Is she _____ happier?   _____ _____ _____
2. Consider the qualifiers *indeed, right, still, just, enough,* and *even.* Which qualifier has a position after, not before, its head?   _____
3. Which two of those qualifiers can occur either before or after the head?   _____ _____
4. Which of those qualifiers can occur in the slot below?

   She is coming _____ now.   _____ _____ _____

B. Prepositions

Prepositions are words like *of, in,* and *to* that are usually followed by a noun, noun phrase, personal pronoun, or noun-substitute, which are called the object of the preposition. The unit of preposition-plus-object of preposition is called a prepositional phrase.

Examples: George sat *between* the two deans.
George jumped *on* it.
George went *from* this *to* that.

English has a small group of prepositions, of which some frequently used ones are *at, by, for, from, in, of, on, to,* and *with.* Others include such two-syllable words as *about, above, after, against, among, before, behind, below, beneath, between, beyond, despite, except, inside, into, onto, outside, over, under,* and *upon.*

Exercise 13–4

In the sentences and questions below, underline the preposition once and the object of the preposition twice. If there is no object of the preposition, write *no* in the blank after the sentence. In some cases you will find that the object of the preposition has been moved up earlier in the sentence or question.

1. The car stopped at the station. _____
2. We walked under the tree. _____
3. He came from the farm. _____
4. Did the party advance into the jungle? _____
5. This is the farm he came from. _NO_ _____
6. These roses are for you. _____
7. The chimpanzee in the cage was yawning. _____
8. The boy stood on a barrel. _____
9. We know what you are looking for. _____
10. The plumber washed in the basin. _____
11. Our train passed beneath them. _____
12. The rose by the window was wilted. _____
13. He walked to the last platform. _____
14. What is it for? _____
15. We invested despite the risk. _____

Some of the words we have been dealing with can be either prepositions or adverbials. Compare

Preposition: She looked *up* the stairs.
Adverbial: She looked *up*.
Preposition: They went *inside* the house.
Adverbial: They went *inside*.

Exercise 13–5

Underline the prepositions once and the adverbials twice.

1. The swimmers waited below. *adverbial (end of sentence)*
2. The swimmers waited below the dam.
3. She liked to sit near.
4. She sat near the window.
5. The paint bucket fell off the porch.
6. The paint bucket fell off. *adv*
7. The refreshments came after. *adv.*
8. The refreshments came after the program.
9. I haven't seen him since. *adv.*
10. I haven't seen him since yesterday.

In addition to the prepositions already mentioned, there is in English a group of *-ing* prepositions that all have a verb as a stem. Here are some of the more common ones: *assuming, beginning, barring, concerning, considering, during, following, including, involving, pending, regarding, succeeding.*[1]

Examples: *Considering* your loss, the bill will not be sent.
Assuming the accuracy of the report, action must be taken at once.
We will delay the papers, *pending* arrival of the contract.

Exercise 13-6

Underline the *-ing* prepositions once and the *-ing* verbs twice.

1. Barring bad weather, the picnic will begin at eleven.
2. There will be a program following dinner.
3. She is only following her orders after all. *Present continuous*
4. May I have a conference regarding my examination?
5. He was regarding the newcomer with curiosity. *past continuous*
6. Considering the time, we had better stop now.
7. The entire squad, including the water boy, will make the trip.
8. I am including damage to my window in the bill.
9. The store will be closed weekends, beginning Saturday.
10. He was vague concerning the details.

The final group is composed of compound prepositions. These are relatively numerous and of various types. Often it is difficult to say whether a word group should be considered a preposition or not. Here is a short list of two types.

Two-Part	**With Noun**
together with	on account of
contrary to	in spite of
ahead of	with regard to
due to	in advance of
apart from	in front of
up to	on behalf of
out of	in place of
away from	in lieu of
up at	in addition to
as for	by way of
inside of	in comparison with
because of	by dint of
owing to	in case of
instead of	by means of
	by way of

---

[1]The stem of *during* is *dure,* an obsolete English verb meaning "to last." The stem of *pending* is *pend-,* which comes from a French base meaning "to hang, suspend."

Those in the first column it is simplest to call compound prepositions. In the second column we seem to have either a compound preposition or two successive prepositional phrases (when an object is added after the last word). One argument for calling them compound prepositions is that we normally do not place modifiers before the noun following the first preposition, as we can do with ordinary prepositional phrases. For example, in *on account of* the word *account* is not modified. Thus we shall refer to the items in both columns above as "compound prepositions."

Exercise 13–7

Underline the compound prepositions.

1. We arrived ahead of time.
2. The game was called off on account of rain.
3. The oldest daughter is up at the camp.
4. Contrary to our expectations, the movie was a delightful spoof.
5. We came by way of Brookline.
6. I want to thank you on behalf of these refugees.
7. They served rice instead of potatoes.
8. They served rice in lieu of potatoes.
9. In spite of her protestations, Harriet was persuaded to join the guild.
10. In case of accident, call your insurance agent.

Finally, here is a little afterthought on prepositions. The name *preposition* implies that this structure word occupies a *pre-* position, that is, one before its object. Such is usually the case. But as you might have realized from some of the examples in exercise 13–4, you can also find it at the end of a few structures:

1. Relative clause: The job (that) he worked *at.*
2. Passive: The lock had been tampered *with*.
3. Infinitive: Clay is fun to play *with*.
4. Exclamation: What a hedge of thorns we stumbled *into!*
5. QW question: Which room did you find it *in*?
6. Set expression: The world *over,*
   your objection *notwithstanding.*

So you can forget the schoolroom superstition that a preposition is an improper word to end a sentence with. In some cases, such as "Where are you from?", any other word order would sound silly or artificial. In other cases you may have a stylistic choice. For instance, "The doctor with whom I was conferring" is formal, whereas "The doctor I was conferring with" is informal. Both are standard acceptable English. We began this chapter with Churchill's response to being corrected for ending a sentence with a preposition. His response, though initially appearing to rearrange prepositions, actually involves a different kind of structure, which we will learn about in a later chapter.

C. Determiners

A determiner is a word that patterns with a noun. It precedes the noun and serves as a signal that a noun is soon to follow.

Example: *The* gymnasium

If the noun is preceded by adjectives and nouns, the determiner precedes these modifiers.

Examples: *The* new gymnasium
The brick gymnasium
The new brick gymnasium

The absence of a determiner to signal a following noun will sometimes produce ambiguity. Here is a case from a newspaper headline:

Union demands increase.

We do not know how to interpret *increase* because a signal is absent. A *will* would show that it is a verb:

Union demands will increase.

A determiner would indicate that it is a noun.

Union demands *an* increase.

The following is a partial list of determiners:

Articles	Prenominal Possessive Pronouns	Demonstratives	Possessive Proper Names
a/an	my	this	John's (or any
the	your	that	• possessive
	his	these	• of name)
	her	those	•
	its		
	our		
	their		

Five of the above determiners—his, this, that, these, those—as well as the whole set of possessive proper names, overlap with a separate list of words that may be used in place of a noun—that is, as noun substitutes.

Examples: *That* will be enough.
I prefer *Elizabeth's.*
What can one do with old cars like *these?*
I can't tell Jim's tennis shoes from *his.*

Exercise 13–8

In the blanks write a D (determiner) or NS (noun substitute) to show the category of the italicized word.

1. Do you like *my* new hat? _____ D
2. Do you like *this*? _____ NS
3. Should you have *a* match? _____ D
4. *These* guys are my new teammates. _____ D
5. *These* are my new teammates. _____ NS
6. We did not disturb *George's* room. _____ D
7. *Its* roots grew under the pavement. _____ D
8. Have you seen *our* formals? _____ D
9. *This* cold is invigorating. _____ D
10. *Smith's* house is for sale. _____ D
11. *His* is the best plan. _____ NS
12. Where are *the* red phlox you planted? _____ D
13. *That* deep pool is a good place for trout. _____ D
14. Jack has *an* interest in grinding rocks. _____ D
15. *Your* slip is showing. _____ D
16. *Sally's* was the winner. _____ NS

Exercise 13–9

Each of these newspaper headlines is ambiguous, that is, can be read in two ways. Add a determiner to each in such a way that a noun will be identified and the meaning reduced to a single one.

1. Police raid gathering _____ Police raid my gathering.
2. Complete faculty at State _____ Complete the faculty at State.
3. Rule book not obscene _____ Rule the book not obscene.
4. Clean model house _____ A clean model house.
5. Girl shows top baby beef[2] _____ A girl shows top baby beef.

D. Auxiliaries

Auxiliaries are closely associated with the verb and are of three kinds. The **first** kind is called modal auxiliaries. There are ten modal auxiliaries:

can	could
may	might
shall	should
will	would
must	
ought (to)[3]	

---

[2]*Baby beef* means calves, which farm boys and girls exhibit at fairs.

[3]This account omits the uses of *dare* and *need* as auxiliaries. You might like to investigate their uses in questions and negative sentences.

The modal auxiliaries are bound together as a group by two characteristics of form: (1) The present-tense form does not take an -*s* in the third person singular; for example, we say "She may," not "She mays." (2) They do not have participle forms, present or past.

These modal auxiliaries precede verb stems and give them special shades of meaning, such as futurity, volition, possibility, probability, permission, and necessity. They are sometimes called verb markers because they signal that a verb is about to follow. The majority of the modals are said to have tense. In the first four pairs—*can, could; may, might; shall, should; will, would*—the second member is the past tense of the first member. This is apparent in indirect discourse:

> I think I *can* help you.
> I thought I *could* help you.

Must and *ought* (*to*) do not have parallel forms, like the others. To express the past tense of *must,* in the sense of necessity, one says *had to,* e.g.,

> This morning I *must* trim the hedge.
> Yesterday I *had to* trim the hedge.

And for the past tense of *ought* (*to*), one uses *ought* (*to*)/*should* plus *have* plus a past participle, e.g.,

> You *ought to* see those strawberries.
> You *ought to have/should have* seen those strawberries.

The negatives of *must* and *ought to* are not regular. If *must* means "is necessary," then its negative means "is not necessary." This negative meaning is expressed by *do not have to* or *need not,* and not by *must not,* which is a forbiddance of the action of the following verb. Thus:

> **Affirm.:** You must return tomorrow.
> **Neg.:** You don't have to return tomorrow.

or

> You need not return tomorrow.

but not

> You must not return tomorrow.

The negative of *ought to* is expressed by *ought not to* or *hadn't ought to* (Northern form) or *should not.* Thus:

> **Affirm.:** You ought to carry that log away.
> **Neg.:** You ought not to carry that log away.

or

> You hadn't ought to carry that log away.

or

You shouldn't carry that log away.

The form *hadn't ought to* is used in speech only, not in writing, and of the three, *shouldn't* is perhaps the most commonly employed.

Often the ideas that modal auxiliaries express do not include an element of time. Here are all ten expressing delicate nuances of meaning exclusive of time, save that a notion of futurity is implicit in all of them.

May I help you?	You ought to be careful.
Might I help you?	Will you come again?
Can I help you?	Would you come again?
Could I help you?	Shall I return it?
You must be careful.	Should I return it?

On the whole the meanings expressed are many and subtly shaded, and you are lucky that, as a native speaker, you already have a command of them.

The **second** kind of auxiliary is the two primary auxiliaries, *have* and *be*. Their forms are

Stem	have	be
Present tense	has/have	am/is/are
Present participle	having	being
Past tense	had	was/were
Past participle	had	been

When immediately preceding a main verb, *have* is followed by a past participle, as in "He has *eaten*," and *be* is followed by either a past participle, as in "The white cat was *found*," or a present participle, as in "They are *studying*."

When auxiliaries are employed in groups of two or three, an obligatory sequence is followed: modal + *have* + *be*.

Examples:	*modal*	*have*	*be*	{-ING vb}/{-D pp}
I	might	have	been	fishing/shot
George	may		be	reading/startled
They		had	been	sleeping/seen
She	must	have		quit

In main-verb sequences only one modal auxiliary is used. With *have* only one form is used in main-verb sequences. But *be* may be doubled, as in "He *was being* punished."

Up to this point we have noted two important sets of auxiliaries: (1) the various modals and (2) the primary auxiliaries *have* and *be* with their various forms. Before proceeding to the third set of auxiliaries it will be helpful to consider the role of the first two sets of auxiliaries in the formation of questions or negative statements. Even though you might think that you don't know much about auxiliaries in English, if you are a native speaker of the language, you know more than you realize, though you don't know it consciously. Indeed, to form questions or to negate statements we are all quite expert at identifying auxiliaries in a sequence. We'll consider this matter in more detail below.

1. When we form questions, we locate the first auxiliary in the string of words that would occur together if the utterance were a statement, and we move it to the front of the utterance, placing it in front of the subject. Of course, if there is only one auxiliary, then it serves as the "first" one. In other words, we invert the subject and first auxiliary. Note also that with regard to this rule as well as the next two we will be listing, the forms of *be,* whether or not they are auxiliaries, are handled as such.[4]

   Examples: "The dog should be licensed" becomes "Should the dog be licensed?"
   "They are happy" becomes "Are they happy?"
   "Jim is teaching history" becomes "Is Jim teaching history?"[5]

2. Most negative statements are formed through the placement of the word *not* or its contracted form after the first auxiliary in a sentence.

   Examples: "The dog should be licensed" becomes "The dog shouldn't be licensed."
   "They are happy" becomes "They aren't happy."
   "Jim is teaching history" becomes "Jim isn't teaching history."

3. Tag questions, which are short questions tacked onto statements, locate the first auxiliary of an utterance and repeat it in the subsequent tag. They also utilize a pronoun form that corresponds to the subject of the sentence. Typically speaking, if the utterance is positive, the tag will be negative and vice versa.

   Examples: The dog should be licensed, shouldn't it?
   The dog shouldn't be licensed, should it?

   They are happy, aren't they?
   They aren't happy, are they?

   Jim is teaching history, isn't he?
   Jim isn't teaching history, is he?

The **third** kind of auxiliary is the periphrastic auxiliary *do.* The auxiliary *do* is a "dummy" form that has a variety of uses. In the discussion above regarding the formation of questions, tag questions, and negative statements, we mentioned that speakers have to locate the first auxiliary. It may have occurred to you, however, that many statements do not even contain an auxiliary (or even a nonauxiliary form of *be*). In such cases we insert an appropriate form of the periphrastic *do,* which not only occupies a slot that would have otherwise been filled by an auxiliary if there were one in the utterance, but also carries the verb tense. Note the examples below:

---

[4]There are some differences between British and American English about the extent to which a few auxiliaries such as *might, must,* or *ought* can be moved forward in questions.

[5]The question examples here involve questions that require "yes" or "no" answers. Wh- questions that begin with words such as *who, what, why* also invert the first auxiliary and the subject. Thus we could ask, "What is Jim teaching?" However, if the wh- word is asking about the subject of the sentence, no inversion takes place (e.g., "Who is teaching history?").

Questions	"Sally studies chemistry" becomes "Does Sally study chemistry?"
	"Sally studied chemistry" becomes "Did Sally study chemistry?"
Negatives	"Sally studies chemistry" becomes "Sally doesn't study chemistry."
	"Sally studied chemistry" becomes "Sally didn't study chemistry."
Tag Questions	"Sally studies chemistry, doesn't she?"
	"Sally doesn't study chemistry, does she?"
	"Sally studied chemistry, didn't she?"
	"Sally didn't study chemistry, did she?"

In addition to what has already been described, the auxiliary *do* may be used in declarative affirmative sentences where it provides emphasis: "The teacher claimed that John never studied. But he *did* study." The auxiliary *do* may also be used in sentences beginning with a negative adverbial such as *seldom, never,* and *not only,* where it is inverted with the subject and carries the verb tense.

Examples: Never *did* I dream of such a thing.
Not only *does* he dream; he has nightmares.

Before proceeding on to some exercises that involve identifying auxiliaries, we caution you to remember that some occurrences of the previously listed words do not constitute the use of an auxiliary. For example, the word *did* is an auxiliary in the sentence "He did not come," but it is a main verb in the sentence "He did the dishes." And the word *have* is an auxiliary in front of a past participle as in "We have eaten," but it is a main verb in a sentence such as "We have a dog."

Exercise 13-10

Give the number of auxiliaries, from 0 through 3, in each sentence or question.

1. I shall be waiting for you. _2_
2. You ought to have done better. _2_
3. Helen should have been working. _3_
4. Mr. Owens has your car. _0_
5. The elephant has been injured. _2_
6. Do you bring the refreshments? _1_

Exercise 13-11

Label the italicized auxiliaries as MA (modal auxiliary), PA (primary auxiliary), or PAD (periphrastic auxiliary *do*).

1. Joyce was *being* attacked by the critics. _PA_
2. *Could* you hold this turkey for me? _MA_
3. *Did* he find the right address? _PAD_
4. The butler *may* have committed the crime. _MA_
5. The net *was* lying in a heap. _PA_

Exercise 13–12

A verb may be preceded by one, two, or three auxiliaries. Underline the auxiliaries. Then write above each one MA (for modal auxiliary), *have,* or *be.* Which sequence, if any, differs from that given on page 189?

1. Those words must be justified.   *M A be*

2. She ought to have written her mother.   *MA have*

3. They could be coming by plane.   *MA be*

4. The car could have been wrecked by that.   *MA have be*

5. You might have mowed it shorter.   *MH have*

The behavior and patterning of auxiliaries differ from those of verbs in several respects. A couple of these differences could be inferred from the previous discussion about the periphrastic auxiliary *do,* but we will still summarize them here.

1. A sentence with a verb can begin a conversation and be satisfactorily understood by the listener. Upon meeting a friend you might say, "I worked like a dog yesterday," and receive a nod of comprehension and sympathy. But if you used only a modal auxiliary in such an introductory sentence as, "I could yesterday," your friend might look at you with concern and reply, "Could what?"

   The point here is that an auxiliary is not used as a full verb. It may be used, however, as a substitute verb for a verb already mentioned, as in

   > He ate an orange and so *did* I.
   > I can drive and so *can* he.

   Or it may be used in reference to a previously stated verb. For example, in reply to the question, "Are you going to the play?" you might say, "Yes, I am."

2. The negative of a verb phrase containing an auxiliary or auxiliaries is made by putting *not* after the first auxiliary in a sequence (e.g., "He has not been attending"). This contrasts with the negative of a verb phrase containing only a verb. This latter case, as we have seen, requires a form of *do* plus *not* preceding the verb unless the main verb is a form of *be* (e.g., "He doesn't attend").

3. To make a question with an auxiliary, the subject and the first auxiliary in a sequence are reversed (e.g., "She can be elected" becomes "Can she be elected?"). In contrast, with a verb, unless the verb is a form of *be,* we formulate a question by following the pattern do {do} + subject + verb stem (e.g., "They studied the constitution" becomes "Did they study the constitution?").

Exercise 13–13

Rewrite each sentence in two ways—as a negative and as a question. Then by using the criteria in paragraphs 2 and 3 immediately preceding this exercise, decide whether the italicized word is an auxiliary or a verb. Indicate your decision by writing Aux or V in the blank at the right.

Example: She *began* working.   Neg. *She did not begin working.*
Q. *Did she begin working?*   *V*

1. He *was* eating.   Neg. <u>He was not eating.</u>
Q. <u>Was he eating?</u>   *Aux*

2. He *quit* eating.   Neg. <u>He did not quit eating.</u>
Q. <u>Did he quit eating?</u>   *V*

3. The worker *was* killed.   Neg. <u>The worker was not killed.</u>
Q. <u>Was the worker killed?</u>   *Aux*

4. The worker *has* gone.   Neg. <u>The worker has not gone.</u>
Q. <u>Has the worker gone?</u>   *Aux*

5. We *should* hurry.   Neg. <u>We should not hurry.</u>
Q. <u>Should we hurry?</u>   *Aux*

6. We *can* hurry.   Neg. <u>We cannot hurry.</u>
Q. <u>Can we hurry?</u>   *Aux*

7. They *are* going.   Neg. <u>They are not going.</u>
Q. <u>Are they going?</u>   *Aux*

8. They *kept* going.   Neg. <u>They did not keep going.</u>
Q. <u>Did they keep going?</u>   *V*

9. He *could* have been sleeping.   Neg. <u>He could not have been sleeping.</u>
Q. <u>Could he have been sleeping?</u>   *Aux*

10. He *will* play.   Neg. <u>He will not play.</u>
Q. <u>Will he play?</u>   *Aux*

E. Pronouns: Personal, Interrogative, Relative

Personal Pronouns

The set of personal pronouns is a closed set. And because it is also a small set, it is relatively easy to familiarize ourselves with its members.

		Singular		
	Subject	**Object**	**Prenominal Possessive**	**Substitutional Possessive**
1st	I	me	my	mine
2nd	you	you	your	yours
3rd **M**	he	him	his	his
F	she	her	her	hers
N	it	it	its	its

	Plural			
1st	we	us	our	ours
2nd	you	you	your	yours
3rd	they	them	their	theirs
Interr. ⎫	who	whom	whose	whose
Relative ⎭				

Let us look at them through the framework terms.

1. **Number.** You are already acquainted with the terms *singular* and *plural,* with their meanings of "one" and "more than one." One difference from noun number here is that *we* does not mean more than one *I* but *I* and somebody else. The singular and plural have the same *you* forms. Earlier in our history the singular forms were *thou, thee, thy, thine.* These were in everyday use by the English who settled our country in the early 1600s, and you meet them in Shakespeare's plays and the King James Bible, both of the same period. They survive today in liturgical or other religiously directed uses of language.

2. **Function Terms.** One dimension of meaning, which we will be giving greater attention to later in the text, involves the function, that is, the grammatical role of particular words in a sentence. In the case of pronouns in English, these functions are signaled by the form of the pronouns. For example, as native speakers we know to say "They are coming," not "Them are coming." Our grammatical knowledge includes the fact that *they* and not *them* is a subject form. As native speakers we know this, even if we don't know the formal grammatical terminology to describe what we know. As you look at the columns in the personal pronoun paradigm you will see four function-related headings: subject, object, prenominal possessive, and substitutional possessive.

   a. The pronouns in the subject column are typically those used in the functions of *subject* of the verb (that which performs the action of the verb, is described, is identified, or about which an assertion is made). The subject form is also used for a *subjective complement* (that which follows *be* or a verb like *become* and identifies the subject).

      Examples: *They* are going to the ballet.
      It was *she* who missed the test.

   b. The pronouns in the *object* column are those that function mainly as objects of the verb and of the preposition. As objects of the verb they may be either a *direct object,* which undergoes the action of the verb, or an *indirect object,* which is the person or thing to or for whom an action is performed.

      Examples: We saw *her* in the car.
      I gave *her* the letter yesterday.
      A package came from *him.*

   c. The prenominal possessives occur before nouns.

Example: With *my* brains and *your* industry we could make a fortune.

d. The substitutional possessives occur as substitutes for nouns (noun phrases). The form *its* is rarely used.

Examples: That lawn mower is *ours* (= our lawn mower).
Yours (= your term paper) was the best.

3. **Person**
a. The first person in the singular denotes the speaker. In the plural it denotes the speaker plus anybody else, one or more.
b. The second person denotes the person or persons spoken to.
c. The third person denotes those other than the speaker and other than those spoken to.

4. **Gender Reference.** Only three of the horizontal rows of pronouns have gender reference—the *he, she,* and *it* rows. The *it* can refer to certain creatures of either gender—*infant, dog, pig*—and to genderless things—*story, stone, justice.*

Interrogative Pronouns

As the first word in a question, the subject form *who* is normally used in cultivated speech, regardless of its function.

Examples: *Who* borrowed my tie? (subject of verb)
Who did you take to the theater? (object of verb)
Who are you referring to? (object of preposition)

In the last two examples *whom* is occasionally used by the ultrafastidious, but it sounds stiff and bookish. The object form *whom* is used directly after prepositions, as in "To whom?" and "With whom did you go?" But in easy conversational style the latter is likely to be "Who did you go with?"

Whose book is this? (prenominal possessive)
Whose is this book? (substitutional possessive)

Other interrogative pronouns include *what* and *which.*

Relative Pronouns

Traditionalists have prescribed the relative pronoun *who* as a subject form and *whom* as object of the verb and object of the preposition. As with the interrogative uses, the distinction between the relative pronouns *who* and *whom* is largely ignored in favor of employing *who* for both subject and object uses, even in Standard English. But understanding the traditional distinction is still important because some situations remain, even if relatively rare, when educated individuals are expected to know and maintain the distinction. If you are trying to maintain a distinction between the two relative pronouns *who* and *whom,* remember that the relative clauses they introduce are embedded sentences in which *who* and *whom* have their own function:

Tom is the boy *who* came = Tom is the boy. *The boy* came. (subject of verb)
Tom is the boy *whom* I saw = Tom is the boy. I saw *the boy*. (object of verb)
The woman *who* bought the business is wealthy = The woman is wealthy. *The woman* bought the business. (subject of verb)
The woman *whom* I admired bought the business = The woman bought the business. I admired *the woman*. (object of verb)
The woman *whom* I voted for won by a close margin = The woman won by a close margin. I voted for *the woman*. (object of preposition)

With this information in mind, now look at the next examples:

The teacher *whose* book I borrowed had an extra copy. (possessive relative)
We had a beautiful maple *whose* leaves turned scarlet in September. (This use of *whose* with nonhuman reference is not uncommon in reputable English.)

As you doubtless noticed from the examples above, *who* and *whom* (interrogative and relative) have human reference, whereas *whose* (interrogative) has human and *whose* (relative) both human and nonhuman reference.

There are two more relative pronouns, *which* and *that*.

Which has nonhuman reference and in its uses parallels those of *who* and *whom*.

Examples: The tree *which* fell was a large oak. (subject of verb)
The tree *which* I prefer is an oak. (object of verb)
The tree *which* we sat under was an oak. (object of preposition)
The tree under *which* we sat was an oak. (object of preposition)

That has both human and nonhuman reference. Its uses parallel those of *which*, but it does not directly follow a preposition.[6]

Examples: The flavor *that* pleases me most is chocolate. (subject of verb)
The teacher *that* I like best is Mrs. Lopez. (object of verb)
The author *that* I am writing about is Camus. (object of preposition)
But
*The author about *that* I am writing is Camus. (ungrammatical)

One more observation about relative pronouns is relevant: When a relative pronoun functions as an object of the verb or object of the preposition, it may be omitted.

Examples: The pet [*which, that*] he wanted to buy was a French poodle.
The carpenter [*whom*] we hired was Mr. Cutter.
The doctor [*whom*] I am waiting for is Dr. Harris.

Exercise: 13–14

Assume you are writing a term paper in a formal style. Fill in the blanks with the relative *who* or *whom*.

---

[6]A further constraint on the relative pronoun *that* is that it must introduce restrictive clauses. These will be explained in chapter 17.

1. The candidate ___whom___ the convention chose had always voted for civil rights legislation.
2. She interviewed a well-known scientist with ___whom___ she had previously corresponded.
3. The doctor ___who___ developed the vaccine warned against possible side effects.
4. The psychiatrist with ___whom___ Carlson conferred was optimistic about the case.
5. All the persons ___whom___ they arrested protested their innocence.

Exercise 13–15

Fill in the blanks with *who* or *which*. After the sentence indicate whether the reference is Hum (human) or Nhum (nonhuman).

1. That's the girl ___who___ won all the honors. _____
2. The council listened to the citizens ___who___ presented the petition. _____
3. It was the spotted kitten ___which___ ran under the porch. _____
4. We spoke about the rising crime rate ___which___ is making life dangerous in cities. _____
5. The bread ___which___ you bought is stale. _____

Exercise 13–16

Consider the blank within each sentence below. In the blank after each sentence indicate whether that sentence would use a prenominal possessive (PP) or a substitutional possessive (SbP).

1. This is ___your___ seat. ___PP___
2. This seat is ___yours___ . ___SbP___
3. Have you seen ___my___ canary? ___PP___
4. I compared it to ___mine___ . ___SbP___
5. ___Mine___ is a poor bathing suit. ___SbP___
6. I'd prefer one like ___hers___ . ___SbP___
7. Where is ___her___ friend today? ___PP___
8. ___His___ bucket is leaking. ___PP___
9. He found it with ___his___ . ___Sbp___
10. She bought ___her___ sister a compact. ___PP___

Some Observations and Applications

This chapter has introduced you to the structure classes. These classes have relatively few members, but they are very important in what they signal about how the structure of a sentence is to be interpreted. In abbreviated speech some structure-class words such as determiners can sometimes be omitted, as frequently occurs in newspaper headlines. This is because determiners are function rather than content words and thus do not carry a heavy semantic load. But because they carry important information about how the structure of an utterance should be interpreted, omitting them poses some risk. Exercise 13–9 illustrated how the absence of a determiner in a headline can lead to ambiguity. If you do specialized writing that requires you to omit function words such as determiners, your linguistic training should prompt you to proofread that writing with particular care.

Another structure-class paradigm related to careful editing is the pronoun paradigm. In most cases, if you are a native speaker of English, your ear will tell you which pronoun forms are correct to use in a given context. But in some contexts you may need to rely on linguistic analysis to help you choose an appropriate form. We have already observed this in relation to the relative pronoun forms *who* and *whom.* And consider also the difficulty that can occur in selecting an appropriate pronoun in a compound noun phrase such as "The decision was not clear to Nancy and _____ ." In a sentence such as this, you may not know whether to use *me* or *I.* Of course you might just try out your ear by omitting the first part of the compound and get "The decision was not clear to _____ ." Your ear would tell you that *me* works there. But it is nice to also verify this with a little grammatical knowledge just to be sure. You could reason that the pronoun must be the object of the preposition because the word *to* is a preposition. The object form is *me* and not *I,* so the word choice should be *me.*

Another important application of grammatical study is in the teaching of a language to others. Being a native speaker of a language is not enough for someone to be qualified to teach that language to others. The teacher must be consciously aware of the rules and patterns that govern the language or else he or she will be unable to explain them to others. Let us consider one illustration of some language rules that you studied in this chapter but would otherwise not have consciously known. In this chapter you have seen that auxiliaries are moved around and inverted with the subject to form questions and followed by the word *not* to form negative utterances. These uses and movements of auxiliaries are performed quite naturally by native speakers but can present a challenge to nonnative speakers. Those who teach English as a second language must be consciously aware of how the language behaves because they must be able to explain it to their nonnative-speaking students.

This chapter has given attention to the morphology of the structure classes. But some attention should also be given to some of their pragmatic behavior, which often escapes the attention of people who typically expect the importance of structure classes to reside exclusively in structural signals. For an illustration of the pragmatic importance of one structure class, let's look at the articles. The definite article *the* is not interchangeable with the indefinite articles *a* and *an.* It is to be used with nouns that have already been specified in the discourse or are known to the listener (e.g., "I saw the president"). The articles *a* and *an* are used with nouns that have not been specified or are not already known ("I saw a dog"). These facts about articles are widely known, but research has also shown that the seemingly insignificant difference between the use of the definite and indefinite article can actually make a significant difference in legal and judicial settings that involve eyewitness reports. Elizabeth Loftus, reporting on empirical research, explains that when a definite article is used in questions directed at an eyewitness (her example is "Did you see the broken headlight?"), it can presuppose the existence of something in a way that an indefinite article wouldn't ("Did you see a broken headlight?") and thus alter the way that some eyewitnesses report what they have seen. Such a question can even alter the subsequent memory of a witness about an event.[7] Such information about the psycholinguistic effect of a structure class should be of interest to people working in law and law enforcement.

---

[7]"Language and Memories in the Judicial System" by Elizabeth F. Loftus in *Language Use and the Uses of Language,* eds. Roger W. Shuy and Anna Shnukal. Washington D.C.: Georgetown University Press, 1980, pp. 257–68.

Part Three

The Syntax
of English

14

Noun and Verb Phrases and Grammatical Functions

In the previous chapter, you briefly considered how the omission of determiners in headlines can lead to ambiguity. The headlines below will illustrate the importance of phrase identification in resolving ambiguity.[1] Often when a headline omits an article, the boundary of a noun phrase or even its identity becomes unclear.

Hershey Bars Protest (The absence of an article in front of the noun *Protest,* allows it to be interpreted as a verb)

Carter Plans Swell Deficit (The absence of an article in front of *Deficit* allows *Swell* to be interpreted as an adjective that forms part of the noun phrase *Swell Deficit*).

Sometimes the headline itself may not have actually omitted an article, but our expectations about headlines can condition us to expect possible omissions and thus can lead to an ambiguity anyway.

Police Discover Crack In Australia (The drug known as "crack" does not require an article because it is a mass noun. But the fact that another type of noun, the "count noun"—such as a *dog,* a *pencil,* a *crack*—, so often appears in headlines without a necessary article leads us to see this headline as possibly ambiguous).

---

[1]These headlines are reported in *Anguished English* by Richard Lederer. New York: Dell Publishing, 1987.

A. Noun Phrases

Up to this point we have examined systematically the phonemic and morphemic structure of English. Now we shall see how words are combined into larger structures—phrases, clauses, and sentences. This is the domain of syntax. The syntactic architecture of the English sentence is extraordinarily complex and can be blueprinted by various methods, none of them perfect. In the presentation that follows you will be shown the main outlines only, with the admonition that there are different ways of interpreting the same syntactic facts and that English syntax contains territories as yet uncharted.

A noun phrase consists of a noun and all the words and word groups that belong with the noun and cluster around it. The noun itself is called the *headword* or *head,* and the other words and word groups are modifiers of the noun.

> **Examples:** The yellow *tulips*
> The yellow *tulips* in the garden
> The yellow *tulips* in the garden which were blooming

In these examples *tulips* is the head. Of the rest of the words, the modifiers, we observe that the single-word modifiers, such as *the* and *yellow,* precede the head and that the word-group modifiers, such as *in the garden* and *which were blooming,* follow the head.

Exercise 14–1

Underline the head of the following noun phrases.

1. the fence
2. the old fence
3. that new aluminum fence
4. the fence between the houses
5. the old fence which was painted green
6. the old fence between the houses which was painted green
7. a worn-out putter
8. my worn-out putter lying in the attic
9. a used car, broken down by abusive driving
10. the children's swings in the park which were in use all day long

Exercise 14–2

Make each list of words into a noun phrase and underline the headword.

1. table, the, small, study — *The small study table.*
2. European, any, opera, great — *Any great European opera*
3. somber, evening, that, sky — *That somber evening sky*
4. my, shoes, roommate's, tennis — *My roommate's tennis shoes*
5. linen, white, handkerchiefs, the, other, all — *All the other white linen handkerchief*
6. soft, a, on the head, pat — *A soft pat on the head*

7. hard, a, which staggered him, <u>blow</u> *A hard blow which staggered him*
8. ski, that, lying in the basement, broken *that broken ski lying in the basement*
9. with a lame leg, a, who was walking on crutches, junior *A junior with a lame leg who was walking on crutches*
10. the, in the front row, whose books he was carrying, girl *The girl in the front row whose books he was carrying*

A noun phrase can be rather complex, containing other noun phrases, or it can consist of just one word (a noun) if that word can occur without any modifiers.

Examples: *Boys* often build dams in the spring.
Small boys who are not in school often build dams in the spring.
Jim wanted *a car.*
Jim wanted *a new sports car with wire wheels which would have a fast getaway.*

Exercise 14–3

Expand the italicized noun phrases by adding modifiers before, after, or both before and after. Then underline these resulting noun phrases.

Example: *The lock* was broken.
Expanded: <u>The rusty lock on the front door</u> was broken.

1. *Sailboats* are beautiful to watch. *white* ... *On a sunny day,*
2. They sailed under *the bridge.* *on the crystal clear water,*
3. He makes *jewelry.* *expensive for affluent people.*
4. The player under the basket is *my brother.* *bald* ... *John.*
5. I gave *the cat* a dish of milk. *fresh cold*
6. Her mother buys *chairs* at auctions and refinishes them. *to sell,*
7. *Camping* is not always fun. *in the winter*
8. She makes *pottery* on her wheel at home. *to sell one day.*
9. It is good exercise to do long cross-countries on *skis.*
10. The doctor remains in *his office* till five. *in the freezing cold*

In a later chapter on modification you will see that the premodifiers that accompany nouns follow a particular word order. Here it is enough for you to recognize that nouns occur in noun phrases that function as a single syntactic unit.

B. Some Syntactic Categories of Nouns

You have earlier seen that nouns do not all behave the same and may be placed in various subclasses according to their behavior. You may recall that collective nouns require particular choices about how accompanying verbs or pronouns display number. And animate nouns differ from inanimate nouns in how they express the possessive notion.

Now we will take a look at three more noun subclasses, which are based on the ways nouns behave with determiners in conjunction with the singular and the plural. These three classes are the count noun, the mass noun, and the proper noun. In the discussion that follows, remember that an asterisk indicates that a particular utterance is ungrammatical.

Count and Mass Nouns

The count-noun class includes everything that is readily countable, such as *beetles, books, sounds, concepts, minutes.* Count nouns have both singular and plural forms. In the singular they must always be preceded by a determiner, e.g.,

A car drove by
The car drove by

but not

*Car drove by.

In the plural they may occur either with or without a determiner:

Cars are dangerous on slippery roads.
Those cars are dangerous on slippery roads.

The mass nouns (sometimes called "non-count nouns") include everything that is not readily countable, such as *steam, music, justice, advice, water, bread, Latin, silk.* Mass nouns have no plural; they occur in the singular under these conditions:

Without a determiner:	*Information* is useful.
With *the*:	*The* information is useful.
But not with *a*:	**An* information is useful.

Many words may be mass nouns in one context and count nouns in a different context, e.g.,

Mass:	*Lemonade* is refreshing in summer.
Count:	They had *two lemonades.* (Remember that mass nouns have no plural. Here *lemonades* is shorthand for two *cups* or two *cans* of lemonade.)
Mass:	*Virtue* is its own reward.
Count:	Her *virtues* were well known.
Mass:	You have *egg* on your chin.
Count:	*Eggs* were served for breakfast.
Mass:	They eat *bread* with every meal.
Count:	Our cafeteria serves several *breads.* (Here *breads* can refer to types of bread such as sourdough, whole wheat, and french.)

As a rule of thumb it is worth remembering that count nouns can be modified by *many* and mass nouns by *much.*

Exercise 14–4

In the blanks write *count* or *mass* to classify the italicized words.

1. The factory releases dangerous *gases* into the atmosphere. _____C_____
2. The price of *gas* jumped over the weekend. _____M_____
3. Hobson enjoys his *leisure*. _____M_____
4. There is *truth* in what he says. _____M_____
5. These *truths* you must never forget. _____C_____
6. Mrs. Lopez buys *juice* every day at the market. _____M_____
7. Please bring me a *juice*. _____C_____
8. Charles studied *Russian* in college. _____M_____
9. Today's world puts a high value on *knowledge*. _____M_____
10. We heard a *Russian* at the United Nations. _____C_____

Proper Nouns

The proper-noun class consists of the names of particular, often unique, persons, places, and things, e.g., Charlotte Brook, the *Mona Lisa*, the *Queen Mary* (ship), Maine, the Rocky Mountains, Mount Washington. They are considered a subclass of nouns because most of them conform in part to the noun paradigm, and they appear in noun positions. Syntactically, they behave like count nouns, with a few restrictions that are worth noting:

1. In the singular proper nouns usually appear without a determiner.

    Examples: *June* is a month for weddings.
    We talked with *Margaret.*
    The inside of *Chartres Cathedral* is beautiful in the sunshine.

    However, a determiner is used with singular proper nouns when such nouns are restrictively modified, as in these cases:

    The June in which she was married was warm.
    It was *a June* to remember.
    The Margaret whom I remember had red hair.

2. Proper nouns that are always plural are normally accompanied by *the,* occasionally by a different determiner.

    Examples: *The Appalachians* are an old mountain chain.
    I don't like *your Bahamas; they* are too commercialized.
    We are going to visit *the Hebrides.*

3. Certain proper nouns are usually singular and take *the.*

    Examples: We took *the Maasdam* (ship) to Rotterdam.
    The Museum of Modern Art has a new show.

He waded across *the Rio Grande.*
We stayed at *the Americana.*
The Atlantic Ocean is rough in winter.

These proper nouns, however, can also be used in the plural:

Several Americanas have been built on the Eastern coast.
There are *two Atlantic Oceans* in the Northern Hemisphere, the
warm one of the tropics and the cold one toward the Pole.

Exercise 14-5

Classify the italicized nouns by *count, mass,* or *proper.* The proper names have been
left uncapitalized.

1. Aunt Tilda's favorite *month* is *may.*   C   P
2. There is *dust* on the *mantelpiece.*   M   C
3. The class had a *picnic* at *riverview park.*   C   P
4. *Cotton* is more absorbent than *linen.*   M   M
5. In the *alps* are many lovely *valleys.*   P   C
6. Do you like *whipping cream* on your *sundae?*   M   C
7. Numerous *injustices* were perpetrated
   by the *invaders.*   C   C
8. Can one expect *justice* in this *court?*   M   C
9. The *americans* are visiting us next *week.*   P   C
10. They sailed on the *statendam* for the
    canary islands.   P   P

C. Verb Phrases

A verb phrase consists of a verb and all the words and word groups that belong with
the verb and cluster around it. The verb itself is called the *headword* or *head,* and
the other words and word groups are the auxiliaries, modifiers, and complements of
the verb. *Complements* is the generic term for the completers of the verb, which we
will later learn to know as direct object, indirect object, objective complement, and
subjective complement. In the phrases below, the head is italicized.

Examples: soon *arrived*
                arrived late
                soon *arrived* at the station
                arrived just as the plane came in
                was *waiting* at the door
                may have been *stolen* by the cashier

Exercise 14-6

Underline the head in these verb phrases.

1. stepped lightly
2. stepped into the room
3. quickly stepped in
4. stepped where he was told
5. at once shouted to the crowd to stand back
6. without hesitation shouted for help
7. were watching for the signal
8. had been eaten by the cat
9. would have driven to the fair
10. spoke loudly

Here are some verb phrases containing complements. Never mind the details now, for you will study them later; just notice that the words in each phrase are connected with the verb.

Examples: *built* a scooter
built his son a scooter
seemed gloomy and dejected
elected George a member of the fraternity
became president of his class

Exercise 14-7

Underline the head of these verb phrases.

1. sold his last semester's books
2. sold me his last semester's books
3. appeared happy in his new job
4. always chose Jim chairman of the dishwashing committee
5. still remained the best candidate
6. cheerfully gave a handsome contribution
7. never paid his bills on time
8. immediately called his uncle a name
9. often was weary after his workout
10. soon returned the book she had borrowed

English sentences can be divided into two parts, one consisting of a noun phrase, the other a verb phrase.

Exercise 14-8

Draw a vertical line separating these sentences into a noun phrase and a verb phrase. Underline the noun head and the verb head.

1. The red pony in the pasture/galloped along the fence.
2. Many students/attended the Christmas party.
3. The senior who sells the most tickets/will be honored at the prom.
4. The pipes in the classroom pounded noisily.
5. The choir in the loft/sang the last hymn softly.

In sentences like these the headword of the noun phrase is the subject of the verb; you will hear more about this shortly. The entire phrase may be called the complete subject. The verb phrase is called the predicate. As with nouns, some verbs by themselves can constitute a phrase.

Exercise 14-9

Add a verb phrase to each of these noun phrases, making complete sentences.

1. The tiny leak in the hose   *created a puddle,*
2. The canoe that he wanted   *was stolen.*
3. The pie   *was delicious.*
4. The steaming apple pie   *smelled delicious,*
5. The passenger in the front seat who
   was watching the speedometer   *sat pensively*

Exercise 14-10

Add a noun phrase to introduce each of the following verb phrases, making complete sentences.

1. . . . . later regretted his decision.   *The doctor*
2. . . . . came after his dog when school was over.   *My neighbor*
3. . . . . will soon return to college.   *John*
4. . . . . always seemed to have a complaint to make.   *The angry customer*
5. . . . . merrily swung the heavy pack on his back
   to begin the long hike.   *The triathlete*

D. Some Syntactic Categories of Verbs

Just as there are differences in the syntactic behavior of noun phrases depending on the type of head noun, there are also differences that occur within the verb phrase depending on the kind of head verb. We will now look at three different verb types that introduce different syntactic requirements in their own verb phrase. The first kind of verb to discuss involves those that are followed by noun phrases (or nominals—to be discussed later) that, loosely speaking, "receive" the action of the verb, as in "Jack brought the car." As you will see later, when we discuss grammatical function, these verbs are called "transitive" verbs, and the noun phrases (or nominals) they introduce are called "objects."

A second type of verb includes those such as *weep*, as in "The distraught parent wept," which involve an action but do not require a following element to receive the action. These verbs are called "intransitive" verbs. Sometimes a verb can function transitively in one sentence and intransitively in another. In the sentence "We are eating the sandwich," the main verb is clearly transitive. However, in the sentence "We are eating," there is no direct object and thus the main verb is intransitive. Some grammarians still like to consider a verb such as *eating* in the latter sentence as a transitive verb, because they argue that a direct object is implied even if it is not expressed. But in our work in this course we will consider a verb as transitive only if it has a direct object that is present within the sentence.

The third type of verb to consider includes those verbs such as *be, become, seem,* and *look,* which introduce a kind of equivalency or descriptive relationship as in "Emily is a doctor" or "Michael looked angry." Verbs that introduce such structures are called "linking" verbs. In the next chapter we will examine the sentence types that involve transitive, intransitive, and linking verbs. But for now it will be helpful to get a little practice in distinguishing among these three different types of verbs.

Exercise 14–11

In each of the following sentences a verb is italicized. Indicate whether the verb is transitive, intransitive, or linking.

1. Carlos *felt* very happy about how he did on the chemistry test. _Linking_
2. She *sang* the anthem beautifully. _Trans_
3. Your haircut *looks* great. _Linking_
4. He wasn't supposed *to look*. _I_
5. Susan *prepared* the manuscript for publication. _Trans_
6. Have you ever *made* taffy? _Trans_
7. When the store owner called, the police *came* quickly. _I_
8. The instructions *were* clear. _Linking_
9. The mold *grew* quickly. _I_
10. The contestant *grew* confident during the competition. _Linking_

Verbs may be classed according to a number of syntactic behaviors in addition to those we have already mentioned. We will not attempt to illustrate the great variety of structural differences that can be classified but will instead provide one more syntactic example of the variability of verbs in the kinds of structures that they introduce. Some English verbs may be followed immediately by a complement that uses either the *-ing* form, as in "walking," or an infinitive, as in "to walk." Those verbs that allow such complements may be classified in one of three ways. The first class contains those followed by the *-ing* form of the verb but not by *to* plus a verb stem:

He enjoyed eating.

not

*He enjoyed to eat.

Those of the second class are followed by *to* plus a verb stem but not by the *-ing* form:

He agreed to come.

not

*He agreed coming.

Those of the third class are followed by either the *to* or the *-ing* form:

He preferred sleeping.

and

He preferred to sleep.

There is no general principle that dictates which form to use immediately after a verb. As a native speaker you know from long experience with our language which forms are permitted with which verbs. But a nonnative speaker must go through the arduous task of learning them one by one.

Verbs taking complements in *-ing* and *to* _____ are called *catenatives* because they can co-occur in chains, such as

He wanted to stop trying to postpone working.

Exercise 14–12

Give the form of the verbal complement that immediately follows each verb by writing in the blank *-ing* or *to* or *both*.

1.	wish	*to*	8.	avoid	*ing*
2.	miss	*ing*	9.	hate	*both*
3.	start	*both*	10.	try	*both*
4.	want	*to*	11.	decide	*to*
5.	postpone	*ing*	12.	risk	*ing*
6.	continue	*both*	13.	cease	*both*
7.	promise	*to*	14.	mention	*ing*

E. Grammatical Function

Up to this point we have looked at words in relation to their part of speech. We have thus classified form and structure classes according to more specific classifications of noun, verb, adjective, adverb, pronoun, and so on. But knowing the part of speech of a particular word yields only a partial understanding about the identity of that word in a particular sentence (or clause). We must also know its grammatical function within the sentence. For example, in a sentence such as "John raked the leaves," we should know that the word *John* is not just a noun. The word *John* bears a special relationship to the verb *raked*. In this case the noun *John* is the performer of the action represented by the verb and is therefore the subject of the sentence. Thus while the word *John* is a noun by its part of speech, it is a subject by its function within the sentence. The function of a particular constituent is highly correlated with its particular location or position in the sentence. For example, the subject usually occupies the first noun phrase position in the sentence. Later on we will discuss some basic sentence types of English, and the common positions of grammatical elements will become more clear.

Below you will find seven functions listed along with a brief description and an example or two to illustrate how they appear in sentences. This is a reference list only, so do not try to master the concepts here and now. But the material should be helpful to you at this point. In the next chapter we will examine some basic sentence types that contain these important functions. Before moving on to this reference list, it is important for you to remember that when we talk about a functional element such as a subject or direct object, you need to be thinking in terms of noun *phrases* rather than just nouns or pronouns. Although some nouns or pronouns by themselves can serve, for example, as a complete subject or direct object, they can do so only if they also constitute a noun phrase. In the sentence "John raked the leaves," the word *John* by itself can serve as the subject because it constitutes a noun phrase. But phrases can, of course, be substantially more complex. Now consider the chart below.

Label of Function	**Grammatical Meaning**
1. Subject of Verb	That which performs the action of a verb, is described or identified, or about which an assertion is made. **Examples:** *The leopard* stalked its prey. *The book* was large.
2. Verb	That which asserts an action or state. **Examples:** Their monkey *climbed* the trees. His claim *seems* ridiculous.
3. Subjective Complement	That which follows *be* or a verb like *become* and identifies or describes the subject. **Examples:** The woman was *a doctor.* The artist seemed *upset.*
4. Direct Object	That which undergoes the action of the verb. (Note that for simplicity of definition, even a verb such as *see* or *believe* is considered to be performing an action that an object can undergo.) **Examples:** Malcolm bought *a chandelier.* She attended *Southern Virginia College.*
5. Indirect Object	That person or thing to or for whom an action is performed. **Examples:** The coach brought *the athletes* some uniforms. The realtor found *the buyer* a nice house.

6. Objective Complement   That which completes the direct object and describes or identifies it.

Examples: We considered the manager *incompetent.*

They elected Henry *treasurer.*

7. Object of Preposition   That which is related to another word by a preposition.

Examples: The dog ran near *the river.*

Sally paid rent for *her mother.*

In addition to the functions listed above there are a few more that will be discussed later. These include modifiers and connectors. The above functions are important to consider at this stage, because an understanding of them is important in the analysis of sentence types, which we will be discussing shortly.

Exercise 14–13

The italicized words below represent the grammatical functions of *subject, verb, subjective complement, direct object, indirect object, objective complement,* and *object of a preposition.* Identify the grammatical function of each of the italicized words below. Note that a complete subject or object, like a complete noun phrase, may consist of more than one word.

1. We sent *Mathilda* a letter.   *Indirect object*
2. We sent a letter to *Mathilda.*   *Object of prep.*
3. *The coach wearing the green shorts* yells a lot.   *Subject*
4. The campaign committee will locate *potential donors.*   *direct object*
5. The unscrupulous salesman has called his customers *suckers.*   *Objective Complement*
6. The scuba diver was *an expert.*   *Sub. Complement*
7. She *read* the book carefully.   *Verb*
8. Jason appeared *confident* with the decision.   *sub. complement*
9. We should buy Waldo *a new suit.*   *direct Object*
10. *They* spoke to Jim about the problem.   *subject*

F. Identifying the Subject

Because the next chapter will be discussing grammatical functions primarily in the context of basic sentence types, it will be important here to discuss one structural phenomenon that operates independently of the particular sentence type that we are dealing with. More specifically, we will examine how the requirements for agreement (sometimes called "concord") in form between the subject and verb can also help us in identifying the subject of a sentence or clause. Let us begin with this simple sentence:

The teacher holds class every day.

If we change the word *teacher* to the plural form *teachers,* we must change the verb to *hold.* We describe this noun-verb relationship by saying that the noun phrase "is tied to" or "agrees with" the verb. And the noun phrase in the sentence that is tied to the verb is the subject of the verb. Thus the tie or agreement shows that *the teacher* is the subject. This "tie" test is the most generally useful way to identify the subject in various kinds of sentences, regardless of the position of the subject.

Here are two simple exercises just to fix the subject-verb relationship in your mind. It will be enough to do them orally.

Exercise 14-14

Change the plural subjects to singular ones and make the necessary changes in the verbs. If you write out this exercise, use a double-pointed arrow to connect the subject and the verb: e.g., Children play.

1. The cats purr.
2. The students study.
3. The houses deteriorate.
4. The vases break.
5. The visitors depart.

Exercise 14-15

Now reverse the process, changing the subject from singular to plural.

1. The cat prowls.
2. The musician plays.
3. The professor teaches.
4. The bus waits.
5. The comedian laughs.

When a noun phrase is in the subject position, it is the headword of the phrase that is tied to the verb and is therefore the headword subject, or as we will call it, "the simple subject."

Examples: The <u>duties</u> of the center depend on the kind of offensive employed.

The <u>height</u> of the bushes varies.

Exercise 14-16

Below each sentence write the simple subject and the verb to which it is tied.

1. The purposes of the training make me eager to begin.
   <u>   purposes   make   </u>
2. The leader of the trainees selects a deputy.
   <u>   leader   selects   </u>

3. One among the flock of swans/maintains guard.

    <u>One</u>   <u>maintains</u>

4. The difference between the two men/appears when they are at a game.

    <u>difference</u>   <u>appears</u>

5. The troublemakers on the squad/were hard to locate.

    <u>troublemakers</u>   <u>were</u>

If a verb is preceded by auxiliaries, the subject is tied to the first auxiliary.

Examples: The visitor has gone.

             The visitors have gone.

Exercise 14–17

Rewrite these sentences, changing the singular subjects to plural ones. Underline the auxiliary that is tied to the subject.

1. The patient is being watched.

    <u>Patients are</u>

2. The janitor has waxed the floor.

    <u>Janitors have</u>

3. The wrestler does not smoke.

    <u>Wrestler do</u>

4. The car has been stolen.

    <u>Cars have</u>

5. The ship was disappearing beyond the horizon.

    <u>ships were</u>

Thus we see that subject and verb, and subject and auxiliary, are tied together by reciprocal changes in form. But there is a difficulty here. Of all the auxiliaries only *be, have,* and *do* have an inflectional -s ending for the third person singular. The others—*can, could, may, might, shall, should, will, would, must, ought*—have the same form throughout the singular and plural.

> **Examples:** Singular: He *will* go.
>   Plural: They *will* go.
>   Singular: The neighbor *may* help.
>   Plural: The neighbors *may* help.

Likewise, the forms of the past tense have no singular-plural change of form that can show a subject-verb tie.

> **Examples:** Singular: I *sang.*
>   Plural: We *sang.*
>   Singular: The thief *ran.*
>   Plural: The thieves *ran.*

How, then, can we find the subject where no tie is perceptible in the form of the verb or auxiliary? It is done this way: Change the verb or auxiliary to another form that is capable of agreement. In the case of a past-tense verb, test its form in the present tense with the third person singular and plural. For example, to find the subject of

The sopranos in the choir *sang* well.

change *sang* to *sings* and *sing:*

The sopranos in the choir *sing* well.
The soprano in the choir *sings* well.

Sopranos sing are the tied forms, or those that are in agreement; hence *sopranos* is also the simple subject in *The sopranos sang.* In the case of an auxiliary verb, such as those mentioned above that do not alter their form, a testing strategy would be to remove it temporarily from its verb phrase and test the next subsequent verb. This becomes necessary because a modal auxiliary such as *can* or *should* is not only uninflected, but also followed by uninflected forms. By removing the modal you may test the next auxiliary or main verb, which can then be inflected. We can see how this works with a sentence such as "The boy could have sung." Although no inflectional distinction occurs between the singular and plural sentence "The boy could have sung" or "The boys could have sung," the removal of "could" gives us an important inflectional distinction in the sentences "The boy has sung" and "The boys have sung." The test then confirms that "the boy" was the subject in our original sentence containing the word *could.*

The following exercise will give you some practice in using verb forms to help identify the subject of a clause or sentence. Remember as you do the exercise that although noun plurals frequently take an *-s* to show a plural, the presence of an *-s* on a verb is a sign of the third person present tense *singular.*

Exercise 14–18

In each of the sentences below, locate the verb (or auxiliary) that you think is tied to the subject and place it in the first blank provided. Then provide a third person present-tense singular and present-tense plural form of that verb. Having done this, you are now able to locate the simple subject of the sentence and test your decisions. The simple subject will be the noun or pronoun that must change its form to accommodate the altered forms of the verb. In the blanks next to the singular and plural verb forms, provide the appropriate form that the subject would have to take to accommodate the two different forms of the verb.

1. The cat with the brown fur slept on the table.
   Verb: _Slept_
   Present singular verb form: _sleeps_   Noun singular: _Cat_
   Present plural verb form: _sleep_   Noun plural: _Cats_

2. After several hours under the tree on a hot day, the schoolboy called softly to his friends.
   Verb: _called_
   Present singular verb form: _Calls_   Noun singular: _schoolboy_
   Present plural verb form: _Call_   Noun plural: _schoolboys_

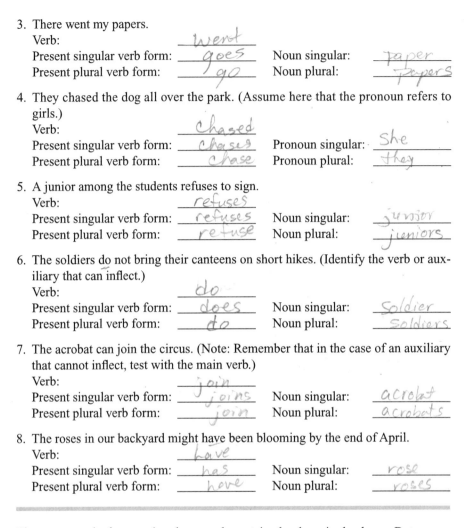

3. There went my papers.
   Verb: _went_
   Present singular verb form: _goes_ Noun singular: _paper_
   Present plural verb form: _go_ Noun plural: _papers_

4. They chased the dog all over the park. (Assume here that the pronoun refers to girls.)
   Verb: _chased_
   Present singular verb form: _chases_ Pronoun singular: _She_
   Present plural verb form: _chase_ Pronoun plural: _they_

5. A junior among the students refuses to sign.
   Verb: _refuses_
   Present singular verb form: _refuses_ Noun singular: _junior_
   Present plural verb form: _refuse_ Noun plural: _juniors_

6. The soldiers do not bring their canteens on short hikes. (Identify the verb or auxiliary that can inflect.)
   Verb: _do_
   Present singular verb form: _does_ Noun singular: _Soldier_
   Present plural verb form: _do_ Noun plural: _Soldiers_

7. The acrobat can join the circus. (Note: Remember that in the case of an auxiliary that cannot inflect, test with the main verb.)
   Verb: _join_
   Present singular verb form: _joins_ Noun singular: _acrobat_
   Present plural verb form: _join_ Noun plural: _acrobats_

8. The roses in our backyard might have been blooming by the end of April.
   Verb: _have_
   Present singular verb form: _has_ Noun singular: _rose_
   Present plural verb form: _have_ Noun plural: _roses_

The sentences in the exercise above each contained only a single clause. But as you might guess, many sentences contain more than one clause. In those cases, the process of identifying the subject of a given clause within the sentence remains the same. Consider the sentences below, each of which contains more than one clause. The verbs (and auxiliaries) in the sentences below have all been italicized.

1. When the insurance agent *came* he *spoke* very frankly to our family.
2. The storybook character *sits* on a wall, and he *has* a great fall.
3. The workers *know* that the horses *have traveled* a great distance.

A second test for locating the subject of a clause or sentence is what we will call the "front-shift" test. We will employ this test to locate the "complete subject" of a sentence. To apply the front-shift test you simply change a statement into a yes-or-no question, as in these sentences:

1. Statement: [That tall man with the yellow checked shirt] is her teacher.
   Yes-or-no question: *Is* [that tall man with the yellow checked shirt] her teacher?

2. Statement: [The student who told me] could have been wrong.
   Yes-or-no question: *Could* [the student who told me] have been wrong?

3. Statement: [The cowboy who was leading the parade] rode a brown horse.
   Yes-or-no question: *Did* [the cowboy who was leading the parade] ride a brown horse?

Now note what happened in these sentences. In the first statement the verb *be* was front-shifted to the beginning of the yes-or-no question. In the second statement the first auxiliary was front-shifted. In the third statement, which has no auxiliary, the auxiliary *did* was supplied and placed in the front-shift position at the beginning of the yes-or-no question. The part of the statement around which the front-shift occurs is the complete subject.

Exercise 14–19

Change each statement into a yes-or-no question. Then underline the complete subject.

1. The boy who mows the lawn was ill.
   Was the boy who mows the lawn ill?
2. Her youngest brother broke his bicycle.
   Did her youngest brother break his bicycle?
3. The students on the debate squad should be excused.
   Should the students on the debate squad be excused?
4. The monkeys playing on the swings are from India.
   Are the monkeys playing on the swings from India?
5. The old gymnasium, which was built in 1907, will be replaced.
   Will the old gymnasium, which was built in 1907, be replaced?

A third strategy for determining the subject of a sentence is to locate the main verb and ask yourself who or what in relation to the verb. For example with a sentence such as "The criminal in the blue jailhouse clothes made a daring escape," we locate the verb phrase "made a daring escape" and ask ourselves, "Who or what made a daring escape?" The answer to this question is the subject. Thus the simple subject is "criminal," and the complete subject is "The criminal in the blue jailhouse clothes."

The ability to identify the complete subject helps in identifying the predicate of the sentence. In English the predicate is the complete verb phrase, including all of its objects and modifiers. Thus unless the sentence has included conjoined material (such as another sentence that has been joined on with the conjunction *and*), everything in the sentence besides the complete subject is the predicate. As it relates to the English language, the term *predicate* can be synonymous with *verb phrase,* but sometimes linguists might prefer using the term *predicate* because some languages other than English use sentences that consist of a subject and predicate and yet do not contain a verb phrase. Speakers of such a language might, for example, say "The instructor angry" rather than "The instructor is angry."

Some Observations and Applications

In this chapter you have learned that noun and verb subclasses may be identified not only by their morphological behavior, as we saw in an earlier chapter, but also according to the kinds of syntactic behavior that they display. In the case of nouns, a recognition of the difference between count and mass nouns has important implications for teaching English to nonnative speakers. Although both count and mass nouns use the definite article *the,* only count nouns may use the indefinite article *a* or *an.* Count nouns may be pluralized, whether that involves an inflection like *-s* or whether it involves mutating their forms, as in the word *geese.* Mass nouns, on the other hand, occur only in the singular form. Similarly, although count nouns use the quantifier *many*, mass nouns use the quantifier *much.* It would be incorrect to ask someone whether they had *many* sugars on hand or whether they had *much* pencils that you could borrow. Thus the distinction between count and mass is signaled in our syntax and morphology and is useful for nonnative speakers to know about as well as for those who teach them.

But the value of being able to distinguish between count and mass nouns is not limited to teaching English to nonnative speakers. There are some stylistic choices related to count and mass nouns that native speakers may not always realize but that careful writers should consider. Although the word *more* can be used to express an increase in a count or mass noun ("more dogs" or "more mud"), expressing a reduction requires us to make a decision between the words *less* and *fewer.* The word *fewer* is used for count nouns whereas *less* is used with mass nouns. Careful writers also maintain a similar distinction between expressions such as "number of" (used with count nouns) and "amount of" (used with mass nouns). For example, it is stylistically preferable to say "We had a large number of people there" rather than "We had a large amount of people there."

The subclasses of verbs play an even more important role in syntax than the subclasses of nouns, because verbs determine the overall pattern of a sentence. The next chapter examines the sentence patterns of English, so we will not show applications of verb phrase knowledge here.

In this chapter we have moved from nouns and verbs to a consideration of noun phrases and verb phrases. This consideration is necessary because nouns and verbs behave as part of phrases and not as individual words. If I were to program a computer to communicate like a speaker of English, I would need to incorporate information about phrase structure. Consider the sentence "The manager gave his employee a book." The noun phrases in this sentence are *the manager, his employee,* and *a book.* If the computer is to answer questions and sound natural (like a native speaker), it must answer with noun phrases rather than just with nouns. For example, to the question "What did the manager give his employee?" a native speaker wouldn't answer with merely *book,* but rather *a book.* A single-word answer, of course, could be appropriate if it constitutes a noun phrase all by itself, as in "Tom brought a gift" in which *Tom* is a subject noun phrase.

This chapter has considered the matter of agreement between subjects and verbs. For most sentences native speakers have no problem deciding whether to use a singular or plural verb form. But there are situations in which speakers can benefit from a greater understanding of what constitutes the subject of the sentence. We will examine this issue further in a later chapter on usage.

15

Basic Sentence Patterns

Consider the structure of the two sentences below. How do the sentences differ? What grammatical function does the word *cars* have in each sentence?

We sold the plastic model cars.

We sold the brunette model cars.

In the previous chapter you saw that the subject of the sentence typically precedes the verb. In a similar way, other grammatical meanings are commonly found in particular positions within the sentence. Consider the difference that position makes in the grammatical interpretation of a noun such as *boy*. If we say "The boy saw the girl," it is clear that the boy is the one who has done the seeing and the girl that has been seen. But if we reverse the position of *boy* and *girl* we get the sentence "The girl saw the boy" in which it is clearly the girl who has done the seeing and the boy who has been seen. Thus although *the boy* can be the subject when it precedes the verb, it can alternatively serve as the direct object when it follows the verb.

But a noun phrase directly following a verb is not always a direct object. As we interpret a sentence we must consider its overall structural pattern, which can influence the grammatical meaning that we attribute to a particular noun phrase. For example, a single noun phrase following a transitive verb is a direct object, but if we perceive two noun phrases directly following a transitive verb, we will analyze the sentence pattern differently and frequently identify the first noun phrase after the verb as an indirect object rather than a direct object. Compare the sentence "Tarzan cooked the dog" with the sentence "Tarzan cooked the dog some meat." In the former sentence the position of the single noun phrase *the dog* right after the verb helps us to interpret *the dog* as the direct object and thus what is being cooked. But in the latter sentence even though *the dog* occupies the same place after the verb, the presence of two noun phrases after the verb causes us to alter our analysis of the sentence pattern and to interpret *some meat* as the direct object (what is being cooked), and *the dog,* fortunately enough, as the indirect object (the person or thing for which the meat is being cooked). As you might expect, our analysis of a particular sentence pattern is also related to whether we interpret a particular verb as transitive, intransitive, or linking.

We can see from this that distinguishing grammatical meanings or functions in a sentence and distinguishing sentence types are related activities. In this chapter we will examine some basic sentence patterns and subpatterns of English. Included within these sentence patterns are specific sentence positions, each representing the home-slot of a particular grammatical meaning (function).[1] Even as we speak of "sentence types," you should realize that we could be discussing the same material in terms of "clause types" because a simple sentence is a single clause.

Pattern 1: SV (Subject + Verb)

Our girls smile.

In the basic patterns we will be looking at, the subject always occurs in the first noun phrase position. In pattern 1 the grammatical meaning of the subject is "that which performs the action." The verb in pattern 1 is intransitive. As you recall, an intransitive verb is self-sufficient; it can stand alone with its subject.

1. The sportsman *fished.*
2. The sportsmen *were fishing.*

It can be modified by words and word groups known as adverbs and adverbials.

Examples: The sportsmen fished *early.*
The sportsmen were fishing *in the stream.*
The sportsmen were fishing *when we drove up.*

But an intransitive verb is usually not completed by a noun phrase (which could involve a noun or pronoun). For example, in

They finished late

finished is intransitive, but in

They finished the game

and

They finished it

finished is not intransitive because it is completed by a noun phrase. If you are in doubt whether a word following the verb is a modifier that goes with an intransitive verb or a completer of a transitive verb, a substitution can settle the matter. If you can substitute *him, her, it,* or *them,* the word is a completer and the verb is not intransitive.

---

[1]The taxonomy of seven basic sentence types, which we will use, is based on a list of clause types provided by Randolph Quirk and Sidney Greenbaum in their book *A Concise Grammar of Contemporary English.* San Diego: Harcourt Brace Jovanovich, 1973, pp. 166–167.

Examples: 1. He hammered fast.
2. He hammered the nail.

In the first sentence you cannot substitute *it* without spoiling the structural meaning. But in the second sentence, *He hammered it* is a suitable equivalent for *He hammered the nail.* Therefore the first *hammered* is intransitive and the second one transitive.

The subject of the verb in pattern 1, and also in patterns 4, 5, 6, and 7 to follow (and sometimes in 3), has the grammatical meaning of "performer of the action."

Some intransitive verbs characteristically do not occur alone but take an adverbial modifier. Examples: *lurk, sneak, lurch, sally, sidle, tamper, lie, live.* The last one, *live,* takes an adverbial modifier in three meanings: "reside" as in "He lives in Mexico"; "stay alive" as in "He lives on soy bean products"; "be alive" as in "He lived in the first half of the twentieth century." Also, intransitive verbs with a passive sense based on transitive verbs take an adverbial modifier, as in "Your car rides comfortably," and "Her book is selling well." If the intransitive verb requires an adverbial modifier in order to be completed, consider that verb to be part of a pattern 3 (to be discussed later).

Exercise 15–1

Write InV after each sentence that contains an intransitive verb. All such InV sentences will be examples of pattern 1, an SV sentence pattern.

1. The audience clapped. _____InV_____
2. The audience clapped loudly. _____InV_____
3. The audience clapped loudly after the main act. _____InV_____
4. The audience clapped their hands. _____
5. They were relaxing quietly at the table. _____InV_____
6. They were drinking bottled water. _____
7. She always paid. _____InV_____
8. He paid his bills on the first of the month. _____
9. Jack left early. _____InV_____
10. Jack left his clothes in the closet. _____
11. We traveled comfortably. _____InV_____
12. A strange man is waiting outside. _____InV_____
13. He studied through the night. _____InV_____
14. Who brought my fishing tackle? _____
15. The children behaved admirably. _____InV_____

Pattern 2: SVC (Subject +Verb + Subjective Complement)

The program became elaborate.
Our friend is a senator.

In pattern 2 the grammatical meaning of the subject is "that which is described or which may be identified as." This pattern will be referred to as an SVC pattern, which means that it consists of a subject, verb, and complement. In a general sense the term *complement* is broadly used for referring to an element that is necessary to complete a phrase, but as we label sentence patterns we will be using the term more specifically to refer to either a subjective or objective complement. In the case of the SVC sentence type that we are discussing here, the complement is a subjective complement, describing or identifying the subject of the sentence. The subjective complement is joined to the subject with a linking verb. This pattern has two main subpatterns that we will consider. The first subpattern is

Subpattern 2A: NP + Linking Verb + Adjective

The food is good.
The manager seems upset.

In subpattern 2A, the third term must be an adjective or adjectival (that is, an adjective-like element[2]).

The verb in this subpattern must be a linking verb. In addition to *be* (or one of its forms) the set of linking verbs includes the following verbs or their respective forms: *seem, appear, become, grow, remain, taste, look, feel, smell, sound, get, continue, or go.* Most of the verbs listed here can occur in other sentence patterns as well, so it is important to know not only which verbs can occur in this subpattern but also how to recognize and distinguish this subpattern from other patterns containing the same verbs. We will provide some tests that should prove useful to you. With a little practice you should be able to distinguish these patterns without such tests, but in the beginning, tests like these can be useful.

The first test involves distinguishing subpattern 2A when it involves the linking verb *be*. The test for this is simple. It involves this expansion:

That food is good > That good food is very good.
That food is poisonous > That poisonous food is very poisonous.

If a sentence will not undergo this expansion, it usually belongs to some pattern other than subpattern 2A. For example, the sentence

My mother is outside

cannot be expanded to

*My outside mother is very outside.

So this sentence does not belong to the subpattern 2A type. The adjective in subpattern 2A is, in grammatical meaning, a modifier of the subject.

Sometimes a prepositional phrase will, as a modifier of the NP, occupy the Adj position, as in

---

[2]We will be examining the positional classes of nominals, verbals, adjectivals, and adverbials in the next chapter.

The teacher was in a bad mood. (= irritable)

His explanation was over my head. (= incomprehensible)

Exercise 15–2

Apply the expansion test to see which of these sentences belong to subpattern 2A. Write 2A after such sentences.

1. The box is large.   _____2A_____
2. The box is here.   _____
3. My mother is kind.   _____2A_____
4. My mother is out.   _____
5. The boys were busy.   _____2A_____
6. The boys were below.   _____
7. The dahlias have been lovely.   ____2A____
8. The party must have been enjoyable. ___2A___
9. The party was afterward.   _____
10. Her brother was hungry.   _____2A_____

The foregoing test for subpattern 2A does not work in all cases. Nor, for that matter, does any grammatical rule or test, unless it is accompanied by exceptions and qualifications. There is a limited number of adjectives that can occur in either the first or the second slot, but not in both, in a subpattern 2A sentence like

The _____ food (= any noun) is very _____ .

For example, some adjectives are used only before a noun, such as *main* and *utter.* Some others appear, in this pattern, after *be + very,* such as *afraid,* but not before the noun. Still others are restricted in various ways.[3] Furthermore, not all adjectives can be modified by *very.* We do not say, for instance, *"the very main speaker." But, apart from such aberrations, the test for subpattern 2A is useful.

The other test, which may be applied to not only a form of *be* but any of the linking verbs, is to see whether the verb in question may undergo substitution with a form of *seem.* The use of *seem* may change the meaning a little, but you are testing to see whether the substitution will work syntactically, not whether the two sentences will be synonymous semantically. If the substitution may be made and if what follows the verb is an adjectival describing the subject of the sentence, then you have a linking verb and a subpattern 2A. But if the substitution can't be made, then your verb is probably not a linking verb, and you probably have a pattern other than 2A. Consider the examples below:

---

[3]For example, *faint* and *ready* go in the first slot when the noun modified is inanimate, as in "a faint breeze" and "a ready answer." But they do not go in the first slot when the noun is animate, that is, in cases like *"a faint player" and *"a ready coach." The last two both sound un-English. Again, consider *due.* We can say "The train is due" but not *"The train is very *due." We ordinarily do not use *due* before a noun, as in *"the due train," but we do use it before a noun in a few set phrases such as "with due respect" and "in due time."

Subject + Linking Verb + Adjectival   1. John appeared weary. (John seemed weary.)

Subject + Verb + Adverbial   2. John grew quickly. (*John seemed quickly.)

In the examples above, only the first sentence could replace its main verb with a form of *seem*. We can say "John seemed weary" but not "*John seemed quickly." Thus we can say that the first sentence is a subpattern 2A and involves a linking verb, whereas the second one does not.

Exercise 15–3

Write the subpattern number *2A* or *other* after each sentence.

1. The milk remained sweet for a week.   *2A*
2. The newcomer remained quietly in her room.   *other*
3. The dog smelled hungrily at the package.   *other*
4. The dog smells bad.   *2A*
5. You look sharp today.   *2A*
6. He looked sharply to the right.   *other*
7. The detective felt cautiously in the box.   *other*
8. He feels cautious about taking the risk.   *2A*
9. That apprentice looks careful.   *2A*
10. The apprentice looked carefully at the new machine.   *other*
11. Our teacher's assignments were easy.   *2A*
12. The book was costly.   *2A*
13. Peter's dogs were outside.   *other*
14. They were sleeping.   *other*

Linking verbs may of course be preceded by auxiliaries.

Examples: The party *may become* lively.

Your sister *must have seemed* friendly.

In addition to the limited number of common linking verbs, other verbs not usually thought of as linking may on occasion be followed by an adjective and therefore conform to subpattern 2A.

Examples: The screw *worked* loose.

The defendant *stood* firm.

His face *went* pale.

The well *ran* dry.

He *proved* true to his cause.

For verbs like these one can substitute *be, become,* or *remain* with no substantial change of meaning.

Exercise 15–4

Write the subpattern number *2A* or *other* after each sentence.

1. The child stood for the flag.   *other*
2. Jameson stood loyal to his firm.   *2A*
3. The students in the back row look sleepy.   *2A*
4. The investigator looked outside.   *other*
5. Penelope turned red at the thought.   *2A*
6. She lay motionless on the hospital bed.   *2A*
7. Jim fell sick during the night.   *2A*
8. The wind blew strongly through the tall pines.   *other*
9. The soda may stay cold until evening.   *2A*
10. You will never keep slender that way.   *2A*

The second subpattern of 2 is

Subpattern 2B: NP¹ + Linking Verb + NP¹

My friend is a doctor.
The girl remained a good student.

The superscript after the second NP indicates that this noun phrase has the same reference as the first noun phrase; that is, in the first sentence both *my friend* and *a doctor* refer to the same person, and in the second sentence both *the girl* and *a good student* refer to the same person. The linking verbs in subpattern 2B mean "be identified or classified as." The first NP (subject) has the grammatical meaning of "that which is identified." The second NP means grammatically "that which identifies the subject" and is a subjective complement just as the adjective is in subpattern 2A. The number of linking verbs that may occupy the verbal position in this subpattern is very small. Among them are *be, remain, become, appear, seem, continue, stay,* and *make.* Sentences that follow subpattern 2B should not be confused with those in which the noun phrase after the verb does not have the same referent as the first noun phrase.

Examples: 2B   Donald *continued* my friend, despite our differences.
other   Donald *met* my friend in the barber shop.
2B   My brother *became* a doctor.
other   My brother was *seeking* a doctor.

Exercise 15–5

Write the subpattern number *2B* or *other* after each sentence.

1. Alma became the class president.   *2B*
2. After two years of faithful service the corporal
   became a sergeant.   *2B*
3. The military police restrained the sergeant from
   entering the hall.   *other*

4. A snake was under the rock. *other*

5. The chief seemed a good fellow. *2B*

6. We saw the fellow. *other*

7. We stayed partners for years. *2B*

8. The governor stayed the execution. *Other*

9. A cowboy is a hard worker. *2B*

10. They appeared friends to all of us. *2B*

11. We shall continue the discussion tomorrow. *other*

12. Johannes had remained a bachelor for reasons of his own. *2B*

13. My sister makes a delicious fruitcake. *other*

14. A fruitcake makes a fine gift. *2B*

15. This is her husband. *2B*

Up to this point, our discussion of subpattern 2B has involved subjective complements that are nouns. But a pronoun can also serve as a subjective complement as in the sentence "This is she." This observation does not invalidate our structural description of subpattern 2B (NP^1 + Linking Verb + NP^1) because, as you will probably recall, the term *noun phrase* does not include only nouns but can also be used to refer to pronouns. Determining the appropriate form of pronoun to serve as a subjective complement has sometimes posed a problem, even for native speakers. But an understanding of the kind of pattern involved and the pronoun paradigm that we have already studied in an earlier chapter should help you understand the grammatical issues involved. Because the subjective complement essentially renames the subject of the sentence, the traditional prescriptive grammar rule requires that any pronoun being used as a subjective complement use the subject form of the pronoun. Thus one would not say "This is her" but rather "This is she" because *her* is an object form.

As it turns out, understanding the traditional rule is a little easier than deciding what might be appropriate for a given context. Some uses that clearly place a speaker in good stead with prescriptive grammarians may not work well for a speaker in a particular social setting. Saying something like "It is I" instead of "It's me" could put a chill on an otherwise friendly and informal conversation. And even when the use of traditional prescriptive rules is expected, the strict application of such rules sometimes sounds incorrect. But being a capable speaker and writer of English requires that a person be able to make informed choices in a given occasion. Informed choices are not available to those who are unfamiliar with the options of formal and informal speech and writing. As a native speaker you are likely to be able to use the informal forms quite naturally, so we will briefly practice the more formal or, as some prescriptive grammarians would say, "correct" forms in the exercise below.

Exercise 15–6

Examine the sentences below. For each sentence decide whether the pronoun form that is used in the subjective complement position follows the traditional rule. Answer either yes or no in each blank provided.

1. The caller to the radio show was him.   _NO_
2. It is me.   _NO_
3. It was they.   _Yes_
4. That is she.   _Yes_
5. I am he.   _Yes_
6. This is it.   _Yes_
7. The people knocking at your door will be them.   _NO_

Some of the sentences in the above exercise likely sound a little different from what you are accustomed to saying in your normal speech. And the kind of prescriptive rule that we have shown you can lead to an occasional sentence that will probably sound absolutely bizarre to a native speaker. Consider the sentence "The people singing on the cassette tape were we." In such a case it becomes important to make a decision about which usage carries the greater risk: (1) using a form that is technically correct according to some traditional grammarians but will sound terrible and unnatural to virtually everyone else, including even educated speakers, or (2) using a form that although it might be incorrect from a prescriptive viewpoint nonetheless will sound correct to most people, including educated people, or (3) recasting your sentence to avoid the issue altogether. In cases such as the one we have been discussing, options 2 and 3 are probably the most desirable.

Pattern 3: SVA (Subject + Verb + Adverbial)[4]

The girl   is   here.

Pattern 3 usually consists of a subject followed by a form of *be* and an adverb or other word(s) that can occupy the same kind of syntactic position and perform an equivalent function to an adverb (we will learn more about such adverbials in the next chapter). Sometimes the pattern involves an intransitive verb such as *reside* followed by an obligatory adverbial as in "The president resides on this street." A pattern 3 sentence such as "Ramon was inside" might superficially resemble a subpattern 2A sentence such as "Ramon was ecstatic." But there are important differences:

1. The verb *be* in this pattern usually has the meaning of "be located" or "occur."

2. Pattern 3 is not capable of taking the subpattern 2A expansion.

3. The third position is occupied by an adverbial rather than an adjectival. Words of this type are typically uninflected words and include *here, there, up, down,*

---

[4]The label of SVA does not indicate a sentence type in which an intransitive verb is followed by an optional adverb (or adverbial) as in "He ran fast." Rather we are following the practice of Quirk and Greenbaum in using this label for the sentence type in which the presence of an adverb (or adverbial) is necessary for the completion of the sentence. The majority of the main sentence types discussed in this chapter could optionally be followed by an adverb or adverbial, so distinguishing each of those additional options would result in an unnecessary redundancy in categories. It will suffice just to acknowledge that most of the sentence types given could accommodate an additional adverb or adverbial.

in, out, inside, outside, upstairs, downstairs, on, off, now, then, tomorrow, yesterday, over, through, above, below, before, after. Up, in, and *out* are partially and/or irregularly inflected with the forms *upper, uppermost, inner, inmost, innermost, outer, outermost, utmost, outmost.* For most words in the third position one can substitute *there* or *then.*

Examples: The pingpong table is downstairs.
The game was yesterday.
The balls are outdoors.

Often a prepositional phrase with a *there* or *then* meaning will occupy the third position.

Examples: The wolf is at the door.
The game will be at three o'clock.

The grammatical meaning of the subject in pattern 3 is typically "that about which an assertion is made," and that of the adverbial is "modifier of the verb."

Exercise 15–7

After each sentence place a number 2A or 3 to identify the pattern it conforms to.

1. The picnic was outside. _____
2. The picnickers were happy. _____
3. The batter is tall. _____
4. The batter is inside. _____
5. They are on the lawn. _____
6. Our appointment is now. _____
7. The meeting will be in an hour. _____
8. The dean is in. _____
9. The dean is benevolent. _____
10. The bunks are below. _____

Pattern 4: SVO (Subject + Verb + Direct Object)

The girl   bought   a   dress.

In pattern 4 the verb is transitive and is completed by a noun phrase, for which one can readily substitute *him, her, it,* or *them.* This noun phrase is called the direct object of the verb and has the grammatical meaning of "undergoer of the action" or "that affected by the verb." As a means for identifying direct objects these descriptions of meaning are roughly adequate, but you must remember that a direct object does not always experience any actual action. This is evident in a sentence such as "We heard the radio" in which "the radio" is the direct object but does not experience any real action.

Normally the direct object is not the same person or thing as the subject. However, with two kinds of pronouns, the direct object does have the same referent as the subject. One is the set of *-self/-selves* pronouns, generally known as the reflexive pronouns. These occur as direct object in sentences such as

She saw *herself.*
The lifeguards splashed *themselves.*

The other set consists of the reciprocal pronouns *each other* and *one another*, which function as direct objects in such sentences as

They found *each other.*
They fought *one another.*

Exercise 15–8

After each sentence write the pronoun that you can substitute for the italicized direct object. In the case of bracketed information, provide the reflexive or reciprocal pronouns that would be necessary to fill in the accompanying blank with an equivalent idea.

1. The salesman sold *the car.*　　　　　　　＿＿＿＿＿＿＿＿＿＿
2. Both soldiers saluted *the colonel.*　　　＿＿＿＿＿＿＿＿＿＿
3. Mrs. Grundy grew *roses* every year.　　＿＿＿＿＿＿＿＿＿＿
4. At the desk we met *the nurse.*　　　　　＿＿＿＿＿＿＿＿＿＿
5. The chauffeur repaired *the tire.*　　　　＿＿＿＿＿＿＿＿＿＿
6. The collision broke *the wheel.*　　　　　＿＿＿＿＿＿＿＿＿＿
7. I met *your sister.*　　　　　　　　　　　＿＿＿＿＿＿＿＿＿＿
8. The veterinarian carried *the dog.*　　　＿＿＿＿＿＿＿＿＿＿
9. We trimmed *the bushes.*　　　　　　　　＿＿＿＿＿＿＿＿＿＿
10. [Jill criticized Sarah, and Sarah criticized Jill.]
    In fact, for two years they criticized ＿＿＿＿＿＿ .　　＿＿＿＿＿　＿＿＿＿＿
11. [Billy taught Billy.] He taught ＿＿＿＿＿＿ .　　＿＿＿＿＿＿＿＿＿＿
12. [Jessica apologized to me, and I apologized to her.]
    We apologized to ＿＿＿＿＿＿＿＿＿＿ .　　＿＿＿＿＿　＿＿＿＿＿

You have seen that a transitive verb such as those in the sentences above contrasts with an intransitive verb of pattern 1, which does not take a direct object.

Examples:　Intransitive:　She sang beautifully.
　　　　　　　Transitive:　 She sang a beautiful folk song.

As shown in the pair of examples above, most English verbs can occur transitively and intransitively, and relatively few can occur only transitively or intransitively.

Examples:　Intransitive only:　The ship had vanished.
　　　　　　　Transitive only:　 We enjoyed the party.

In this exercise you are to distinguish, as a review, among linking verbs, intransitive verbs, and transitive verbs. After each sentence place an LV, InT, and TV to label the head verb. In the second blank write the number of the sentence pattern.

1. The center *passed* the ball to the quarterback. _____ _____
2. She *is* inside. _____ _____
3. Chris *became* a skillful tennis player. _____ _____
4. The sheriff *was* the leader of the posse. _____ _____
5. The sheriff *was leading* the posse. _____ _____
6. Your doughnuts *smell* delicious. _____ _____
7. Who *is leading* now? _____ _____
8. Harris *remained* the assistant coach. _____ _____
9. The dean *made* an important announcement. _____ _____
10. Your violin tone *sounds* rather squeaky. _____ _____
11. The announcement *may be* helpful to you. _____ _____
12. The firm *sent* a form letter to all its customers. _____ _____
13. A French poodle *makes* an affectionate pet. _____ _____
14. The driver *turned* sharply. _____ _____
15. The driver *turned* the car around. _____ _____
16. Emily Walton *was* the judge in the case. _____ _____

A transitive verb has two forms, which we call active and passive. The active form is the one that is followed by the direct object, which we have seen in pattern 4. From this active form we can make the passive form. Here is an illustration:

Active: The chef cooked the meal.

Passive: The meal was cooked (by the chef).

In this process there are four things to notice:

1. The object of the active form becomes the subject of the passive form. This is shown above in the shift of *meal.*

2. The passive is made up of a form of the verb *be* plus a past participle, as in *was cooked.*

3. The subject of the active verb may be made the object of the preposition *by,* or it may be suppressed.

4. In the passive, two grammatical meanings are shifted around. The performer of the action, *chef,* is now the object of the preposition, and the undergoer, *meal,* is the subject.

These sentences contain transitive verbs in the active form. Change the sentences to the passive form.

1. The servant opened the window.
   The window was opened by the servant.
2. He rolled the dice.
   The dice was rolled by him.
3. Most adolescents enjoy dancing.
   Dancing is enjoyed by most adolescents.
4. We chose the mountains for our vacation.
   (past tense)   *The mountains were chosen for our vacation.*
5. Jim has never read *King Lear*.
   King Lear has never been read by Jim.
6. The tourists burned wood in the fireplace.
   Wood was burned in the fireplace by the tourists.
7. The shepherd counted the sheep.
   The sheep were counted by the shepherd.
8. We began the game at four o'clock.
   The game was begun at four o'clock.
9. The Smiths built a new house on the river.
   The new house on the river was built by the Smiths.
10. The nature club spotted a pileated woodpecker.
    A pileated woodpecker was spotted by the nature club.

Exercise 15–11

These sentences contain transitive verbs in the passive form. For each verb construction underline the *be* auxiliary once and the past participle twice. Then change the sentences to the active form. In cases where there is no *by* phrase, you will have to supply a subject.

1. The rat was killed by the terrier.
   The terrier was killed by the rat
2. The pancakes were turned by the cook.
   The cook turned the pancakes
3. Much corn is raised in Iowa.
   Iowa raises much corn.   *Farmers raise much corn in Iowa.*
4. An early folk tune was heard.
   We heard an early folk tune
5. The dishes have been washed.
   They have washed the dishes.
6. A good time was had by all.
   They all had a good time.
7. Jane was teased by Allison's boyfriend.
   Allison's boyfriend was teased by Jane.
8. The flag had been lowered.
   He lowered the flag.
9. The motorcycles were stopped by the traffic officer.
   The traffic officer stopped the motorcycles.

10. A carillon concert is played at 7:45 in the morning.

At 7:45 the musician plays Carillon a concert.

English also has a passive in which *be* is replaced by *get,* e.g.,

Active: The teacher excused Bill.
Passive: Bill got excused by the teacher.
Active: Helen rewarded him.
Passive: He got rewarded.

This *get* passive is useful in avoiding the occasional ambiguity of the *be* passive, as in

The gate was closed at ten o'clock.

This can mean either "Someone closed the gate at ten" or "The gate was not open at ten." With *got* only the first meaning is possible:

The gate got closed at ten.

Not all verbs accept the *get* passive, e.g.,

*The fiesta got enjoyed by the guests.

There is in English a tiny group of transitive verbs called middle verbs that do not form the passive. These are illustrated in the sentences below. Try turning each sentence into the passive and see if the result sounds English to your ears.

The box contains a pair of shoes.
She lacks the necessary money.
A wondrous adventure befell our hero.
Your humor eludes me.
He can afford a new car.
My mother has a new car.
The apple cost fifty cents.
They parted company.

Verbs with reflexive pronouns are not made passive, e.g.,

He scratched himself.

Pattern 5: SVOO (Subject + Verb + Indirect Object + Direct Object)

The mother   bought   the girl   a dress.

In pattern 5 there are some important matters to be observed:

1. The verb of this pattern must be transitive.

2. We see two grammatical objects after the verb *bought*. These two objects are called, in order, the indirect and the direct object. If we omit the first one, the pattern becomes number 4 and *dress* is seen to be the direct object.

3. The indirect object may often be replaced by a prepositional phrase beginning with *to* or *for*, or occasionally with a different preposition.

   Examples: He sold *the student* a ticket.
   He sold a ticket *to the student.*

   He built *them* a playpen.
   He built a playpen *for them.*

   He played *me* a game of chess.
   He played a game of chess *with me.*

   He asked *her* a question.
   He asked a question *of her.*

4. The verbs that can be used in pattern 5 are in a restricted group. Some of the common ones are *give, make, find, tell, buy, write, send, ask, play, build, teach, assign, feed, offer, throw, hand, pass, sell, pay.*

5. A pattern 5 sentence may be transformed into the passive by making either the direct or the indirect object the subject of the passive verb:

   A dress was bought the girl by her mother.
   The girl was bought a dress by her mother.

   In some cases, however, the passive transformation does not sound fully natural and seems to demand a preposition, as in

   The sergeant found the recruit a rifle.
   A rifle was found (*for*) the recruit by the sergeant.

6. The grammatical meaning of the indirect object is "beneficiary of the action of the verb-plus-direct-object."

7. If the direct object is a pronoun, it must precede the other object, which is moved back within a prepositional phrase:

   The mother bought *it* for the girl.
   Not *The mother bought the girl *it.*

   This movement occurs even if both objects in the sentence are pronouns:

   The mother bought *it* for her.
   Not *The mother bought her *it.*

Exercise 15–12

The following sentences follow pattern 5. Replace the indirect object by a prepositional phrase. Put the latter where it sounds most natural.

1. The librarian found me the pamphlet.
   The librarian found the pamphlet for me.

2. He assigned Jack the toughest job.

   He assigned the toughest job to Jack.

3. The spaniel brought his master the stick.

   The spaniel brought his master the stick.

4. Susie fed the baby robins some juicy worms.

   Susie fed some juicy worms to the baby robins.

5. Her mother sent her a new sweater.

   Her mother sent a new sweater to her.

Exercise 15-13

These sentences also follow pattern 5. Transform each one into two sentences by making first the indirect and second the direct object the subject of a passive verb.[5]

1. She gave him a dirty look.

   He was given a dirty look by her.

   A dirty look was given to him by her.

2. The company made the manager a fine offer.

   The manager was made a fine offer by the company.

   A fine offer was made to the manager by the company.

3. The dealer dealt me a bad hand.

   I was dealt a bad hand by the dealer.

   A bad hand was dealt to me by the dealer.

4. He offered his roommate the car.

   The roommate was offered to him, the car.

   The car was offered to his roommate.

5. The instructor asked her a question.

   The question was asked by her instructor.

---

[5]When a pattern 5 sentence is made passive, one object becomes the subject and the other is retained after the verb. The latter is called a retained object. Examples:

   Bill gave George a tennis racket.
               RO
   George was given <u>a tennis racket.</u>
               RO
   A tennis racket was given <u>George.</u>

Pattern 6: SVOC (Subject + Verb + Direct Object + Objective Complement)

We considered Salvatore noteworthy.
The coach made their sister a manager.

Pattern 6 is much like pattern 2 except that in this case the complement describes or completes the direct object rather than the subject of the sentence. As with pattern 2, the complement may involve either an adjective or a noun (or pronoun). Thus the adjective complement in the sentence "We considered Salvatore *noteworthy*" functions like the predicate adjective complement in subpattern 2A ("The food is *good*"). And the noun complement in the sentence "The coach made their sister a manager" functions like the predicate nominative complement in subpattern 2B ("Our friend is a senator"). And even though the main verb of pattern 6, unlike the main verb of pattern 2, is a transitive rather than a linking verb, a linking verb is at least implied between the object and its complement. This is suggested by the way many SVOC sentences, though not all, can be changed in form to use a linking verb while preserving the same meaning. In the three sets of sentences below, note how the SVOC sentence represented by each sentence A can be altered to render the B and C versions:

1. A. The voters elected him president.
   B. The voters elected him to be president.
2. A. He considered her brilliant.
   B. He considered her to be brilliant.
   C. He considered that she was brilliant.
3. A. I thought the caller you.
   B. I thought the caller to be you.
   C. I thought that the caller was you.

Exercise 15–14

Translate each pattern 6 sentence into one of the two forms shown in the B and C sentences above.

1. The committee declared Isabelle the winner.
2. She believed George honest.
3. I imagined her capable.
4. We thought him a great scholar.
5. The owner of the newspaper appointed Marcos editor-in-chief.
6. The inspector found the premises clean.

As pattern 6 is most commonly exemplified by an NP in the final position, we will restrict our attention to this form of the pattern. Pattern 6, like its predecessor pattern 5, has two NPs following the verb, as in the sentence "The basketball team chose Charlotte captain." But it differs from pattern 5 in three respects:

1. In pattern 6 the first of the two NPs is the direct object. In some sentences, if we eliminate the second NP, we are left with pattern 4, which contains only the direct object after the verb:

   The basketball team chose Charlotte.

   The second NP is called the objective complement, because it completes the direct object.

2. In pattern 6 both NPs following the verb have the same referent; that is, both *Charlotte* and *captain* refer to the same person.

3. In pattern 6, only the direct object can be made the subject of a passive verb. We can transform the pattern sentence into

   Charlotte was chosen captain

   but we cannot make the objective complement such a subject, for

   *Captain was chosen Charlotte

   makes no sense.
   In the passive of pattern 6 the subject comes from the direct object of the active.

   DO   OC

   Example: Active: He appointed Ruth secretary.
                Passive: Ruth was appointed secretary.

Only a very small group of verbs can be used for pattern 6. Among them are *name, choose, elect, appoint, designate, select, vote, make, declare, nominate, call, fancy, consider, imagine, think, believe, feel, keep, suppose, find, prove, label, judge.*

Exercise 15–15

In each sentence determine the sentence pattern involved and confirm your decision by striking out the indirect object or the objective complement. Then write the pattern number, 5 or 6, after the sentence.

1. She taught him a trick.   _____
2. We appointed Evelyn the committee chair.   _____
3. You threw us a curve.   _____
4. The student body selected Arabella their representative.   _____
5. The faculty chose Sieverson the head counselor.   _____
6. We found her a sandwich.   _____
7. The dealer sold me an air mattress.   _____
8. She gave the baby a toy.   _____
9. The city elected Mouchy mayor.   _____
10. He named his new boat Belle.   _____

Pattern 7: SVOA (Subject + Verb + Object + Adverbial)

Mr. Jensen set the cup on the table.

For most of the sentence patterns we have previously listed, an adverbial may accompany the verb but is not required. But pattern 7 is listed here as its own pattern because of the obligatory nature of the adverbial element.[6] In this regard it is like pattern 3 except that pattern 3 involved *be* or intransitive verbs whereas pattern 7 contains transitive ones. The determination of whether an adverbial is required or not of course depends on the verb. With some verbs, such as *set,* leaving the adverbial out makes the sentence sound ungrammatical as in an utterance such as *"We set the book." With other verbs, the sentence does not sound ungrammatical, but the meaning of the verb is significantly changed without the accompanying adverbial. For example, consider what happens to the meaning of the verb *kept* in the sentence "We kept the smelly dog outside" if the adverbial *outside* is removed from the sentence. Without the adverbial it sounds as if the point of the sentence is that we kept the dog (as opposed perhaps to selling it). But the meaning of the verb in a sentence containing the adverbial *outside* relates to how we maintain the dog.

With pattern 7 we complete the list of the basic sentence patterns in English.

Exercise 15–16

After each sentence write the number of the pattern it represents. Remember that the presence of an adverbial does not change the sentence pattern unless the adverbial is crucial to the sentence structure or meaning.

1. Your recital was wonderful. _____
2. Mabel was here a moment ago. _____
3. The rancher told his guests a tall tale. _____
4. The archers were not successful hunters. _____
5. The frogs croaked in the marsh. _____
6. Jerry thought the proposal a mistake. _____
7. She had been a secretary. _____
8. The Romans won the first battle. _____
9. The judges believed Lightning the best horse in the show. _____
10. The director found him a new costume. _____
11. My uncle remains the worst bridge player in town. _____
12. The coach designated Jan the new manager of the team. _____
13. Migrant workers pick the strawberries in early June. _____
14. The pickles are near the wieners. _____
15. We considered his offer a fine gesture. _____
16. Her brother laid the camera on the park bench. _____

---

[6]For a discussion of this sentence type, as well as some examples of the verbs that are used within it, see Randolph Quirk et al. *A Comprehensive Grammar of the English Language.* London and New York: Longman, 1985, pp. 55–56. For additional information consult also a learner's dictionary, such as the *Oxford Advanced Learner's Dictionary.*

17. Your cologne smells so good. _____
18. He has always seemed a serious boy. _____
19. Who is at the cottage this week? _____
20. They stayed roommates for three years. _____
21. The board elected Mr. Stoopnagel the president. _____
22. Don't leave the car in the parking lot. _____

Exercise 15–17

Unless we recognize the pattern of a sentence, we do not know what the sentence means. The following sentences illustrate this thought. Each one is ambiguous because we do not know which of two patterns it represents. After each sentence write the numbers of the patterns that it can represent. In the case of a pattern 2, indicate whether it is 2A or 2B.

1. He found her a pig. _____ _____
2. The girl looked forward. _____ _____
3. They are discouraging transfers. _____ _____
4. I'm getting her socks. _____ _____
5. The man gave the library books. _____ _____
6. It was a little uniform. _____ _____
7. He accepted Wednesday. _____ _____
8. Thorne taught himself during his young manhood. _____ _____
9. The doctor made them well. _____ _____
10. He found the mechanic a helper. _____ _____
11. Our spaniel made a good friend. _____ _____
12. The judges designated the girl winner. _____ _____
13. The detective looked hard. _____ _____
14. Mary called her mother. _____ _____

Other Sentence Types

You should be aware that there are other types of sentences. Sometimes they represent merely an expansion of one of the types above. For example,we could join two SVO sentences together to get a sentence like "I brought the bowl, and Mortimer lost it." Or a direct object of the SVO sentence type could itself be a sentence, as in "I knew (that) you were coming." In this SVO sentence the direct object of *knew* is the embedded sentence "(that) you were coming," which is itself an SV sentence type.

But there are also sentence types that we have not discussed because they are not basic types, though some of them are related to types already listed. We will acknowledge just a few of them here. Two types seem similar to pattern 6 as they provide more information about the object of the verb, but instead of using a noun or adjective they use a present participle or a past participle form as in "I imagined her eating" or "I believed him seated."

Another important set of sentences includes those involving an expletive such as *there* or *it*. These sentence types deserve particular attention. First we will look at the kinds beginning with *there + be* as in the following:

There is a sock under my bed.

Here *there* is an expletive, that is, a meaningless slot-filler occupying the normal position of the subject. The subject itself comes after the *be*. Sentences beginning with the expletive *there* are rearrangements of basic pattern sentences, and most of them conform to one of three types.

The first type, illustrated both above and below, follows the pattern of *there + be* + subject + adverbial of place or time, as in

There are two socks under my bed.

This type is a rearranged form of pattern 3:

A sock is under my bed.
Two socks are under my bed.

The second type is illustrated by this sentence:

There was a police officer looking for you.

This second type follows the pattern of *there + be* + subject + *-ing* participle + Ø or remainder. It is usually derived from patterns 1, 4, or 5 employing an *ing* verb.

Examples:
a. Pattern 1: A politician was speaking.
   There + be: There was a politician speaking.
b. Pattern 4: Some boys were eating apples.
   There + be: There were some boys eating apples.
c. Pattern 5: Several jockeys were giving their horses water.
   There + be: There were several jockeys giving their horses water.

The third type comes from the passives of patterns 4, 5, or 6, with pattern 6 being the most frequent.

Examples:
a. Pattern 4: The police found a shotgun.
   Passive: A shotgun was found by the police.
   There + be: There was a shotgun found by the police.
b. Pattern 5: The company made him an offer.
   Passive: An offer was made him by the company.
   There + be: There was an offer made him by the company.
c. Pattern 6: They elected a Swede captain.
   Passive: A Swede was elected captain.
   There + be: There was a Swede elected captain.

The pattern of the preceding sentences is *there + be* + subject + *-ed* participle + remainder or Ø.

In all of these cases the expletive *there* was followed by *be*. Now and then a few other verbs appear in this structure, for example:

There remained only three doughnuts.
There stood a handsome lad in the doorway.

The expletive *there* should not be confused with the adverbial *there*. Although the expletive *there* is merely a slot filler, the adverbial *there* refers to a location (even if sometimes only metaphorically). Furthermore, the expletive bears weak or third stress whereas the adverbial has secondary or primary stress.

Examples:

Thĕre (expletive) are sóldiers in town.
Thêre (adverbial) go the sóldiers.
They are thére (adverbial).
Thêre (adverbial) they áre.

Exercise 15–18

Change each sentence into one beginning with the expletive *there*.

1. A rabbit is in your garden.

2. Some squirrels were cracking nuts.

3. A moon craft was pictured by *Life*.

4. Some idiot was chosen commissioner.

5. Five men have been working on the rules.

Another expletive is *it,* which occurs as a "dummy" in the subject position before the verb. It takes the place of the real subject, which follows later in the sentence, as in

It is nice that you could come.

If you apply here the subject-finding rule of thumb—Who or what is nice?—the answer will give you the subject ". . . that you could come." The subject is always a word group in this kind of sentence.

Exercise 15–19

Underline the subject in these sentences.

1. It is odd that the tree fell in that direction.
2. It occurred to me that the road might be impassable.
3. It is hard to see the difference.

4. It doesn't matter whether she wears the green or the yellow suit.
5. It is necessary that you write a tactful letter.

The expletive *it* may also represent a following direct object, as in

I think it a shame that she lost the match.

Here ". . . that she lost the match" is the direct object.

Exercise 15–20

Underline the direct object represented by a preceding expletive *it.*

1. She makes it a practice to revise all her papers.
2. I believe it unwise to set out in this storm.
3. He felt it unnecessary that we postpone the game.
4. The dean found it difficult to deny their petition.
5. I thought it strange his leaving so suddenly.

The expletive *it* should not be confused with the impersonal *it,* which also occurs at the sentence beginning as a "dummy" subject. This *it* is usually found in short sentences referring to weather, time, or space.

It is raining.
It seems cold.
It is seven-thirty.
It is a long way to London.

There are also idiomatic uses of *it* that are neither expletives nor impersonals.

We hoofed it to the fair.
You're going to get it when mom and dad get home.
Beat it. (= go away)
I'll have it out with you.
How goes it?
It looks bad for the White Sox.

Exercise 15–21

Indicate whether the *it* in each sentence is an Exp (expletive) or an Imp (impersonal).

1. It is too bad that you can't attend.   _____
2. It is bad outside.   _____
3. She considered it incomprehensible that he should fail. _____
4. It is snowing.   _____
5. It is ten after three.   _____

Three Modes of Classification

As a preliminary to the next chapter it will be useful to examine briefly the three major modes of classification that you must keep clearly in mind.

1. **Classification by Function.** In classification by function, you will recall, specific positions in specific patterns signal grammatical meanings. In

   > The boy gobbled the hamburger

   the position of *hamburger* signals that its grammatical meaning, or FUNCTION, is that of undergoer of the action, and this FUNCTION is labeled direct object of the verb.

2. **Classification by Form.** In chapter 12, "Parts of Speech: Form Classes," you classified words by word-form alone, using inflectional and derivational suffixes to determine the individual classes. The result was four form classes: nouns, verbs, adjectives, and adverbs. But this was not satisfactory as a complete part-of-speech catalog because an embarrassingly large number of words were unclassifiable as noun, verb, adjective, or adverb and had to be put in a miscellaneous file called non-suffixing words. This unsatisfactory situation will be remedied in the next chapter, where you will encounter parts of speech as distinguished by position.

3. **Classification by Position.** In classification by position it is the part of speech, not the function, that is associated with positions. Certain groups of positions are normally occupied by particular parts of speech. For instance, the positions that bear the functions of subject of the verb, subjective complement, direct object, indirect object, objective complement, and object of the preposition are frequently occupied by nouns. Thus we think of these six positions as noun positions, and any word or word group occupying them, whether a noun or not, we label a *nominal* by position, regardless of its function or form class. A few cases will make this clear. In the illustrative sentences that follow, the items in brackets are all **nominals.** The function of each is given in parentheses.

   1. [The prettiest] sat in the center. (Subject)
   2. [Whoever desired] sat in the center. (Subject)
   3. [Now] is the time to study. (Subject)
   4. [Under the pines] is the place to study. (Subject)
   5. That is [she]. (Subjective complement)
   6. That is [whom I saw]. (Subjective complement)
   7. He chose [the prettiest]. (Direct object)
   8. He chose [whatever he wanted]. (Direct object)
   9. She gave [whomever she met] a cheery smile. (Indirect object)
   10. Hard practice made Evelyn [a good swimmer]. (Objective complement)
   11. Hard practice made me [what I am]. (Objective complement)
   12. Can you see from [where you sit]? (Object of preposition)

Note that you can readily put a noun in each of these positions because each is the customary abode of a noun.

Similarly, any word or word group occupying slots normally filled by a verb, adjective, or adverb is by POSITIONAL classification a verbal, adjectival, or adverbial. The *-al* (or *-ial*) is the suffixal signal that tells you that you are dealing with a major positional class.

In addition the small closed parts of speech—such as determiner and auxiliary—are known as structure classes. You studied them in chapter 13.

Here are three examples to illustrate this threefold classification, although they will become fully meaningful to you only after you have completed the next chapter. Take the sentence

> The *shouting boys* will play *tennis.*

1. *Shouting* is a modifier by function, a verb by form, and an adjectival by position.
2. *Boys* is the subject of the verb by function, a noun by form, and a nominal by position.
3. *Tennis* is the object of the verb by function, a non-suffixing word and thus indeterminate by form, and a nominal by position.

Some Observations and Applications

Some people make usage decisions about which of two possible forms is more "correct" based on what sounds right. But this practice is sometimes risky because what sounds right to them may just be what they are accustomed to hearing. A better alternative is for them to know the rule on which some particular prescriptive grammar rules are based so that they do not have to rely on their ear alone but can make informed and conscious choices about some of the forms that they will use. The ability to recognize sentence patterns and to distinguish one sentence pattern from another is important for understanding why some usage choices are sometimes prescribed over others. And even if you don't agree with all of the traditional prescriptive rules, in some situations it is important at least to understand the nature of the prescribed choices.

We have earlier noted the usage issue of deciding between subject or object pronoun forms in a pattern like "It is _____." If we recognize this as a subject + verb + subjective complement pattern, then the prescriptive rule can be easy to remember. The subjective complement blank needs to be filled with a pronoun form that matches the subject. This is clearly a pronoun form such as *he, she,* or *I.* In a related situation, an analysis of sentence or clause structure is also useful when making a choice between *who* and *whom.* The use of *whom* is disappearing from the language, but once again, there are some formal occasions or tasks in which an educated person is at least expected to know how to make the distinction. In the case of a relative pronoun the choice is determined by its function within the relative clause. Thus the sentence "The engineer who designed the bridge appeared at the ceremony" uses the relative pronoun *who* to represent the subject of the relative clause "(the engineer) designed the bridge." In a later chapter we will provide more information on relative clauses, but we wish at least to acknowledge here the importance of recognizing sentence or clause patterns when making usage determinations.

In another situation we might have to decide between "I feel bad" and "I feel badly." If we recognize that *feel* is a linking verb when it refers to our current mood or disposition, then we understand the traditional rule which prescribes an accompanying adjective—in this case *bad*. If, on the other hand, we intend the less likely meaning of *feel*, to express what we do as we reach out and touch things, then we have an SV pattern that allows a following adverbial such as *badly.*

The recognition and analysis of sentence patterns and types can also be useful for interpreting literary works because authors sometimes alter normal speech patterns to achieve particular effects. Although such syntactic alterations may occur in poetry in order to achieve a particular rhyme or meter (just as they occur in lyrics to songs), they can have interpretive significance, as is evident in some of the poetry of E. E. Cummings. Departures from normal syntactic behavior can also play an interpretive role in literary prose. For example, Roger Fowler shows that one of the characters in Faulkner's *The Sound and the Fury* displays unusual linguistic behaviors including, within one passage, a "preponderance" of intransitive verbs. And even with one transitive verb that the character uses repeatedly in the passage, there is no accompanying direct object. Fowler explains that this linguistic behavior shows the character to have "little sense of actions and their effects on objects: a restricted notion of causation."[7]

A knowledge and understanding of nouns, verbs, and the patterns that they fit into is very important for those who develop products and software that rely on such knowledge. Most people are probably not acquainted with what are called *learner's dictionaries.* These dictionaries are very useful to nonnative speakers of a language and differ from conventional dictionaries because they provide not only the definitions of words but also the syntactic information necessary for using those words correctly in a sentence. For example, in addition to defining a verb and identifying its morphological behavior, a learner's dictionary provides specific information about the kinds of sentence patterns that a particular verb requires. You have seen that some verbs are intransitive, some are transitive, some are linking, and some can be used either transitively or intransitively. Furthermore some transitive verbs vary in the degree to which they may be used in SVO, SVOO, SVOA, and SVOC patterns. And although nearly any transitive verb may be used in a passive sentence, a learner's dictionary can alert a student of the language about any verb that might resist such a transformation. In a similar way, learner's dictionaries also provide important information about other form and structure classes in the language.

The kinds of grammatical information that have made learner's dictionaries valuable for students of the language have also been important to those engaged in programming computers. We have previously noted the field of artificial intelligence, which works to program machines to perform tasks and produce output similar to what is done by humans, including language-related tasks such as speech production and recognition as well as machine translation. Information about the syntactic requirements of particular words and the kinds of patterns they require is essential to the development of such language capabilities.

---

[7]"Studying Literature as Language" in *Linguistics and the Study of Literature,* ed. Theo D'haen. Amsterdam: Rodopi, 1986, pp. 187–200.

16

Parts of Speech: Positional Classes

"Who climbs the grammar-tree, distinctly knows
Where noun, and verb, and participle grows." (Dryden)[1]

An English sentence is an arrangement of words, not as words but in their capacity as parts of speech. If we do not, as listeners or readers, grasp the identity of these parts of speech, we cannot understand with certainty the message being communicated. Consider, for example,

> They are encouraging reports.

Here the word *encouraging* is the stumbling block. It may be a verb, so that the sentence means

> They encourage reports

or it may be an adjectival, giving the meaning of

> These reports are encouraging.

Not knowing the part of speech of this one word, we find the sentence ambiguous. In a carefully controlled context, of course, this sentence might not be ambiguous.

As native speakers we already have an operational command of the parts of speech. Now we will continue to approach them analytically and study the specific ways by which we identify them.

But first here is a schematic overview of the parts of speech. If you will refer to it occasionally, it may keep you from getting lost in a thicket of details.

    I. Form classes. These are large and open classes, admitting new members. They are based on changes in form that a word can undergo, though as we noted in

---

[1]"Sixth Satire of Juvenal," Line 583 as cited in *Hoyt's New Cyclopedia of Practical Quotations,* compiled by Kate Louise Roberts. New York: Funk & Wagnalls, 1940, p. 426.

the chapter on form classes, some words belong to a form class and yet have no distinctive change in form.

A. Noun
B. Verb
C. Adjective
D. Adverb

II. Structure classes. These are small and closed classes, rarely admitting new members. Members of these classes are normally uninflected, and we recognize them by position alone. You have already studied the first six below.

1. Determiner	8. Predeterminer
2. Personal pronouns	9. Postdeterminer
3. Auxiliary	10. Subordinating
4. Qualifier	conjunction
5. Preposition	11. Coordinating
6. Expletive	conjunction
7. Restricter	12. Relative

III. Positional classes. These are based on the positions occupied by the form classes. The members of these classes are both words and word groups. You have already seen brief references to the terms below as we have examined sentence patterns.

1. nominal
2. verbal
3. adjectival
4. adverbial

A. Nominals

Certain sentence positions are characteristically the habitation of nouns. You already know that these positions are those occupied by items having these functions:

Subj Subject of verb
SC   Subjective complement
DO   Direct object of verb
IO   Indirect object of verb
OC   Objective complement
OP   Object of preposition

But occupancy of these positions does not positively identify nouns because words of other form classes can occupy them as well. Here are a few illustrative cases involving the Subj position.

Pattern 3: The *rich* live on the bay.

Here the Subj slot is occupied by an adjective, recognizable as such because it can be inflected with *-er* and *-est,* e.g.,

> The *richest* live on the bay.

Pattern 2:   *Steadily* is the best way to work.

Here an adverb, formed of the adjective *steady* plus the adverbial derivational suffix *-ly,* sits comfortably at home in the Subj slot.

Pattern 4:   *Swimming* develops the lungs.

We recognize *swimming* as a verb in form, a verb stem *swim* plus the verbal {-ING vb}. You may be tempted to call it a noun, but observe: (1) It cannot take a noun inflection, either the {-s pl}, as in "Your paintings are beautiful," or the {-s ps}, as in "the meeting's end." (2) It does not contain a noun-forming derivational suffix. So in form it cannot be declared a noun.

In the three illustrative sentences above we have seen an adjective (*rich*), an adverb (*steadily*), and a verb (*swimming*) each occupying a noun position. What we will do is to set up a positional class called nominal. Any word, whatever its form class (noun, verb, adjective, or adverb), will be tabbed a nominal if it occupies one of the six noun positions listed above. This gives us a double-track classification for parts of speech, one by form and the other by position. Such a procedure is perfectly sound, for any given entity may be classified in various ways by using different bases of classification. You yourself, for example, might be classified "female" by sex, "junior" by class, "brunette" by hair pigmentation, "Unitarian" by church affiliation, and so on. The double-track classification also helps us to classify words that don't have characteristic suffixes that could help determine their membership in one of the form classes. A few more examples may be pertinent.

1. We enjoyed the *game.*

   Game is a noun by form, because it can be pluralized in its context, and a nominal by position, because it occupies the DO slot.

2. What can one expect from the *young*?

   Young is an adjective by form because it is inflected by *-er* and *-est.* One could say "from the younger" but not "from the youngs." It is a nominal by position because it is in the OP slot.

3. *Now* is the best time.

   Now is a non-suffixing form that does not take any kind of suffix to indicate its part of speech, but it is a nominal by position, occurring in the Subj position.

Exercise 16–1

The italicized words are nominals because they occupy the sentence positions that are the home territory of nouns. The occupants of these positions perform the FUNCTIONS of Subj, SC, DO, IO, OC, and OP, but BY POSITION they are NOMINALS.

In the first blank give the form class of the italicized nominal, using N (noun), V (verb), Aj (adjective), or Av (adverb). If it is a non-suffixing word, write NS.

In the second blank indicate the particular function of the position the nominal occupies, the function of Subj, SC, DO, IO, OC, or OP.

	Form	Function of position
Example: The *poor* grew troubled.	Aj	Subj

1. The *cheapest* are on that counter.
2. The *seniors* held a class meeting.
3. The *hearings* were postponed.
4. He hated *starving.*
5. Can you see the game from *here*?
6. The winners were the *men* from Homburg Hall.
7. That car is a *gas-guzzler.*
8. We believed the letter a *hoax.*
9. The safest way to drive is *carefully.*
10. We gave the *upstairs* a good scrubbing.
11. *Below* was dangerous.
12. Her roommate disliked the *chaos* in Jo's room.

Word groups as well as individual words can be nominals, and they occupy the usual noun positions. In the sentence

About a plateful is my limit.

the opening word group *about a plateful* is a prepositional phrase occupying the Subj position and is a nominal because the Subj is the position of a noun. In the next sentence

A chipmunk emerged from under the porch.

the prepositional phrase *under the porch* is the object of the preposition *from.* Because it occupies an OP position it is a nominal by position.

Exercise 16–2

The italicized word groups are nominals. In each blank indicate the function of the group by Subj, SC, DO, IO, OC, OP.

1. Jerry knows *that history is never completely true.*
2. His greatest ambition is *to win the match.*
3. You made me *what I am.*
4. He assigned *whoever was late* an extra problem.
5. Do you object to *what I wrote?*
6. *Petty gossiping* makes one unpopular.
7. *Under seventeen* requires an accompanying parent.

Whether or not a word group is a nominal can be tested by substitution. A word group is a nominal if it can be replaced by one of these: a noun or noun phrase, *this, that, these, those, he/him, she/her, it, they/them.*

Exercise 16–3

The italicized word groups are nominals. Write in the first blank one of the substitutes mentioned above. In the second blank indicate the function of the group.

1. *To win the match* was his greatest ambition.

_____   _____

2. Can you see from *where you sit*? (Try a noun phrase).

_____   _____

3. I brought a scarf for *my favorite aunt from Peoria.*

_____   _____

4. He did not give *finding the cat* a second thought.

_____   _____

5. *Where we are going* has not been decided.

_____   _____

6. She became *what she had hoped.*

_____   _____

7. He hated *arriving late.*

_____   _____

8. We found *what we wanted.*

_____   _____

9. *That she is beautiful* is evident to all.

_____   _____

10. They made him *what he had always wanted to be.*

_____   _____

11. We never anticipated *all of the problems.*

_____   _____

Exercise 16–4

Underline each nominal word group. In the blank give the function of the word group.

1. They heard what we said.   _____
2. What you do is legal.   _____
3. That was what I thought.   _____
4. You must succeed with what you have.   _____
5. Jack made whoever came there pancakes.   _____
6. We will do whatever his grandfather wishes.   _____
7. We came in the car.   _____
8. I'll take whichever is the most durable.   _____
9. Betty forgot to bring the notes.   _____

10. George postponed mailing the letter.   _____
11. To speak of her contributions is important.   _____

B. Verbals

Verbals are those forms that occupy verb positions. The kingpin verbal position is that of the main verb. It comes after the opening NP slot. The verb by form is a verbal by position.

Examples: The golf team may *play* tomorrow.
They have been *loitering* near the bank.
The victim must have been *shot* from the side.

Exercise 16–5

Underline the verbal in each sentence.

1. The activity clubs had been making floats.
2. A survey is being made of TV watchers.
3. He has left for the summer.
4. Your tennis racket may have been stolen.
5. Gertrude had sung a solo.

To identify the other verbal positions, we must first make a distinction between two kinds of verb forms. Certain verb forms and verb phrases have complete assertive power; they are needed to make a sentence go. Here are some examples:

a. I *choose* carefully.
She *chooses* carefully.   } Contrastive inflection for person

b. She *chooses* carefully.
They *choose* carefully.   } Contrastive inflection for number

c. They *choose* carefully.
They *chose* carefully.   } Contrastive inflection for tense

d. She *has* been chosen carefully.
We *have* been chosen carefully.   } Contrastive inflection for person and number

e. I *am* being chosen.
They *were* being chosen.   } Contrastive form for person, number, and tense

Two characteristics are noteworthy about these utterances:

1. You can comfortably place a period after each one; each has sentence completeness because each contains a fully assertive verb or verb phrase.

2. Each pair contains contrasting forms. Here are the explanatory details:

In *a,* the verb form *chooses,* inflected for third person, contrasts with the uninflected form in *I choose.*

In *b,* the verb form *chooses,* inflected for singular number, contrasts with the uninflected form in *They choose.*

In *c,* the verb form *chose,* indicating past tense, contrasts with the uninflected form in *They choose.*

In *d,* the primary auxiliary *has,* inflected for person and number in one form, contrasts with the uninflected form in *We have.*

In *e,* the irregular primary auxiliary *am* contrasts with the verb form in *He is* for first person, with the verb form in *We are* for singular number, and with the verb form in *I was* for present tense. And the irregular primary auxiliary *were* contrasts with the verb form in *He was* for plural number and with the verb form in *They are* for past tense.

Verb forms that are capable of full assertion in a sentence and of changing their form to indicate person, number, and tense are called **finite verbs** and by position they are finite verbals.

The second sort of verb forms is the **nonfinite.** These do not assert fully and do not change their form to indicate person, number, or tense. There are three nonfinite verb forms: the present participle {-ING vb}, the past participle {-D pp}, and the infinitive (to) + verb stem. Do not be confused by the labels "present" and "past" participle. These labels actually refer to words that are neither present nor past. In fact they have no tense at all. Note that in a construction such as "is growing" or "was growing," the tense is carried by the auxiliary verbs preceding the so-called present participle rather than by the present participle itself. The terms *present participle* and *past participle* are traditional terms that are widely used, and so we will continue to use them here, but it is important to note that descriptively they are not very accurate. The nonfinite verb forms frequently appear in sentence portions, like the following:

1a. *Shaking* his fist
1b. *Being* angry
1c. The willow *bending* in the wind

2a. *Having crushed* the invaders
2b. *Having stayed* calm
2c. The guide *having disappeared*

3a. *To stop* this nonsense
3b. *To be* sensible
3c. His cousin *to come*

Oral Exercise 16–A

Add something to each of the nine foregoing sentence portions to make a sentence of each. Do not change the wording of the sentence portion.

You may have observed that each sentence portion above conforms in part to one of the seven basic sentence patterns. In 1a, 2a, and 3a there is a direct object, respectively *fist, invaders,* and *nonsense.* This is a partial pattern 4. In 1b, 2b, and 3b there is a linking verb + an adjective, *angry, calm,* and *sensible.* This is a partial pattern 2. In 1c, 2c, and 3c there is a subject, namely, *willow, guide,* and *cousin,* used with an intransitive verb. This is characteristic of pattern 1.

All of the verb forms above are nonfinite and participate partially in one of the seven sentence patterns, but they do not have the full assertive power of the main verb. These forms we call **nonfinite verbals.**

Exercise 16–6

Indicate the number of the sentence pattern that each of the italicized nonfinite verbals participates in. Your pattern analysis is not of the entire sentence but rather the portion involving the nonfinite verbal.

1. *Picking* strawberries was her favorite occupation. _____
2. Perkins did not approve of *assigning* students long papers. _____
3. *To give* generously is a Christian virtue. _____
4. *Being* a minister, Prentiss spoke gently. _____
5. We regretted the warblers *leaving* for the South. _____
6. *Remaining* a conscientious objector, Harkness did not
   return to his native country. _____
7. Seeing the photos is not *being* there. _____
8. *Having been* competent in camp activities, Juanita was
   invited to return as a counselor. _____
9. He wanted *to call* the lawyer a fraud. _____
10. Heinrich congratulated Gretchen for *becoming* slender. _____
11. We watched George *throw* the discus. _____
12. We watched George *throwing* the discus. _____
13. We wanted George *to throw* the discus. _____
14. The camp director needed *to put* the tent poles in the truck. _____

Exercise 16–7

Underline the nonfinite verbals and accompanying verbal group. Indicate in the blanks the basic sentence pattern each verbal or verbal group participates in.

1. Having sprinkled the lawn, he turned off the water. _____
2. She remembered seeing the play before. _____
3. Do you like to be there? _____
4. We urged the guests to remain for dinner. _____
5. She was proud of being a member of the band. _____
6. He wanted the teacher to give him an A. _____
7. After having been cheerful for weeks, Chuck was now depressed. _____
8. Keeping quiet, she peered through the window. _____

9. Harris made his brother repay the loan. _____
10. Calling Josephine an artist was a compliment. _____
11. Jim's father did not object to his becoming a Marine. _____

When a nonfinite verb form—present participle {-ING vb}, past participle {-D pp}, and (*to*) + verb stem— appears alone in a noun position, it is labeled a nominal, as in

To err is human. (Subj position)
She enjoys *skiing*. (DO position)
Her hobby is *gardening*. (SC position)

Likewise, the whole sentence portion containing a verbal and occurring in a noun position is labeled a nominal, as in

Playing field hockey is her favorite pastime. (Subj position)
He liked *to play the piano*. (DO position)
Their specialty is *raising turkeys*. (SC position)
Jim got paid for *mowing the lawn*. (OP position)

Exercise 16–8

The italicized parts of the sentences below are nominals by position. Indicate the function of each, using these abbreviations:

Subj	subject of verb	DO	direct object of verb
SC	subjective complement	OP	object of preposition

1a. *Motorcycling* always gives Genevieve a thrill. _____
 b. *Riding a roller coaster* always gives Genevieve a thrill. _____
2a. Fred earned money by *delivering*. _____
 b. Fred earned money by *delivering papers*. _____
3a. Charlotte likes *to swim*. _____
 b. Charlotte likes *to play volleyball*. _____
4a. What can he do besides *complain*? _____
 b. What can he do besides *play the drums*? _____
5a. Jerry enjoys *fishing*. _____
 b. Jerry enjoys *playing bridge*. _____
6a. Its only purpose was *swindling*. _____
 b. Its only purpose was *soaking the rich*. _____

Complements of the Verbal. The main verb, as we saw in the basic sentence patterns, can be complemented by nominals functioning as subjective complement, direct object, indirect object, and objective complement. These same kinds of complements can follow not only the main verb but other verbals in the sentence as well. A few examples will make this clear.

Her hobby was *making prints*.

Here the main verb *was* has as its subjective complement the nominal *making prints.* Within this nominal *prints* is the direct object of the verbal *making.*

He enjoys *playing golf.*

In this case the main verb *enjoys* has as its direct object the nominal *playing golf,* and within this nominal the verbal *playing* has *golf* as its direct object. Here is another:

We wanted *to teach her a lesson.*

In this example, the main verb *wanted* has as its direct object the nominal *to teach her a lesson.* And within this nominal the verbal *to teach* has an indirect object *her* and a direct object *a lesson.* In the next sentence,

George asked *her to drive the car*

we say that the main verb *asked* has the direct object *her to drive the car* and that, within this nominal, *her* is the subject of the verbal *to drive* and *the car* the direct object.[2] This analysis is supported by the possibility of substituting a nominal clause like this:

George asked *that she drive the car.*

Exercise 16–9

In the preceding exercise you investigated the function of nominals (embodying a verbal) in the sentence. Now we will look inside such nominals to ascertain the functions of their parts relative to the embodied verbal. Each nominal embodying a verbal is italicized, and after each such nominal, its function in the sentence is given in parentheses. Within the nominal one or two words are printed in small capitals. Indicate the function within the nominal of each word printed in small caps.

Example: *Eating CHOCOLATES made her sick. (Subj)*   <u>DO</u>

This tells you that *eating chocolates* is a nominal embodying a verbal (*eating*), that it is the subject of the main verb *made,* and that you are to indicate the function of *chocolates* within the nominal. *Chocolates* is, of course, the direct object of the verbal *eating.* You will probably also notice that *eating chocolates* is a partial pattern 4.

For your answers, use these abbreviations:

Subj	subject of the verb	IO	indirect object
SC	subjective complement	OC	objective complement
DO	direct object	OP	object of preposition

---

[2]An alternate analysis is to consider the slot before the verbal (i.e., _____ to drive the car) an indirect object and the rest, the direct object. This is supported by the passive form of the sentence:

She was asked to drive the car by George.

1. She hated *to miss the* PARTY. (DO)   _____
2. Dimitri tried *to remain* CALM. (DO)   _____
3. *Shooting* QUAIL takes a great deal of skill. (Subj)   _____
4. I expect YOU *to be* TRUTHFUL. (DO)   _____ _____
5. *Finding the* TRAIL *again* was no easy matter. (Subj)   _____
6. Thank you for *washing* DISHES. (OP)   _____
7. *Being a golf* CHAMPION was exhilarating to Olga. (Subj)   _____
8. I saw THEM *break the* WINDOW. (DO)   _____ _____
9. The doctor advised HIM *to stop* SMOKING. (DO)   _____ _____
10. *Electing* BETTY PRESIDENT required a lot of campaigning. (Subj)   _____ _____
11. He wished *to give* HAROLD *a* BICYCLE. (DO)   _____ _____
12. Fleming thought *visiting* MUSEUMS an exciting excursion into the past. (DO)   _____

Verbals and sentence portions containing verbals occur not only as nominals but also as adjectivals and adverbials, functioning as modifiers. These will be dealt with at the end of the next chapter.

C. Adjectivals

Adjectivals, like nominals and verbals, occupy certain characteristic sentence positions.

1. The first position is that between the determiner (that is, words such as *a, the, this, that, these, those, his, her, our, their, Johnny's*) and the noun, for example,

   That *joyful* freshman[3]

   In this noun phrase *joyful* is an adjective by form—the source noun *joy* plus the derivational suffix *-ful*—and an adjectival by position. This position may be occupied by two other form classes and by some non-suffixing forms. The noun is shown in

   That *college* freshman

   The verb appears in

   That *laughing* freshman
   That *recommended* freshman

   And here are non-suffixing words in this adjectival slot:

   An *inside* job
   Her *inmost* thoughts

---

[3]The determiner is also an adjectival by position, and it is a modifier by function.

A series of adjectivals may occur between the determiner and the noun, as in

The many earnest university seniors

Here there are three successive adjectivals in a fixed and unchangeable order. Because these are not interchangeable—that is, not mutually substitutable—we will set up subclasses of adjectivals, which will be discussed in the next chapter under "Prenominal Modifiers."

Exercise 16-10

The italicized words are adjectivals. Indicate the form class of each with the symbols N (noun), V (verb), and Aj (adjective). If it is a nonsuffixing word, write NS.

1. A *clean* apron	_____	11. These *broken* boxes	_____
2. An *evening* party	_____	12. An *inside* connection	_____
3. The *college* dormitory	_____	13. Their *garage* door	_____
4. The *class* dance	_____	14. The *office* typewriter	_____
5. A *hopeful* sign	_____	15. Our *school* principal	_____
6. Their *back* yard	_____	16. The *above* statement	_____
7. Those *neighborhood* cats	_____	17. That *funny* hat	_____
8. Sally's *new* radio	_____	18. A *scenic* drive	_____
9. That *paper* book	_____	19. Those *chattering* girls	_____
10. A *fighting* rooster	_____	20. His *glass* eye	_____

The preceding exercise illustrates the first and most common adjectival position.

2. The second adjectival position is the third slot in pattern 2:

NP	LV	Aj
Those boys	are	*young.*
The boat	remained	*shiny.*
The man	appeared	*aware.*
The man	seemed	*in the money* (= rich).

Exercise 16-11

Underline the adjectivals in the following sentences and indicate whether they occupy the first or second type of adjectival position.

1. The old farmer worked hard. _____
2. The forest seemed dark. _____
3. The visitor was very afraid. _____
4. The scouts seemed asleep. _____
5. This frog appears alive. _____
6. The student athlete came. _____

7. The hedge grew tall. _____
8. The contestant was becoming angry. _____
9. The contestant was becoming. _____
10. The professor taught the history class. _____
11. The catamaran remained dirty. _____
12. The villagers looked hostile. _____

3. The third adjectival position is the one after the noun. It accepts adjectives, adverbs, verbs (participles), non-suffixing words, and word groups.

Examples: adjectivals: The waitress, *old* and *weary*, sat heavily down.
The blondes *especially* → wore blue.
That girl *jogging* is my sister.
The floor *below* is rented.

When an adjective is in this postnoun position, it usually does not occur alone but with another adjectival, as in

A fire, *red* and *yellow,* threw shadows around the room.

or with a modifier, as in

The plumber, rather *angry,* threw down his wrench.

There are occasional instances, however, in which the adjective does appear alone after the head noun. Examples: *money necessary, resources available, court martial, God Almighty, time immemorial, consul general, sum due.*

Exercise 16–12

Underline the adjectivals occuring in the third adjectival position, and in the blanks indicate the form class by using the symbols: Aj (adjective), Av (adverb), V (participle). If the word is non-suffixing, write NS.

1. One person alone heard the message. _____
2. Those coeds there are sophomores. _____
3. The surface, black and smooth, reflected the sunshine. _____ _____
4. The weather today suggests a thunderstorm. _____
5. We started our trip homeward. _____
6. The woman speaking became our vice president. _____
7. His demeanor, excessively grim, annoyed the guests. _____
8. Selmer canceled his trip abroad. _____
9. The coach particularly ate in silence. _____
10. The door ajar worried the janitor. _____

In this postnominal position we find word-group adjectivals of different structures:

It is time *to go.* (Infinitive)

Andy watched his dog, *which was swimming after a stick.* (Relative clause)[4]

Andy watched his dog, [which was] *swimming after a stick.* (Reduced relative clause)[5]

He was a man *who was disturbed by many phantasies.* (Relative clause)

He was a man [who was] *disturbed by many phantasies.* (Reduced relative clause)[5]

The sweater *that I prefer* is the striped one. (Relative clause)

The sweater *I prefer* is the striped one. (Reduced relative clause)

Mount Washington is the place *where we spent a strenuous week.* (Relative clause)

The second chapter *of the book* presented the problem. (Prepositional phrase)

This is a medicine *good for gastritis.* (Modified adjective)

Exercise 16–13

Underline the word-group adjectival and encircle the word it modifies.

1. This will be a day to remember.
2. The chap sitting in that cubicle is Marge's friend.
3. This is not the size I ordered.
4. The drugstore on the corner sells the *Times.*
5. Our guests came on the week when I was housecleaning.
6. A girl spoiled by her mother is not a good roommate.
7. Just choose a time convenient to yourself.
8. Who is the head of this club?
9. Have you finished the book I lent you?
10. He was a sight to behold.

4. A fourth position for adjectivals occurs in written English. This is the slot at the beginning of a sentence before the subject:

> *Angry* and *upset,* the applicant slammed the door.

But this presubject position is also an adverbial position:

> Angrily, the applicant slammed the door.

In the former sentence we consider *angry* and *upset* to be adjectivals, not adverbials, because they can be used in other positions that are clearly the territory of adjectivals:

---

[4]The relative clause adjectival is presented in the next chapter.

[5]Another name for a reduced relative clause employing a present or past participle is participle phrase.

The applicant was *angry* and *upset.*
The applicant appeared *angry* and *upset.*
The *angry* and *upset* applicant . . .

In a nominal position they would of course be nominals:

The angry make few friends.
The upset sometimes need treatment.

5. "Something" adjectival. Words composed of *any-, every-, no-,* or *some-* plus *-body, -one, -place,* or *-thing* can be followed by an adjectival.

Nothing *good* was on the table.

Exercise 16–14

Underline the postnominal adjectivals.

1. Would you like something sweet?
2. We cannot find anyplace desirable.
3. Nothing exciting happened.
4. Everybody interested is invited to appear.
5. An invitation was extended to everyone concerned.

D. Adverbials

A positional description of adverbials presents some significant challenges. One difficulty is that there are numerous subclasses of one-word adverbials, and each subclass has its own positions in the various sentence patterns. To illustrate, let us look at the traditional adverbial subclasses of time, place, and manner. We'll choose two examples of each class:

Time:	a. soon	b. tomorrow
Place:	a. here	b. outside
Manner:	a. well	b. skillfully

Now we'll take a simple sentence of pattern 4 and see how these adverbials assume their positions in this pattern. We'll begin with the *a* group.

	1	2	3	4	5
	He	will	play	tennis.	
Time:	Soon	soon	soon	_____	soon
Place:	Here	_____	_____	_____	here
Manner:	_____	_____	_____	_____	well

Next let's look at the *b* group of the same three adverbial subclasses—time, place, and manner.

	1	2	3	4	5
		He	will	play	tennis.

Time:	Tomorrow	_____	_____	_____	tomorrow
Place:	outside	_____	_____	_____	outside
Manner:	skillfully	_____	skillfully	_____	skillfully

Here it is evident that the members of the group *a* adverbials of time, place, and manner have a distribution that does not necessarily coincide with their mates in group *b*. In other words we have positional sub-subclasses.

Exercise 16–15

Here is a simple pattern 2 sentence, with adverbial positions numbered above it. Below the sentence are three adverbials. In the blanks write the numbers of the positions in which each adverbial sounds natural in spoken English. Compare these positions with those in the preceding example. The point is that each pattern dictates its own adverbial positions.

	1	2	3	4
	NP	LV	Aj	
Pattern 2:	The leaves	turned	brown.	

Time:	recently	_____
Place:	everywhere	_____
Manner:	gradually	_____

Next we divide adverbials of time into three subclasses.

Adverbials of definite time, answering the question "When?":
   yesterday, last week, at three o'clock, tomorrow, early, late, soon, then, now.

Adverbials of frequency, answering the question "How often?":
   always, never, seldom, rarely, frequently, often, sometimes, generally.

Adverbials of duration, answering the question "How long?":
   hours, for hours, a week, the whole night, until dawn, since yesterday.

Each of these subgroups of time adverbials has its favored or admissible positions, as the next exercise will show.

Exercise 16–16

A. In these two sentences which one of the three subclasses of time adverbials normally occupies the empty slot?

1. Pattern 3:   The game was _____.   _____
2. Any pattern, preverb
   position: We _____ played ball.   _____

B. In the next sentence which two positions seem to be the most natural ones for adverbials of duration, such as *all afternoon?*

	1	2	3	4	
3. Pattern 4:	Jim	studied	chemistry.		_____

With this brief discussion you may begin to suspect the complexity of the problem of describing adverbial positions. In addition there are further complicating circumstances that we cannot pursue here. So we will limit this description to a general statement of five common adverbial positions, moving position by position from the first one (at the beginning of the sentence) to the last one (at the end).

1. Before the pattern, with or without juncture:

Really, you should know better.
Now it's time to go.

2. After the subject and before the auxiliary or verb:

She *often* would forget her keys.
He *actually* expects to marry her.

3. After the auxiliary or the first auxiliary:

He would *seldom* make the effort.
They could *easily* have made another touchdown.

4. After the verb in pattern 1 and after *be* in patterns 2 and 3:

He drove *recklessly.*
Her brother is *always* a gentleman.
She is *seldom* late.
She is *outside.*

5. After the complement of the verb (SC, DO, OC):[6]

Hoskins will be quarterback *tomorrow.*
Hoskins will play football *tomorrow.*
They may choose Hoskins captain *tomorrow.*

The postcomplement position of a pattern 4 sentence overlaps with the OC position of pattern 6:

They elected Monty *captain.*
We considered her *reasonable.*

There need be no trouble here. Because *captain* is a noun and *reasonable* an adjective, we obviously have in these sentences a nominal and an adjectival, not adverbials. This positional overlap, however, can produce ambiguity, as in

---

[6]You will recall that even though our discussion of sentence types such as SVC has limited the term *complement* to those elements that may serve as a subjective or objective complement, in a general sense the term can include any element that serves to complete a verb.

He considered the applicant *hard.*

Here *hard* can be looked at two ways. It is an adverbial at the end of pattern 4, as you can substitute for it an adverb, like *carefully.* But it is also an adjectival in pattern 6, as it permits a substitute like *unsuitable,* hence the ambiguity.

In any of these five positions we can label a word an adverbial, unless we have an instance of positional overlap. In such cases the form class that occupies a slot or that can be substituted will determine the positional classification. Here is an illustration of each case.

He eats *doughnuts.*

The postverb position admits nominals, adjectivals, and adverbials. In this example the postverb slot is occupied by the form class of noun (*doughnuts*) so that the word is positionally nominal. In the second illustration,

He eats *fast,*

we can substitute the adverb *quickly* for *fast.* Thus *fast* is called an adverbial.

The passive transformation offers another test to distinguish nominals from adverbials in this postverbal position. If we compare

He ate Wednesday
He ate sandwiches

we see that the first cannot be made passive, for no one would say

*Wednesday was eaten by him

Hence *Wednesday* is not a nominal but an adverbial. But we can say

Sandwiches were eaten by him.

Therefore, in "He ate sandwiches," the word *sandwiches* is a nominal.

Another way to spot adverbials is by their mobility. Most adverbials can be moved to one or more positions in the sentence without disturbing the sentence pattern or sounding un-English. In the illustrative "tennis" sentences, for instance, five of the six adverbials were movable.

As a last resort for identifying adverbials, try elimination. If the term in question is not a nominal, verbal, or adjectival—and not a structure word—then it is by elimination an adverbial.

It must never be forgotten that we are dealing with a positional class and that any form class can be an adverbial, e.g.,

Noun:	He will come *Sunday.*
Verb:	They stood *eating.* (= thus)
Adjective:	They played *dirty.*
	Come *quick.*
Adverb:	Come *quickly.*

In the word-stock of English there are many non-suffixing[7] words often employed in adverbial positions, and it may be useful to you to inspect a sample of them before proceeding with the next exercise. They follow below:

1. Non-suffixing words used both as adverbials and prepositions:
   above, about, after, around, before, behind, below, down, in, inside, on, out, outside, since, to, under, up.

2. "-ward" series, with optional -*s*:
   afterward, backward, downward, forward, inward, outward, upward.

3. "Here" series:
   here, herein, hereby, heretofore, hereafter.

4. "There" series:
   there, therein, thereby, therefore, thereafter.

5. "-where" series:
   anywhere, everywhere, somewhere, nowhere.

6. "-way(s)" series:
   crossways, sideways, anyway.

7. "-time(s)" series:
   meantime, sometime, anytime, sometimes.

8. Miscellaneous:
   today, tonight, tomorrow, yesterday,[8] now, then, seldom, still, yet, already, meanwhile, also, too, never, not, forth, thus, sidelong, headlong, maybe, perhaps, instead, indeed, henceforth, piecemeal, nevertheless, downstairs, indoors, outdoors, offhand, overseas, unawares, besides, furthermore, always.

Exercise 16-17

Underline each one-word adverbial. In each blank of the first column write the number that shows which of the five numbered adverbial positions it occupies:

1. before the pattern, with or without juncture
2. after the subject and before the auxiliary or verb
3. after the auxiliary or the first auxiliary
4. after the verb in pattern 1 and after *be* in patterns 2 and 3
5. after the complement of the verb (SC, DO, OC)

In each second blank identify the **form** class of the adverbial by N (noun), V (verb), Aj (adjective), Av (adverb), or NS (non-suffixing word).

---

[7]Some of the non-suffixing words contain an -*s*, which at one time may have constituted an inflection but probably no longer does and thus such words will not be considered to be suffixed.

[8]A few of these words have noun homophones, e.g., "And all our *yesterdays* have lighted fools / The way to dusty death."

1. Bob should talk loud.   _____   _____
2. Indeed, bring him with you.   _____   _____
3. He drove the car madly around the track.   _____   _____
4. I certainly will.   _____   _____
5. They entered singing.   _____   _____
6. He frequently reads in bed.   _____   _____
7. The deer was standing below.   _____   _____
8. I'll see you inside.   _____   _____
9. I will eventually make a report.   _____   _____
10. We usually stopped for tea.   _____   _____
11. They stood around for ten minutes.   _____   _____
12. Will you set the plant here?   _____   _____
13. It is still a long distance to Albany.   _____   _____
14. The vice president had already signed the contract.   _____   _____
15. The bus approached rapidly.   _____   _____
16. We had seldom walked to the park.   _____   _____
17. Meanwhile Giovanni started the fire.   _____   _____
18. The ride was also tiresome.   _____   _____
19. They rode Saturday.   _____   _____
20. The ants were everywhere.   _____   _____

Word groups as well as single words can occupy adverbial positions and thereby be classified as adverbials. Here are some illustrative groups in the five positions.

1. Before the pattern, with or without juncture:

   With a sharp ax you can do wonders.
   By using a little red here, you can balance your colors.
   Unless you follow the printed directions, the set will not fit properly together.

2. After the subject and before the auxiliary or verb:

   Angelina *in her own way* was a darling.

3. After the auxiliary or first auxiliary:

   You may *in this way* be of great assistance.

4. After the verb in pattern 1 and after *be* in patterns 2 and 3:

   He drove *with abandon.*
   She is *at any event* happy.
   He is *without doubt* an expert.
   The wolf is *at the door.*

When an infinitive (*to* + verb) follows the verb, it may be in one of two positions:
Adverbial, after verb in pattern 1, as in

They waited *to escape.*

Nominal, position 3 in pattern 4, as in

They expected *to escape.*

If *in order to* can be substituted for *to,* the infinitive is in the adverbial position: "They waited *in order to* escape." If *that* or *it* can be substituted for the infinitive, it is in the nominal position: "They expected *that/it.*"

5. After the complement of the verb (SC, DO, OC):

My brother was a doctor *for twenty years.*
Tom put his watch *where he could find it in the dark.*
They believed the man crazy *after questioning him.*

A prepositional phrase after the object of the verb may be ambiguous:

They watched the hunter *with the binoculars.*
She spied the dog *on the corner.*

In these two sentences the prepositional phrase is either adjectival or adverbial.

Exercise 16–18

The adverbial word groups are italicized. In the blank indicate by number the adverbial position of each.

1. I'll dress *while you shave.*　_____
2. *When the dinner is ready,* blow the whistle.　_____
3. He might *under the circumstances* agree to the job.　_____
4. Our guide split the log *with ease.*　_____
5. *Eating his food slowly,* Antonio studied the manual.　_____
6. A hungry trout rose *to the surface.*　_____
7. *By that time* the fish were no longer biting.　_____
8. *To find the camp,* just follow the creek downstream.　_____
9. *From the hilltop* you can see the sawmill.　_____
10. Jake hunts *to make a living.*　_____
11. You must hold the knife *this way.*　_____
12. My sister *for a variety of reasons* came later.　_____

Exercise 16–19

This is a review of the four positional parts of speech. In the blanks identify each italicized element by N-al (nominal), V-al (verbal), Aj-al (adjectival), or Av-al (adverbial).

1. Last *Monday* was a holiday.　_____
2. The *Monday* washing is on the line.　_____
3. Mrs. Reed always jogs *Mondays.*　_____
4. Won't you come *in*?　_____
5. The outs were angry with the *ins.*　_____

6. They stomped *upstairs.* _____
7. They slept in the *upstairs* room. _____
8. One can see the airport from *upstairs.* _____
9. Jake was *wrestling* with his math. _____
10. The *wrestling* roommates were exhausted. _____
11. Juniper found *wrestling* exciting. _____
12. They came in *wrestling.* _____
13. The student movie is presented *weekly.* _____
14. The student movie is a *weekly* occurrence. _____
15. His *way* is the best. _____
16. He did it *his way.* _____
17. The mechanic ran the engine *full speed.* _____
18. *By this means* he burned out the carbon. _____
19. He raised the hood *because the engine was hot.* _____
20. They found the cabin *just what they wanted.* _____

Exercise 16–20

This is a review of the four form-class parts of speech. Classify the italicized words by writing in the blanks N (noun), V (verb), Aj (adjective), Av (adverb), or NS (non-suffixing word). Remember to use derivational as well as inflectional criteria.

1. Minnie is fond of Siamese *cats.* _____
2. The island was *colonized* by the Northmen. _____
3. One of her *stockings* is torn. _____
4. What *punishment* do you think should be administered? _____
5. Fritz *always* says the wrong thing. _____
6. Her room was in a state of *chaos.* _____
7. We'll *gladly* refund your money. _____
8. The nurse puts a *disinfectant* on the cut. _____
9. Carl sleeps late *mornings.* _____
10. How *peaceful* the house seems today! _____
11. You should *shorten* that dress. _____
12. The salesman quietly turned *away.* _____
13. Our ladder is not *tall* enough. _____
14. The class listened to a *reading* from Shakespeare. _____
15. I don't know *offhand.* _____

E. Verb-Adverbial Composites[9]

The form we are about to examine is extraordinarily intricate in its behavior. As you progress through the explanations, all may appear clear-cut and simple. But if you

---

[9]This structure has various names: "verb-adverb combination" (A. G. Kennedy), "phrasal verb" (Dwight Bolinger), "verb-particle combination" (Bruce Fraser), "two-word verb" (G. A. Meyer).

stray from this carefully laid-out path to inquire into instances of your own finding, you may meet with variations, exceptions, and impasses. So be warned that beneath the specious simplicity of what is to follow lies a tangle of complication.

A verb-adverbial composite consists of two words, a verb followed by an adverbial such as *up, down, in, out, over.* There are two kinds, intransitive and transitive, each with partially different structural and transformational characteristics.

Intransitive Verb-Adverbial Composite (VAC)

We will begin with an example that illustrates the characteristics of the intransitive verb-adverbial composite.

He *turned up* (= appeared) at seven o'clock.

There are three characteristics to be noted here which tend to be common to intransitive VACs and which can be used as VAC tests.

Test A—Meaning. The meaning of *turned up* as a unit is different from that of the individual meanings of the two parts added together. Other examples:

We *took off* (= departed) for Memphis.
The violence of the storm may *let up* (= lessen) soon.

Test B—Immovability. The adverbial element of an intransitive VAC is not movable, for you would be unlikely to say

*Up he turned.
*Off we took.
*Up the storm let.

Test C—Inseparability. The two parts of an intransitive VAC are inseparable. A modifier separating them results in a strange or non-English locution, as in

*He turned suddenly up at seven o'clock.
*We took immediately off for Memphis.
*The violence of the storm may let soon up.

All three of these traits are not necessarily characteristic of every intransitive VAC, and the meaning test in particular may result in uncertain decisions. Let us say, therefore, that if the expression in question shows ONE of the three characteristics, we can label it an intransitive VAC.

In contrast to the intransitive VAC there is the simple verb plus adverbial, as in

He climbed up.

This does not have any of the three characteristics noted above for the intransitive VAC:

A. The meaning is that of *climbed* plus that of *up,* as shown by the question "Where did he climb?" "Up."
B. The *up* can be moved, as in

Up he climbed with the agility of a squirrel.

C. The two parts can be separated by a modifier, as in

He climbed nimbly up the tree.

Classify the italicized words as VAC (intransitive verb-adverbial composite) or V +
A (verb plus adverbial).

1. The two friends *fell out.* (=quarreled)   _____
2. The two friends *walked out.*   _____
3. England will always *carry on.*   _____
4. Willard *went in.*   _____
5. After drinking heavily, he suddenly *passed out.* (lost consciousness) _____
6. You should *keep on* with your investigation. (=continue)   _____
7. The dean *gave in* to the request of the committee. (=acceded)   _____
8. He *fell down* unexpectedly.   _____
9. The shop may *close down.*   _____
10. Betsy likes to *show off.*   _____

Transitive Verb-Adverbial Composite (VAC + O)

The transitive verb-adverbial composite has an object, as you would expect, and is
symbolized by VAC + O. Here is an example:

He *turned down* (= rejected) the offer.

A distinction must be made here between the VAC + O and the verb plus prepositional phrase, V + PP. The latter is illustrated in

He *turned* down the driveway.

There are three useful tests that enable us to make this distinction; and, as was the
case with the intransitive VAC, we will label a verb a VAC + O if it passes ONE of
these tests.

Test A—Adverbial Postpositioning. In a VAC + O sentence the adverbial
can be placed after the object of the verb:

He *turned* the offer *down.*

This change is impossible with the preposition:

*He turned the driveway down.

Furthermore, when the object of the VAC + O is a personal pronoun, the adverbial
MUST be placed after the pronoun object and only there:

He *turned* it *down.*

If one said

He turned down it

the last two words would be a preposition and its object.

Using Test A, classify the italicized words as VAC + O (verb-adverbial composite and object) or V + PP (verb and prepositional phrase).

1. I will *turn in the requisition.*   _____
2. I will *turn in the street.*   _____
3. We *called up the plumber.*   _____
4. Mother *called up the stairs.*   _____
5. He *broke in his new car.*   _____
6. The windshield *broke in his new car.*   _____

Test B—Inseparability. The verb-adverbial in the VAC + O cannot be separated by a modifier, but a modifier can occur between a verb and a prepositional phrase. For example,

VAC + O: He *turned up* (= discovered) a new manuscript.
V + PP: He *turned* (sharply) up the country road.

Insert a modifier wherever you can after the verb. Then classify the italicized words as VAC + O or V + PP.

1. The wind *blew down* the canyon.   _____
2. The wind *blew down* the tree.   _____
3. Jean *ran up* a bill.   _____
4. Jean *ran up* a hill.   _____
5. Will you *turn on* the light in that room?   _____
6. My car can *turn on* a dime.   _____

Test C—Relative Transformation. The V + PP sentence can be transformed into a relative structure in which the preposition is followed by a *which* or *whom,* thus:

V + PP: She ran *down* the hill

can be transformed into

The hill *down which* she ran.

In this relative structure, note that the preposition *down* is separated from the verb *ran.*

In the VAC + O sentence, this form of the transformation is not possible. For instance,

VAC + O: She *ran down* (= criticized adversely) her roommate cannot become

*Her roommate *down* whom she *ran*.

Instead, the two parts of the VAC + O must remain together:

Her roommate whom she *ran down*.

Exercise 16–24

For each sentence that permits it make a relative transformation, following the first example under Test C above as a model. Then label the italicized parts of each sentence as VAC + O or V + PP.

1. The police *ran in the criminal.* _____

2. The horses *ran in the pasture.* _____

3. The teacher stood *drinking in the moonlight.*
   (= observing with pleasure) _____

4. The teacher stood *drinking in the moonlight.* _____

5. Alice *pricked up her ears.* _____

6. Keith *looked over her painting.* _____

7. We *prevailed on the dean.* _____

8. He *knocked over the chair.* _____

9. He *stepped over the chair.* _____

10. Jake *closed down his shop.* _____

Exercise 16–25

Apply all three tests to each pair of italicized words. Indicate by letter (A, B, C) which tests show the item to be a VAC + O.

1. The butler *carried in* the tray. _____
2. Marge *made up* her mind. _____
3. Marge *made up* the story. _____
4. She *turned over* the pancake. _____
5. Father *turned off* the light. _____
6. The Senate *brought about* a change. _____
7. Ed always *puts out* the fire. _____
8. The clerk *wrapped up* the meat. _____

9. Will you *take over* the job? _____
10. Willie soon *wore out* his shoes. _____

Some sentences similar to those we have been discussing may seem to have two adverbials, as in

He can't *get along with* them. (= tolerate)

Such expressions are most simply analyzed as being composed of an intransitive VAC (or a verb plus adverbial) followed by a prepositional phrase. It may seem to you that *with* should belong with the verb and adverbial in a three-part verb because no other preposition can replace it. But remember that many verbs are linked to one specific preposition; for instance, we object *to,* flirt *with,* exclude *from,* and compensate *for.*

That the preposition is not a part of the verb is suggested when we make questions with such forms, as in

With whom can't he get along?

Exercise 16–26

Make a question of each sentence, following the model just above.

1. She *looked down on* her former friends. (= scorned)

_____

2. McBride *made off with* the child. (= stole, kidnapped)

_____

3. We *made up with* the girls.

_____

4. They won't *put up with* that spoiled child. (= endure)

_____

5. We should *look in on* the Smiths. (= visit)

_____

Some Observations and Applications

One of the most important concepts taught in this chapter is that a sentence position normally occupied by a member of one form class may sometimes be occupied by members of another. In such situations the actual part-of-speech identity is secondary in importance to the position and function of the word in the sentence. Thus although the word *swimming* is definitely a verb by its form-class identification, it can constitute a nominal by its position in a pattern such as "He taught swimming." The recognition that *swimming* is a nominal then helps in recognizing that, despite its form, it can behave in ways normally associated with nouns. It can, for example, undergo the passive when it follows a transitive verb. Thus the sentence "The lifeguard taught swimming" could be altered to become the passive "Swimming was taught by the lifeguard." Once again, a native speaker does not need to learn such information consciously in order to speak the language, but a conscious awareness of positional classes could be useful for a variety of applications. This is certainly true for teaching English as a second language (ESL) and programming computers with language capabilities. But it can also relate to improving stylistic choices that native speakers might make in their writing. For example, students who overuse the passive voice in their writing could become better at recognizing when they are using it if they are aware not only that the passive can use *get* as an auxiliary but also that the transposed nominal in the passive could belong to other form classes besides a noun, including even the form class of verbs.

In this chapter you also learned to distinguish between finite and nonfinite verbs. By this point in the course you should recognize that subclasses of nouns and verbs exist because of syntactic behavior that distinguishes members of one subclass from another. What is important about the distinction between finite and nonfinite verbs? Finite verbs are vital to the formation of complete sentences. You have probably heard the claim that every sentence in English requires a subject and a verb in order to be complete. But it would be more precise to note that every sentence needs a subject and a FINITE or modal verb within the main clause. Thus an utterance such as "My friend Jenny having seen only two or three snakes in her whole life" is not a complete sentence because there is no finite verb or modal in the main clause. This can be remedied in different ways. For example, one could provide a finite auxiliary verb such as *has* to create *has seen,* or include a main verb that is finite as in "My friend Jenny having seen only two or three snakes in her whole life **came.**"

Modification

The following three jokes or humorous sayings all result from a postmodifier that relates ambiguously to more than one preceding verb or noun. These kinds of ambiguities are commonly found in student writing, but in some cases jokes have actually been built around them.

"I feel like I'd like to punch the boss in the jaw again."
"Gosh! Did you say AGAIN?"
"Yeah. I felt like doing it once before today."[1]

One morning I shot an elephant in my pajamas. How he got into my pajamas I'll never know.[2]

Bert: "I know a man with a wooden leg named Smith."
Uncle Albert: "What's the name of the other leg?"[3]

The seven basic sentence patterns that we studied in chapter 15 were exemplified by somewhat skeletal sentences in order to reveal the structure without interference from unneeded parts. But in our actual speaking and writing we seldom use sentences so spare and bony. Instead we flesh out our sentences with many kinds of modifiers.

---

[1]Lupton, Martha, ed. *The Treasury of Modern Humor.* Indianapolis: Maxwell Droke, 1938, p. 329. *Again* could modify either *feel like* or *punch.*

[2]Attributed to Groucho Marx. *In my pajamas* could modify either *shot* or *elephant.*

[3]From the film *Mary Poppins* as cited in *More Anguished English* by Richard Lederer. New York: Delacorte Press, 1993, p. 181. *Named Smith* could modify either *man* or *wooden leg.*

A modifier is a subordinate element in an endocentric structure.[4] It is a word or word group that affects the meaning of a headword in that it describes, limits, intensifies, and/or adds to the meaning of the head. In the noun phrase *the blue shirt,* for example, the word *blue* describes the shirt; it limits by excluding other colors; and it adds to the plain meaning of *shirt.*

Modifiers may appear before or after the heads they modify, and sometimes they are separated from the head by intervening words. Here are some examples of modifiers with heads.

Modifier	Head	Modifier
dirty	dog	
that	dog	
	dog	there
	dog	across the street
	dog	barking angrily
	dog	to be feared
	dog	which was howling
extremely	dirty	
	reads	rapidly
	reads	standing
	reads	when he wants to relax
	reads	nights
	reads	to calm his mind
often	reads	
quite	often	

The position of a modifier sometimes shows the head that it modifies:

The _____ flower

This slot, which we call adjectival, is the position of a modifier of the following noun, whether the slot is filled by an adjective (*lovely*), noun (*garden*), or a verb (*blossoming*). At times there is no positional cue to show what is modified:

---

[4]An endocentric structure has the same function as one of its parts or is replaceable by one of its parts.

Endocentric Structure	*Replacement*
those dirty dogs	dogs
extremely dirty	dirty
dog across the street	dog
dog which was howling	dog
reads rapidly	reads
reads to relax his mind	reads
often reads	reads
quite often	often

The replacing part is the head. The other words and word groups are the modifiers. The replacing part may retain a determiner from the endocentric structure because a certain class of nouns (count nouns) requires a determiner in the singular:

Elise bought *a shiny new bicycle.*

Replacement: Elise bought *a bicycle.*

A butterfly in the garden *which was fluttering among the flowers.*

In this sentence it is the meaning that reveals that the *which* group modifies *butterfly* and not *garden.* At other times we rely on formal cues, not position or meaning, to keep the modification clear:

The flowers in the garden which *were* blossoming beautifully.
The flowers in the garden which *was* blossoming profusely.

When neither position nor formal signals reveal the modification, and when the meaning does not make it clear, we have an ambiguity, as in

A flower in the garden which was blossoming beautifully.

Exercise 17–1

Rewrite these sentences, replacing each italicized endocentric structure by its head. Retain the determiner when necessary.

1. His laughter was *extremely loud.*

2. *The jar on the shelf* is filled with dates.

3. McPherson was *a dour man who seldom smiled.*

4. The two *strolled through the park after they had finished work.*

5. The constable *laughed nastily.*

6. We heard *the loud rattling clank of the chain.*

7. *The angry squirrel in the pine* scolded the blue jays.

8. *The contract that he signed* had paragraphs of fine print.

9. The searchers found *the car lying on its side.*

10. Claribel *jumped into the deep pool.*

In the above exercise the parts that you left out were modifiers, both single-word and word-group modifiers. Take another look at these modifiers before going on to the next exercise.

Exercise 17–2

Write down the one-word heads that are modified by the italicized words.

1. A *noisy* motorcycle sputtered there.   _____
2. A noisy motorcycle sputtered *there.*   _____

3. The motorcycle *in the yard* had not been recently used.   _____
4. He stopped *for a second.*   _____
5. She stopped *to pick up the agate.*   _____
6. It was *very* nice of you.   _____
7. Lisa came to the shop *rather* often.   _____
8. He stopped *when the clock struck twelve.*   _____
9. That fellow *making his bed* is the supervisor.   _____
10. Gerald owned a long black whip, *which he could snap expertly.*   _____

The two exercises above illustrate modification. Modification is a function, and a word or word group that performs this function is a modifier. A modifier belongs not with the form classes or the position classes but with the function classes, such as the subject of verb, subjective complement, direct object, indirect object, objective complement, and object of preposition. Words, you remember, have a threefold classification—by form, by position, and by function. Here is an example by way of reminder:

The *jolly* minstrel sang a ballad *energetically.*

In this sentence *jolly* is classified as an adjective by form, an adjectival by position, and a modifier by function; and *energetically* is called an adverb by form, an adverbial by position, and a modifier by function.

Now we are ready to look at modification systematically.

A. Sentence Modifiers

A sentence modifier is an adverbial that modifies, as its head, all the rest of the sentence, and is often set apart by terminals—rising, sustained, or falling.[5]

Example: Naturally, he behaved at the party.

Here *naturally* modifies *he behaved at the party.* Compare this

He behaved naturally at the party.

In this sentence *naturally* modifies the verb *behaved,* and the meaning is different from that of the former sentence. Here are examples of seven structures that are commonly used as sentence modifiers.

1. Single-word adverbial:
   Luckily, I knew how to swim.
2. Clause adverbial:
   Since the door was closed, we climbed in the back window.
3. Prepositional phrase:
   In fact, the contract is invalid.

---

[5]For a review of terminals, consult chapter 5.

4. Absolute structure:[6]
   The guests having departed, we resumed the normal household routine.
5. Infinitive phrase:
   To keep dry in a tent, you should be provided with a fly.
6. Participial phrase in *-ing:*
   Considering the circumstances, he was lucky to escape alive.
7. Relative in *-ever:*
   Wherever she is, I will find her.

Each of these, we note, is in initial sentence position, the most common one for sentence modifiers. However, sentence modifiers may appear in medial and final positions as well.

Exercise 17–3

Rewrite the seven sentences above, placing the sentence modifiers in positions other than initial.

1. _____
2. _____
3. _____
4. _____
5. _____
6. _____
7. _____

It is not always possible to distinguish a sentence modifier from one that modifies a part of the sentence. But often there is a difference between the meaning of a sentence modifier and that of an identical expression that does not seem to be a sentence modifier. The next exercise will illustrate.

Exercise 17–4

Identify the sentence modifiers.

1. Oliver did not die happily.
2. Happily, Oliver did not die.
3. He was anxious to tell the truth.
4. He was anxious, to tell the truth.
5. Hopefully, we are going to London.
6. We are going to London hopefully.
7. Honestly, he is going to sell his car.
8. He is going to sell his car honestly.

---

[6]A noun plus a present or past participle or both. This structure is a sentence portion but never a complete sentence.

9. Frankly, I do not wish to speak.
10. I do not wish to speak frankly.

B. The Noun Phrase: Prenominal Modifiers

The noun phrase, you will recall, consists of a noun head together with all the modifiers that accompany it, before and after.

NH
Example: All my many old school friends of other days who have passed away

We shall take up first those modifiers that precede the head. These are known as prenominal modifiers and constitute subclasses of the adjectival. Let us begin with the simple modification structure of determiner plus noun head, e.g.,

D   NH
the fence

In case your memory has misted over, here are the determiners again:

Article	Poss. Aj.	Poss. of Names	Demonstrative
the	her	John's	this
a/an	his	•	that
	its	•	these
	my	•	those
	our		
	their		
	your		

Between the determiner and the noun head is the position for adjectives:

D   AJ   NH
that   low   fence
your   sturdy fence

The same position is also occupied by nouns that modify the noun head, e.g.,

D   N   NH
our   garden fence
their   wire   fence

When an adjective and a noun both precede the noun head, the adjective precedes the modifying noun, thus:

D   AJ   N   NH
our   sturdy garden fence
that   low   wire   fence

Exercise 17–5

Make each list of words into a noun phrase following the pattern of *D   Aj   N   NH*

1. a, street, village, narrow   _____
2. large, dormitory, college, this   _____
3. players, tall, those, sophomore   _____
4. photogenic, swimmer, that, girl   _____
5. this, counselor, enthusiastic, senior   _____
6. wool, blue, necktie, George's   _____
7. leather, her, shoes, old   _____
8. desk, hardwood, large, his   _____
9. cheap, ballpoint, these, pens   _____
10. computer, laptop, my, portable   _____

This pattern of *D   Aj   N   NH* is often ambiguous, as the adjective may modify either the first noun or the second noun. Consider

a decent college graduate.

This phrase may mean either "graduate of a decent college" or "decent graduate of a college." The overlapping of stress patterns may play a part in such ambiguities, as in

Those hôt cár dèals.

Here the modifier-plus-noun stress pattern of ˆ ´ (hôt *cár*) overlaps with that of the compound-noun ´ ` (*cár* dèals). Thus the meaning can be either "hot car-deals" (car deals that are hot) or "hot-car deals" (deals in hot cars).

Exercise 17–6

Give two meanings for each of these ambiguous noun phrases.

1. A smâll árms fàctory   a. _____
                                b. _____

2. That grêasy kíd stùff   a. _____
                                b. _____

3. The bâsic bóok sèrvice   a. _____
                                b. _____

4. A fôreign lánguage tèacher   a. _____
                                b. _____

5. An ôld cár enthùsiast   a. _____
                                b. _____

We can now add to the prenominal modifiers another group, one that precedes the determiners and whose members are called predeterminers. This group consists of *all, both, half, double,* and a few others, as in

PRE/D	D	AJ	N	NH
all	my	old	school	friends

Make each list into a noun phrase, beginning with a predeterminer.

1. blocks, your, cement, half, new   _____
2. long, copper, wires, all, the   _____
3. engagement, both, lovely, her, rings   _____
4. fresh, those, flowers, prairie, all   _____
5. young, both, rabbits, baby, my   _____

The possessive of common nouns (not proper nouns) appears between the determiner and the noun head. Let us examine its possible positions, using the pattern

D	AJ	N	NH
the	red	garden	roses

We will use the noun possessive *summer's* and see where it fits.

D		AJ	NH
the	summer's	red	roses

D	AJ	N	NH
the	red	summer's	roses

D		N	NH
the	summer's	garden	roses

D		AJ	N	NH
the	summer's	red	garden	roses

All these sound like normal English. But we would not say

D	N		NH
the	garden	summer's	roses

So it appears that the possessive of common nouns occurs anywhere between the determiner and the noun head, except between N and NH. Yet what about

D	N		NH
a	cotton	man's	shirt?

This too sounds English. It is likely that different subclasses of the noun or the noun possessive permit different positioning patterns. This is a matter that requires investigation. With this limitation in mind we can say here that the possessive of common nouns can occur anywhere between the determiner and the noun head.

These noun possessives at times make for ambiguity in the noun phrase. For example, we can interpret *the late summer's roses* as "the roses of late summer" or "the late roses of summer." Such ambiguities in the written words sometimes disappear in the spoken form because of the ability of the suprasegmentals to distinguish meanings. The noun phrase *her new doll's house* is ambiguous to the eye, but the ear will distinguish between *hèr nêw dôll's hóuse* and *hèr nêw dóll's hòuse.*

Exercise 17–8

Give two meanings for each of these noun phrases in their written form.

1. An old girl's bicycle
    a. _____
    b. _____

2. The world women's congress
    a. _____
    b. _____

3. A nice woman's fur coat
    a. _____
    b. _____

4. A large woman's garment
    a. _____
    b. _____

5. An advanced learner's dictionary
    a. _____
    b. _____

The next step is to enlarge the class of determiners. The fourteen determiners you have learned can all be preceded by the predeterminers *all, both,* and *half.* But besides these fourteen there is a second set of determiners, and these are not preceded by predeterminers. There are twelve of the latter:

another	either	neither	what (a)
any	enough	no	which
each	much	some	whose

These belong in the determiner class because they precede adjectives and are mutually exclusive both with one another and with the members of the first set.[7] The first set we will label the *the* determiners, subset A; the others are the *another* determiners, subset B.

The order of the prenominal modifiers we have examined so far may be shown thus:

V	IV	III	II	I	NH
Pre D	*Det*	*(Class yet*	*Aj*	*Noun*	
	A. *the*	**to come.)**			
	B. *another*				

Exercise 17–9

Place above each modifier the number of the class to which it belongs. In this and the following exercises be careful about two successive nouns. They may be either a noun modifying a following noun, as in *côllege déan,* or a single compound noun, as in *cláss pìn.*

---

[7]Don't be misled by cases like *this much cider.* Here *this* is not a prenominal modifier. It does not modify *much cider* or *cider;* it is a qualifier like *very* and merely modifies *much.*

	IVb	II	I	NH
Example:	any	small	cloth	rag

1. Another huge glass ornament
2. Each rural pumpkin patch
3. Some long winter vacations
4. All our friendly neighborhood dogs
5. Either short cotton dress
6. Enough college friends
7. Both my studious roommates
8. No cold cheese sandwich
9. Much evening enjoyment
10. Neither tall Christmas tree

Above you noticed a blank Class III. This contains words that follow determiners and precede adjectives and are called postdeterminers. The list is as follows:

ordinal numbers: first, second, . . . last
cardinal numbers: one, two, three . . .

every	most
few	other
less	same
little (quantity)	several
many (a)	single
more	such (a)

This is an untidy class. Not all postdeterminers can follow all determiners, but each one can follow at least one determiner. And within the group there are complicated orders of precedence. For example, *other* usually follows, not precedes, another postdeterminer, as in *many other boys, several other boys, most other boys, few other boys;* but when *other* is combined with a cardinal number, either order is allowed: *the three other boys, the other three boys.* If you try to plot the precedences of these postdeterminers, you will end with about six columns. For our purpose it will suffice to recognize the class as a whole without exploring its internal complications.

Exercise 17–10

Place the class number—V, IV, III, II, or I—above each modifier. In the case of class IV, remember to specify a or b.

1. The last three pickles
2. His every wish
3. Many fine university seniors
4. Some other bad book reports
5. Much more white sand
6. Those same hungry ants

7. Both those two aimless fellows
8. Any such childish pranks
9. Harry's few acquaintances
10. What other foolish ideas

Exercise 17–11

Make each list of words into a noun phrase. Above each modifier write the number of the class to which it belongs.

1. summer, several, flowers, pink   _____
2. garden, both, old, his, hoes   _____
3. junctures, three, these, all, terminal   _____
4. bad, schedule, another, examination   _____
5. two, silk, my, dresses, pretty   _____

Exercise 17–12

Make each list into two noun phrases, and write above each modifier the number of the class to which it belongs.

1. truck, delivery, any, large   _____

    _____

2. that, steel, heavy, construction   _____

    _____

3. excellent, some, factory, parts   _____

    _____

4. vacation, summer, long, student's, the   _____

    _____

5. dog, first, good, her, house   _____

    _____

One final class of prenominals remains, the restricters. This is a very small set of words such as *just, only, even, especially, merely.* Like the other prenominals these can modify the noun head alone—

    just girls
    even water
    especially candy

or the noun head with its modifiers—

    just college girls
    just romantic college girls
    just another romantic college girl.

These precede the predeterminers and are therefore in column VI.

Make a noun phrase of each list and write above each modifier its class number.

1. guests, all, our, especially _____
2. skills, photography, particularly, her _____
3. the, expensive, even, gift _____
4. white, socks, athletic, some, just _____
5. only, ten, minutes, short _____

A summary of the prenominal modifiers is given in the chart on page 289.

This brief look at the six subclasses of prenominal adjectivals is perhaps enough to give you an inkling of the complexity of the modifications that we practice in our daily speech. We have left numerous questions of prenominal order unexplored, and we might take just a quick look to see what they are like. Here are a few:

1. What is the position of these classes?

a. non-suffixing adjectivals: an *inside* look
b. {-ING vb} verbs: an *approaching* stranger
c. {-D pp} verbs: the *fallen* snow

2. In Class I which nouns precede which other nouns? For example, you would probably say "an iron garden gate" but not "a garden iron gate." What principle of precedence is operative here?

3. In Class II which adjectives precede which other adjectives? Would you say "a pink Chinese flower" or "a Chinese pink flower"? "A wonderful little book" or "a little wonderful book"? There are subclasses of adjectives in terms of precedence, e.g., those of color, nationality, and shape-size—and those inflected with -*er* and -*est* as opposed to those taking *more* and *most*. What orders of precedence do we as native speakers follow in using these different subclasses?

C. The Noun Phrase: Postnominal Modifiers

Modifiers of the noun headword may be placed after the headword as well as before it.

Examples: 1. The apartment, spotlessly *clean*
2. The apartment, *large* and *empty*
3. The apartment *downstairs*
4. The freshmen *especially*
5. The weather *this morning*
6. The apartment *in front*
7. The apartment *standing empty*
8. The apartment *located in the rear*
9. The apartment *to rent*
10. The apartment *which is empty*
11. The apartment, *the home of the Snopeses*

PRENOMINAL MODIFIERS

VI Restricter	V Predeterminer	IV Determiner	III Postdeterminer	II Adjective	I Noun	Noun Head
EXAMPLES:	EXAMPLES:	A. ARTICLES	CARDINAL NUMBERS	EXAMPLES:	EXAMPLES:	
especially	all	a/an	1, 2, 3, . . .	red	school	
even	both	the	ORDINAL NUMBERS	blue	college	
just	half	POSSESSIVE ADJS.	first, second	green	dormitory	
merely	double	her	. . . last	old	house	
only		his	every	new	garden	
particularly		its	few	young	fence	
almost		my	less	big	garage	
nearly		our	little (quantity)	little (size)	gate	
		their	many (a)	large	summer	
		your	more	small	rock	
		POSS. OF NAMES	most	high	wool	
		John's	other	low	silk	
		DEMONSTRATIVES	same	tall	steel	
		this	several	short	iron	
		that	single	thick	clay	
		these	such (a)	thin	plastic	
		those	POSS. OF COMMON	intellectual	cloth	
			NOUNS	dogmatic	brass	
		B. another		thoughtful	copper	
		any		commendable	leather	
		each		excellent	nylon	
		either		prevalent	brick	
		enough		Japanese	cement	
		much		Chinese	paper	
		neither		American	shoe	
		no		silken	coat	
		some		woolen	skirt	
		what (a)		wooden		
		which		POSS. OF COMMON		
		whose		NOUNS		

After the next exercise these postnominal modifiers will be described in the order of the examples above.

Each of the italicized expressions above has the function of modifying the headword, but each is different in form. In the following sentences similar noun modifiers are italicized. After each sentence place the number of the modifier above to which it corresponds.

1. We watched the brown river, *swollen with rain.*　　＿＿＿＿＿
2. I want to rent the bicycle *outside.*　　＿＿＿＿＿
3. It was a large outdoor swing, *the property of our neighbor.*　　＿＿＿＿＿
4. The fireworks were a sight *to behold.*　　＿＿＿＿＿
5. The hoe *leaning against the house* is dull.　　＿＿＿＿＿
6. The mountaintop, *high* and *craggy,* was hidden in a cloud.　　＿＿＿＿＿
7. The building *which is near the library* is new.　　＿＿＿＿＿
8. The fan *in the corner* has only one speed.　　＿＿＿＿＿
9. I'll see you the day *before you go.*　　＿＿＿＿＿
10. The skiing *last winter* was good.　　＿＿＿＿＿
11. The car *that is in front* is mine.　　＿＿＿＿＿
12. There stood Jane, miserably *tired.*　　＿＿＿＿＿
13. The seniors *especially* arrived early.　　＿＿＿＿＿

Forms of Postnominal Modifiers

1. Modified Adjective. A bare adjective modifying a noun often occurs in the prenominal position. But an adjective in the postnominal position is usually modified by a qualifier.

> The mailman, exuberantly *happy,* whistled merrily.
> He had never seen a woman more *lovely.*

2. Compounded Adjective. When two or more adjectives modify a noun, they can occur after the noun.

> The mail carrier, *weary* and *wet,* trudged along in the rain.
> A woman *old* and *gaunt* stood at the door.

Underline the postnominal adjectivals.

1. A new blossom, scarlet and exotic, excited his attention.
2. The emerald ring, inordinately expensive, was beyond his means.
3. There stood the quivering horse, stalwart and proud.
4. He tossed the bag, new and glossy, into the luggage compartment.
5. The problem, extremely complicated, would not yield to his operations.

3. Non-suffixing Word. Nouns may be modified by some of the non-suffixing words that are often adverbial.

> The people *upstairs*
> The poker game *now*

The uninflected word in this position usually has a place or time meaning.

Exercise 17–16

Underline each postnominal modifier and put a wavy line under the noun it modifies. Insert primary stresses and juncture arrows.

> **Example:** The <u>river</u> <u>belów</u> → wound through the górge.

1. The paragraph above is too long.
2. The students here are a courteous group.
3. This matter too must be discussed.
4. The party yesterday had a large attendance.
5. The weather outside is foul.

4. Adverb. An adverb may modify a noun that precedes it.

> My meaning exactly
> The blue dress particularly

Structures like 3 (non-suffixing word) and 4 (adverb) above will now and then be ambiguous in writing, as in

> The blue dress particularly interested her.

This happens because the postnominal position coincides with the preverbal position. In such cases the suprasegmentals usually show whether the word in the ambiguous position modifies the preceding noun or the following verb; thus in speech the ambiguity is eliminated.

> The blue dress partícularly → ínterested her.
> The blue dréss → partícularly interested her.

Exercise 17–17

The sentences below are ambiguous. For each put in the primary stress and the sustained juncture arrow that will indicate that the word in the ambiguous position goes with what follows it.

> **Example:** The méetings → thereafter took place in the Georgian Lóunge.

1. My older brother especially likes to go fishing.
2. The discussion later was heated.
3. Her fiancé then was Elmer Jukes. (*then* = at that time)
4. The rabbits also enjoyed our lettuce.
5. The members only were allowed to buy shares.

Read aloud each sentence in the preceding exercise as you have marked it. Then read each one aloud in a different way to show a sustained juncture AFTER the modifier instead of before it.

5. Noun Phrase Adjectival. A noun phrase may modify a preceding noun.

> The party *last night*
> Our vacation *next summer*

Exercise 17–18

Underline each noun phrase that modifies a noun.

1. The decision that time was correct.
2. The lecture this morning was sparkling.
3. Your dinner the next time had better be good.
4. My course last fall converted me.
5. Your class the third hour always begins late.

6. Prepositional Phrase Adjectival

> The bend *in the river*

7. Participle or Participial Phrase, *-ing*, Adjectival[8]

> The woman *weeping* was escorted to the door.
> The hawk, *spotting his prey,* swooped to the meadow.

8. Participle or Participial Phrase, *-ed*, Adjectival

> They refused to pay the money *demanded.*
> The snow, *driven by the wind,* sifted through the cracks.

9. Infinitive Phrase Adjectival, *to____*

> I have a lesson *to study.*

Exercise 17–19

Underline the words or phrases of the preceding four types of postnominal modifiers (6–9). In the blanks indicate by number the type of modifier.

1. The majority of the voters appeared satisfied. _____
2. There was Al, licking his ice-cream cone. _____
3. She gave him a sandwich to eat. _____

---

[8]In 7 and 8 the entire participial phrase is an adjectival modifying the preceding noun—*hawk* and *snow.* Within these phrases, *spotting* and *driven* are verbals. Other analyses are possible.

4. Johnny wanted the red scooter with the white trim.   _____
5. We watched the fullback, urged on by the crowd, fight his
   way forward.   _____
6. Do you have something to do?   _____
7. The sailboat gliding across the bay looked majestic.   _____
8. On the river bank sat little Robert, covered with mud.   _____
9. The roof of the garage was beginning to leak.   _____
10. The puppies tugging at the rope soon gave up.   _____
11. No man living has seen this tomb chamber.   _____
12. She was disappointed in the results obtained.   _____

10. Relative Clause Adjectival. A noun may be modified by a relative clause.
In the examples that follow, the relative clauses are italicized.

1. The trees *that had mistletoe* were half dead.
2. The old carpenter, *who had been laying the floor,* stood up and straightened
   his back.
3. The partner *whom she selected* was a bashful, red-headed boy.
4. In the bargain basement he found his sister, *whom he had been looking for.*
5. It was the vice president *to whom I sent the letter.*
6. The client *whose stock he was handling* died.
7. The boat *he wants* is a catamaran.
8. The success *that you become* depends on your initiative.

With the help of these examples we can easily learn to identify relative clauses,
which have these characteristics:

   a. A relative clause is introduced by a relative: *that, who, whom, whose, which,*
      and Ø (= zero or omitted).
   b. The relative has a function in its own clause. For instance, in sentences 1 and
      2 *that* and *who* are subjects of the verb. In sentence 3 *whom* is the direct ob-
      ject. In sentences 4 and 5 *whom* is the object of a preposition. In sentence 6
      whose is a modifier. In sentence 7 the relative is omitted. Such a zero relative
      can always be replaced by a *that* functioning as the direct object or subjective
      complement. In sentence 8 *that* is a subjective complement.

Exercise 17–20

Underline each relative clause, double-underline the relative, and tell in the blank
the function of the relative, using these abbreviations:

   Subj = subject of verb   SC = subjective complement
   DO = direct object   Md = modifier
   OP = object of preposition   Ø = relative omitted

1. The composer whom he studied with was Hindemith himself.   _____
2. The doctor who performed the operation was Bernard Diamond.   _____

3. That is the book I ordered. _____
4. The bait that Jack used was an old-fashioned spinner. _____
5. This is Roger Stuffy, whose mother is president of the PTA. _____
6. The old battered boathouse, which had long been our meeting
   place, was torn down. _____
7. She is not the woman that her mother was. _____
8. He was a young, blue-eyed pilot, who immediately won our hearts. _____
9. Another boy who helps me is Skunky Hooper. _____
10. The girl whom I met at the play disappeared during the intermission. _____

We will next divide relative clauses into two kinds, a division that is useful for punctuation and for control of meaning. The two kinds are traditionally called restrictive and nonrestrictive clauses.[9] Let's begin with examples:

Restrictive: He walked to the garage *which he liked best.*
Nonrestrictive: He walked to the garage, *which was a mile away.*

Do you sense the difference in the structural meaning of the two relative clauses? The first clause points out one garage among many. Of all the garages, he walked to the particular one that he preferred. This can be called a defining clause. In the second sentence, however, there is only one garage, and as additional information we learn that it is a mile away. This can be called a commenting clause. In short, the restrictive clause restricts the meaning to part of the total, but the nonrestrictive clause makes no such limitation. This is the semantic way of distinguishing the two kinds of relative clauses.

Now we will distinguish them structurally by means of terminal junctures. Look at these two cases:

2   3 2 2   3   2 2   3   1

Nonrestrictive: The bóy → who often úshers → has been cálling me ↓

2   3 2 2   3 1

Restrictive: The boy who úshers → is my latest stéady ↓

The key is in the **word that precedes the relative**—in these examples, the word *boy.* If this preceding word is lengthened (i.e., if it is followed by a terminal juncture), the relative clause is nonrestrictive, as in the first example above. But if no terminal juncture is present at this point, the relative clause is restrictive, as in the second example. Here are two more examples:

3 1

Nonrestrictive: Billie whistled to Rágs, ↓ who thumped his tail on the floor.
("Rags" is lengthened, i.e., is followed by a terminal.)

---

[9]Note: The restrictive-nonrestrictive distinction is characteristic of all postnominal-phrase modifiers: prepositional phrases, participial phrases in *-ing* and *-ed*, infinitive phrases, appositives, and noun phrases. This is not surprising, as all of these can be considered as elliptical forms of relative clauses.

$$\overset{3}{}\qquad\overset{2}{}$$

Restrictive: They didn't like the hédge that I planted. ("Hedge" is not lengthened, i.e., is not followed by a terminal.)

Exercise 17–21

Read each sentence aloud in a natural manner, using the punctuation as a guide. If you lengthen the **word preceding the relative,** insert the appropriate terminal juncture after the word.

At the end of the sentence place an R or NR to indicate whether the relative clause is restrictive or nonrestrictive.

Examples: 1. The daughter who was eighteen won the pretzel-baking
                     contest.[10]   R
              2. Chris married the youngest daughter, ↓ who was a
                     winsome lass of eightcen.   NR

1. The blouse that she preferred was made of sea island cotton.   _____
2. She wore an old blue blouse, which had always been her favorite. _____
3. The house, which he had long admired, was built of bricks.   _____
4. The house that he built was of steel.   _____
5. Jane, who is fond of dictionaries, bought the new *Webster's Third.* _____
6. The man whom I marry must have curly hair.   _____
7. I'll take a man who respects me.   _____
8. The car I want is a BMW.   _____
9. The student whose purse he returned offered Dick a generous reward. _____
10. Thomas bought a silk, red-and-gray-striped necktie, which his
    roommate admired.   _____

By this time you have probably noticed the relation between the type of relative clause and its punctuation: a nonrestrictive clause is set off. And now you should have no trouble in punctuating them. But here are a few practical hints:

1. A *that* clause is always restrictive.
2. A clause with a zero relative is restrictive.
3. If you can substitute *that* for *who, whom,* or *which,* the clause is restrictive.
4. After a personal or geographical name, such as Elmer Perkins or Brandy Branch, the clause is usually nonrestrictive.

Relative clauses may also begin with *when, where, why, after, before,* and similar words, e.g.,

---

[10]Here you may lengthen *eightéen,* producing a juncture, but this has nothing to do with the R/NR distinction, for in speaking we normally place a juncture between the complete subject and the verb, when the subject is long. It is what happens at *daughter who* that counts. Here nothing happens, so the clause is restrictive. But in 2, you have

$$\overset{3}{}\qquad\overset{1}{}$$

. . . *dáughter* ↓ *who;* hence the clause is nonrestrictive.

The hour *when we leave* has not been decided.

These relatives function as adverbials within the relative clause.

Exercise 17–22

Underline the relative clause and write the relative in the blank at the right.

1. Do you know the reason why she deserted him?   _____
2. The woods where we camp are filled with mushrooms.   _____
3. The year after he enlisted was a momentous one.   _____
4. Let me know the minute when he comes in.   _____
5. I cannot find the place where I lost it.   _____

The relative *that* belongs in the **structure class of relatives.** It should not be confused with the *that* which is a member of the **structure class of subordinating conjunctions.** These will be taken up very soon. The subordinating conjunction *that* stands outside the sentence pattern of its clause and performs no function in it. Example: I know *that* he is sick.

Example 17–23

Circle each relative and indicate its function. Underline each subordinating conjunction.

1. The lawyer said that the will must be filed.   _____
2. The lawyer that he chose was a shyster.   _____
3. It cannot be doubted that he is competent.   _____
4. Are you sure that you returned the book?   _____
5. The book that cost me a fine was *The Castle.*   _____

Similarly, the relatives *when, where, why, after,* and *before* should not be confused with their homophones, which are subordinating conjunctions connecting nominal or adverbial clauses with the rest of the sentence. Here are five illustrative sentences with the nominal or adverbial clauses italicized.

Exercise 17–24

Underline the subordinating conjunction in each sentence, noting that it stands outside the clause and serves the function of connector.

1. Phone me *when you are about to leave.* (adverbial clause)
2. Did you find out *where she lives?* (nominal clause in DO slot)
3. We always pick up the litter *after we have picknicked in a public park.* (adverbial clause)
4. You must mow the lawn *before you leave to play tennis.* (adverbial clause)
5. I know *why he bought the car.* (nominal clause in DO slot)

11. Appositive Adjectival. The final postnominal modifier that we will study is the appositive. The two examples following show what an appositive is.

2   3 2 2   3   2 2   3   1
The *Bailey Búgle* → a college néwspaper → appears wéekly ↓
2   3   1 2   3   1
The top awards were won by two sísters ↓ horsewomen in the ríding set ↓

In these sentences the expressions *a college newspaper* and *horsewomen in the riding set* are the appositives. From these sentences we observe that

1. An appositive is a noun phrase:

   a college newspaper
   horsewomen in the riding set

2. An appositive follows a noun phrase:

   The *Bailey Bugle,* a college newspaper
   two sisters, horsewomen in the riding set

   Occasionally an appositive occurs in a position other than after a noun phrase, e.g.,

   That was what he wanted, *a riding horse.*

   A promising lad of eighteen, Harry was soon a favorite among his classmates.

3. An appositive and the noun phrase it follows have the same referent—that is, they refer to the same entity. In our examples the *Bugle* and *a college newspaper* are the same thing; the *sisters* and *horsewomen* are the same persons.

Exercises 17–25

Underline each appositive.

1. His heart was set on Alpha Gamma Beta, the debating club.
2. Mary Evans, a graduate in journalism, became a feature writer for *The Saturday Review.*
3. The three puppies, offspring of registered parents, were taken to the veterinarian's office.
4. A Republican from Olga Valley, Ivanovitch sat at the speaker's table.
5. We pushed off with the boat into the river, a sluggish, slowly winding stream.

Appositives may be divided into two kinds, restrictive and nonrestrictive, distinguished by the suprasegmentals that accompany them. Note the following:

                              2   3   1
Restrictive: Richard visited his friend the dóctor. ↓

$$\overset{2}{\text{Nonrestrictive:}} \quad \text{Richard visited the } \overset{3}{\text{d\'octor,}} \overset{1}{\downarrow} \overset{2}{\text{ a friend from }} \overset{3}{\text{c\'ollege days. }} \overset{1}{\downarrow}$$

With the restrictive appositive there is no juncture between the noun phrase and its following appositive—in the first example above, between *friend* and *the doctor*. But with the nonrestrictive appositive there is a terminal juncture at this point, shown in writing by a comma. This terminal is usually a sustained → or a rising ↑ juncture. However, it is likely to be the fading juncture ↓ if at this point the sentence pattern may be considered complete. For example,

$$\overset{2\quad 3}{\text{The m\'otorcycle,}} \rightarrow \overset{2\quad 2}{\text{a secondhand contr\'aption,}} \rightarrow \overset{3\quad 2\quad 2}{\text{was in good sh\'ape }} \overset{3\quad 1}{\downarrow}$$
$$\overset{2}{\text{They stopped before the }} \overset{3\quad 1}{\text{h\'ouse,}} \overset{2}{\downarrow} \text{ a decorated Victorian } \overset{3\quad 1}{\text{m\'ansion }} \downarrow$$

Exercise 17–26

Underline each appositive. Supply the marks of stress, pitch, and juncture on the word before each nonrestrictive appositive. In each blank indicate, by R and NR, whether the appositive is restrictive or nonrestrictive.

1. We saw *Hamlet,* a play by Shakespeare.   ————
2. Next week they will present the play *Hamlet.*   ————
3. My brother Keith is a good tennis player.   ————
4. Keith, my oldest brother, is a good tennis player.   ————
5. The poet Shelley wrote "Adonais."   ————
6. The river Severn is wide at the mouth.   ————
7. William the Conqueror crossed the English Channel.   ————
8. The class was studying Byron, a fiery, Romantic poet.   ————

In writing, two postnominal modifiers are often placed in succession after the noun head. This practice causes structural ambiguity when it is not clear what the second modifier refers to. For example:

Many institutions are now offering plans other than straight savings accounts that offer premium interest.

Here the second modifier, *that offer premium interest,* can modify either *plans* or *accounts*. The next case contains an ambiguity that had to be settled by the courts:

The law requires that the applicant be "conscientiously opposed to participation in war in any form."

The question was whether *in any form* modifies *war* or *participation*.

Oral Exercise 17–B

Point out the ambiguities caused by two successive postnominal modifiers. These modifiers are set off by brackets.

1. The poem was about the land [next to the poet's own] [which Mr. Edwards uses in the summer].
2. There were two stairways [leading to each floor] [which could accommodate all the people in case of emergency].
3. Prominent people who have been robbed include Lord Peel, [a descendant of Sir Robert Peel,] [who lost $19,200 worth of antiques].
4. Few couples [with children] [that are not rich] can afford to live in Manhattan.
5. We enjoyed the party [after the game] [yesterday].

D. The Verb Phrase: One-Word Adverbials

A verb phrase, as you have already seen, consists of a verb and all the modifiers and complements that cluster around it. The one-word modifiers are the adverbials which you have already studied in some of their characteristic positions. All adverbials in these positions are part of the verb phrase, except those that serve the function of sentence modifiers. We classified the three common kinds of adverbials as expressing time, place, and manner. Then we subdivided the time adverbials into three subclasses—adverbials of definite time, frequency, and duration. Although these five categories account for the majority of one-word adverbials, there are also others that are outside these classes, e.g.,

> . . . will *perhaps* drive.
> . . . should do it *anyway.*
> . . . may dance *instead.*

Here a short review exercise may be helpful.

Exercise 17–27

Underline the **one-word** adverbials in these verb phrases. After each sentence classify them as P (place), M (manner), DT (definite time), F (frequency), D (duration), and O (other).

1. . . . shouted angrily.   _____
2. . . . often drove without her license.   _____
3. . . . rarely drove carelessly.   _____   _____
4. . . . felt fearfully in the drawer.   _____
5. . . . never work long.   _____   _____
6. . . . was walking ahead.   _____
7. . . . could even smell him.   _____
8. . . . had always lived there.   _____   _____
9. . . . was sewing inside.   _____
10. . . . may still snow.   _____
11. . . . were happily chatting on the patio.   _____
12. . . . put it anywhere.   _____

13. . . . cautiously looked sidewise.   _____   _____
14. . . . read the story aloud.   _____
15. . . . tasted the ginger timidly.   _____
16. . . . studies nights.   _____
17. . . . gnashes his teeth sleeping.   _____
18. . . . ate seated.   _____
19. . . . played cleaner than the others. _____
20. . . . came prepared.   _____

E. The Verb Phrase: Word-Group Adverbials

In the verb phrase we find various kinds of word groups operating to modify the verb headword. They are the following:

1. Prepositional phrase adverbials: eats *in the kitchen*
2. Noun phrase adverbials: eats *every hour*
3. Clause adverbials: eats *when he is hungry*
4. Infinitive phrase adverbials: eats *to satisfy his appetite*
5. Participial phrases in *-ing* as adverbials: came *running to the table*
6. Participial phrases in *-ed* as adverbials: returned *wounded in the leg*

1. Prepositional Phrase Adverbials. Prepositional phrases that modify the verb headword often come right after the verb, in adverbial position 4:

The car slid *into the garage.*

Two such modifying phrases may appear in succession, each modifying the verb:

The car slid *into the garage with its headlights on.*

Positions before the verb (position 2) and within the auxiliary-verb combination (position 3) are also possible:

Harry *at that time* was studying Akkadian.
Harry was *at that time* studying Akkadian.

And after the direct object one may often find a prepositional phrase modifying the verb head (position 5):

He put the chair *on the lawn.*

Two of the positions mentioned above are subject to ambiguity. You can guess which ones if you remember that in the noun phrase a prepositional phrase modifies an immediately preceding noun, e.g.,

The chair *on the lawn*
The garage *with the lights on*

They are the postnominal positions, of course—the one after the object of the preposition and the one after the direct object. Here is what can happen:

> The car coasted into the garage with the lights on.
> He found the chair on the lawn.

Each sentence here is structurally ambiguous.

Exercise 17-28

After each sentence write N if the italicized prepositional phrase modifies a noun headword, V if it modifies a verb headword, and Amb if it is structurally ambiguous.

1. He greeted the girl *with a smile.* _____
2. The child *in the blue rompers* ran *into the kitchen.* _____ _____
3. Jake was fishing *from the bridge for the first time.* _____ _____
4. He looked at the girl *with the binoculars.* _____
5. We watched the game *on the front porch.* _____
6. We had never *until that time* visited the tomb. _____
7. She hurried *to the auditorium for her interview.* _____ _____
8. The flower *between the pages* was flat and dried. _____
9. She pressed the flower *between the pages.* _____
10. Georgia waited *in her room for the news.* _____ _____

2. Noun Phrase Adverbials. Noun phrases are used as modifiers in the verb phrase to modify the verb head or the head with auxiliaries, as in

> . . . held the hammer *that way.*
> . . . will pay *the next time.*

Exercise 17-29

Underline the modifying noun phrases in these verb phrases.

1. . . . will see you this Friday.
2. . . . sold the cat the following day.
3. . . . had come the whole way.
4. . . . work a little while.
5. . . . return another time.

3. Clause Adverbials.[11] Clause adverbials in this context are those word groups that have a subject and predicate and begin with such words as *after, although, as, as if, as soon as, because, before, if, once, since, that, unless, until, when, where, in case (that), in order that.* These words are called **subordinating conjunctions.** Unlike the

---

[11]Also called adverbial clauses.

relatives they have no function within the clause they introduce. They state a relation-ship, e.g., cause, time, condition, and, in the function of connectors, make the clause a part of a larger grammatical structure. When such clauses are separated from the rest of the sentence by juncture, they are sentence modifiers, as we have learned. But when they occur in the verb phrase with no junctural separation, they are modifiers of the verb or modified verb.

> **Examples:** The terrified lad ran *until he was exhausted.*
> Call *when you need me.*
> I'll scream *unless you let go.*
> She telephoned *as soon as she could.*
> He looked at the toad *as if it were poisonous.*

Subordinating conjunctions constitute another part of speech, not a form class but a structure class. The structure classes, you recall, are small and closed classes that we identify by position. So far you have met the structure classes of determiner, auxiliary, personal pronoun, qualifier, relative, and preposition, each occupying its characteristic position.

Subordinating conjunctions perform the grammatical job of connecting, and so, in function, are connectors. Some words in those other structure classes are also connectors by function: prepositions and relatives, which you have already met, and coordinating conjunctions, which will appear shortly.[12]

Exercise 17–30

Identify the structure class of the italicized words, using Aux (auxiliary), D (determiner), P (preposition), Q (qualifier), and SCj (subordinating conjunction).

1. *Each* student *can* have one ticket.   _____   _____
2. Please shut *the* door *when* you leave.   _____   _____
3. She has been very happy *since* he asked her *to* the prom.   _____   _____
4. It looks *as if* it *may* rain.   _____   _____
5. The job will be *quite* easy *after* you have started.   _____   _____

Exercise 17–31

Identify the function class of the italicized words, using Md (modifier) and C (connector).

1. They ran *around* the track.   _____
2. Jake bought *a* motorbike.   _____
3. Come early *if* you can.   _____
4. Georgie seems *rather* gloomy today.   _____
5. I'll wait *until* class is over.   _____

---

[12]Relatives have a double function: that of connector and that of the relative's function in its clause, that is, Subj, DO, etc.

6. They walked *to* the pool. _____
7. We'll be late *unless* you hurry. _____
8. The door *of* the room was open. _____
9. *Those* planes are easy to fly. _____
10. Jim lost the race *because* he stumbled. _____

Exercise 17–32

The modifying word groups in each verb phrase are italicized. Identify each one as PP (prepositional phrase), NP (noun phrase), or CAv (clause adverbial).

1. Come *as you are.* _____
2. Gerald has been working on his paper *the whole afternoon.* _____
3. I'll wait for you *where the road forks.* _____
4. I'll just sit *a while.* _____
5. The blue jay perched *on the eaves.* _____
6. Ellen has not written *since she left.* _____
7. Don't touch that wire *with your bare hands.* _____
8. Please mail this *before the post office closes.* _____
9. Bernie walks *two miles* to school *every day.* _____ _____
10. Let me know *if you need assistance.* _____
11. Why don't you come over *this evening?* _____
12. We must get home *before the sun rises.* _____
13. I'll write that letter *the first thing* in the morning. _____
14. You can't stop *once you have started.* _____
15. He will be at the office *until it closes.* _____

4. Infinitive Phrase Adverbials. It is necessary to distinguish between the infinitive phrase as adverbial modifier and as a direct object of the verb. The distinction can easily be made by substitution, as you learned in the section on adverbials. These sentences will remind you:

Adverbial Modifier: He works *to* (= *in order to*) *succeed.* (Sentence pattern 1)
Object: He wants *to succeed* (= *it/that*). (Sentence pattern 4)

Exercise 17–33

In each blank label the italicized infinitive phrase as AM (adverbial modifier) or DO (direct object of verb).

1. The children like *to gather hazelnuts.*
2. They waited *to see the result.*
3. O'Brian wanted *to be relieved of the office.*
4. O'Brian dieted *to reduce his weight.*
5. She studied long hours *to make an A in the course.*

5. Participial Phrases in *-ing* and in *-ed* as Adverbials.

You have previously met participial phrases in *-ing* and *-ed* as modifiers of the noun. Their function as modifiers in the verb phrase is similar, as these sentences will show:

Modifier of noun: The girl *eating the sundae* is a freshman.
Modifier of verb: The girl sat *eating a sundae.*
Modifier of noun: The sonata *played at the recital* was Beethoven's *32nd.*
Modifier of verb: He returned *defeated by the weather.*

Exercise 17–34

The participial phrases are italicized. Point out what they modify by NM (modifier of noun) and VM (modifier of verb).

1. He gulped his juice *standing up.* _____
2. She sat *fascinated by the music.* _____
3. Mary left *encouraged by the interview.* _____
4. The girl *laughing at his sally* is a flatterer. _____
5. Hal spends every evening *watching TV.* _____
6. Professor Doolittle had a good time *arguing with his students.* _____
7. The dog lay *drowned by the high tide.* _____
8. The bicycle *smashed by the truck* was a total loss. _____
9. He stood *addressing the crowd.* _____
10. The child entered *singing a light tune.* _____

Exercise 17–35

Using numbers 1 to 6, classify the italicized word-group adverbials in the verb phrase as

1. Prepositional phrase   4. Infinitive phrase
2. Noun phrase   5. Participial phrase in *-ing*
3. Clause adverbial   6. Participial phrase in *-ed*

1. The patient lay *on the operating table.* _____
2. She labored *to improve her flower garden.* _____
3. We must send them a card *this Christmas.* _____
4. He fell *wounded by the arrow.* _____
5. Open your eyes *when you hear the bell.* _____
6. She danced *keeping her eyes closed.* _____
7. Bring a chair *if you can.* _____
8. Jim's work had much improved *by that time.* _____
9. You can do the problem *either way.* _____
10. She sat *splashing the water.* _____

Oral Exercise 17–C

Adverbial modifiers in the verb phrase, both single and successive modifiers, can be a source of ambiguity. In the sentences below, such modifiers are enclosed in brackets. Explain the ambiguity in each sentence.

1. She washed the chair [on the porch].
2. I want a copy of the picture [in the paper].
3. He searched among the ruins I had sifted [for artifacts].
4. Cuba called [for planes] [to aid its radar].
5. Carl had been found guilty [of gambling] [in the municipal court].
6. He promised to call [at ten o'clock].
7. Take the big bag [upstairs].
8. It was a plot to sell industrial secrets worth millions [to the Dupont Company].
9. His work was drawn on [largely] by later dictionary makers.
10. Harriman, who headed the negotiating team in Moscow, Russia, invited the congressmen [to explain the situation].

Verbals Again. In the previous chapter, exercise 16–8, we dealt with sentence portions that contained verbals and were nominals by position. In this chapter, we have observed sentence portions that contain verbals (infinitive phrase, participial phrase in *-ing* and *-ed*) and that are not nominals, but adjectivals and adverbials. Now, let us solidify your grasp of verbals by an exercise which contains sentence portions that are nominal, adjectival, or adverbial. It may pay you to review section A, near the beginning of this chapter, to refresh your mind on sentence modifiers.

Exercise 17–36

In each sentence below, a sentence portion containing a verbal is italicized. Indicate whether it is a nominal, adjectival, or adverbial by using the abbreviations Nom, Aj, or Av.

1. Jim wants *to become a physical therapist.* _____
2. *To become a physical therapist,* one must have five years of college training. _____
3. His ambition *to become a physical therapist* was strong. _____
4. That is a movie *to see.* _____
5. *The weather having cleared up,* we continued our game. _____
6. The player, *dispirited and protesting,* strode to the dressing room. _____
7. *Having been picking strawberries all morning,* we were quite tired. _____
8. The text *chosen by the instructor* was up to date. _____
9. Jenny admired the chip shot *performed by Nicklaus.* _____
10. Sue objected to *taking the test over.* _____
11. The girl *taking the test over* was Sue. _____
12. Karl opened his book bag *to look for his term paper.* _____
13. The desire *to finish his term paper* kept nagging at Karl. _____
14. His desire was *to finish his term paper early.* _____
15. The coach, *having diagrammed the play,* waited for questions. _____

F. Beyond Modification

1. Non-Modifying Complements

In this chapter you have looked at relative clauses, noting how they modify particular nouns. But before leaving this chapter, we should examine some complement clauses that might superficially appear to be relative clauses but which actually function differently. The term *complement* has primarily been used thus far to mean any nominal completer of the verb, such as a subjective complement and direct object. Now we will broaden the term to include two more kinds of completers. First we will begin by looking at some complements of nouns.

a. Complement of the Noun. Complements of nouns sometimes resemble relative clauses but are in fact different. As a point of comparison we will briefly look at an example of a relative clause, a complement of a verb, and a complement of a noun. Compare the three sentences below:

> The fear *that he has* is dangerous. (contains relative clause)
> I fear *that they are lost.* (contains complement clause of a verb)
> My fear *that they are lost* has caused my depression. (contains complement clause of a noun)

In the first sentence "that he has" is a relative clause. It describes or modifies the noun *fear.* As we have noted, one feature that helps to identify relative clauses is that the words introducing them (relatives such as *that, who, whom, whose,* or *which*) have a function in their own clause. In the sentence "The fear that he has is dangerous," the relative pronoun *that* functions as a direct object in its own clause. In the second example, the clause "that they are lost" is not introduced by a relative but rather a subordinating conjunction. The word *that* has no function within the subordinate clause. The entire clause is a complement of the verb and serves as a direct object. In the third example, the clause "that they are lost" might initially appear to be a relative clause since it follows a noun (not a verb) and begins with the word *that.* Closer examination, however, reveals that once again *that* is not a relative since it has no function within its own clause. Rather, *that* is a subordinating conjunction, which stands outside the clause and connects it with the noun *fear.* In this case the clause functions as a complement of the noun.

Some complements of a noun could arguably be called "appositive clauses." In a sentence such as "The fact that Henry came surprised everyone," the clause "that Henry came" tells us something about *the fact,* serving to define or rename the fact. For this reason, we might be tempted to label the modifying clause as an appositive. But such an approach would ignore the similarities that exist between this kind of complement and a complement of a verb. The sentences

> He contended *that war is evil.*
> His contention *that war is evil . . .*

bear a special relationship to each other. The first sentence contains a complement of a verb that functions as a direct object. The second one, which we are saying has a complement of a noun, contains a noun (*contention*) that is clearly related morphologically to *contended* in the first sentence. In the first sentence the complement completes the verb *contended,* whereas in the second sentence, the complement completes the noun *contention.* In some cases we can provide a pair of sentences in which the complement of the noun accompanies a noun that doesn't merely relate morphologically to a corresponding verb but is in fact homonymous with it as in the following sentences:

> We hope *that they will come.*
> Our hope *that they will come* . . .

Now let us look at a sequence of illustrative sentences:

> 1) I believe *that Henry is lazy.*
> 2) My belief *that Henry is lazy* . . .
> 3) My idea *that Henry is lazy* . . .
> 4) The fact *that Henry is lazy* . . .

Here again the first two sentences appear to contain a complement of the verb (DO) and a complement of the noun, respectively. But the third, which means substantially the same as the second, has a noun *idea,* for which the English language happens to have no generally used corresponding verb, that is, a verb meaning "to possess or form an idea." In the fourth, *fact* is still further removed from any verb in English, and the "that" clause begins to look like a modifier of the noun, such as an appositive. Should we call the *that* clauses in sentences 2–4, and all similar clauses, complements of the noun, or should we make a distinction between complements and modifiers of the noun? Here, as often in grammatical analysis, we must make a hard and somewhat arbitrary decision. In this book we will apply the concept of the complement of the noun to any *that* clause like those in examples 2–4, regardless of whether or not the noun has a related verb.

Exercise 17–37

Underline complements of the noun once and relative clauses twice.

1. The assertion that women are poor drivers does not hold up under investigation.
2. We entertained a suspicion that Mink had been cheating.
3. The principle that water runs only downhill seems sometimes to be contradicted by our senses.
4. The canoe that leaked badly was an old wooden one.
5. His conviction that the stars influence our lives could not be shaken.
6. His notion that the stars influence our lives could not be shaken.

An infinitive phrase may also serve as a complement of the noun. In these two sentences,

> She decided *to tell the truth.*
> Her decision *to tell the truth* . . .

it looks again as if we have a complement of the verb (DO) and a complement of the noun. And again the noun (*decision*) has a corresponding verb (*decide*). But with this structure we will say that only nouns with related verbs can take a complement of the noun in infinitive form. This means nouns such as *refusal, desire, intention, promise, hope.* If the noun is not of this kind, the infinitive following it will not be a complement of the noun but probably a postnominal modifier. Compare:

Complement of the noun: His refusal *to submit without a fight* was courageous.
Postnominal modifier: He was not a man *to submit without a fight.*
Complement of the noun: His desire *to consider the motion* was thwarted.
Postnominal modifier: The next thing *to consider* is the stage set.

Infinitive structures are many and varied and complex, and this procedure will work best with the system you are studying here.

Exercise 17–38

Underline complements of the noun once and postnominal modifiers twice.

1. His offer to buy the whole lot was accepted.
2. We heard of Tom's attempt to raise money for the needy.
3. Agatha needed somebody to love.
4. They did not approve of Harry's intention to register late.
5. It was a thrilling game to watch.
6. Their hope to win was strong.
7. Robert's resolution to practice daily soon faded away.
8. There is a man to admire.
9. Father's order to stay away from the telephone was sullenly obeyed.
10. We approved Josephine's determination to live within her budget.

b. Complement of the Adjective/Adjectival.

The other kind of complement that has not yet been discussed is the complement of the adjective or adjectival. As you will see a little later on, this kind of complement can sometimes resemble an adverbial and thus can be mistakenly considered as a modifier. We will introduce complements of adjectives or adjectivals by once again looking at some examples:

I fear *that they are lost.* (complement of the verb)
I am fearful *that they are lost.* (complement of the adjective)

By now you will recognize that the first sentence contains a nominal clause that is a complement of the verb and that functions as a direct object. The second sentence closely parallels the first in meaning and form. But in this case, the clause "that they are lost" does not complete a transitive verb but rather follows an adjective and serves to complete its meaning. We thus have a clause functioning as a complement of the adjective *fearful.*

The next set of sentences is similar and illustrates in addition the prepositional phrase as complement of the adjective.

He hoped *that a change would occur.* (complement of the verb)
He was hopeful *that a change would occur.* (complement of the adjective)
He was hopeful *of a change.* (complement of the adjective)

Likewise, an infinitive phrase can be a complement of an adjective:

He hesitated *to see her.* (complement of the verb)
He was hesitant *to see her.* (complement of the adjective)

Many adjectives that do not have a related verb, as those above do, also take complements of the adjectives, for example:

I want *to see her.* (complement of the verb)
I am eager *to see her.* (complement of the adjective)

Sentence patterns that contain adjectives (or adjectivals) in the third position, can be extended by means of this particular complement, as these examples show:

I am happy *that you are here.*
Her roommate became tired *of studying.*
She is indifferent *whether you come or not.*
Jim is certain *to succeed.*

It is not always easy to make a clear-cut distinction between an adverbial and a complement of an adjective. One can perhaps say that in natural speech the complement of the adjective is not transposable but retains its position after the adjective, whereas the adverbial is movable, e.g.;
Complement of the adjective:

She was glad *that he was safe,*

but not

**That he was safe* she was glad.

Adverbial:

She was glad *when he arrived.*

and also

When he arrived she was glad.

Exercise 17-39

Indicate whether the italicized word groups are

DO   direct object of verb
CAj   complement of the adjective/adjectival
Av-al   adverbial

1. Jim doubts *that he can pass the course.* _____
2. Jim is doubtful *that he can pass the course.* _____
3. Jim is doubtful *of passing the course.* _____
4. We were reluctant *to leave.* _____
5. Jane learned *that something unpleasant had happened.* _____
6. Jane was conscious *that something unpleasant had happened.* _____
7. Juliet forgot *that she had a job to finish.* _____
8. Juliet became forgetful *of her duties.* _____
9. Jerry was sick *when the game began.* _____
10. Jerry was sick *of watching.* _____
11. Penelope was anxious *to be sure.* _____
12. Penelope was anxious, *to be sure.* _____
13. The lad was afraid *of venturing into the deep water.* _____
14. Are you sure *of it?* _____
15. Mrs. Hawkins is devoted *to her daughter.* _____

2. Coordination

In this chapter about modifiers we have dealt with the phenomenon of subordination, for a modifier (as well as a complement) is always subordinate to its head. But subordination is not the only relationship that can exist among constituents within a sentence. We now consider the matter of coordination.

In English we have a small structure class consisting of eight structure words called **coordinating conjunctions.** These are *and, but, for, nor, not, or, so, yet.* These conjunctions connect grammatical equivalents—form classes or position classes or structure words or grammatical structures or sentences. A few cases will illustrate this connection of equivalents.

Connection of equivalent form classes

Nouns	1. The library *and* the gymnasium are nearby.
Adjectives	2. George is powerful *but* clumsy.
Verbs	3. He studied hard, *yet* failed.
Adverbs	4. Arabella dances lightly *and* gracefully.

Connection of equivalent position classes

Adjectivals	1. My business *and* academic friends . . .
	2. He was popular *and* in good health.
Adverbials	3. Is it upstairs *or* in the garage?
Nominals	4. He did what he pleased, *not* what was expected.
Verbals	5. We watched him rowing hard *but* getting nowhere.

Connection of equivalent structure words

Auxiliaries	1. You can *and* should help your brother.
Prepositions	2. Was the witness walking to *or* from the scene of the accident?

Connection of equivalent grammatical structures

Prepositional
    phrases   1. You can sleep on the beach *or* in the woods.
Relative
    clauses   2. Bess was a girl who could swim *but* was afraid to dive.

Connection of sentences

        Ned began nodding, *for* the room was hot.

Since coordinating conjunctions fulfill the grammatical function of connecting, they belong to the function class of connectors, as do prepositions, relatives, and subordinating conjunctions.

All the coordinating conjunctions except *not* can occur between two sentences, changing them into a single sentence, but in other positions their distribution is limited. In other words, not all of them can be used to connect the same equivalents. For example, we do not use *for, nor,* or *so* to connect two adjectives.

In writing, these coordinating conjunctions are sometimes used to begin a sentence, as in

Jane was never on time. But that made no difference to Bob.

This would be uttered with a fading terminal juncture after *time* whether the punctuation mark were a comma, semicolon, or a period. Hence this way of beginning sentences can be considered simply as a writing convention that in no manner changes the classification of the coordinating conjunction.

Exercise 17–40

Underline each coordinating conjunction, and below each sentence identify the grammatical items that it connects.

    Example: Samuel was equally happy hunting ducks <u>or</u> playing chess.
                <u>participial phrases</u>

1. You and I ought to play them.

2. Winterbottom ran swiftly yet gracefully.

3. I don't know who you are or what you want.

4. We worked fast, for darkness was approaching.

5. These flowers are for Helen, not for you.

6. Bill had studied late, so he slept in until noon.

7. She smiled but remained silent.

8. I have not cleaned the fish, nor do I intend to.
    (*Nor* produces an inversion)

_____

9. Do you want to play now or wait till evening?

_____

10. Rising and stretching, Harry yawned and began to dress.

_____   _____

These conjunctions are sometimes doubled up, as in *and yet, and so, but yet,* and *but not.* Compare, for instance, these two sentences:

1. He was tired *but yet* he couldn't sleep.
2. He was tired *but* he couldn't sleep *yet.*

The first *yet* is a coordinating conjunction; the second is an adverbial with a different meaning.

In addition to the set of eight coordinating conjunctions there is a second set that occurs in pairs:

either . . . or
both . . . and
neither . . . nor
not (only) . . . but (also)
whether . . . or

These are a subclass of coordinating conjunctions known as correlative conjunctions.

Exercise 17–41

Underline the correlative conjunctions, and below each sentence identify the grammatical items that are connected.

1. Either you leave or I will call the police.

_____

2. They stood both in the aisles and on the platforms.

_____

3. Jenkins had neither the time nor the energy to finish the job.

_____

4. Our navigator was not only knowledgeable but careful not to make errors.

_____

5. The main requirement for this position is not specialized knowledge but the ability to handle people tactfully.

_____

6. The question is whether to stay or go.

_____

Some Observations and Applications

One potential pitfall that writers must avoid is unintended ambiguity. Clear and un-ambiguous expression is essential in most writing that we do whether we are engaged in writing a business proposal, drafting legislation, or preparing a set of instructions for someone else to follow. In this chapter you have learned about modifiers and the positions that they take in English. This kind of study can be useful in addressing ambiguity, because many of the ambiguities that occur in writing result from the nature and positional placement of modifiers. In fact, in several places in the chapter we have pointed out where a particular type of ambiguity can easily occur. Some attention to this information could help writers to be more aware of potential ambiguity in their writing and thus more sensitive to ambiguity as they proofread their writing.[13]

An awareness of the nature and distribution of modifiers as well as the structure of clauses and sentences can be useful background for teachers or materials developers who are helping students to generate more syntactically complex sentence patterns. One area of overt grammatical instruction that has appeared to make a difference in the writing skills of students (not merely in the students' proofreading and editing skills) involves sentence combining. Sentence combining exercises are designed to provide students with practice in taking a series of short, choppy sentences (each containing a relatively limited amount of information) and transforming them into a single more complex sentence that is more densely packed with information. In doing so, students learn to spot modifiers or potential modifiers that can be more carefully integrated into a single sentence whether they are included as single word modifiers, as phrases, or as embedded relative clauses. Thus the sentences

> The police officer was well-trained.
> He had a dog.
> The dog was barking.
> It was loud.
> The officer spotted the criminals.
> They were dangerous.
> A caller had reported them.

---

[13]Norman Stageberg has published a number of articles that identify various types of structural ambiguity. Perhaps the most helpful one to students of writing is his article entitled "Ambiguity in College Writing (To a College Freshman)." This article appeared in an anthology titled *Introductory Readings on Language,* 4th ed., ed. Wallace L. Anderson and Norman C. Stageberg. New York: Holt, Rinehart and Winston, Inc., 1975. It was later anthologized again by Dallin D. Oaks in *Linguistics at Work: A Reader of Applications.* Fort Worth: Harcourt Brace College Publishers, 1998.

On the other hand, for a discussion showing how grammatical knowledge could enhance a person's ability to deliberately create structural ambiguities for word plays used in advertising and humor, see 1) "Structural Ambiguities and Written Advertisements: An Inventory of Tools for More Resourceful Advertisements in English" by Dallin D. Oaks in the *Journal of Technical Writing and Communication* 25:4 (1995): 371–392. 2) "Creating Structural Ambiguities in Humor: Getting English Grammar to Cooperate" by Dallin D. Oaks in *Humor: International Journal of Humor Research* 7:4 (1994): 377–401.

can be combined into the sentence

> The well-trained police officer, who had a dog that was barking loudly, spotted the dangerous criminals that a caller had reported.

In learning to do sentence combining, the students do not need much grammar instruction, but those who teach sentence combining or who help develop its teaching materials would probably be more effective if they have an understanding of modifiers and their structure. If teachers or materials developers are themselves informed about modifiers only to the extent that native speakers are already informed about them (an unconscious understanding that allows them to generate and recognize well-formed constructions but not to analyze and identify the elements involved), gaps are likely to occur in the instruction. Thus they might design lessons or exercises involving relative clauses that modify the subject of the sentence, but they might not even think to include exercises in which clauses could be embedded to modify objects or subjective complements. Or as far as the internal structure of the relative clause is concerned, they might not notice that their examples and exercises all use a relative that serves as a subject within its own clause, forgetting to include other types in which the relative could serve other functions. They might also forget to include examples that could involve restrictive as well as nonrestrictive clauses. It might also not occur to them to involve modifiers of verbs as well as those that modify nouns.

As we looked at relative clauses, we noted the difference between restrictive and nonrestrictive clauses. The distinction between the two types of clauses has a relevance beyond mere linguistic classification. As we noted in the chapter, it relates to punctuation differences. Restrictive clauses are not set off by commas, whereas nonrestrictive clauses are. In the next chapter we will briefly revisit this topic and provide some practice in comma placement as it relates to restrictive and nonrestrictive clauses.

This chapter has looked briefly at coordinating conjunctions. Like the matter of restrictive and nonrestrictive clauses, a recognition of coordinating conjunctions is important for proper comma placement. If two independent clauses are joined by any of the coordinating conjunctions other than *not* (*and, but, or, nor, for, yet,* or *so*), then a comma is usually required.

Part Four

Further Perspectives

Usage†

"To our language may be with great justice applied the observation of Quintilian, that speech was not formed by an analogy sent from heaven. It did not descend to us in a state of uniformity and perfection, but was produced by necessity and enlarged by accident, and is therefore composed of dissimilar parts, thrown together by negligence, by affectation, by learning, or by ignorance."—Samuel Johnson[1]

The term *grammar,* as this text has so far used it, refers to the structures of language as well as their formal description and analysis. At the beginning of this book it was noted that this larger sense of grammar includes the systems and patterns of the language whether at the phonological, morphological, or syntactic level. Our approach in this type of grammatical study has been primarily a descriptive one, describing the kinds of knowledge a native speaker of English has, even if that knowledge is largely unconscious. But the term *grammar,* as was noted earlier, has also been commonly used for a prescriptive approach to language, in other words, an approach that prescribes what people should say. The kind of grammar that treats the more socially prescribed forms in a language is what linguistics now usually refers to as "usage." This latter meaning of grammar is what people usually intend when they say that someone has used "bad grammar." What they mean is that a speaker or writer has used a nonstandard variant, such as *ain't* or a double negative ("I don't have no . . . ")—usages ordinarily attributed to people with less education. Throughout this chapter we will frequently use the term *usage* rather than *grammar* as we speak of issues related to notions of correct/incorrect, proper/improper, good/bad, right/wrong, and standard/nonstandard. It is important to note that the forces that determine the preferable variant nearly always lie outside the language.

When we speak of proper usage in English we are often speaking of what constitutes the standard dialect of the language. In college coursework and public settings or formal situations, people are expected to use a standard variety of English.

---

†This chapter is coauthored by Don Norton and Dallin D. Oaks.

[1]Cited in *Attitudes Toward English Usage: The History of a War of Words* by Edward Finegan. New York: Teachers College Press, 1980, p. 18.

Standard English is no more logical than the nonstandard varieties. In fact, many nonstandard varieties display features that are even more logical than the corresponding forms in the standard dialect. Historical reasons led to one dialect being used over the others. With the selection of the standard dialect, all others became nonstandard by definition. But this was not through any deficiency inherent in the nonstandard dialects.

Many of the stigmatized forms of the nonstandard dialects are in fact variations from irregularities in the standard dialect. In fact, the standard dialect contains many irregularities. When people say "He don't care" they are regularizing a pattern. Rather than using the contraction of *do not* for every present-tense pattern except the third person singular, they have removed the exceptional *does not* from the verb paradigm and replaced it with the more regular pattern.

Consider also the matter of the form *ain't*. This form is highly stigmatized but would serve a very useful purpose in the standard dialect. Our paradigm for the *be* verb when it is contracted with the word *not* contains the following forms: you aren't, he isn't, she isn't, it isn't, we aren't, and they aren't. Notice that there is no contraction to go with the pronoun *I*. We can contract the pronoun and *be* verb, as in *I'm not,* but this belongs to the separate paradigm of *you're not, he's not, she's not, it's not, we're not,* and *they're not.* The missing form in the first person part of the paradigm explains why tag questions such as "You are healthy, aren't you?"; "He is healthy, isn't he?"; and "We are healthy, aren't we?" must resort to a sort of bizarre corresponding first person form such as "I am healthy, aren't I?" We would expect a form other than *aren't*. In fact, this situation shows the need for a form such as *ain't*. But *ain't* has been so highly stigmatized that it is not available for use in the standard dialect. Thus we resort to *aren't*, which makes very little sense logically, since we would never say something like "I are happy."

A. Identifying Standard Usage

Identifying what constitutes the standard variety of English is not always easy. Over the last several centuries, as speakers of some other European-based languages set up language academies that determined the standard forms of their languages, the speakers of English settled into a practice of relying on the normative use of educated speakers of the language. Consequently, there is no ultimate source in the English-speaking world to which we may turn for an official and authoritative pronouncement of which forms are correct and which are not. Instead we must observe what educated speakers do. Thus in contrast to the practice followed in some language communities, English follows a bottom-up rather than top-down resolution of what is correct and incorrect in the language. Many speakers do not realize this when they turn to so-called authoritative sources to find out what is "correct" in the language.

One very useful tool for learning about current usage expectations is a usage dictionary. Many people are unaware that such dictionaries even exist, but these dictionaries can be enormously helpful. A usage dictionary differs in several important ways from the sort of dictionary that most of us use to settle questions about spelling or definitions. A usage dictionary does not, for example, define words (except as a definition may relate to a usage issue), and it does not even have an entry for each word that we might use. It essentially catalogues and discusses debated points of usage in the language. So a usage dictionary wouldn't have an entry for "spoon" because that word is not involved in a usage issue. But it would likely have an entry for the contraction *ain't,* in which it describes the problematic issues surrounding this form. The listed entries in a usage dictionary may also be set up according to names or descriptions of issues rather than specific words. Thus a usage dictionary is likely to have the entry "double negative," which refers to a usage issue. In this regard, the entry is more like an encyclopedic entry than a dictionary entry.

Serious students of language should be familiar with what a usage dictionary is and how to use one. Even as they consult one, they should be aware that usage dictionaries do not address all the same issues; and even when treating the same usage issues, some differences will exist in their observations and directives with regard to those issues. This is a natural consequence of not having a language academy. Although educated people agree on many usage points such as avoiding the use of *ain't,* they may also disagree on some usage points. This fact underscores the advisability of a writer or editor consulting more than one usage dictionary when trying to make an informed decision about a particular usage item. The following exercise will illustrate.

Exercise 18–1

Consult at least two usage dictionaries for each of the words or issues below. Report whether the usage dictionaries have an entry, and if so, very briefly summarize what they suggest with regard to the word or issue in question. For a list of usage dictionaries, see the end of this chapter.

1. *disinterested* vs. *uninterested*
2. *hopefully* as a sentence modifier (as in "Hopefully, she will be there.")
3. *appreciate* to mean "thank you"

Standard speakers are not generally aware of all the various usage rules. But even if they are, they do not seem to regard all usage violations with the same degree of seriousness. Some violations of usage rules carry a more serious stigma than others. For example, the prescriptive rule against *hopefully* as a sentence modifier, as in "Hopefully, he will come to school," usually carries little if any stigma against speakers who violate this usage rule. On the other hand, if someone during a job interview were to say "That don't matter," this kind of subject-verb agreement problem would, depending on the type of job, possibly destroy any chances the prospective employee might have of landing the job. Studies have been made into the relative frequency of and social stigma attached to the violation of particular prescriptive rules. In a book about the teaching of composition, Noguchi briefly summarizes and reports the results of a study by Robert J. Connors and Andrea A. Lunsford on error frequency, and a study performed by Maxine Hairston on attitudes by working professionals toward particular types of errors. Such studies, as Noguchi shows, have important implications for teachers with limited classroom time to address grammar teaching. Noguchi explains that of particular concern are those errors that are both common and carry serious social costs.[2] It is beyond the scope of this chapter to enter into an analysis of the relative weights that should be given to each of the various usage points in the classroom, but the reader is invited to look at articles by Connors and Lunsford, as well as Hairston.[3]

On the topic of grammar and usage, it is important that people be realistic about what the study of grammar and usage can do for someone and what it should not realistically be expected to do. The most effective way to acquire a standard usage is to grow up speaking it and to be around those who speak it regularly. It is unrealistic to think that merely by being informed about a usage rule, someone who has grown up using nonstandard forms can suddenly change spontaneous speech habits that have been ingrained over a period of years. Such change requires practice and reinforcement. But an awareness of grammar and usage rules could presumably help people in editing and proofreading their own written work. Written communication allows considerably more time to consider and revise than does oral communication. Editing one's work for usage problems is certainly not all that one needs to do to improve writing. This still leaves such important issues as content, topic development, and organization. But even the most lucid and intelligent ideas in the world won't persuade some readers to your side if those readers are overly distracted by usage problems that undermine your credibility at every turn.

People often think of usage choices as choices of right and wrong. But language issues are more complex than that. Some forms, although common in formal writing, may seem highly unusual in speech, even standard speech. And etiquette might even suggest that some traditionally correct forms which could sound pretentious should perhaps be avoided in some contexts to avoid making others feel uncomfortable. Part of being educated is knowing how to make appropriate choices in language and to make adjustments as necessary. In this regard, language usage is a little bit like the choice in clothing. Even though a tuxedo is the most formal piece of clothing a person is likely to wear, it is not invariably the most appropriate. There are times when its use would even be much less appropriate than casual slacks. The analogy is not a perfect one, but it illustrates that any approach to usage that ignores the larger set of contextual circumstances is superficial.

B. Applying Structural Knowledge to an Understanding of Usage Issues

The study of grammar can be helpful not only in describing some of the issues addressed by prescriptive grammarians, but also in learning and understanding the

---

[2]See *Grammar and the Teaching of Writing* by Rei R. Noguchi. Urbana, Illinois: National Council of Teachers of English, 1991. This book contains some significant ideas and suggestions for teachers of writing. Among the most interesting ones, Noguchi suggests some strategies for using the unconscious language knowledge possessed by native speakers to help them learn to consciously identify such things as a subject and verb rather than using time-consuming grammatical discussions. The identification of subject and verb can then be used to correct particular usage errors.

[3]"Frequency of Formal Errors in Current College Writing, or Ma and Pa Kettle Do Research" by Robert J. Connors and Andrea A. Lunsford in *College Composition and Communication* 39 (1988): 395–409. See also "Not All Errors Are Created Equal: Nonacademic Readers in the Professions Respond to Lapses in Usage" by Maxine Hairston in *College English* 43 (1981): 794–806.

nature of their prescribed forms. Throughout the previous chapters as the grammatical content has prompted relevant connections, we have looked at some particular usage issues. But many additional usage issues remain with which careful users of the language should acquaint themselves. It would not be practical or even possible to address all these issues in this chapter, so we will just attempt to illustrate the relevance that the kind of grammatical information that you have studied throughout this book has for usage. In what follows, we will look at some selected usage issues in a sort of encyclopedic way, giving a brief introduction to each issue as well as some observations. The issues will be organized according to the first three major sections of this book: phonology, morphology, and syntax. Again, our focus will not be to illustrate every application of these three areas to usage but rather to show some examples representing applications of the grammatical knowledge you have studied within each of the three areas.

Except when noted, our observations will apply particularly to American English. In the examples accompanying some of the headings, the use of an asterisk indicates that an example would be considered incorrect by traditional prescriptive grammarians.

Phonetics and Phonology

Our consideration of phonetics and phonology in relation to usage items is not intended to suggest that American English has a standard pronunciation. As has been indicated earlier, it does not. But while most of the general pronunciation characteristics of the various dialects may be standard, some particular phonological features and word pronunciations carry some negative social consequences when used among many segments of the population. We will look at just a few of these from the added perspective of the phonetic and phonological material you have studied. In this section we will also look at some usage issues that are not based on phonetics or phonology per se but involve decisions that can be aided by a greater awareness of the sound system of our language.

Interdental Fricatives

Some speakers of English do not use interdental fricatives /θ/ and /ð/ where most speakers of the standard would, using an alternative sound instead. The nature of the alternatives will vary according to the specific dialect and the location of the phoneme within the particular word. It is common, however, for alveolars, such as /t/ and /d/ or a labiodental such as /f/, to be used in the place of an interdental.

Predictably enough, the variants correlate with voicing principles you have learned. Thus if a speaker uses /t/ and /d/ instead of an interdental, the voiceless /t/ will occur in those environments where /θ/ would have been used, and /d/ will occur where /ð/ would otherwise have been used. Historically as well as phonologically there has been a relationship between /ð/ and /d/. In fact, several hundred years ago, the words *burden* and *murder* were frequently written as *burthen* and *murther.*

Nevertheless, the substitution of an alveolar stop or labiodental fricative for an interdental fricative will likely be viewed negatively by many speakers.

Word Pronunciations Resulting from Epenthesis and Metathesis

Among the pronunciations that occasion some stigma are those related to phonological processes, such as epenthesis and metathesis, that we identified in an earlier chapter. As you will recall, epenthesis involves the addition of a sound, and metathesis involves a rearrangement of sounds.

One common example of epenthesis is found in some people's pronunciation of the word *wash* as /wɔrš/. This particular pronunciation rarely goes unnoticed by some individuals. An example related to epenthesis is evident in the pronunciation some people give to the word *grievous,* wherein they add an extra vowel to yield /griviəs/ rather than /grivəs/.

Examples of metathesis include the words *nuclear* and *relevant.* In the former word, the vowels are sometimes reordered to give a pronunciation like /nukyulər/. In the latter word the consonants /l/ and /v/ are reversed, giving /rɛvələnt/. But one of the most unfavorably viewed cases of metathesis is found in the dialectal form /æks/ for the word *ask.* As will be pointed out in the next chapter, this form of the word has historical precedent. But usage attitudes are frequently formed arbitrarily.

A vs. *An* Immediately Preceding Multisyllable Words Beginning with an Unstressed /h/

Examples: a/an hysterical, a/an historian

The choice of whether to use *a* or *an* as the indefinite article depends on the initial sound of the word that directly follows. If the word begins with a consonant sound, then we typically use *a.* If it begins with a vowel sound, then we use *an.* Some confusion, however, exists with what to do about words beginning with an unstressed /h/. In speech, the choice between *a* or *an* ultimately depends on whether or not a speaker pronounces /h/ at the beginning of a word. In writing, there's a tendency to use *a,* under the assumption the /h/ *is* pronounced, but you will find both "a historical" and "an historical." The choice in article is one usage issue in which some variance occurs between British and American English.

Oral Exercise 18–A

Look at each of the following noun phrases and determine which form of the indefinite article that you would use. Explain your choice. Remember that dialects may vary on the pronunciation of some words beginning with /h/.

1. _____ habitual liar
2. _____ historical moment
3. _____ hypnotic state

Could of

Example: *We could of been there last night.

This written form results from an attempt by some people to represent in spelling the best approximation of what they think they are pronouncing. The presence of the past participle *been,* however, indicates that the vowel and labiodental fricative [əv] are part of a reduced form of the auxiliary *have* rather than the preposition *of.* Both forms are pronounced the same, so the confusion is understandable. But the written form *could of* should nonetheless be avoided.

To/Too

When spelling, some students, particularly in the lower grades, struggle with the distinction between *to* and *too.* The word *to* is used as a preposition as in "to the store" and as the first part of a verb infinitive as in "to go." The word *too,* on the other hand, is an adverbial that is used as a synonym for "also" or to indicate excessiveness, as in "too nervous." College students should have mastered the difference between the two words. But it is understandable that younger students could still struggle. For younger students, any grammatical explanation of the difference in the two forms could be confusing. An alternative approach to distinguishing the two forms could use phonetic information. Both the preposition and infinitive use of *to* may be pronounced using the schwa vowel /ə/, whereas the adverbial *too* must be pronounced with /u/. This makes for an easy explanation. A teacher could explain therefore that if the word in question can be pronounced /tə/, then spell the form as *to.* If the word in question cannot be pronounced /tə/, then spell it *too.* Of course students do not have to know anything about the phonetic symbol or the name of the schwa vowel. It is enough for them to hear the teacher pronounce the difference between the two vowel sounds.[4]

Every Day/Everyday

Examples: We passed his house every day.
        We experienced everyday problems.

The choice between *every day* and *everyday* is ultimately a choice between whether the words are used adverbially or adjectivally. But the distinction is also one that can be approached through the phonological features of stress and juncture. The adverbial use of *every day* contains a stress on both words, as well as a brief pause between

---

[4]One notable exception to the simplified rule given here is to be found in the case of an infinitive that has undergone ellipsis. This can occur in a sentence such as "I didn't want to go, but the teacher told me to." This kind of sentence would pronounce the final *to* as /tu/, yet it should still be spelled with *to.* This case is not as exceptional as it appears. If one supplied the verb that has been ellipsed ("I didn't want to go, but the teacher told me to go."), then the infinitive marker *to* would still be pronounced as a schwa, and the rule would hold. Another exception would involve a relative clause in which the relative pronoun functions as an object of a preposition within its own clause ("I know the house that he went to."). Such exceptions, however, are probably unlikely to be among the sentences that younger spellers would be trying to spell.

them. In contrast, the adjectival *everyday* has stress on the first part of the compound and no pause between the two parts of the compound.

Exercise 18-2

Each of the following sentences contains a blank and a pair of choices. Using your knowledge of grammar as well as pronunciation, select the appropriate choice to fill in the blank.

1. She comes to our house _____. (every day/everyday)
2. We wanted to meet some _____ people. (every day/everyday)
3. We wanted to meet some people _____. (every day/everyday)
4. Those three girls could _____ necessity be cautious. (of/have)
5. The mail carrier should _____ seen that the mailbox was full. (of/have)
6. If he would _____ helped them, they would be here by now. (of/have)
7. The wrapping paper was _____ colorful. (to/too)
8. We attended that university _____. (to/too)
9. In order _____ be successful in your job, you should work hard. (to/too)
10. You have made _____ many mistakes. (to/too)
11. The student walked all the way _____ the library. (to/too)

Hyphenation of Compounds

The use of a hyphen within a compound is often an attempt to clarify an otherwise ambiguous expression. Thus although the *Chicago Manual of Style* explains that "the trend in spelling compound words has been away from the use of hyphens," it shows that in some cases, hyphens clarify intended meaning. It provides the example of "a fast sailing ship" and explains that if *fast* modifies *sailing ship,* no hyphen is necessary. But if *fast* modifies only *sailing,* then this relationship can be indicated by *fast-sailing.*[5] Appropriate decisions may be made through a consideration of modification, but phonetic criteria may also be useful. Earlier you saw that the stress and juncture of compound nouns (such as *greenhouse*) are pronounced differently from the way they are handled with noun + modifier structures (such as *green house*). Similarly, the two different intended meanings of *fast-sailing ship* and *fast sailing ship* are also indicated by a difference in stress and juncture. An awareness of these two suprasegmental features can help in determinations of whether or not to use a hyphen. For *fast sailing ship,* the two heaviest stresses come on *fast* and *sailing,* with a brief pause after *fast.* On the other hand, for *fast-sailing ship,* the two heaviest stresses are on *fast* and *ship,* with a brief pause after *sailing.*

Restrictive/Nonrestrictive Clauses and Comma Placement

You have previously used a semantic notion to distinguish between restrictive and nonrestrictive clauses. If clauses are necessary for limiting a particular noun phrase, then they

---

[5]*The Chicago Manual of Style,* 14th ed. Chicago: University of Chicago Press, 1993.

are restrictive; otherwise they are nonrestrictive. The difference in the two clauses relates to a punctuation difference. Nonrestrictive clauses are set off by commas, whereas restrictive are not. As you have seen earlier, the two types of relative clauses may also be distinguished through other means, including the suprasegmental feature of juncture. When a relative clause is nonrestrictive, it is preceded by a terminal juncture.

Exercise 18-3

Insert commas and hyphens when necessary to clarify the intended meaning of the potentially ambiguous sentences below. The intended meaning is indicated in the parentheses after each sentence. Some sentences can be left as they appear. Confirm your decisions by noting the stress and juncture differences that correspond with the intended meanings.

1. The price will be a little cost effective on January 12. (The cost begins on January 12.)
2. The price will be a little cost effective on January 12. (The financial arrangement will be economical.)
3. The major had received no nonsense orders from the general. (The orders were direct and to the point.)
4. The major had received no nonsense orders from the general. (No orders that were nonsensical had been issued to the major.)
5. I had seen his changing tables in the back of the building. (He owned tables for changing babies' diapers.)
6. I had seen him changing tables in the back of the building. (He was changing the linens on the tables.)
7. She wanted to get some free loading advice. (Advice on how to take advantage of other people's generosity.)
8. She wanted to get some free loading advice. (Free advice on how to load things.)
9. The salesman was put in charge of a big wig convention. (A convention about marketing wigs that are big.)
10. The salesman was put in charge of a big wig convention. (A convention attended by very important people.)
11. The book which was written in just 30 days was a little disorganized. (This book, not the other book, was disorganized.)
12. The book which was written in just 30 days was a little disorganized. (The book was disorganized; it was written in 30 days.)
13. My sister who lives in Rockford will be visiting us soon. (This particular sister as distinguished from any of my other sisters.)
14. The thief who was really quite careless left a driver's license on the counter. (There was only one thief, so the fact about his carelessness does not serve to distinguish him from others.)
15. Waldo purchased the book that had a polka-dot cover. (There was only one book with a polka-dot cover.)
16. His animosity which was completely unexplainable shocked the senator. (The animosity is not being distinguished from other animosities.)

Morphology

Morphology relates to a number of usage issues. Some issues considered in this section concern the word-formation processes involved in generating particular words. Other usage issues are included in this section because an understanding of them depends on a knowledge of form or structure classes.

Acronyms

Acronyms are an important part of our language, but at least two usage issues should be considered in relation to their use. First, as *Webster's Dictionary of English Usage* cautions, some care should be taken that the intended meaning of the acronym be clear to the audience. *Webster's Dictionary of English Usage* also points out that some acronyms do not last for long.

Another issue to remember with regard to acronyms relates to how they should be represented on the page. New acronyms typically show themselves with capital letters and sometimes even some indication that they are based on an abbreviation of different words as, for example, *MASH* or *M.A.S.H.* for mobile army surgical hospital. Over time, however, this designation may fade and the word may be represented in lowercase letters as with *mash.* A writer should be aware of the current conventions for a given acronym.

Back-formations

In an earlier chapter on the processes of word formation you looked at back-formations, which result when a new word is formed from one mistakenly assumed to be its derivative. New back-formations frequently find themselves at the center of usage controversies, though many ultimately achieve full respectability. In English the verb *donate* originated as a back-formation from *donation* and was condemned by many, but it has now become such common usage that virtually no one is afraid of using it, even in formal texts. But one should be cautious with more recently derived back-formations, such as *burgle* (from *burglar*) and *enthuse* (from *enthusiasm*).

Clippings

Another common word-formation process is clipping, by which a longer word is reduced to a shorter one, as with *fan* (from *fanatic*) or *ad* (from *advertisement*). Like back-formations, clippings may not initially be accepted by more careful speakers and writers of the language. If you are aware that a word is a clipped form, it might be a good idea to consult a "regular" or usage dictionary to get a sense of how accepted the term is.

The Suffix -ee

Some commentators on language are perfectly comfortable with a particular morpheme until they begin to feel as if it is getting overused. This has happened to some extent with the derivational suffix *-ee* in words that share a relationship with other words using the agentive suffix *-er.* Thus although there is no complaint against words such as *employer* and *employee,* we can find some objection to *-ee* on words such as *tutee* or *helpee.* One might argue that the morpheme *-ee* is a victim of its own success.

The Suffix *-ize*

Like the suffix *-ee,* the suffix *-ize* is very productive, serving to change nouns or adjectives into verbs. Again, some speakers object to what they see as an overuse of this morpheme as in words such as *finalize, prioritize, Americanize,* and *popularize.* But new *-ize* verbs do gradually gain acceptance, and some have existed in the language for some time. Usage texts usually inveigh against what they consider "cheap" creations, such as *sloganize.* A recent example of just how productive this morpheme is can be seen in the advertisements for Midas Mufflers that tell us to "Midasize" our cars.

Foreign Plurals

Foreign borrowings occasionally present a problem to speakers of our language, such as when a determination needs to be made about the plural forms of these words. In chapter 11 you saw that the plural of some foreign borrowings, such as *soprano* (plural *sopranos*), are regularized. Some retain the pattern of their native language such as *phenomenon* (plural *phenomena*). And others, such as *syllabus,* allow either option (plural *syllabuses* or *syllabi*). The insecurity that some speakers have about just which forms should be used may stem from the changing nature of our language. For example, though *datum* was originally borrowed as a singular form with *data* as the plural, the word *data* has increasingly been used as a singular rather than a plural. This is evident in the frequent use of the word with the singular verb *is.* Another possible cause for insecurity might go back to the time in which a particular word entered the language. With no language academy to establish the so-called correct plural form in the first place, there can be confusion from the start, to say nothing of what happens as the language continues to change. An academy could perhaps have declared just which form we should use for the plural of *octopus. Webster's Dictionary of English Usage* shows that two forms are used: *octopuses* and *octopi,* with *octopodes* sometimes being considered as a possible variant. Speakers and writers who wish to avoid controversy in their choice of plural forms should consult a usage dictionary for words they question. And while usage dictionaries cannot make authoritative pronouncements about the correctness of any particular form, they can often provide a clue about the relative acceptance of various forms.

Adverbs without the Suffix *-ly*

Examples: *They ran *slow.*
*He walked *crooked.*
*She was *real* happy.

As a form class, adverbs are frequently identified through the use of the suffix *-ly*. In Old English, there were two adverbial suffixes: *-lice* (or *-lic*), and *-e*. Through time the suffix *-e* eventually dropped from the end of many adverbs, and many grammarians subsequently assumed that the presence or absence of *-ly* (the later form that had developed from *-lice*) was an essential factor in distinguishing between adjectives and adverbs. This assumption about the necessity of *-ly* to signal an adverb ignores the historical reality that some adverbs have never commonly employed the *-ly* ending. Others nearly always take the *-ly*, especially when they can be confused with non *-ly* words: *hard/hardly, fair/fairly*. Many words take either form. In those situations where the adverb has both forms, the non *-ly* form is usually the more vernacular, the more forceful, casual, spoken choice; the *-ly* form is the usual form in more formal speech and writing.

Excessive commitment to the idea that adverbs must have *-ly* has led to such "overcorrections" as *thusly* (an affectation), and *muchly*, either a hypercorrection or a usage that carries a tone of humor or novelty (as in "Thank you muchly"). Although *muchly* has been around for centuries, it has never gained approval in standard usage.

Exercise 18–4

Some of the italicized words below would likely be objectionable to prescriptivists. Others merely resemble words that could present a usage problem. For each italicized word, determine whether it represents a potential usage problem. If it does, label what aspect of the word would cause some to object to it. If there is no usage issue, then answer No problem.

1. Because there will be no time afterward, they will *commentate* during the broadcast.
2. The book had several *appendixes* in the back.
3. I prefer a full beard rather than a *goatee.*
4. He pledged money to *madd* for their efforts against drunk driving.
5. The runner was sick at that time and ran *slow.*
6. We would like you to examine some of the *cactuses* on the property.
7. Their preacher will *sermonize* to the congregation one more time.
8. Thank you *muchly* for you assistance.
9. He planned to do some *SCUBA* diving while in Hawaii.
10. It seemed *right.*
11. The children lived in a *prefab* house.
12. As the interrogator prepared further questions, the *interrogatee* waited nervously.
13. You should not *characterize* him that way.

Comparative (and Superlative) Absolutes

Examples: *more unique
*more perfect
*most black

*most complete
*less perfect
*least unique

Comparative and superlative absolutes are usually edited out of serious writing, though they are common in the informal speech of educated people. The use of comparative and superlative forms with absolute forms has probably developed through analogy with other adjectives which freely admit such forms. The objection to comparative and superlative absolutes resides in logic. Logically, something that is perfect or unique should not be capable of being compared. If something is unique and thus one of a kind, it cannot be more unique than something else. And something cannot be more or less perfect, because perfection, logically speaking, must either be possessed in its entirety, or it is not perfection. Although many people recognize the comparative and superlative use of *perfect* and *unique* as a violation of the prescriptive rule against such absolutes, fewer people realize that words such as *black, circular, complete, chief, extreme,* and *equal* could present a similar problem.

Usage authorities vary widely in their tolerance and condemnation of comparative and superlative absolutes. Even conservative prescriptivists must admit that such phrases as "more/most unique; more/most perfect" are common (see the Preamble to the U.S. Constitution: "in order to form a more perfect union"). Comparative and superlative absolutes are more common in informal educated speech, though they have been used for centuries among even the best speakers and writers in nearly all situations.

Ain't

As we noted earlier in this chapter, we have no contraction for "am not" in English. It is precisely for this reason that *ain't* could be so useful in our language. In fact, the contraction may have originally derived from a contraction of "am not" (*an't*), which was once a common variant, used by the educated as well as uneducated. Unfortunately, this particular contraction has become one of the great shibboleths in the language, probably because it has been used with other pronouns ("we, you, he, she, it, they ain't").

Prescriptive grammar (usage) texts now condemn the form categorically, and its use marks a person as uneducated or of low social standard, except perhaps in some specialized contexts in which it might be used to achieve a casual, earthy, or humorous effect.

Irregular Verbs

Some of the problems native speakers encounter in making appropriate choices in past tense and past participle verb forms can be traced back to the history of our language. Old English had a number of different verb classes, each with its own characteristic set of forms. Some of these verb classes are still present in Modern

English, though because so many verbs have conformed to the pattern of using *-ed* in both the past tense and past participle, we label any that do not do so as "irregular." But in Old English times these alternative paradigms had many members. We can still see some evidence of the varying classes in the patterns that are visible as we compare the base form, the past tense, and the past participle forms of particular verbs. For example, one set of verbs, such as *ride, drive,* and *write,* changes the inner vowel of its verb according to one kind of pattern (r*i*de, r*o*de, r*i*dden), whereas another set of verbs, such as *sing, ring,* and *drink,* changes the vowel according to another pattern (s*i*ng, s*a*ng, s*u*ng).

Even as some of what now would be considered "irregular" verbs have become regular, other regular verbs have become irregular. And many verbs now have both kinds of forms competing equally (*broadcast/broadcasted; knit/knitted; lighted/lit*). Some have older and more recent forms (*strive, strived/strove, strived/striven*). And some archaic forms are locked into idioms (*new-mown, clean-shaven, cloven-hoof* but *cleft palate, wrought* [worked] *iron*). There are even verbs with three past-participle forms: *wake, woke/waked, woke/waked/woken; plead, pleaded/plead/pled, pleaded/plead/pled* (*pled* also being used in the past tense). And some verbs have British versus American preferences: *proved/proven, burnt/burned, dreamt/dreamed, dwelt/dwelled, got/gotten.* There are also colloquial forms: *beat* for *beaten, busted* for *burst, drug* for *dragged, snuck* (now accepted in speech) for *sneaked, boughten* for *bought* ("store *boughten*" bread or dress), and so on.

Adding to the confusion, some verbs have specialized meaning. In such cases one verb form corresponds to a particular meaning, whereas the other verb meaning requires the other form. For example, *flew* is appropriate to one meaning, whereas *flied* is appropriate for the other: "The bird flew out the window"; "The batter flied out in the 8th inning." Other verbs displaying this dual behavior include *born/borne* and *hanged/hung,* though the distinction is breaking down in *hanged/hung.*

With all of this variation and change in verb forms, we could expect some confusion. If you are a native speaker and are unsure of which past tense or past participle form to use with a particular verb, the chances are that the verb causes problems for other speakers as well. In this case, there is likely to be a treatment of it in a usage dictionary.

Less/Fewer; Amount/Number

As you have seen in an earlier chapter, count nouns require different structural concatenations than noncount nouns. Native speakers are accustomed to using *many* with count nouns and *much* with noncount. But there is less consistency surrounding the use of the words *less, fewer, amount,* and *number.* Traditional prescriptive rules require that *fewer* and *number* be used with count nouns, and *less* and *amount* be used with noncount nouns. But in fact, *less* before count nouns has been around for a long time and is gaining in popularity, as in the common claim by advertisers that their product has "less calories." The use of *amount* before count nouns is common in speech; though it still sometimes occurs in serious writing, it is usually edited out.

Shall/Will

The old usage rule calls for *shall* in the first person (I, we) for simple future and *will* for second and third person. In instances of determination or obligation, the rule reverses: I, we will; you, he, she, it, they shall. These rules are not generally observed in American English, except in very formal settings. In instances where *will* conveys the wrong meaning, *shall* is standard: "What shall we do?" "Shall we dance?" This book does not maintain a distinction between *shall* and *will*.

Double (or Multiple) Negatives

Old and Middle English featured the double, triple, and even quadruple negative idiomatically, to emphasize the negation:

> "I will not budge for no man's pleasure." (Shakespeare)
> "And that no woman has; nor never none
> Shall mistress be of it." (Shakespeare)
> "He nevere yet no vileynye ne sayde
> In al his lyf unto no maner wight." (Chaucer)

In the eighteenth century, amateur grammarians formulated a rule against multiple negatives. Their reasoning, based on formal logic, was that more than one negative could make a positive. This conclusion, however, ignored actual language usage, for speakers do not interpret two negatives to mean a positive except in an idiom like "I couldn't not go to her wedding" or in an utterance that combines "not" with a word containing a negative prefix: "It was not incorrect."

After a couple of centuries of proscriptions against multiple negatives, most educated people would now avoid saying something like "I don't see no paper." But even among some educated speakers we might find some nonstandard uses of multiple negation. Some speakers seem unaware that such words as *hardly* and *scarcely* are considered negative. Such speakers might therefore utter something like *"I can't hardly understand" or *"She couldn't scarcely walk there."

Ending a Sentence with a Preposition

It is a myth that you should not end a sentence with a preposition. This myth may have arisen from the name of that part of speech itself: pre-position. As some prescriptivists probably reasoned, if a preposition by its name should precede the noun it is associated with, then it should never follow it—and certainly not at the end of the sentence.

But ending a sentence with a preposition is idiomatic, and the practice is long-standing. It appears to be John Dryden who set grammarians' teeth on edge regarding the placement of prepositions, though he later rued his proscription. But the amateur grammarians had already picked it up, and the rule became canonized.

The avoidance of a preposition at the end of a sentence (or clause) is certainly more common in writing than in speech. And in some instances, earlier placement of the preposition does sound more formal: "The authority to whom we've just listened spent three years in Tibet" versus "The authority we've just listened to spent three years in Tibet." But labored attempts to avoid a preposition at the end of a clause or sentence are unnecessary.

Part of the confusion surrounding this usage issue results from the fact that some of what are considered by prescriptivists to be prepositions are in fact part of the verb itself. You may recall the discussion of verb-adverbial composites in chapter 16. There is a difference between "We ran down the hill" and "We ran down our roommate." You can say "The hill down which we ran," but not "The roommate down whom we ran." "To run down someone" or "to run someone down" involves a two-part verb. Thus to refer to "the apartment we've just cleaned up" involves no preposition at all, but rather the adverbial part of the composite (sometimes called a "particle"). Verb particles are involved in some humorous examples. Winston Churchill, in protest to his editors, who were fiddling with his idioms, is purported to have said something like "This is the sort of nonsense up with which I shall not put" (In *put up with* it is arguable whether the verb is followed by two particles or by a particle and a preposition). And one well-known example involves an accumulation of prepositions and verb particles in an entirely idiomatic sentence a child speaks to her father, who's carrying a book upstairs: "What are you bringing that book that I don't want to be read to out of up for?"

In some constructions, the preposition must come at the end of the clause or sentence: "The rule is one that most people have heard of. It's something we have all heard of." Resorting to an "of which" alternative would sound unnatural. A number of grammatical constructions in fact call for postponement of the preposition.

Split Infinitive

One commonly discussed usage violation is the split infinitive. An infinitive verb is said to be "split" when an adverbial modifier occurs between the *to* and the verb. Perhaps one of the most controversial split infinitives in the history of television was the one used in the television show *Star Trek*. In the original *Star Trek* series the introduction to each episode proclaimed "To boldly go where no man has gone before." This use apparently outraged a number of armchair grammarians who felt that this prominent use of a split infinitive was detrimental to usage standards of the community. The complaints of grammarians were apparently not as influential as the complaints of feminists, since the later *Star Trek* series retained the split infinitive but changed the "no man" to "no one."

The split infinitive was uncommon before the nineteenth century, probably because the *to* + verb construction itself was not common, though the introduction of this form of the infinitive dates to Middle English (Old English usually used a suffix to indicate the infinitive). With the increased usage of the *to* + verb construction came a proscription against splitting it, probably by comparison with the prestigious languages Latin and Greek, in which the infinitive is a single word (as it was in Old English) and thus cannot be "split."

The continued prejudice against the split infinitive is strong enough that writers probably do well to avoid the split if the ear tolerates it. But it is nonetheless true that despite the textbook rule, the split infinitive occurs in all levels and varieties of English, though more often in speech than in writing. And in some constructions, it becomes necessary to split the infinitive to preserve intended meaning. Compare the difference in meaning between "The policy was intended to generally guide future decisions " and "The policy was intended generally to guide future decisions." This book has occasionally split an infinitive when it seemed appropriate to do so.

Exercise 18-5

For each of the sentences below, answer yes or no to indicate whether the italicized word(s) would be compatible with even the most traditional prescriptive rules as they have been explained above.

1. The senator's intention was *to quickly wrap up* her business and leave Washington.
2. While interacting with the guests, the child demonstrated the *most polite* behavior that we had ever seen in someone so young.
3. We *cannot hardly* believe what he said to the media.
4. I believe that I *shall* be able to be there tomorrow.
5. Angela thought that my presentation was the *most unique* one at the conference.
6. We never expected to see such a large *amount of pencils* in his desk.
7. The Greeks traveled *to friendly shores* where their landing was unopposed.
8. The gas station attendants *shall* probably return your money.
9. I *did not see* her anywhere.
10. They were *more capable* than we had thought.
11. Is she the person you were going to watch the movie *with*?
12. There was *less garbage* on the lawn this morning.
13. *I don't believe no one.*
14. The two of us *shall* decide on that issue after it becomes necessary.

Syntax

In this section we will consider those usage issues whose understanding relies on a knowledge of syntactic information. Some of the usage issues, such as subject-verb agreement, require not only a recognition of the subject, but an understanding of phrases, for example, which part of the noun phrase is the head and thus the part that must agree with the verb phrase. Other usage issues, such as those involving the case form of personal, interrogative, or relative pronouns (e.g., *I* vs. *me, who* vs. *whom*), require an understanding of sentence or clause types, the kinds of verbs that construct them, and the function of particular phrases within those sentences or clauses. A basic understanding of the necessary requirements of a sentence relates to decisions about how to edit fragments, comma splices, and fused sentences. And an understanding of modifiers relates to decisions involved with ambiguity and the forms that sentence or adjectival modifiers must take. We will now turn to these syntactic issues.

Subject-Verb Agreement

Historically, such great writers as Shakespeare, Malory, Milton, and Swift enjoyed freedom from the rigid rules that dictated how "a verb must agree with its subject in number." These rules were formed in the eighteenth century and became codified in the nineteenth century, in many instances contradicting the practices of the educated. Today, in most instances, writers and editors follow in written English the established conventions. Below we will briefly summarize some rules that are prescribed for written Standard English though frequently not well-known among English speakers.

1. When a sentence or clause contains a construction like "either . . . or" or "neither . . . nor," agreement of the verb is with the closer subject.

   Example: Either the boy or the girls are going.

   Note that stylists recommend putting the plural subject last, to meet aural expectations. Thus it would be considered a little awkward to say "Either the girls or the boy is going," though technically it would be "correct."

2. When working with such words as *each, either,* or *neither,* use a singular verb.

   Example: Neither prefers the orange ball.

   This remains true even when *each, either,* and *neither* are separated from the verb by intervening words such as a prepositional phrase: "Each of the men was . . . ." In addition, the singular form of the verb is also used with the pronouns *anyone, someone, everyone* (and other indefinite pronouns).

3. In sentences involving a subjective complement, the agreement is with the subject.

   Example: Radio and TV are his favorite pastimes.
   But
   His favorite pastime is radio and TV.

   This rule also applies to inverted sentences in which the subject is not found at the beginning of the sentence, for example, "On the counter were three oranges." In sentences beginning with *there is* or *there are,* locate the subject: "There are three boys in the yard." However, "*There's* + a plural subject" is all but standard in informal spoken English: "There's three points I'd like to make."

4. Compound subjects (subject + *and* + subject) take a plural verb. This rule has exceptions in the case of "plural" subjects that are perceived as a single unit, such as in the sentence "Macaroni and cheese is a popular dish." The expression "as well as" has an equivalent meaning to "and" but is handled differently in regard to subject-verb agreement. When joining two singulars with "as well as," some prescriptivists suggest that a comma makes a difference: "The president, as well as members of his cabinet, was lying," but "The president as well

as members of his cabinet were lying." There is probably some disagreement on this point. Our best suggestion is to let your ear guide you.

5. Collective nouns, such as *group, team, class, family,* may be either singular or plural: "My family *gathers* on holidays to enjoy one another's company" or "My family *gather* on holidays to enjoy one another's company." American ears like the singular verb, British ears the plural. Good ears make the agreement logical—whether the user implies unit or individuals. Often the presence of an additional singular or plural noun helps make the decision: "The crowd were waving their programs," versus "The crowd was a large one."

Exercise 18–6

Consider the agreement rules you read above. For each of the sentences below, select the appropriate form of the verb within the parentheses.

1. Neither of these books (is, are) worth reading.
2. The only drawback to the apartment (is, are) the lack of reliable air conditioning and heating.
3. The recurrence of like sounds (helps, help) students learn this passage of poetry.
4. There (is, are) in my estimation three theories that account for the higher incidence of cancer in Roseville's north section.
5. Professional basketball and football on TV (is, are) his main diversion.
6. His main diversion (is, are) professional basketball and football on TV.
7. Neither they nor I (was, were) averse to dancing.
8. Neither I nor they (was, were) averse to dancing.
9. Running counter to these theories (is, are) the theory of Einstein.
10. Either two book reports or a term paper (is, are) required in this course.
11. Each of the items (is, are) considered important.
12. There (was, were) found at each of the sites evidence of vandalism.
13. One of the two teachers (is, are) eligible for promotion this year.
14. The senior judge, as well as three junior judges, (is, are) to attend the seminar.
15. Either my sister or my parents (drives, drive) me to music lessons twice a week.
16. A list of local high school honors students occasionally (appears, appear) in the local newspaper.

Bad vs. *Badly* after a Linking Verb

Example: *I feel *badly.**

The usage issue of whether to use *bad* or *badly* relates to the syntactic requirements of the main verb in the sentence, and thus the sentence type that is involved, since the kind of verb used is integrally connected to the sentence type. Prescriptivists have traditionally cautioned against using an adverb such as *badly* after a linking verb such as *feel* or *look,* preferring instead that the linking verb be followed by an adjective. Adverbs would be used after "action" verbs. Another way of saying this is that adjectives, not adverbs, serve as subjective complements. But an expression such as "I feel badly" has become so common, even among educated users of the language, that most usage authorities consider it standard. In other words, *badly* in this usage has come to be treated like an adjective. More conservative speakers and writers, however, will still use "I feel bad."

It Is I/It's Me

"It is I" seems never to have been a natural idiom of English. Some authorities speculate that it originated in the Middle English "Hit am I" (or perhaps Old English "Ic hit eom"). Perhaps because *hit* can't agree with *am, am* became *is,* and the idiom was created. The recognition that the pronoun following the linking verb must be a subjective complement helped in determining that the appropriate pronoun form should be the subject form *I* rather than the object form *me.*

Despite its use over the centuries, "It is I" is restricted to formal speech and writing, and it has always conveyed a stuffy tone. Curiously, the construction "It is I who am/is expecting consideration" sounds more natural, though it raises the subsequent subject-verb agreement issue.

Many usage authorities argue for the very natural sounding "It's me," often by citing the standard French idiom "C'est moi." Also, *me* is clearly in "object territory" (occurring in a position following the verb), where it could be mistakenly presumed to be a direct object despite its function as a subjective complement.

Although all modern usage authorities allow "It's me/It is me," some editors still insist on the traditional and prescriptive "It is I," just as they would require the somewhat stilted though much more common "This is she/he."

Reflexive Pronoun for Subject and Object Meanings

Example: *He incorrectly identified John and myself.

The use of *myself* for *I* or *me* appears to have increased greatly over the last century or so. By rule, *myself* and other "self" pronouns (*himself, yourself,* etc.) are reflexives or intensives. Reflexive pronouns are used in an object position when an object of the verb and its subject are the same: "John washed himself." Intensive pronouns emphasize the noun or even pronoun that they accompany: "I myself would never have accepted the assignment" or "We gave it to Henry himself."

Although the use of *myself* for the subject form may be part of a movement to avoid overuse of *I,* and thus to deflect attention from one's self, some grammarians think that its use stems from an insecurity about which case (object or subject) to use. In fact, the pronoun *myself* is in common use in both subject and object functions. As a subject, it replaces *I,* though it does sometimes sound forced: "After three alternates and myself were designated, we met and reviewed our options." It is more likely to occur as a substitute for *I* when it is in a compound following a *be* verb, or when it follows the conjunction *than*: "The three designees were Oaks, Skousen, and myself." "No one knows that better than myself."

Myself for *me* is also common, again especially in compound constructions, occurring in a variety of object positions:

"Not wanting to involve Davis, Harrington and myself in a controversy, we simply conceded." (compound direct object)

"The boss gave the secretary and myself our choices of times for the lunch break." (compound indirect object)

"Completion of the task will be up to three consultants and myself." (compound object of the preposition)

Who/Whom

The choice of whether to use *who* (a subject form) or *whom* (an object form) is related to the function of the pronoun in its sentence or clause: "I brought the boy who wrote the paper" (*who* = the boy. The boy wrote the paper); "I brought the boy whom they saw" (*whom* = the boy. They saw the boy).

The distinction between *who* and *whom* is not consistently maintained, even among standard speakers. In ordinary speech, *who* for *whom* is common in relative clauses mainly because the ear perceives the position of the relative pronoun as a sort of "subject territory" (the relative pronoun precedes the verb), and thus *who* sounds more normal. But as we indicated, the choice should be based on function rather than position. The distinction between the two pronoun forms is not generally preserved in speech except in speech that is self-consciously pedantic. But the distinction is generally maintained in formal speech and edited writing.

Among the insecure social strivers, *whom* is a common overcorrection for *who.* And many journalists and other writers never quite get the rule right: *"Give the package to whomever comes to the door." Many construe *whomever* to be the object of the preposition *to,* though of course it is not. The object of the preposition is the entire clause, "whoever comes to the door." Indicative of the kinds of problems that the choice can present is the response of Theodore Bernstein, of the *New York Times,* writer of a nationally syndicated column on usage. A few decades ago he called for a "I'm for whom's doom" movement—because of the difficulty people have in determining the appropriate form. Historically we also cannot rely on older texts to guide our current usage in the choice between *who* and *whom.* Note, for example, the King James translation of the Bible, which reads, "Whom say men that I am?"

Subject of a Nonfinite *-ing* Verbal

According to current prescriptive rules dating from the nineteenth century, the subject of nonfinite *-ing* verbals (sometimes called "gerunds") must be in the possessive case. Earlier, in the eighteenth century, some grammarians had argued for the object or common case.

Eighteenth century: We objected to him being nominated for vice president.
                     We objected to Perry being nominated for vice president.

Nineteenth century: We objected to his being nominated . . .

We objected to Perry's being nominated . . .

Thus despite the prescriptions of conservative textbooks, both possessive and objective/common case substantives enjoy time-honored usage. In fact, both forms have been around among the educated for three hundred years.

In spite of the current prescriptive rule, even traditionalists allow exceptions to the use of the possessive:

1. If a word has no possessive form: "We were happy with both (not both's) receiving an award." (Compare also *that, this,* and *many*)
2. If there are intervening words: "The party objected to Wilbur (not Wilbur's), a convicted felon, being considered for the post."
3. If the subject is a plural noun: "There are laws in most states against teenagers (not teenagers') getting a license before the age of sixteen."
4. If the subject is an inanimate noun: "Some reviewers objected to the book (not book's) being subsidized." "We were fearful of the roof (not roof's) collapsing."

Exercise 18–7

Within the sentences below, circle the form prescribed by traditional grammarians. For the purposes of this exercise, do not concern yourself with whether some of the forms would sound pedantic or overly formal.

1. The boy brought Waldo and (me, myself) a road almanac.
2. (Jessica, Jessica's) traveling with Jeremy is a bad idea.
3. (Who, Whom) did you expect?
4. I saw Linda and (me, myself) in the mirror.
5. I watched as John praised the person (who, whom) had done so much for the college.
6. Your opinion about the person (who, whom) we discussed was important in our decision.
7. Bill did not approve of (you, your) being hired.
8. His voice sounded (bad, badly).
9. Kim was perfectly agreeable to (Ted, Ted's), who was my friend, coming along for the ride.
10. He was surprised by the (protestors, protestors') complaining about the new policy.
11. Her brother sang (bad, badly) because of his laryngitis.
12. Tammy purchased new umbrellas for Tony and (me, myself).
13. Sam and (I, myself) will be traveling to the game that evening.
14. (Who, Whom) would be willing to sew the patches of the quilt together?

Lie/Lay

Forms of *lay* for *lie* have been common for centuries. Grammarians have taught that *lie* is intransitive, whereas *lay* is transitive. But historically, this distinction has never been fully and consistently maintained by speakers of the language, though the distinction is always made in edited writing (except when a casual tone is desired). In light of what you have learned about verb paradigms, now consider the following forms of *lie* and *lay*:

	stem	present participle	past tense	past participle
intransitive verb:	lie	lying	lay	lain
transitive verb:	lay	laying	laid	laid

Very few speakers, even those who are well-educated, are able to determine the "correct" forms of *lie* and *lay* in spontaneous speech, because the standard forms are so rarely heard. The most common "error" occurs in the past tense as *laid* is used for *lay*: *"The weary worker laid down for a half-hour nap." The past participle *lain* is also uncommon, as is the present participle *lying*: *"The weary worker had laid down for a half-hour nap. *She had been laying down for twenty minutes when the phone rang."

It may be helpful to note that the forms of *lay* parallel with the verb *set*: to place something. Both *lay* and *set* are transitive and may thus be used in the passive (see the next usage item). *Lie* parallels with *sit* (which is usually intransitive) and means to rest or remain. The forms of *lie* are often followed by an adverbial: "The child had lain quietly in the crib for ten minutes without making a sound."

Some common expressions follow the rule; some do not: it's the "lie" of the ball in golf, but the "lay" of the land (the British say "lie" of the land).

Exercise 18-8

For each of the blanks below, select the traditionally prescribed form of *lie* or *lay*.

1. The sunbathers were (lying, laying) out in the sun.
2. He (lay, laid) the cup gently on the saucer.
3. We have already (lain, laid) that matter to rest.
4. Last Friday, Donna just (lay, laid) in bed all day.
5. Our lazy dog has (laid, lain) on the back porch for hours at a time.
6. Don't just (lie, lay) there; do something!
7. Between here and there (lies, lays) a very treacherous path.
8. The camera was (lain, laid) there hours ago.
9. Her children had been (lying, laying) clothing on the deck to dry.
10. Now I understand why hens (lie, lay) eggs.
11. (Lie, lay) down before you get dizzy and fall.

Passive Voice

The passive voice is formed from an active sentence by making a subject of the direct object, changing the main verb to a past participle preceded by a form of *be,* and either deleting the former subject or relegating it to an optional prepositional phrase that begins with *by*:

> The professor failed the lazy student.   (active sentence)
> The lazy student was failed (by the professor).   (passive sentence)

A common myth among teachers of writing is that the active voice is always more forceful, and hence more appropriate, than the passive voice. But the passive has its place and is well established in English. Although it is usually not appropriate in narrative or descriptive prose, it is useful in some kinds of prose, especially when the agent (or performer of the action) is unknown or unimportant, or when the writer wants to be impersonal or diplomatic:

> A clinic was firebombed late last evening.
> The senator was pronounced dead on Sunday.
> In the Soviet Union, many political prisoners were consigned to gulags.

Use of the passive is unacceptable, however, when it forms part of a calculated strategy to avoid personal responsibility: "It was decided yesterday that you be released from your position." And it is ineffective when used simply for stylistic variety.

In casual spoken usage, the verb *get* may act as a passive marker: "The neighbor child got hit by a car last evening."

Like as a Conjunction

Example: *The dog acted like someone was invading the house.

By rule, *like* is a preposition and is thus followed by a noun phrase: "He staggered down the street like a drunk man." Prescriptivists condemn the use of *like* as a conjunction when it introduces a following clause, as in *"He acts like he's king of Bunker Hill." Historically, the conjunctive *like* has occurred in serious literary works, by some of the greatest writers of our language. Some usage authorities, for example, Evans and Evans, accept the conjunctive *like* as a well-established idiom, in writing as well as in speech. Indeed, the more realistic usage scholars who simply believe in "telling it like it is," and like it has been for centuries, accept *like* as a conjunction. Still, published writing does not often contain sentences such as "Few English authors have been able to write like Shakespeare did." Of course the sentence would be acceptable if the single word *did* had been left out, because it is what changes the phrase to a clause.

Often the word *as* forms part of a construction that may usefully be substituted for *like* when a conjunction meaning is intended. This is evident in sentences such as "To the children, it seemed like/as if the meeting would never end" or "The couple were dressed like/as though they were going to a costume ball."

Back in the 1960s when many people were apparently more concerned about the harmful effects of "poor grammar" than they were about the harmful effects of tobacco, one cigarette advertiser ran a television campaign with the slogan "Winston tastes good like a cigarette should." In response to insulting complaints from viewers about the incorrect use of *like* as a conjunction, advertisers ran a follow-up advertisement that said, "What do you want, good grammar or good taste?"

Although *like* as a conjunction remains extremely common in casual, even informal speech, it is not seen very often in carefully edited writing.

Than as a Preposition

Example: *Shirley is taller than me.

The word *than* presents a usage contrary to that of the word *like.* In this case prescriptive grammarians insist on its use as a conjunction to introduce a clause rather than as a preposition to introduce a noun phrase, though a part of the clause often undergoes ellipsis and is removed. The example above should therefore be "Shirley is taller than I (am tall)." In this example, as the prescriptive argument would suggest, the first person pronoun should be the subject form *I* rather than the object form *me* because the pronoun is the subject of its own clause rather than an object of a preposition. But *than* is commonly used as a preposition in speech and informal writing: "Her hairdo is different than my hairdo"; "He weighs more than me."

The same requirement of *than* to be used as a conjunction explains why prescriptivists would warn against its combination with *different* in a sentence, such as *"I am different than those people." In this case the preposition *from* would be preferred over *than.*

Exercise 18-9

For each of the sentences below, indicate with yes or no whether traditional prescriptive rules would accept the italicized form as correct.

1. You look *like* Tom.
2. It looked *like* Tom had already spoken with them.
3. The vine was *like* a snake winding around the nearby vegetation.
4. The man was more angry *than* I have ever seen him.
5. I thought that you were different *than* the rest of them.
6. We behaved badly *like* you said we would.
7. She seemed more self-assured *than* him.
8. He offered to pay for the damage *as* he should have.

Fragments, Fused Sentences, and Comma Splices

Some of the common problems that occur in student writing result from a lack of understanding of what constitutes a sentence or clause. You should have become aware by now that a sentence requires a subject and a finite verb (or a modal auxiliary) in its main clause. Thus a construction such as "The man known only as Jack" is not a sentence because even though it has a subject, its verb is nonfinite. The construction is thus a fragment. If a finite verb (or modal auxiliary) is only to be found in a subordinate clause, such as an adverbial or adjectival (relative) clause, then we also have a fragment as in "The girl who ate the sandwich" or "After we visited the store."

A fused sentence constitutes a separate problem. In this case, two or more independent clauses have been strung together without any kind of proper connecting device such as a conjunction. Thus you might have an utterance such as *"Mathilda opened the can of soda it sprayed all over the place." In this example, two independent clauses ("Mathilda opened the can of soda" and "it sprayed all over the place") have been joined incorrectly. This kind of error can be corrected either by separating the two clauses with a period or semicolon or by joining them with a coordinating conjunction and comma, as in "Mathilda opened the can of soda, and it sprayed all over the place."

When using a comma to join independent clauses, it is essential that you remember to include the coordinating conjunction. Otherwise you will have a comma splice: *"Mathilda opened the can of soda, it sprayed all over the place."

Exercise 18–10

Label each of the numbered utterances below according to whether it is OK or Not OK. If it is Not OK, then identify whether it is a fragment, fused sentence, or comma splice.

1. Because of the difficulty of the test, most of the students failed.
2. The accountant who had helped the police pinpoint the money laundering operation and who had left the country under the witness protection program.
3. I knew that he was coming. It was just a matter of time.
4. The police used undercover agents. In order to catch the criminals.
5. He doesn't want to be rude, he just wants to help you understand the situation.
6. Our neighbor rarely spoke with us, but his children were frequently at our house.
7. Don't come.
8. Walter thought about it a long time then he gradually changed his mind.
9. There was one person we needed to contact. The man who had lived in Moscow.
10. Mrs. Jensen, knowing that she wouldn't live much longer.
11. Jacob slept.
12. Before Jacob slept.
13. We donated lots of money, it wasn't enough.
14. I had seen the movie already, and I wasn't impressed with it then either.
15. It was very easy to do well in the course. Until you came to the unit on paleontology.
16. We waited by the railroad tracks, it was a very cold morning.
17. The nanny, hoping that the train would still be there, left.

Above as an Adjectival or Nominal

> **Examples:** The *above* sentence requires some attention. (*above* as an adjectival)
> Please see the *above*. (*above* as a nominal)

Some usage authorities question the use of *above* as an adjectival or nominal, preferring instead that *above* be used only as a preposition or adverbial. The adjectival and nominal uses are common, despite purists' objections, but if overused, these uses call attention to themselves. Other authorities allow for *above* as a nominal or adjectival but insist that it refer only to something on the same page. This latter requirement, however, is also not supported in general usage.

More Important/Importantly

Example: *More importantly, you should never lose your passport.

Some traditionalists argue that an adjective form is required in the example above, "(What is) more important" being implied. But common usage frequently employs the adverb form *importantly,* interpreting *importantly* as a sentence adverbial.

Whose vs. Of Which

The presciptive rule says that the relative pronoun *whose* should not refer to a non-human referent. Thus by this rule we can say "The house the roof of which blew off" but not *"The house whose roof blew off." This rule is pretty much ignored, except in very formal contexts.

Exercise 18–11

Some of the sentences below contain modifier usages that have troubled some grammarians. For each sentence indicate with a yes or no whether the italicized words as they are used in the sentence would likely be acceptable to a very traditional, prescriptive grammarian.

1. *More important*, you should never play near railroad tracks.
2. The manager, *whose* apartment always had loud music playing, had the nerve to criticize us for talking loudly one evening.
3. When you read the *above,* you will understand.
4. The water dripped from *above* the pipes.
5. We immediately recognized it as the book *whose* cover had been changed.
6. *More importantly,* if you change the oil in your car, dispose of it properly.
7. If you examine the *above* photograph, you will see hidden messages.

Dangling and Misplaced Modifiers

Examples: *While investigating the crime scene,* the wind howled fiercely.
(dangling modifier)
Being a writer, the differences between written and spoken English are very important. (dangling modifier)
*The sergeant yelled at the dog with colorful language. (misplaced modifier)

The term *dangling modifier* is commonly used to refer to a modifier that describes an element not present in the sentence. In the first example above, "while investigating the crime scene" has nothing to which it may attach itself logically. It therefore appears to be modifying "the wind." Of course our world knowledge tells us that the wind can't logically be the person or thing modified by the phrase "while investigating the crime scene." And often we figure out what someone has meant when they use a dangling modifier. But the careless use of dangling modifiers is a distraction and should be avoided in careful writing, though we often allow greater latitude in speech. A dangling modifier is often a participial phrase, though it need not be. It might, for example, be an infinitive phrase as in "To run efficiently, proper oiling is needed."

Some kinds of dangling modifiers occasion little criticism, for example, "On further examining relevant evidence, the conclusion became apparent," in which an implied "examiner" suffices. Other "dangling" modifiers that have come to gain acceptance include *concerning, based on, regarding, providing, failing,* and *excepting.* For example, few would object to the dangling modifier in "Regarding the new applicant, the consensus is that we should hire her." Some participles evolve idiomatically to what we call "absolute" status and occasion little if any complaint: "Weather permitting, we'll have a cookout" or "All things considered, our decision will be to impeach." But these latter kinds of modifiers are not what most people have in mind when they speak of a dangling modifier. The prototypical kind of dangling modifier that we mentioned earlier should be avoided.

A related sentence problem is the **misplaced modifier.** A modifier is said to be "misplaced" when structurally it appears to modify something the writer does not intend it to modify. This often occurs when a modifier is not placed next to the element that it is intended to modify, for example, "We fed the cheese to our pet goat that was moldy."

A variety of phrase and clause types may occur as misplaced modifiers. Consider a few examples below:

The bank approves of loans to individuals *of any size.* (prepositional phrase)
Having been mutilated by the printer, the secretary discarded the crumpled
   paper. (participle phrase)
To play tennis well, a good racquet is needed. (infinitive phrase)
We bought the chair for my cousin *that had only three legs.* (relative clause)

Like the dangling modifiers, the intended meaning of a sentence containing a misplaced modifier is usually clear, but ambiguity can result. And even when the meaning is clear, the presence of such careless expressions in writing is distracting and can undermine the credibility of a writer. Misplaced modifiers are a rich source of hilarity. The popular collections of illogical and absurd sentences sent to social workers, insurance adjustors, and TV talk show hosts are often based on misplaced modifiers.

Exercise 18–12

Each of the italicized modifiers in the sentences below is either dangling or misplaced. Label each italicized modifier according to the type it represents, and rewrite the sentence to correct the problem.

1. *While sleeping in bed,* the smoke detector started buzzing.
2. *Already tired and angry,* the final straw occurred when the dishwasher broke.
3. *To purchase a car,* the money a person needs is phenomenal.
4. We took the dogs to the veterinarian *that had fleas.*
5. *Leaking gas dangerously,* the children avoided the car.
6. *Having taught the class,* the chalk and eraser were no longer needed.
7. The attorney brought a case to the jury *without a leg to stand on.*

Some Observations and Applications

The specific usage items we have discussed in this chapter were selected, at least in part, to review the phonological, morphological, and syntactic information contained in earlier chapters and to show its relevance to understanding and making informed choices about usage as you edit and proofread your own writing. In addition, this chapter should have acquainted you with some larger usage issues. You have learned about the nature and purpose of usage dictionaries. Many people are unaware that such dictionaries even exist, yet these dictionaries can be very helpful reference works for people who want to write professionally. Consulting such dictionaries not only helps people to become more acquainted with particular usage issues they have already encountered, but may also alert them to issues they have never considered.

You have also learned that the English language has no academy, and you have seen that disagreement exists on some particular usage items among the so-called experts. These facts alone should make you less linguistically dogmatic in asserting a "correct" answer on the basis of having consulted a single source, since that source may simply reflect a personal bias of its author(s). You have also seen that prescriptive rules are not always based on logic and clarity but can in some cases be quite arbitrary. Such an awareness may help you to be less judgmental and more understanding of particular forms that are found in the nonstandard dialects, even as you may decide to avoid using those forms yourself.

Bryant, Margaret M., ed. *Current American Usage.* New York: Funk & Wagnalls, 1962.

Burchfield, R. W., ed. *The New Fowler's Modern English Usage,* 3rd ed. Oxford, 1996.

Copperud, Roy. H. *American Usage and Style: The Consensus.* New York: Van Nostrand Reinhold, 1980.

Ebbitt, Wilma R., and David R. Ebbitt. *Index to English,* 8th ed. New York: Oxford UP, 1990.

Evans, Bergen, and Cornelia Evans. *A Dictionary of Contemporary American Usage.* New York: Random House, 1957.

Finegan, Edward. *Attitudes toward English Usage.* New York: Teachers College Press, 1980.

Leonard, Sterling A. *The Doctrine of Correctness in English Usage, 1700–1800.* Madison: The University of Wisconsin Studies in Language and Literature: No. 25, 1929.

Webster's Dictionary of English Usage. Springfield, Mass.: Merriam-Webster Inc., 1989.

Note: In addition to usage dictionaries, other helpful sources also exist. William Safire has for years written a column for the *New York Times*, occasionally publishing book-length collections of his articles. College writing handbooks have fairly extensive sections on standard usage, with a focus mainly on common writing "errors" among college students. Some "regular dictionaries" now also include brief discussions of some selected usage points.

19

Language Variation: Historical, Regional, and Social

Old English of about 1000 A.D.

The Lord's Prayer[1]

Fæder ūre,
þū þe eart on heofonum,
sī þīn nama gehālgod.
Tōbecume þīn rīce.
Gewurþe ðīn willa on eorðan swā swā on heofonum.
Ūrne gedæghwāmlīcan hlāf syle ūs tō dæg.
And forgyf ūs ūre gyltas, swā swā wē forgyfað ūrum gyltendum.
And ne gelǣd þū ūs on costnunge,
ac ālȳs ūs of yfele. Sōþlīce.

Our attention so far has been on the phonological, morphological, and syntactic structure of the English language as it exists today. Such a synchronic view could by its very nature imply that our language is static. But this is certainly not the case. Any living language continues to change and develop. By "living," we mean a language with native speakers who must use the language and adapt it for their own purposes. This is in contrast with so-called dead languages, like Latin, which no longer have any native speakers and thus do not continue to change. Tracing language change is not like tracing the growth and development of an individual human being along a single continuum. This is because our language does not consist of one dialect but rather many dialects, each with its own development. We should

---

[1] *A History of the English Language,* 4th ed., by Albert C. Baugh and Thomas Cable ©1993. Reprinted by permission of Prentice-Hall, Inc., Upper Saddle River, NJ.

therefore acknowledge that our study of English has in one sense been incomplete since it has been limited to Standard American English.

Studying Standard American English is of course perfectly appropriate in a course such as ours since this variety continues to be the most influential and widely accepted variety in our country. But we should realize that any description of English has necessarily limited its data for consideration. This is even true of a historical consideration of English since even the Old English of King Alfred's time (about 1,100 years ago) had various dialects, and that was in a time before the dispersion of the English language across the globe.

Having said that, let us examine some of the historical variation that has occurred in the language. Such an examination will not only provide insights into the current nature of our language but also present a useful context for looking at some of the phonological, morphological, and syntactic information that we have already considered. Later in this chapter we will also consider the matter of dialectal differentiation. Rather than provide a thorough account of historical and dialectal differentiation, our intent is to contextualize some of the principles and concepts we have been discussing throughout this text.

A. Some English Language History

English belongs to a set of languages that derive from a single common ancestral language that we now call "Indo-European." This mother tongue ultimately gave rise to many languages found in a geographical area of the world extending from India to Europe (hence the term *Indo-European*). Subsequent colonialism has stretched the influence of these languages even further across the world. The Indo-European family contains a variety of languages. Among these are the Romance languages such as Latin and the languages derived from it such as French, Spanish, Italian, Portuguese, and Romanian; the Slavic and Baltic languages such as Russian, Polish, Lithuanian, and Latvian; the Germanic languages such as German, Swedish, Norwegian, Dutch, Danish, and English; the Celtic languages such as Irish, Gaelic, Welsh, and Manx; and the Hellenic languages such as Greek. It also includes the Iranian languages as well as Sanskrit and Hittite.

How did one language give rise to so many other languages? The first fact that must be remembered is that language always changes. Because language change is gradual, we may not even notice some changes that occur within our language since we adjust our language together with other speakers over the course of time. But if one set of speakers is separated from another set of speakers for a prolonged period, then the differences can become quite dramatic. This is what happened anciently with Indo-European. As groups of speakers migrated outward and were separated from each other, they experienced change independently of each other. No ancient records exist of the Indo-European language. Our knowledge of its form and characteristics comes from careful reconstruction based on comparative linguistic scholarship of the existing languages as well as ancient records of individual Indo-European languages such as Latin, Sanskrit, and Greek. But the important role of separation in the process of language diversification can be observed with more recent language change for which we do have some written records. Latin gave rise to a number of modern languages, which developed as Latin speakers spread out into different areas. What had begun as individual dialectal variation eventually developed through time into the modern languages of French, Spanish, Portuguese, Italian, and Romanian. This kind of change has repeated itself in numerous languages through thousands of years. At one time in the past, some of the major subbranches of Indo-European were once merely dialectal variants of Indo-European. Then they gradually became different languages from which new dialects and eventually languages began to emerge.

In order to get a better idea of how languages can change through time, let's look at one feature that distinguishes many speakers of southern dialects of American English from speakers of more northern varieties. This feature is illustrated in the pronunciation of the word *greasy*. Whereas in the North the alveolar fricative within the word is the voiceless [s], in the South it is commonly the voiced [z]. You will recall from our discussion of the sound system of English that whether a sound is voiced or voiceless depends on whether the speaker switches his or her vocal cords on or off. Just as modern dialects can develop differences in how they voice consonants in particular words, ancient dialects and languages sometimes did the same thing. Some voicing differences, for example, arose historically among the dialects and subsequent languages that developed from Latin. The following exercise will illustrate some of the differences that developed between Latin and two of its descendant languages, Italian and Spanish.

Exercise 19-1

In each of the Spanish and Italian words below, change the voicing of the underlined consonant sound in order to form the corresponding Latin word from which the Spanish or Italian word was developed. Note that the sound /k/ was spelled as a "*c*" in Latin.

Spanish	Latin
1. lobo (wolf)	lu__us
2. amigo (friend)	ami__us
3. cabeza (head)	ca__ut
4. lugar (place)	lo__us
5. sobra (over)	su__er
6. lado (side)	la__us
7. abierto (open)	a__ertus
8. vida (life)	vi__a

Italian	
9. gola (throat)	__ollum
10. padre (father)	pa__er
11. gatto (cat)	__attus

Changes in voicing did not just occur among descendant languages of Latin. They had also occurred even earlier as the branch of Indo-European that later developed into the Germanic languages began to differentiate itself from the rest of the Indo-European languages. For some reason as yet unknown, the Germanic branch, which gave rise to a number of languages, including English, systematically and consistently changed particular consonants from one kind of sound to another. Some of the sound changes involved voicing. But others involved the manner of articulation. Because other languages that descended from Indo-European did not make these same changes, we can look at words in the other languages and compare some of their differing sounds with a Germanic language such as English in order to understand which sounds underwent change in the Germanic branch. Below you will find an exercise that illustrates some of those sound changes.

Exercise 19–2

Compare the words below, which come from various Indo-European languages, with their English counterpart. By examining the underlined consonants, fill in the subsequent chart which outlines some of the sound changes that affected the Germanic branch of Indo-European. Remember that the sound /k/ is spelled as a *c* in some of the words. In historical linguistics, an asterisk in front of a word means that it is a reconstructed form.

Indo-European Language Words
(Non-Germanic)[2]

Indo-European Language Words (Non-Germanic)[2]	English Words
kannabis (Greek)	hemp
diente (Spanish)	tooth (Germanic *tanthuz)
due (Italian)	two
pater (Latin)	father
grano (Italian)	corn
corno (Italian)	horn
collina (Italian)	hill
pur (Greek)	fire
tres (Spanish)	three
agro- (Latin)	acre
kuon- (Classical Greek)	hound
edere (Latin)	eat
kardia (Greek)	heart

Some changes from Indo-European to Germanic:

1. Indo-European /b/ became Germanic _____.
2. Indo-European /d/ became Germanic _____.
3. Indo-European /g/ became Germanic _____.

---

[2]See the *American Heritage Dictionary of Indo-European Roots*, revised and edited by Calvert Watkins. Boston: Houghton Mifflin, 1985. See also Baugh and Cable, pp. 87–90.

4. Indo-European /p/ became Germanic ____.
5. Indo-European /t/ became Germanic ____.
6. Indo-European /k/ became Germanic ____.

The significance of such a chart is in what it shows about systematic sound correspondences. Even while two particular words may look very different, such as *kardia* and *heart,* if the differences between them are part of a systematic set of differences that have occurred again and again within other words, we are probably dealing with words that are from a common origin. The sound changes you noted are part of a group of sound changes that were first described by a German linguist Jacob Grimm, and the full set of changes has come to be referred to as "Grimm's law."

Knowing something about the specific sound changes that affected the Germanic branch of Indo-European can help us to make some educated guesses about which English words or roots are part of our original Germanic wordstock that ultimately traces back through Indo-European versus which ones appear to have been borrowed from another Indo-European branch more recently. Consider for example a situation in which you have two words or roots that appear related in meaning and contain consonants that can be correlated with each other through the operation of the sound changes outlined in Grimm's law. This situation occurs with the words *canine* and *hound.* We know that Grimm's law specifies that the Indo-European /k/ became the germanic /h/ rather than vice versa. Thus the word *hound* is probably original to our language and *canine* is a later borrowing from a separate Indo-European branch. If *canine* had been inherited through our Germanic line, it would have undergone the changes described by Grimm's law. This approach must be used carefully and supplemented with other information for you to be absolutely sure of your conclusions, but it will provide you some measure of insight into the origin of a number of vocabulary words in our language. The following exercise will give you some additional practice with Grimm's law.

Exercise 19–3[3]

Examine the word pairs below. Each word pair consists of two English words that have come from the same Indo-European root. One of the words in each pair has come down to us through Germanic, and one has come into the language through a later borrowing. In the blank to the side of each word pair, indicate which word has come through the Germanic line (in other words, native to the English language). We have underlined the consonants to which you should pay particular attention.

1. druid   tree   _____
2. fishy   piscatorial   _____
3. eat   edible   _____
4. agnostic   know [think of the historical
                  pronunciation /k/]   _____

---

[3]Ibid.

5. labial   lip   _____
6. podiatrist   foot   _____
7. fatherly   paternal   _____
8. capital   head (Old English "heafod")   _____
9. kind   genus [use the historical pronunciation /g/
                       rather than the modern /ǰ/]   _____

As you have seen, Grimm's law, which describes the sound changes that the Germanic languages underwent as they developed from Indo-European, is important to the study of the historical development of English because English is a Germanic language. English developed from the ancient Germanic language just as Germanic developed from Indo-European. English wasn't even spoken in England until the fifth century when some Germanic tribes known as the Angles, Saxons, and Jutes invaded the island. The island was inhabited at that time by Celtic people who also spoke languages that derived from Indo-European. The Angles, Saxons, and Jutes ultimately displaced the Celts, and the island came to be named for the Angles, hence the name *England* (Angle-land). The language spoken by the Germanic peoples in England also became known as *English* ("Anglish"). Through time these Germanic peoples who had invaded England were themselves invaded by others. Beginning in the late eighth century and continuing for over two centuries, Vikings and other Scandinavian peoples, who spoke North Germanic languages, invaded England, for a time even occupying the English throne. Later, in the eleventh century, William Duke of Normandy invaded England, and for the next couple of centuries, the English throne was occupied by speakers of French.

These historical events brought extensive changes to our language. Although English had not been dramatically affected by its contact with Celtic (English speakers borrowed primarily place names) and Latin (at that time primarily vocabulary related to Christian contact), the influence of the Viking and Norman conquest in contrast brought dramatic changes to the language, as speakers of these languages eventually began to adopt English and infuse the language with some of their own vocabulary. This was particularly true with French.

If you have studied Spanish or Italian, you have seen many words in these languages that resemble words in English. Some of these similarities are of course the result of borrowing Italian and Spanish terms into English. But in most cases the similarities result from the number of French loan words that English borrowed hundreds of years ago. Because Italian, Spanish, Portuguese, Romanian, and French are closely related "sister" languages to each other, borrowings from French or Latin would naturally provide our language with words resembling the vocabulary of the other Latin-based languages as well. Thus it should not surprise us that the word *communication* in English resembles the word *communicación* in Spanish and "communicazione" in Italian. On the other hand, the resemblances that English has in some of its vocabulary with Germanic languages occur because English is historically a Germanic language.

The effect of French and Scandinavian speakers on English was not limited to vocabulary. Speakers of these languages likely contributed significantly to the loss of inflectional complexity in our language. Indo-European had been a highly inflected language and passed this feature on to its descendant languages, including Old English. In an earlier chapter you saw that Modern English has only nine inflectional endings (or eight, depending on whether you lump the two possessives together). This represents a vast reduction from what it once had in Old English times (about 450–1100 A.D.). Some scholars believe that the extensive loss of inflectional endings on nouns, verbs, adjectives, and adverbs resulted from the imperfect acquisition of English by the speakers of the Scandinavian and French languages.[4]

Among the grammatical notions conveyed by the heavy inflectional component of Old English was the grammatical function of the individual words. The inflectional ending of nouns and adjectives as well as the forms of pronouns and articles could indicate whether they were functioning as or as part of a subject, direct object, indirect object, or possessive. Under this system, word order was not as important as it now is. The subsequent loss of inflections, however, has made word order vital to the interpretation of grammatical function. For example, whether we put a noun phrase before or immediately after a verb can change whether the noun phrase is interpreted as a subject or direct object. Despite the substantial loss of inflectional endings, some have survived to the present day but in a slightly different form.

Exercise 19–4[5]

In each numbered entry below you will find a grammatical description as well as an Old English word with an inflection that corresponds to the grammatical description. Compare each inflected form below with what you know about the form of its modern counterpart. If a form has survived into present-day English, even if in a slightly altered form, fill in the blank with the form as it occurs in English today. If it has instead been replaced or disappeared altogether, write "gone" in the blank.

1. Subject/Direct Object plural (form of "heaven") heofon<u>as</u> _____
2. Indirect Object plural   heofon<u>um</u> _____
3. Possessive singular   heofon<u>es</u> _____
4. Possessive plural   heofon<u>a</u> _____
5. Present participle verb (form of "perform")   fremm<u>ende</u> _____
6. Third person singular present-tense verb   freme<u>þ</u>
                                     (þ is pronounced like /θ/) _____
7. Second person singular present-tense verb   frem<u>est</u> _____
8. First person singular past-tense verb   frem<u>ede</u> _____

Another important change in the English language occurred sometime around the sixteenth century and affected the pronunciation of long vowels (By "long" vowels, we refer primarily to the duration of the vowel—how long it is held). This change,

---

[4]Baugh and Cable, pp. 101–102.

[5]Confer *Bright's Old English Grammar & Reader,* 3rd ed., ed. Frederic G. Cassidy and Richard N. Ringler. New York: Holt, Rinehart and Winston, 1971.

which has since been known as "The Great Vowel Shift," moved long vowels upwards to the nearby tense vowel position.

Other than in the case of the vowel [a:] which became [e], and high vowels that could not move any higher and thus became diphthongs, the vowel shift did not change the front versus back positions of the affected vowels. The high front and high back vowels, which couldn't be raised to anything higher, became the diphthongs /ay/ and /aw/, respectively.

Exercise 19–5

For each of the long vowels below, provide the appropriate phonemic symbol to represent what it has become as a result of the Great Vowel Shift. (A colon after a vowel indicates that it is long.)

1. [a:]   _____
2. [ɛ:]   _____ (same as # 1)
3. [e:]   _____
4. [i:]   _____
5. [ɔ:]   _____
6. [o:]   _____
7. [u:]   _____

One consequence of the Great Vowel Shift was that it put an even greater distance between our spelling and pronunciation. Because the printing press had already been introduced into England and many spellings had already become common, the subsequent change in the pronunciation of some of our vowels increased an already existing disparity between the sound and symbol correspondence that has continued in many ways to the present day.

The changes within our language have not just been morphological and phonological. There have been some syntactic changes within the language as well. As we noted, the loss of inflectional endings brought with it more rigid requirements of word order. Now we virtually expect the subject of a sentence to appear in the initial position unless we note the presence of an initial adverbial or the operation of some kind of movement rule. Other changes have involved the syntactic requirements of specific nouns and verbs. Some verbs that were once transitive can now be used intransitively as well, thus altering the kinds of sentence structure they may appear in. And some nouns have changed in how they handle the count/mass distinction. This of course affects not only how they agree with verbs but also how they are combined with articles.

The combinations of verbs and auxiliaries have also become more complex over the last several hundred years. Though the language had the simple present, simple past and even present and past progressive or perfect, it has since developed more elaborate combinatorial possibilities which can create such constructions as the modal perfect progressive, for example, "could have been moving," or even the past perfect progressive passive, for example, "had been getting moved" (note the use of the "get" auxiliary, which can sometimes replace "be" in the passive).

One kind of syntactic change that continued to develop, even after the time of Shakespeare, involves the formation of questions and negative statements. While the Early Modern English of Shakespeare's time allowed options in forming questions and negative statements, the Modern English of today has settled into a more uniform pattern.

Exercise 19–6

Examine the following utterances from the play Hamlet[6] and describe how their formation contrasts with the usual formation of questions and negatives in the English of today. You may wish to consult chapter 13 for a review of the current rules.

1. Goes it against the main of Poland. . . ? (IV.iv.15)
2. If you love me, hold not off. (II.ii.291)
3. I have not the skill. (III.ii.362)
4. I like him not, nor stands it safe with us to let his madness range. (III.iii.1–2)
5. Say you so? (V.ii.300)
6. Sailors, my lord, they say, I saw them not. (IV.vii.39)
7. Nay, I know not. (V.i.178)

Another important area of change is in the lexicon (vocabulary) of a language. Words change meanings or acquire additional meanings through time, even as the same words may continue to exist in the language. Interesting examples of this may be found in connection with new technology. Today we still sometimes call a particular foodwrap "tin foil" even though it is now made of aluminum rather than tin. And what we call a "lamp" now is very different from what people had in mind a couple of hundred years ago when they spoke of a "lamp."

Other lexical changes involve words that eventually acquire more general or more restricted meanings. For example, the word *holiday* has a more general meaning than it once did. As its form suggests, it once referred specifically to holy days. Later it came to mean virtually any festive day. In contrast to words that have acquired more general meanings, there are words such as *meat* which have acquired more specialized meanings. *Meat* once referred to food of any kind. Now of course the word refers to the specific food we obtain from animals. The older meaning of *meat* is evident in a compound such as *mincemeat.*

Some words have acquired more positive meanings through time such as *knight,* which once referred to a young person without conveying any particular honor. And many have acquired a more negative meaning such as *vulgar,* which once referred merely to something characteristic of people generally. This older meaning can be seen in the name of a biblical translation which was made available to the larger public and known as the "Vulgate Bible."[7]

---

[6]Cf. "Hamlet" in *the Riverside Shakespeare,* ed. G. Blakemore Evans. Boston: Houghton Mifflin, 1974.

[7]For a discussion of some of the above examples of lexical change, as well as others, see the following sources: Thomas Pyles and John Algeo, *The Origins and Development of the English Language*, 4th ed. Fort Worth: Harcourt Brace Jovanovich College Publishers, 1993, pp. 241–246.; C. M. Millward, *A Biography of the English Language*, 2nd ed. Fort Worth: Harcourt Brace College Publishers, 1996, pp. 294–295; Victoria Fromkin and Robert Rodman, *An Introduction to Language*, 6th ed. Fort Worth: Harcourt Brace College Publishers, 1998, p. 463.

B. Regional and Social Varieties of English

> An Australian tourist was run over in London and taken to a hospital. "Was I brought here to die?" he asked when he gained consciousness.
>
> "Oh, no," answered the orderly, "you were brought here *yesterdie*."[8]

We earlier noted that language constantly changes, and we examined some of the changes that have distinguished Modern English from earlier varieties. But language differentiation is not just evident across time; it is also apparent in simultaneously occurring varieties of the same language across different geographical areas. This is true not only among national varieties such as American, British, Australian, South African, or Indian English (as spoken in India), but also among regional varieties within a national variety. Speakers of American English in the southern United States speak differently from speakers in the Rocky Mountain states. Similarly, there are differences among speakers of American English in New England and speakers in the Midwest. Dialectal differentiation occurs within these regions as well. Southern English varies among Virginia, Georgia, and Texas, each localized area having its own characteristics that serve to distinguish it from others. And even within a very localized speech community, there are differences. In fact, each person has his or her own idiolect, that is, personal dialect. If there are ten people in a room, there would be ten different idiolects spoken, even if those ten individuals are members of the same family or close friends of each other. It would be impractical to discuss the millions of American English idiolects, or even the local dialects, for that matter. So we will continue to speak of varieties used by larger speech communities.

Exercise 19–7[9]

The list of words below consists of British English vocabulary words that are not used in American English or that have a different sense from the way the words are used in American English. Look up each word in a dictionary and provide a word from American English that means the same thing.

1. Solicitor (legal)   _____
2. Pram   _____
3. Hoarding   _____
4. Draughts   _____
5. Nappy   _____
6. Chemist (a type of business)   _____
7. Torch   _____
8. Bonnet (a car part)   _____
9. Crisps (a type of food)   _____
10. Plimsolls   _____

---

[8] *1000 Howlers for Kids,* by Joel Rothman. New York: Ballantine Books, 1986, p. 83.

[9] The words and answers here are adapted from a list provided in David Crystal's book *The English Language.* London: Penguin, 1988, pp. 249–250.

11. Drawing pin _____
12. Dustbin _____
13. Lorry _____
14. Boot (a car part) _____
15. Waistcoat _____
16. Windscreen _____
17. Spanner _____

It is common for people to assume that they have no distinctive dialectal features. For example, some may assert that they have no accent, though they are convinced that they can tell when others do. The fact is that all of us, regardless of the dialect we speak, have an accent. It is true that a kind of Midwest accent has become largely accepted as the most normative in television. But while there is a standard grammar for American English, there is no standard pronunciation. A southern pronunciation is just as "correct" as a Midwest or New England pronunciation.

Linguists working in dialectology identify the features of a particular dialect by conducting interviews and surveys with speakers of that dialect.[10] The most useful speakers for identifying the traditional dialects of a region have been those speakers who were less likely to have been affected by influences external to their own speech community. Thus it has been more helpful to interview or survey older speakers, for example, since they are less likely to use slang and trendy speech styles. Dialectologists also prefer to study speakers who have not had advanced education and who have not lived elsewhere. On the basis of information gleaned from interviews and surveys it is possible to chart out areas where dialect boundaries seem to occur. This is done by comparing where a series of differences occurs between one area and another. Let's say, for example, that a dialectologist tests speakers for the pronunciation of the word *oil*. He or she would likely find that some speakers use the diphthong /ɔy/, whereas others use the simple vowel /ɔ /. If the interviewer takes the results of the interviews for this feature and marks on a map where each interviewee lives and which variant he or she uses, then a pattern will likely emerge, and a line can be drawn on the map indicating where the dividing line is for the choice among speakers between /ɔyl/ and /ɔl/. This line is an isogloss. It shows the dividing line separating groups of speakers with regard to one linguistic variant. If the interviewer finds that plotting the occurrence of several other features produces similar isoglosses in the same location on the map (in other words a bundle of isoglosses in the same place), then he or she can begin to identify the boundary between two dialects.

When most people think of differences between dialects, they usually think of the lexical (vocabulary) and phonological differences. The lexical differences among dialects frequently center around the use of one kind of word versus another as in the choice between *pail* or *bucket, bag* or *sack, soda* or *pop* (or even *tonic*), and

---

[10]For a discussion and illustration of recent work in identifying and describing a dialect, see "The Utah Dialect Project" by Paul Baltes and Diane Lillie. *Newsletter of the American Dialect Society*. May 1999. Vol. 31:2. See also Diane Lillie's 1998 MA thesis treating the same topic.

skunk or *polecat*. Phonological comparisons most commonly involve vowels, though sometimes consonant differences also occur. The following exercise will illustrate some of the kinds of vowel and consonant sounds that a dialectologist might listen for in different speakers.

Oral Exercise 19–A

In a film produced some years ago, a linguist assembled speakers from different parts of the country and asked them to pronounce sets of words.[11] Most of his word sets are listed below with the particularly relevant sound underlined. Be prepared to discuss your own pronunciation of the words below and what kinds of alternative pronunciation differences you may have heard in the speech of others.

1. merry, marry, Mary
2. It's greasy.
3. Put it on.
4. off, dog, often
   lot, log, sorry
5. wash, water
6. ash, ask
7. father, park, part
8. Yes I can.
   I want it in a can.
9. law, paw
10. about the house
11. first, bird
12. any, many, penny

In addition to the differences in the lexicon and phonology that serve to distinguish various dialects, there are also some important differences in their morphology and syntax. In fact, a study of phonology, morphology, and syntax is vital to work in the field of dialectology just as it is in the field of historical linguistics. As dialectologists observe and identify the distinctive features of dialects, they must be able to express what it is that they are observing. The next exercise will illustrate some of the terminology that you have encountered through the previous text material and how it can be used in the identification and description of forms that you may encounter and discuss in dialectology.

Exercise 19–8

Each of the numbered items below contains a description of a particular form and an example that illustrates that description. Fill in each blank in order to complete the structural description or the illustrative example.

---

[11]The film was titled *Dialects* and featured Dr. Henry Lee Smith, Jr. It was produced by the Metropolitan Educational Television Association. The film was directed by Frank Jacoby.

1. The use of *what* as a _____ pronoun. Example: *He is the man what spoke to me.*
2. Double _____. Example: *We might could bring you to our house.*
3. The use of *do* as an _____verb. Example: *He done prepared a cake for us.*
4. Double comparative. Example: *He is _____ happier than I have seen him in a long time.*
5. The use of a high front _____ vowel [ɪ] rather than a high front _____ vowel [i]. Example: /krɪk/ is sometimes pronounced rather than /krik/.
6. The use of an alveolar nasal rather than a velar nasal for the present participial suffix. Example: *cook* ____
7. The use of a past participial form of *see* where the standard dialect would use the past tense form. Example: *I _____ you do that.*
8. A third person singular masculine reflexive form that attaches *-self* to a possessive pronoun rather than to an _____ pronoun form. Example: *hisself*
9. The absence of a _____ in the dipthongs /ay/ and /ɔy/. Examples: "tie" /ta/ and "boil" /bɔl/

Some of the morphological and syntactic features of regional dialects are nonstandard. But just because they are nonstandard does not mean they are any less logical than what is found in Standard English. Several hundred years ago before the dialect of the East Midland region of England became the standard dialect in that country (a selection subsequently affecting the form that American English later took), it was just one of a number of dialects in England with no more inherent claim to superiority than any of the others. It was certainly no more logical than the others. With its selection as the standard, however, all other dialects by definition became nonstandard. The various dialects have their own systems. To outsiders unacquainted with the systems of these dialects, there may be a tendency to judge the dialects as somehow deficient. But these dialects have rules, though the rules may be different from what prevail in the standard dialect. And if history had played itself out a little differently, then one of the current nonstandard dialects would be the object of our grammar study in school. Let us consider one set of rules that we might have to be studying in school if traditional Appalachian English were the standard dialect.

You have perhaps heard a participial form like *a-goin'*. Ronald Williams and Walt Wolfram explain that this form can be used in Appalachian English for "progressives, as in *I knew she was a-tellin' the truth* or as certain types of adverbials, as in *I went down there a-huntin' for them, She just kept a-beggin', He woke up a-screamin'.*" Williams and Wolfram show that there are certain additional constraints that operate on how this participial form is used:

1. It is not used as a nominal or adjectival.
2. It is not used with a word that starts with a vowel or "an unstressed syllable."[12]

---

[12]"A Linguistic Description of Social Dialects" by Ronald Williams and Walt Wolfram in *Social Dialects: Differences vs. Disorders,* prepared by Ronald Williams and Walt Wolfram. ed. Irma K. Jeter. Rockville, MD: American Speech and Hearing Association, 1977, p. 22.

Exercise 19–9

Examine the uses of the present participle in each of the sentences below. In the blank accompanying each sentence, indicate with a yes or no whether the rules of Appalachian English as they have been explained above would allow the use of the distinctive Appalachian participle.

1. His discussion was a-fascinatin'. _____
2. She is a-singin'. _____
3. A-joggin' will keep your body in shape. _____
4. The farmer was a-eatin' on the porch. _____
5. John was a-reportin' about the family. _____
6. We could be a-plantin' the crop right now. _____
7. There is no a-smokin' allowed in that building. _____
8. We came a-playin' the drums. _____
9. The story was a-depressin'. _____
10. The scout troop was a-campin'. _____

In addition to the kinds of structural knowledge that have been shown to be important to the collection and interpretation of dialectal differentiation, there are also pragmatic and discourse features that distinguish the speech of people in one area from those in another and should be considered. Deborah Tannen has shown, for example, that there can be differences in how speakers from various speech communities interpret the significance of loud speech. Some might assume that it indicates anger; others would not. Tannen also shows that speakers from different areas of the country vary in their expectations about turn-taking in conversations. Some expect the end of a speaker's "turn" to be signaled by a longer pause time than others do. Cross-cultural misunderstanding can thus occur as speakers of different dialects communicate with each other since the speaker who is accustomed to a shorter pause time will unintentionally and unknowingly be interrupting the other speaker who hasn't quite finished what he or she wanted to say.[13] The area of discourse analysis is beyond the subject matter of this text, but for serious students of language, it merits some important consideration.

Dialect differences do not just correspond with geographic areas but also occur along social dimensions. Among the social factors that affect the forms of language that a speaker uses are gender, age, occupation, religion, and ethnicity. We will very briefly look at each of these.

Gender

Male speakers tend to be less concerned with speaking correctly than are female speakers. In addition, linguistic research has shown that female speakers also dis-

---

[13]*That's Not What I Meant! How Conversational Style Makes or Breaks Your Relations with Others* by Deborah Tannen. New York: Ballantine Books, 1986.

play important lexical differences from males. For example, women tend to be familiar with or use more color terms. Moreover, it has been claimed that women use more tag questions than men do. Important differences between men and women's speech also occur in discourse and conversational features. We previously noted that the expectations that people have about the appropriate length of time needed to signal the end of a speaker's turn can vary according to the geographical region of the country. But Deborah Tannen indicates that it can also vary by gender, with women generally expecting a longer pause time than men do.[14]

Age

Older speakers are often linguistically conservative in a couple of ways: they sometimes preserve speech forms that are no longer in use by younger speakers, and they are less inclined toward adopting new slang or passing fads in language than are younger speakers. For example, several years ago it was common to hear youth modeling their speech after some comedians who would place the word *not* after the end of a sentence, rather than after an auxiliary verb (as in "I'm coming to the dance. Not!"). This was a passing fad that would not likely have influenced older speakers. Vocabulary items also distinguish younger speakers from older ones. For example, some older speakers use the term *two bits* to refer to twenty-five cents, but this usage is now probably rare among younger speakers. Other kinds of vocabulary differences can be found in exclamations. One generation might say, "Radical!" whereas an older group might say, "Great Scott," and an even older one could exclaim, "My stars!"

Occupation

Anyone who has listened to a conversation among doctors, lawyers, engineers, soldiers, or others within specialized occupations has noticed that some vocabulary is specific to those who work within a particular occupation. Oftentimes some of the most distinctive lexical differences are found in the acronyms that are used by individuals in a profession. A nurse, for example, will know that NCS is a directive for a patient to be given "no concentrated sweets." Others are not likely to know this.

Religion

Religions often contain vocabulary that those outside the faith are unfamiliar with. For example, the ecclesiastical grouping of congregations that a Catholic would call a "diocese" roughly corresponds to what a Mormon (a member of the Church of Jesus Christ of Latter-day Saints) would call a "stake." Even if people from separate religious communities use the same terms, the way that those terms are used and the connotations they have for the members of those communities may be very different. Mormons and Catholics both use the words *bishop* and *saint*. But what those words convey to the two religious communities are quite different. Religious communities

---

[14]*You Just Don't Understand: Women and Men in Conversation* by Deborah Tannen. New York: Ballantine Books, 1990. p. 95.

also sometimes use acronyms that others outside their community may or may not recognize and understand.

Ethnicity

In American English, the two ethnic varieties that have probably occasioned the most study are commonly called "Black English" (or African American Vernacular English) and "Chicano English." It is important to understand that even as we speak of an ethnic variety such as Black English, no claim is being made that all blacks speak Black English. People speak the language they grow up hearing in their home and neighborhood. Some whites speak Black English, and many blacks speak the standard variety of the language. Linguistic research has identified a number of systematic rules that seem to govern the use of Black English, showing that Black English is not a "degenerate" form of English but rather a variety that has its own rules and features. For example, Black English uses a present progressive which has developed a distinction that Standard English does not even have in its progressive. When Standard English expresses a sentence such as "Jason is studying chemistry at the college," it can be unclear whether Jason is studying right now or off and on throughout a longer period of time such as a semester or term. In other words it is unclear whether what is being described is happening instantaneously or habitually. Black English, on the other hand, uses two different forms for these notions. The instantaneous usage would be expressed as "Jason studying chemistry at the college," whereas the habitual sense would be "Jason be studying chemistry at the college." It is not that Standard English cannot express these two separate notions. Although Standard English sometimes uses the progressive verb construction ambiguously, it can clearly distinguish the two notions by using the progressive for the instantaneous, and the simple present ("studies") for the habitual. Both Black English and Standard English have their own system and sets of rules. From a linguistic standpoint, the nonstandard system is not inferior, merely different. Of course social considerations come into play, and we can suggest that people who speak a nonstandard dialect, of whatever variety, should become conversant with the standard dialect. But this is for factors other than anything inherently inadequate with a nonstandard dialect.

Nonstandard dialects, whether regional or social, sometimes preserve older features of our language that have since disappeared from the standard dialect. This fact may surprise some people who are used to thinking of nonstandard dialects as newer dialects that have somehow mutated from the standard dialect through time. As we have shown, however, some nonstandard dialects have as long a history as the standard dialect. They just didn't happen to be the dialect chosen when decisions were made about which dialect should be used for the standard one. If they had a feature that was later lost in the standard, then the continued use of the feature in a nonstandard dialect was then viewed as somehow less legitimate, even if historically it had a long history.

Exercise 19–10

Below you will find some samples from earlier writings in English, more specifically the plays of Shakespeare and the King James Translation of the Bible (KJT) of

1611. In each excerpt, identify which feature would now be considered nonstandard in American English (at least by some prescriptivists) and briefly indicate what it is about the feature that would be considered nonstandard.

1. From Shakespeare: "The red-plague rid you for learning me your language."[15]
2. From Shakespeare: "Thou art right welcome, as thy master is."[16]
3. From Shakespeare: "This was the most unkindest cut of all."[17]
4. From Shakespeare: "She cannot love, nor take no shape nor project of affection."[18]
5. From Shakespeare: " . . . how slow this old moon wanes!"[19]
6. From Shakespeare: "There is tears for his love."[20]
7. From KJT: ". . . which the children of men builded." (Genesis 11:5)
8. From KJT: "Simon Peter saith unto them, I go a fishing." (John 21:3)
9. From KJT: " . . . and the thorns sprung up, and choked them." (Matthew 13:7)
10. From KJT: " . . . every scribe which is instructed. . . . " (Matthew 13:52)

Other forms in nonstandard dialects exist, not because they have a long history but because they result from common linguistic tendencies. These same tendencies are frequently apparent in the standard dialect. As an example of this consider what happens with palatalization. Palatalization, which was discussed in some detail in chapter 2, is a type of assimilation in which the alveopalatal glide /y/ (or a high front vowel like /i/) affects the place of articulation of the preceding consonant, usually an alveolar, causing it to become an alveopalatal consonant as well. This is what occurs with words such as *education.* In this word, the presence of an alveopalatal glide between the alveolar /d/ and the back vowel /u/ pulls the alveolar back to the alveopalatal region, thus causing the /d/ to be pronounced as [ǰ].

Because palatalization represents a natural tendency among speakers, it shouldn't be surprising that it could exist in standard as well as nonstandard dialects, though the specific words it affects can vary from one dialect to another depending on the phonology of the dialect. Palatalization, as we noted earlier, can operate across word boundaries. Speakers of the standard dialect are accustomed to palatalizing the last consonant of such words as *hit, hate,* and *want* when those words precede the word

---

[15]This line comes from *The Tempest* as cited in *The Language of Shakespeare* by G. L. Brook. London: Andre Deutsch, 1976, p. 45.

[16]From *As You Like It* as cited in Brook, p. 87.

[17]From *Julius Caesar* as cited in *Introduction to Early Modern English* by Manfred Gorlach. Cambridge: Cambridge U.P., 1991, pp. 84, 321

[18]From *Much Ado About Nothing* as cited in "double negative" in *Webster's Dictionary of English Usage.* Springfield, MA: Merriam-Webster, 1989.

[19]From *Midsummer Night's Dream* as cited in "slow, slowly" in *Webster's Dictionary of English Usage.* Springfield, MA: Merriam-Webster, 1989.

[20]From *Julius Caesar* in *The Riverside Shakespeare,* ed. G. Blakemore Evans. Boston: Houghton Mifflin, 1974.

you. And even though standard dialect speakers might look down on a nonstandard dialect speaker who palatalizes the final consonant sound of *with* before the word *you,* producing a form like [wɪču], the nonstandard speaker is applying the same kind of palatalization rule that standard speakers use. Those who pronounce [wɪču] do so because their dialect uses an alveolar /t/ rather than an interdental in the word *with.* This sets up the word *with* to be palatalized in the same way that *want* would be palatalized in front of the word-initial /y/ of *you* by standard speakers. Thus speakers of standard and nonstandard dialects both employ palatalization, though the specific words in which it occurs may vary.

Languages and dialects, whether social or regional, will contain varying registers, styles, and levels of formality according to the task at hand. For example, a legal contract might require the use of a register that includes such expressions as "the afore-mentioned" or "the said Thomas Jones," despite the fact that lawyers do not use such otherwise unnatural language in their regular speech. Speakers belonging to a religious community might sometimes use forms such as "brethren" or "thee" and "thou" on particular occasions, even if those forms are not a part of their regular speech register. Some occasions, such as delivering an inaugural address, require considerable formality; other situations, such as joke-telling, do not.

Writing, for a variety of reasons, often requires that we express things a little differently than when we speak. Some inexperienced writers incorrectly believe that using big or obscure words makes good writing. The exercise below, however, illustrates that some of the most memorable expressions within our language are expressed in a relatively straightforward style.

Exercise 19–11[21]

Each of the sentences below corresponds to a famous expression in our language. Change the inflated language of the sentences below into the language of the expression as it is commonly heard.

1. It is futile to attempt to indoctrinate a superannuated canine with innovative maneuvers.
2. Pulchritude possesses exclusively cutaneous profundity.
3. Everything is legitimate in matters pertaining to ardent affections and international armed conflicts.
4. Members of an avian species of identical plumage congregate.
5. It is fruitless to endure lacrimation over precipitately departed lacteal fluid.
6. Pulchritude reposes within the optic parameters of the perceiver.
7. Where there are visible emissions from carbonaceous materials, there exists conflagration.
8. Hubris antedates a gravity-impelled descent.
9. Consolidated we maintain ourselves erect; bifurcated we plummet.

---

[21]The sentences in this exercise as well as the accompanying answers are taken from a larger list in *The Play of Words* by Richard Lederer. New York: Pocket Books, 1990, pp. 220–223, 235–236.

10. A feathered biped in the terminal part of the arm equals the value of a brace of such creatures in densely branched shrubbery.
11. Individuals who make their abode in vitreous edifices of patent frangibility are advised to refrain from catapulting petrous projectiles.
12. Missiles of ligneous or osterous consistency have the potential of fracturing my osseous structure, but vocalized appellations eternally remain benocuous.
13. Fondness for lucre constitutes the tuberous structure of all satanically inspired principles.
14. You cannot estimate the value of a bound narrative from its exterior vesture.
15. Although it is within the realm of possibility to escort equus caballus to a location providing a potable mixture of hydrogen and oxygen, one cannot coerce said mammal to imbibe.

Some Observations and Applications

In one sense, this chapter has been an extended illustration of how the phonological, morphological, and syntactic material you have previously studied in this text can be applied to a greater understanding of dialects and historical linguistics. But we will also consider how historical linguistics or dialectology can themselves be usefully applied.

Perhaps the most self-evident application of studying the history and development of languages relates to the interpretation of older writings. Without an understanding of how a language has changed, it might be very difficult to interpret particular texts accurately. To get an idea of how difficult and inaccessible an older text of a language can be, even to native speakers who speak a more recent variety of the language, consult again the Old English text at the beginning of this chapter. For many readers this Old English text is probably more decipherable than some other Old English texts since it corresponds to a passage that many already know in its modern version. As our language continues to change, an increasing number of people will be unable to understand and interpret some of the great texts of our cultural past. Already many individuals struggle with Shakespeare's writings. And his language is only a few hundred years removed from us.

Another interesting area of application of historical linguistics involves using a reconstruction of a protolanguage to learn about an ancient culture. When determining which languages appear to be related, linguists can use comparisons of words in the related languages as well as linguistic knowledge about how sounds within particular patterns typically change, to reconstruct to some extent what a particular ancestral language might have looked like. This kind of reconstruction provides important clues into the nature and location of an ancient culture. Thus even without archaeological ruins or artifacts like pottery, we can still know something about an ancient culture just by knowing something of its words, since words are created to refer to items or ideas within a culture. On the other hand, words that are significantly different in the various descendant languages and whose differences cannot be accounted for through any systematic sound correspondences (of the type that we saw outlined in Grimm's law, for example) probably correspond to items or concepts that developed after the once-united people separated from each other. The reconstruction of forms and the mass comparison between languages has been used to learn not only about Indo-Europeans but also to arrive at some conclusions about the migratory patterns of other ancient peoples.[22]

The study of dialects and varieties of language has a number of very interesting applications. Some of the most important ones are in education. These applications range from decisions that must be made about educational policy to decisions made by individual teachers in the classroom. On the level of educational policy, the more that educators and administrators understand about the dialects and needs of their students, the more effective their decisions are likely to be. At the very least, they will avoid policies that assume some kind of intellectual or cognitive deficiency on the part of the students who speak nonstandard dialects.

The material in this chapter is not intended to suggest that schools should abandon their attempts to teach students to use the standard dialect effectively. Rather, students who speak a nonstandard dialect should be encouraged and assisted in acquiring proficiency in the standard dialect, thus becoming bidialectal. Whether the situation is fair or not, the reality continues to exist that there are frequently social and economic costs associated with an inability to work in the standard dialect. As a teacher helps students to acquire proficiency in the standard dialect, it is important that he or she be informed about and respectful of the students' nonstandard dialect since for many people, their self-identity is strongly wrapped up in the language they speak. If teachers aren't careful, any misplaced contempt they feel toward a child's dialect may be interpreted by the child to extend toward the child's own family, culture, and identity.

One important skill or insight that teachers may gain from a study of dialects is a greater ability to distinguish between issues related to a particular teaching task and dialectal issues that might be better addressed in a different time and setting. As children learn to read, it is important that their teacher be able to distinguish between genuine reading errors and merely pronunciation differences between the children's dialect and the teacher's dialect.[23] If a British student reads "part" without an -r, most teachers would probably recognize that that is not a reading error but rather relates to the phonology of the student's particular dialect, which drops -r in certain linguistic environments. But what about a student whose dialect pronounces

---

[22]As examples of the kind of historical information that linguistic reconstruction can provide, see "Indo-European and the Indo-Europeans" by Calvert Watkins in *The American Heritage Dictionary of Indo-European Roots.* Revised and edited by Calvert Watkins. Boston: Houghton Mifflin, 1985, pp. xi–xxiv. See also "Linguistic Origins of Native Americans" by Joseph H. Greenberg and Merritt Ruhlen in *Scientific American* (Nov. 1992): 94–99.

[23]For a discussion of the importance of distinguishing between reading errors and dialectal pronunciations, see "Knowledge into Practice: Delivering Research to Teachers" by Robert Berdan in *Reactions to Ann Arbor: Vernacular Black English and Education,* ed. Marcia Farr Whiteman. Arlington, VA: Center for Applied Linguistics, 1980. pp. 77–84. See also "Recognizing Black English in the Classroom" by William Labov in *Black English: Educational Equity and the Law,* ed. John W. Chambers, Jr. Ann Arbor: Karoma Publishers, 1983. pp. 29–55.

a word-final interdental [θ] as [f] in words such as *with* and *math*? Would a teacher be as likely to recognize this as a dialectal difference which has nothing to do with a student's reading ability? Or would the teacher conclude that the student needed remedial reading help?

A knowledge of dialectology would also be useful for those preparing assessment materials. Walt Wolfram has shown that one diagnostic test which was prepared in part to help in assessing students' reading readiness contains a grammatical closure test that puts speakers of Appalachian English and Black English at a disadvantage. In the test students are given statements that they have to complete. For example, students are given "This man is painting." They then have to fill in the blank of the following: "He is a _____." Those who score the test are expecting a noun phrase answer such as "a painter" or "a fence painter." But for speakers of Appalachian English, it would be perfectly natural to say "a paintin'." Unfortunately, such a nonstandard response would not be considered correct by those scoring the test, even though the test is not intended to assess acquisition of the standard dialect.[24] If the test scores are to be useful in assessing reading readiness, then very clear instructions should be given to those grading the test so that they are prepared to accept alternatives based on dialectal differences.

Elsewhere, Walt Wolfram and Natalie Schilling-Estes show that even the common testing tasks that ask children to identify rhyming words or homophones can "result in misclassifying cases of dialect-appropriate symbol-sound relationships as incorrect responses."[25] Once again, in such cases a child's reading skills should not be judged as inadequate just because his or her pronunciation differs from that of the person who designed (or scored) a particular assessment test.

Dialectal knowledge has also been helpful in criminal cases in which a criminal has left behind a spoken or written speech sample. In such cases, investigators have used dialectal knowledge to narrow a list of suspects or to construct a profile of the criminal.[26] In a different setting, Deborah Tannen has researched discourse patterns in businesses that have experienced gender-based communication problems in the workplace. Her research about discourse differences between men and women, can be helpful to companies wishing to foster a more positive and productive work environment.[27]

[24]"Beyond Black English: Implications of the Ann Arbor Decision for Other Non-Mainstream Varieties" by Walt Wolfram in *Reactions to Ann Arbor: Vernacular Black English and Education,* ed. Marcia Farr Whiteman. Arlington, VA: Center for Applied Linguistics, 1980. pp. 10–23.

[25]*American English: Dialects and Variation* by Walt Wolfram and Natalie Schilling-Estes. Oxford: Blackwell Publishers, 1998. pp. 300–301.

[26]For one example of how dialectal information has provided important evidence in a case, see "The Judicial Testing of Linguistic Theory" by William Labov in *Linguistics in Context: Connecting Observation and Understanding,* ed. Deborah Tannen. Norwood, NJ: Ablex Publishing, 1988. pp. 159–182.

[27]"The Power of Talk: Who Gets Heard and Why" by Deborah Tannen in *Harvard Business Review* (Sept.–Oct. 1995). pp. 138–148.

Appendix A

A Basic Introduction to Tree Diagramming

In this book you have learned that nouns and verbs act as part of a phrase structure. A noun constitutes the head of a noun phrase (NP), whereas a verb is the head of a verb phrase (VP). A noun phrase may consist of a single noun or one that is accompanied by determiners and other modifiers. And a verb phrase may consist of a single verb, or it may include additional elements such as noun phrases, prepositional phrases, and adverbs. Linguists frequently use a special kind of diagramming known as **tree diagramming** to illustrate the syntactic relationship that exists within and among phrases in a particular utterance. A basic understanding of tree diagrams is helpful in analyzing and illustrating the syntax of various structures. It is also essential for understanding grammatical models like the Transformational grammar developed by Noam Chomsky, which is briefly outlined in appendix B. For these reasons, it is important for you to have some idea of how to interpret and construct tree diagrams, though our treatment here will be very basic and indeed a little oversimplified.

Tree diagramming gets its name from the fact that its diagrams with their branching features look like upside down trees. This can be seen in the simplified tree diagram below:

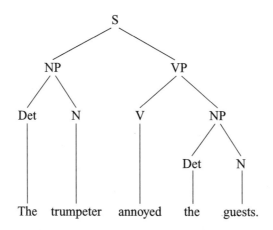

In a tree diagram the S stands for sentence or clause. As you know, sentences (or clauses) have a subject and verb. Thus in the tree diagram the S branches into an NP and VP. Even if the subject of the sentence is a solitary noun, you should continue to diagram that subject noun as an NP, though your diagram would show the NP tracing through a single node (N) rather than branching out. The same is true for verb phrases. Even if a verb phrase consists solely of an intransitive verb, you should still show the S as branching into an NP and VP. Thus the sentence "Michael cried" would be diagrammed as

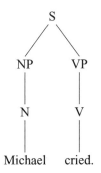

Diagramming phrases rather than just nouns and verbs is important because some syntactic behavior such as movement rules is better described in relation to entire phrases rather than individual nouns and verbs.

The ability of a tree diagram to represent phrases that branch out as well as those that do not is, of course, necessary to account for structural requirements found in connection with particular nouns and verbs. As you will recall, mass nouns and personal names, for example, may occur without a determiner (represented in the diagrams as "Det"). Thus in the case of a mass noun, although we can say "The snow hit the ground," we could also just say "Snow hit the ground."

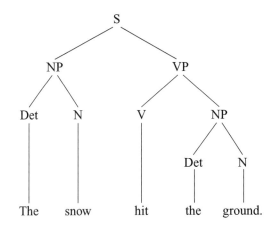

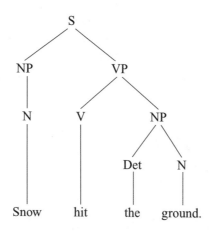

Within a verb phrase, a transitive verb requires branching since that verb phrase must contain an NP object. Intransitive verbs, on the other hand, do not by themselves require such branching. We can contrast the difference between an intransitive and transitive verb phrase by the two tree diagrams below:

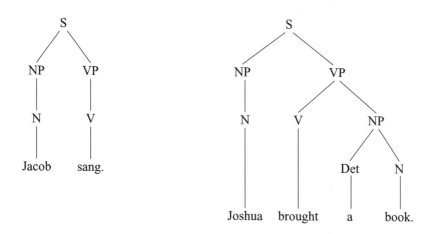

Our diagrams above show very basic phrase structures for noun phrases and verb phrases. It is true that noun phrases may consist of a single noun or a determiner and noun. And verb phrases may consist solely of an intransitive verb or a transitive verb followed by a simple noun phrase. But your studies in this book also show that noun and verb phrases may be accompanied by other modifiers. A system of tree diagramming must therefore take such matters into account.

A modifier's phrase structure placement depends on what it modifies. In the sentence "The happy boy left," we know that the modifier *happy* describes the noun *boy*. It is thus attached to the noun phrase node, occurring between the determiner *the* and the head noun *boy*. In the case of an adverb that modifies a preceding verb, we could expect a tree diagram that attaches the adverb to the verb phrase node. Thus we would diagram the sentence "The happy boy left quickly" as

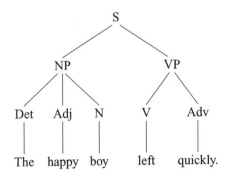

Another common type of modifier that we have studied is the prepositional phrase (PP). Prepositional phrases consist of a preposition and a noun phrase and thus branch into P and NP. The noun phrase in turn can branch out as we have shown earlier. The sentence "Hyrum brought a dog into the store" would therefore be diagrammed as

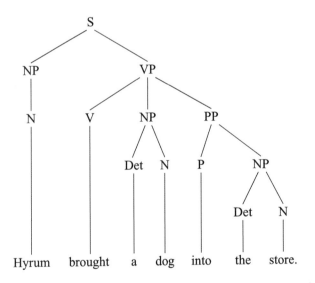

Prepositional phrases can modify a noun or a verb. Because of this fact we have studied them as a type of adjectival and adverbial. When diagramming a prepositional phrase you must consider what it modifies, for this will help you to determine the appropriate node to which it should be attached. If the prepositional phrase describes the verb, it should be attached to the VP. If it describes the noun, it should be attached to the NP.

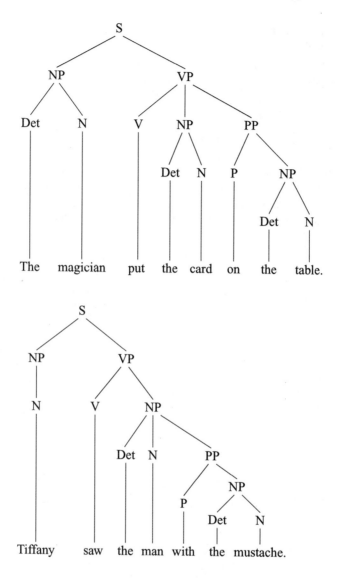

We will now have you practice with some tree diagrams.

Exercise A–1

For each of the following sentences draw the appropriate tree diagram. Remember that possessive pronouns are determiners.

1. The angry man left.
2. Our sister watched the man.
3. Marleen saw gray cats.

4. The answer to the question surprised Jim.
5. John sneezed.
6. The student wrote her paper with the computer.
7. Large deficits lead to problems.
8. My sympathy for her problems diminished.

Our discussion has only served to introduce you to some basic tree diagrams, as we have limited our examination here to SV and SVO sentence (or clause) types. A more thorough discussion would be necessary to show you how to diagram a greater variety of possible sentence types, including those which contain subordinate clauses. Diagram systems also frequently involve special conventions for representing inflectional suffixes on verbs. Such details, however, are unnecessary in your initial exposure to tree diagramming.

Appendix B

An Introduction to Transformational Grammar

Paul Baltes

Introduction

How is it that native speakers of a language produce and understand sentences that they have never heard before? How can there be an infinite number of sentences within a language? These are the essential questions that motivated Noam Chomsky to develop a theory of language known as Transformational Grammar, sometimes called Transformational Generative grammar (abbreviated as TG). In this chapter, I shall simplify some of the most difficult concepts of TG so we might more readily focus on the principles behind the concepts. These principles are important to understand because while the specifics of TG have been abandoned by Chomsky and most other linguists, the principles still influence and form the basis for almost every modern linguistic theory of grammar.

Chomsky introduced Transformational Grammar to the world in the 1957 monograph *Syntactic Structures*.[1] He followed this up with a more complete explanation of the theory in his 1965 book, *Aspects of the Theory of Syntax*.[2] In each, Chomsky declares that language can be explained as a system of rules, based on mathematical principles, which can generate an infinite number of sentences. Although he wasn't the first to come up with this idea (Wilhelm von Humboldt had argued a similar

---

[1]See Noam Chomsky, *Syntactic Structures*. The Hague: Mouton & Co., 1957.

[2]See Noam Chomsky, *Aspects of the Theory of Syntax*. Cambridge, MA: The M.I.T. Press, 1965.

view over a century earlier and the Port Royal Society before that), Chomsky proposed a specific framework which revolutionized the way we think about language.

Chomsky's theory is a way to explain what is going on when people use and interpret language (called *explanatory adequacy*) rather than to represent exactly what is going on in the brain during language use (*representational adequacy*). Linguists believe that we are each born with the capacity for language already in place. Every human, barring damage to the brain, is born with the ability to learn any language. This entails that there must be something shared by all humans that enables them to learn any language, and that there must be something shared by all languages.

TG suggests what an ideal native speaker of a language must already know about language in order to use and interpret it. Most of this knowledge is subconscious. Most English speakers have probably never been told, for example, that numbers precede colors in a string of adjectives, but very few people would say, "the blue two sweatshirts" rather than "the two blue sweatshirts." Ordering constraints also apply to adjectives dealing with material. Most of us would say that the phrase "the green wooden bench" sounds better to our ear than "the wooden green bench." This knowledge, as well as all of our knowledge of language, both conscious and subconscious, is called a speaker's *competence.* Because of our linguistic competence we understand that two sentences can be related or have the same meaning even though they appear different, or that conversely, one sentence may have different meanings. We also understand the structure of sentences, and can therefore make judgments as to which are grammatical and which are not.

Competence is usually distinguished from *performance,* the actual language that someone produces when speaking. This includes not only normal communication but also hesitations, slips of the tongue, repair strategies, and various kinds of speech errors, or in other words, what actually comes out when we speak.

How TG works

The focus of TG is on describing the production of structurally well-formed sentences, matching the inborn native speaker's competence. To do so, TG separates syntax (the structure of language and languages) from semantics (the meaning within language and languages) since, Chomsky argued, the structure of a language works independently from any consideration of meaning. His famous example, *Colorless green ideas sleep furiously,* illustrates this point. The sentence is considered "grammatical" or, in other words, "well-formed" because every part of it works according to the rules of English grammar. The adjectives *colorless* and *green* both modify the noun *ideas*; the adverb *furiously* modifies the verb *sleep* (telling how the sleeping occurs); and the subject, *Colorless green ideas,* and the predicate, *sleep furiously,* agree with each other. If the sentence seems odd, it's because it doesn't seem to make sense. Things that are green in color, cannot therefore be colorless. Similarly, we don't usually think of ideas as colorless or green, unless we're using a metaphorical sense of the words (colorless to mean "bland" and green to mean "new," for example). We also don't normally think of ideas being able to sleep, nor do we think of sleeping as something that can be done furiously.

When we hear the term *grammar* we usually think of right and wrong ways to speak. Utterances that are called *ungrammatical* often refer to sentences using the word *ain't* or other slang, or violating some usage prescription, such as "Don't end a sentence with a preposition," or "Don't split infinitives." For many people, the notion of grammar also includes knowing the difference between *affect* and *effect* or using correct punctuation or capitalization. Some of these ideas are taught to us in school, along with how to identify subjects, predicates, and various parts of speech, including nouns, verbs, adjectives, and prepositions. We're used to using traditional grammar definitions (such as "nouns are people, places, things, and ideas" and "verbs express action or state of being"), or descriptions of grammatical functions (such as "adjectives modify nouns" and "adverbs modify verbs").

In TG, the term *grammar* refers to how the structure of language operates. Linguists use the term *ungrammatical* to indicate that a particular utterance isn't well-formed, according to the linguistic knowledge, unconscious or conscious, we have about the structure of language. Utterances that are considered grammatical conform to the system of rules which generate well-formed structures in a language.

Rules describe the way a language actually works. Linguistics is a descriptive study, meaning that linguists describe the way they observe language working, based on their observations of real language users. They represent patterns of linguistic behavior as rules. If we ask someone where they're going and they reply, "The grocery store," we can make certain judgments about the phrase. We can say that *store* is a noun and the words preceding it, *grocery* and *the* are giving us more information about *store,* namely what kind of store, and that there is a particular one that the speaker has in mind. Even if we didn't know what *grocery* meant, we could speculate (and then verify with additional observation) that it was giving us more information about *store.* Certainly we would recognize with more observations that phrases similar to *the grocery store* exist. We might hear "the dollar store," "the candy store," or "the toy store." After a while we might write a description of these types of phrases as "the _____ store." Later we might formulate more significant generalizations of the phrase such as "Article + Adjective[3] + Noun," which represents an even larger number of occurrences of similar phrase structures.

Repeated patterns in language behavior are often expressed in generalizations which fit the patterns. The more generalizations a theory can make, the more explanatory power it has. If each sentence or each phrase needed to be explained by its own individual rule or description, then for an infinite number of sentences or phrases in English, there would be an infinite number of rules. We would never be able to produce or understand a sentence we had never heard before, without then understanding its unique behavior. Instead, language seems to behave in patterns such that if we know the structures and the rules for combining these structures, we have the knowledge to create and interpret new structures, in other words, new

---

[3]In TG, a premodifier, such as "grocery," because of its function, would probably be considered an adjective in the broad sense. A structural grammar, on the other hand, would note that a word such as "grocery" forms a plural by adding an *es* suffix and is thus a noun that can serve as a premodifier.

phrases or sentences. All sentences in English, for example, can be represented as the symbol S. Each S consists of a noun phrase (NP) and a verb phrase (VP). We can formalize this expression as the rule

$S \rightarrow NP\ VP$

Rules such as this one, called *phrase structure rules,* represent the basic or *underlying* structure of each of the various types of phrases in English. Phrase structure rules in other languages would reflect their underlying structural specifications. The formula of the phrase structure rules indicates that we can rewrite the left side of the rule according to the information on the right side. For the rule above, a sentence can be written as a noun phrase plus a verb phrase. Similarly, we can expand the right side of the rule further, with parentheses indicating optional elements. Each noun phrase can be rewritten as either

$NP \rightarrow (Det)\ (Adj)^*\ N\ (PP)$
$NP \rightarrow Pro$

The first of these two rules basically states that a noun phrase can begin with a determiner (articles, such as *the, a,* or *an;* possessive pronouns, such as *your, my, her;* demonstratives, such as *this, that, these, those;* or vague quantities, such as *some, few, several,* or *many*), then has the possibility of containing an unlimited number of adjectives (indicated by the asterisk to the right of the parentheses. It's important to remember, however, that in actual speech or writing, we don't tolerate very many adjectives). Notice that the noun phrase could also end in a prepositional phrase, but again, this isn't required. The only required element of the phrase structure is a noun since the noun is the *head* of the noun phrase. Of course any or all of the optional elements could be present in a noun phrase (each of these elements, required or optional, is called a constituent). The second rule means that a noun phrase can also be rewritten as a pronoun.

Based on the NP phrase structure rules above, we could create noun phrases such as

John (N)
Boxes (N)
Jazz (N)
She (Pro)
The dogs (Det + N)
The dogs in my neighborhood (Det + N + PP)
The loud rabid dogs (Det + Adj +Adj + N)
The mangy vicious loud rabid dogs in my neighborhood (Det + Adj* + N + PP)

With these simple structures, we could generate an infinite number of noun phrases. The same is true of verb phrase structures, such as

$VP \rightarrow V\ (NP)\ (Adv\ P)^*\ (PP)^*$

which states that the verb phrase consists of a verb (the head of a verb phrase), and then could contain all, some, or none of the following: a noun phrase, an adverb phrase, or a prepositional phrase. Examples of verb phrases that demonstrate this rule would be

sleeps (V)
eats an apple (V + NP)
eats an apple slowly (V + NP + Adv P)
talks quickly (V + Adv P)
talks in the hallway (V + PP)
puts the book on the desk (V + NP + PP)
places the book carefully on the table (V + NP + Adv P + PP)

Often, the structure of the verb phrase is determined by the verb itself. Different verbs require the presence of different constituents. Some verbs, such as *sleep* or *talk,* can be complete in themselves, as in the sentences

She sleeps.
The dinosaur talked.

These verbs are called *intransitive* verbs. Notice that they can be modified by adverbs or prepositional phrases, but they cannot take a following NP object (linguists mark sentences that are not well-formed with an asterisk preceding the sentence).

She sleeps quietly.
She sleeps in her bed.
*She sleeps the bed.
The dinosaur talked loudly.
The dinosaur talked under his breath.
*The dinosaur talked the swamp.

Verbs which require the presence of a following noun phrase are called *transitive* verbs. This noun phrase is called the *direct object* in traditional grammar.

Ross ate the entire pie.
Mark Maguire hit the baseball out of the park.
Rachel rode the bus home.
Cynthia Cooper shot the ball smoothly through the hoop.

Some linguists and grammarians believe that a third class of transitivity exists for those verbs which seem to require a noun phrase at some times and not at others. A few of these verbs are *to eat, to drink,* and *to dance* as in the examples

I ate dinner late last night.
I ate late last night.
Sam drinks fruit punch.
Sam drinks.
Terry danced the Macarena.
Terry danced.

Other linguists, however, feel that the distinction is an artificial one, since the noun phrases for these verbs are often redundant and therefore can be cut out or *ellipsed.* It would strike most of us as odd to hear "I ate food last night." "What would the other options be?", we might ask. In the same way, speakers will not usually say, "Terry danced a dance," although certainly it is possible to say so. *Drink,* on the other hand, is a verb that when used without a noun phrase usually indicates *drinks alcohol,* but since it is understood, it is unnecessary to utter the entire phrase. In the sentence *That dog bites,* the fact that the dog bites *people* is ellipsed for the same reason; any other option is not important enough to even mention.

Other important phrase structure rules include

PP → Prep NP
VP → Aux V
Aux → tense (modal)
NP → N S
VP → V (that) S

The first two read, respectively, that a prepositional phrase consists of a preposition and a noun phrase, and that a verb phrase can contain an auxiliary (Aux) and a verb. The third rule defines what an auxiliary can contain; in this case the rule indicates the tense of the verb and the additional possibility of a modal, such as *can, could, will, would, shall, should,* among others.[4] Some linguists don't list Aux as a separate rule, choosing instead to incorporate the information directly into the verb structure. The last two rules mean that a sentence can be a part of a noun phrase or a verb phrase, following the head of the phrase. Examples of each of these are

Emeril, who cooked the incredible meal (N + S)
think that I am going to the park (V + that + S)

Since a sentence consists of a noun phrase and a verb phrase (S → NP VP), and a noun phrase or a verb phrase can contain another sentence within them, then the rules can be rewritten to show that a noun phrase can contain a noun, a noun phrase, and a verb phrase (NP → N NP VP); then that verb phrase can contain a verb and another noun phrase and a verb phrase (VP → V NP VP). Such rules, where a symbol can occur on both the right side and the left side of a rule, are called *recursive* rules. These rules indicate another way to generate the possibility of an infinite number of structures.

Although phrase structure rules help us understand the basic or underlying structure of the language, Chomsky's unique contribution within TG was that he was able to account for those structures which on the surface look as if they operate differently from the phrase structure rules, such as the structures represented by the passive voice, Yes-No questions, WH-questions, ellipses, embedding, and nominalizations.

Chomsky argued that knowing the structure of the language means that a speaker of a language knows three levels of structure: the basic or underlying structure, called *deep structure*; the way the sentence appears in actual speech, called *surface structure*;

---

[4]The grammatical tense of a sentence is a part of the structure of a VP, rather than part of the verb itself. It becomes attached to the first verb of a phrase, not necessarily to the main verb (which will be the last verb of a verb phrase with multiple auxiliaries, including the *have* and *be* auxiliaries of the perfect and progressive aspect). If a modal is present, it's always the first verb of the verb phrase, but, unlike other verbs, it does not change form in any way. This can be illustrated by the sentences: *She must be going to the store* and *She is going to the store.* See also the discussion of the passive below.

and the rules which connect the surface structure to its corresponding deep structure. The semantics of a language is a component of deep structure, and the phonetic interpretation is a component of the surface structure. The deep structure of every English sentence can be formalized as the rule S → NP VP, where the NP functions as the subject and the VP functions as the predicate. Some linguists, to clarify the functions of the NP and VP, represent the deep structure of the English sentence as

Subject Verb Object (SVO)

which means that the subject of the sentence precedes the verb which then precedes its object (if the verb is transitive) or other complement. The surface structure of simple declarative sentences such as

I love a cappella music.
The plane is leaving.
You need to wash your dishes.

most closely approximates their deep structure representations. Other surface structures do not seem to follow the SVO pattern. Examine the following common sentence patterns:

Passive voice	The ball is thrown to Jerry Rice by Steve Young.
Yes-No question	Have I gone to the store?
WH-question	What did you eat for dinner?
Ellipsis	Victor guesses he did.
Nominalization	Their refusal to participate annoyed the teacher.
Embedding	Emeril, who cooked that fantastic meal, is one of the best chefs in the world.

Compare these to

Steve Young throws the ball to Jerry Rice.
I have gone to the store.
You ate what for dinner?
Victor guesses he did prepare for class.
They would not participate. This annoyed the teacher.
Emeril cooked that fantastic meal. He is one of the best chefs in the world.

We intuitively know that sentences in the first set are related to corresponding sentences in the second set even though they have different surface structures. Chomsky understood that if native speakers could recognize the connection then linguists should be able to account for and describe it. He suggested that the surface structures were connected to their deep structures by a set of rules called *transformational rules*. The connections themselves are called *transformations*.

Speakers reorganize the sentence structure for various reasons, from ordering the information contained in the sentence in order of importance (in English the most common ordering is from least important to most important information) to varying the complexity of sentences for stylistic effects. Not every potential reorganization is considered well-formed. Constituent structure plays an important role in what can be transformed. This knowledge is part of the linguistic competence involved in transformations.

To illustrate, let's look closely at a few transformations. To form the passive voice, a speaker must start with some input in deep structure and then be able to specify the output transformation. Passive transformations, for example, only work with transitive verbs. At least six steps are incorporated into this transformation.

Steve Young throws the ball to Jerry Rice.

1. Move the (direct) object to the subject position.
2. Move the subject to the object of a prepositional phrase beginning with the word *by*.
3. Insert the preposition *by*.
4. Insert the auxiliary verb *to be* before the main verb.
5. Add the tense to the auxiliary (since the tense always attaches to the first verb of a verb phrase).
6. Change the main verb to its past participle form (usually an *-en* or *-ed* ending).

The ball is thrown to Jerry Rice by Steve Young.

Other transformations act differently. Yes-No questions require switching the subject and auxiliary verb (sometimes called *SUBJ-AUX inversion*). WH-questions involve fronting the pronouns which begin with 'w' or 'h' (who, whom, what, where, when, why, which, how, how many, how much). We ellipse when we decide that the hearer can understand the information without our having to specify it. The sentence *Victor guesses he did* is an appropriate answer to the question *Did Tony study?* Other transformations, as exemplified by the nominalization or the embedding instances above, are ways of combining constituents of one sentence within constituents of another to indicate that they are connected in the speaker's mind. In TG there were many more transformations than we will discuss here, but Chomsky eventually abandoned cataloging each of them in favor of a single generalization, which he called α (the Greek letter alpha). This later version used the terminology, *move* α to indicate that a transformation occurs.

Representing Sentence Structure

To represent sentence structure, linguists use both the phrase structure rules and a mathematical graphing called tree structures. Tree structures, also referred to as *syntactic trees, tree diagrams,* or just the elliptical *trees,* allow us to see various aspects of our inborn knowledge of constituent structure. Rewriting the phrase structure rules for the sentence *Steve Young throws the ball to Jerry Rice* would look like

$S \rightarrow NP\ VP$
$NP\ (of\ S) \rightarrow N$
$N \rightarrow Steve\ Young$
$VP \rightarrow Aux\ V\ NP\ PP$
$NP\ (of\ VP) \rightarrow Det\ N$
$PP \rightarrow Prep\ NP$

NP (of PP) → N
V → throw
Aux → tense
Tense → present
Det→ the
N → ball
Prep → to
N → Jerry Rice

There are several levels involved in this rewriting: the sentence level (S), the phrase level (NP, VP, PP, etc.), the categorical level (N, V, Prep, etc.), and the terminal symbol level (the last set of symbols which cannot be rewritten any further, in this case the representations for the words in the sentence, "Steve Young," "to," "ball," etc.).

The tree structure for the same sentence incorporates these levels and would look like

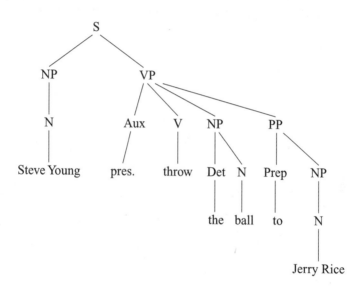

Tree structures help us understand both the constituent structures and the modification relationships within the sentence. Each relationship is discussed in terms of a mother-daughter metaphor called node-daughter configurations. The higher symbol is a node, and the lower one a daughter. We say nodes *dominate* their individual daughters. For our example sentence, S dominates the two daughters NP and VP, which are *sisters* to each other. This NP (of the sentence), in turn, dominates the node N, which dominates the terminal symbol "Steve Young." We can also talk about them in reverse order. We say the daughter "Prep" *is dominated* by the node PP, which is dominated by the node VP, and so on.

The node-daughter relationships reveal the constituent structure of a sentence. Our own competence tells us that "Steve Young," "Jerry Rice," "throws the ball (to Jerry Rice)," "to Jerry Rice," and "the ball" are all constituents of the sentence. They can be used as ellipsed answers to various questions about the sentence: Who throws the ball? Whom is the ball thrown to? What does Steve Young do? Where does he throw the ball? What is thrown to Jerry Rice? Each answer is a daughter of a different node. The tree structure also illustrates that because they are not independent node-daughter relationships, phrases such as "*Steve Young throws" or "*Steve Young the ball" are not constituents.

To graph a sentence in a tree structure, first rewrite the sentence so it looks as close to its deep structure representation as possible. If you're graphing a passive voice sentence, rewrite it in active voice. If you're working with a Yes-No question where the subject and the auxiliary verb have been inverted, invert them back. For embedded sentences or nominalizations some linguists will separate them into individual sentences, but others will leave the embedding in the tree structure to demonstrate the way that they're modifying another constituent. For our example, *Emeril, who cooked that fantastic meal, is one of the best chefs in the world,* the relative clause *who cooked that fantastic meal* is functioning adjectivally. To retain that relationship, its tree structure might look like

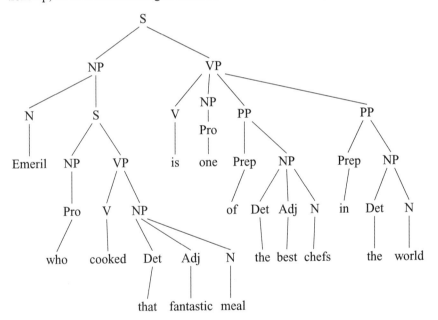

To generate a tree structure, first rewrite the sentence so that it's in Subject NP + VP structure. After you've done this, label the parts of the sentence according to their grammatical categories. Here's an example:

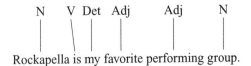

Next connect these categorical daughters to phrase-level nodes. It's easiest to start from the right and work back to the left. Remember, if there's a noun or a pronoun present, there will be a noun phrase at the phrase level; if there's a verb, there will be a verb phrase, etc.

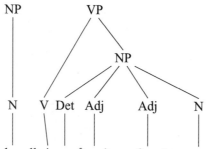

Rockapella is my favorite performing group.

Lastly, link the subject NP and the predicate VP to the node S:

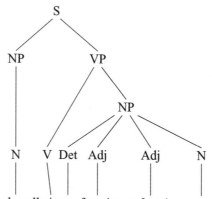

Rockapella is my favorite performing group.

One advantage of tree structures is that they can demonstrate how we disambiguate sentences which on the surface seem to be the same, but actually have more than one meaning. Take the old joke: Tracy walks into the clothing store and asks the salesperson, "May I try on those clothes in the window?" "Certainly," replies the salesperson, "but we have dressing rooms in the back." The joke relies on the ambiguity between trying on clothes from a window display and using the store window as a dressing room. Tree diagrams show that the ambiguity in the surface structure results from two distinct underlying sentence structures, in other words two distinct deep structures. In this particular case, each prepositional phrase (PP) in the two sentences modifies a different constituent. Using the sentence *Tracy tries on the clothes in the window,* we can represent this ambiguity with the following two trees:

Tracy tries on the clothes in the window (trying on clothes from a window display).

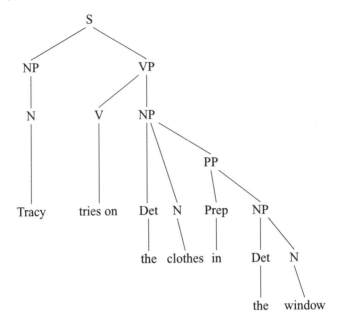

Tracy tries on the clothes in the window (using the store window as a dressing room).

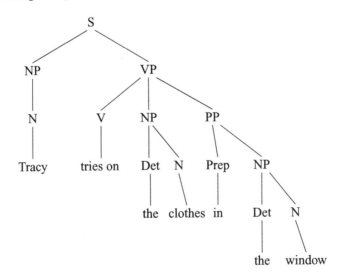

While there are more particulars to TG than we have addressed here, this description provides the fundamentals to understanding modern syntactic theory. The goal of any linguistic theory is to describe what a native speaker knows about language. TG, and its subsequent evolution, accounts for the structural knowledge on which language seems to operate, as well as our notions of paraphrases and related sentence structures, and ambiguity. For Chomsky, language is interconnected with the human mind in such a way that to understand the way language works is to understand the way the mind works. Because of this idea, he is one of the most quoted active scholars. His theories of language have been adapted to the fields of psychology, communication, and education. His ideas have completely revolutionized the field of linguistics and all its applications, from the teaching of grammar to native speakers of English, to teaching English to speakers of other languages (ESL, TESL, EFL), and to programming computers to use natural language (Natural Language Processing or NLP). Though not all linguists and language scholars agree with Chomsky's ideas, all of them have been significantly affected by the theoretical principles which govern Transformational Generative grammar.

Answers to Exercises

IMPORTANT: At times your answer may be correct and yet not agree with the answer given here. In the phonology this will happen because there are many variations of pronunciation, both dialectal and idiolectal, in American English, and your pronunciation may be one of these. In other parts of the grammar your "wrong" answer may represent a variant usage or a different but legitimate way of viewing a particular form or structure. Therefore, whenever you are in doubt about an answer, do not hesitate to bring up the matter in class.

Also, you should use these answers intelligently. Suppose, for example, that you are asked to find an English word that begins with the sounds /gw-/. If your own mental resources, aided by a desk dictionary, do not yield the answer in a reasonable time, don't spend further effort on it; simply look at the answer and then go on with the assignment.

Exercise 1–1

The nasals are the final sound in *rim, bin, sing, trim, pain, wrong*. The other final sounds are orals.

Exercise 1–2

The voiced sounds are the final sound in *hum, pin, among, fin*, and *song*. The other final sounds are voiceless.

Exercise 1–3

The first sound in each of these words is voiced: *vine, then, zeal, late,* and *rate*. The other initial sounds are voiceless.

Exercise 1–4

The first sound in each of these words is voiced: *bin, dime,* and *goop*. The initial sound in each of the other three words is voiceless.

Exercise 1–5

1. p	b	6. r	t	11. d	t		
2. b	d	7. f	v	12. d	k		
3. l	r	8. z	t	13. l	m		
4. p	k	9. h	g	14. t	n		
5. g	s	10. s	w	15. n	ŋ		

Exercise 1-6

1. pæk	8. kɪp	15. kɪk	22. gɛt
2. kɛp	9. kɪd	16. kæp	23. gæt
3. pit	10. kæt	17. pɛk	24. bæk
4. pɪt	11. bik	18. pɪk	25. bek
5. pet	12. bɪg	19. pik	26. tæp
6. pɛt	13. det	20. gæd	27. tep
7. pæt	14. dɛt	21. gɛt	28. tɪp

Exercise 1-7

1. fud	6. šo	11. vudu	16. zu
2. fʊt	7. ðo	12. šuk	17. θat, θɔt
3. fo	8. θa, θɔ	13. hu	18. ðoz
4. fat, fɔt	9. sup	14. ho	19. oθ
5. šu	10. at, ɔt	15. zon	20. vɪžən

Exercise 1-8

1. pər	4. gofər	7. wʊdəd	10. hərd
2. mərdər	5. čərčəz	8. foldəd	11. hərt
3. čɪldrən or čɪldərn	6. rəbz	9. ritərn	12. hət

Exercise 1-9

1. ərǰ	6. əbəv	11. ližər	16. pakət
2. stap	7. bərd	12. ərbən	17. təde
3. kət	8. rəst	13. ad	18. kəbərd
4. sofə	9. rən	14. əfɛkt	19. ǰərni
5. rəg	10. bərč	15. əfɛkt	20. hat

Exercise 1-10

(Numerous variations are possible here.)

1. wɪr	10. mornɪŋ	19. pɛr
2. gɪr	11. mornɪŋ	20. pe-ər
3. ðɛr	12. nɔrθ	21. stɛr
4. ðɛr	13. nɔrðərn	22. ste-ər
5. kɛr	14. flɔr	23. mɛr
6. mɛri	15. hɪr	24. me-ər, mɛr
7. mɛri	16. lur	25. park
8. mɛri	17. hɔrs	26. pər
9. barǰ	18. hɔrs	

In exercise 1–10 these groups are especially likely to show dialectal variation: 6, 7, 8; 10, 11; 17, 18. Also, pronunciation may vary according to the position in the sentence. Compare, for example:

1. The stair /stɛr/ is crowded.
2. He ran up the stair /ste-ər/.

Exercise 1-11

1. sɪt   1
2. ɪnfɛkt   2
3. pɛpər   2
4. dɪsɪnčænt   3
5. ənastəntešəs, ənɔstəntešəs   5

Exercise 1-12

1. may	6. ǰɔy	11. hay	16. tray
2. tɔy	7. čayvz	12. awč	17. strayp
3. haw	8. ðaw	13. mayti	18. rawdi
4. tay	9. šay	14. rɔyl, rɔyəl	19. kɪlrɔy
5. kaw	10. ray	15. kɔy	20. dɪstrɔy

Exercise 1-13

1. pɪp	6. gæg	11. fæst	16. flɪkər
2. bɪb	7. stapt	12. fæsən	17. sɪks
3. tat	8. stapgæp	13. uzd	18. gɛst
4. did	9. hɪkəp	14. hænd	19. kip
5. kot	10. səbpɔynt	15. hænz	20. kup

Exercise 1-14

The /k/ of *coop* is far back and is rounded because of the influence of the following /u/, which is back and rounded. The /k/ of *keep* is further front and is unrounded because of the influence of /i/, which is front and unrounded.

Exercise 1-15

1. inəf	7. wɪθ, wɪð	13. haws	19. anəst
2. wayf	8. sɛnt	14. həzbənd	20. haməǰ, aməǰ
3. wayvz	9. klos	15. ləkšəri, ləgžəri	
4. fɪfθ, fɪθ	10. kloz	16. ləgžəriəs	
5. sawθ	11. nuz	17. mɛžər	
6. səðərn	12. nuspepər	18. həmbəl	

Exercise 1-16

Examples (other examples are certainly possible):

1. baynd	4. bəs	6. ǰæm	8. ædər
2. bes	5. dim	7. lərk	9. seŋ
3. bol			

Exercise 1–17

1. fud
2. fyud
3. i-an
4. yan, yɔn
5. jəǰ
6. saləm
7. ič
8. sɪŋər, sɪŋgər
9. lɪŋgər
10. straŋ, strɔŋ
11. straŋgər, strɔŋgər
12. ɪlužən
13. fok
14. mɪlk
15. yuz
16. əpɪnyən
17. tray
18. wɛr
19. wɛr, hwɛr
20. biret

[Exercise 1–18 omitted]

Exercise 1–19

1. frog
2. sorry
3. why
4. room
5. room
6. pretty
7. woman
8. women
9. chiefs
10. lives
11. sends
12. sense
    cents
    scents
13. pounds
14. across
15. affect
    effect
16. wash
17. wash
18. wash
19. horse
    hoarse
20. horse
    hoarse
21. something
22. language
23. contact
24. contact
25. Tuesday

1. Let me go.
2. I'm going to cry.
3. Who asked you?
4. I told him.
5. We told them.
6. I should think he would.
7. She's pretty cheeky.
8. They could have bought them.
9. I'll miss you.
10. I'll treat you.

Exercise 2–1

1. lɛd̲ər
   bad̲əl
   fɔr̲di
2. saw̲θ
   saðərn
3. ɪt
   ɪd̲ɪz
4. wərθ
   wər̲ði
5. gat
   ayv gad̲ɪt
6. kəp
   kəbərd̲
7. šət
   šəd̲əp
8. hæv
   ay hæf̲tə fɪš
   ay hæv tu fɪš
9. haw mɛni gɛs wɪl yə hæf̲tə fid
   haw mɛni gɛs wɪl yə hæv tə fid
10. yuzd
    hi yus̲tə dæns
    hi yuzd tu ɛgz

Exercise 2–2

Singular	Plural		Singular	Plural
1. stap	staps		11. sən	sənz
2. rayt	rayts		12. saŋ, sɔŋ	saŋz, sɔŋz
3. kek	keks		13. dal	dalz
4. məf	məfs		14. fɪr	fɪrz
5. brɛθ	brɛθs		15. glæs	glæsəz
6. mab	mabz		16. roz	rozəz
7. rayd	raydz		17. dɪš	dɪšəz
8. frag, frɔg	fragz, frɔgz		18. məraž, mɪraž	məražəz, mɪražəz
9. wev	wevz		19. dɪč	dɪčəz
10. səm	səmz		20. ɛǰ	ɛǰəz

Answer to question 1: The three forms of the plural are /-s/, /-z/, and /-əz/.

Answer to question 2: A singular form ending in an s-like sound—/s/, /z/, /š/, /ž/, /č/, /ǰ/—is followed by /-əz/. As for the remaining, /s/ follows a voiceless sound, and /z/ follows a voiced sound.

Exercise 2–3

Present	Past		Present	Past
1. pæs	pæst		11. həg	həgd
2. læf	læft		12. rev	revd
3. map	mapt		13. mɪl	mɪld
4. bæk	bækt		14. stər	stərd
5. rəš	rəšt		15. rat	ratəd or radəd
6. rɛnč	rɛnčt		16. lod	lodəd
7. rab	rabd		17. sit	sitəd or sidəd
8. sim	simd		18. sad	sadəd
9. lon	lond		19. nid	nidəd
10. raŋ, rɔŋ	raŋd, rɔŋd		20. ripit	ripitəd or ripidəd

The answers are just what you expected:
1. The -ed suffix has three forms: /-t/, /-d/, and /-əd/.
2. The /-əd/ follows a /t/ or /d/. The /t/ follows other voiceless sounds, and /d/ follows other voiced sounds.

Exercise 2–4

1. strɛnθ, strenθ	/ŋ/ becomes /n/ because of /θ/. Both /n/ and /θ/ are dentals or interdentals. This pronunciation is an occasional variant.
2. ðɪšugər	/s/ becomes identical with /š/. They are adjacent sounds.

3. græmpa	/nd/ becomes /m/ because of /p/. Both /m/ and /p/ are bilabials.
4. græma	/nd/ becomes /m/ because of /m/. Both /m/ and /m/ are bilabials.
5. hæŋkərčɪf, heŋkərčɪf	/nd/ becomes /ŋ/ because of /k/. Both /ŋ/ and /k/ are velars.
6. kaŋkər	/n/ becomes /ŋ/ because of /k/. Both /ŋ/ and /k/ are velars.
7. hi lɛfθə tawn	/t/ is lost because of difficulty of articulation. /ð/ becomes /θ/ because of /f/. Both /f/ and /θ/ are voiceless.
8. ǰəsθɪŋk	/t/ is lost because of difficulty of articulation.

Exercise 2–5

1. arduous
2. glacier
3. Parisian
4. impetuous
5. fracture
6. congratulate
7. Please wait your turn.
8. What was your idea?
9. Did you come?

Exercise 2–6

1. The assimilated /mp/, with two bilabials juxtaposed, is easier to say.
2. *Emplane* is more likely to become the standard form, for reason given in answer above.
3. *Condemn* contains the alveolar /n/ because the next sound, /d/, is also alveolar. *Congress* contains the velar /ŋ/ because the next sound, /g/, is also velar.
4. The /t/ of *writing* is often voiced, becoming /d/ because it occurs between two vowels.
5. The /n/, which is alveolar, is assimilated to the /p/, bilabial, becoming /m/, also bilabial.
6. a. The /t/ of *patre* is between two voiced sounds and thus becomes voiced as /d/.
   b. In *donna* the VL (Vulgar Latin) /m/ of *domna has become identical with the following /n/.
      In *damme* the VL /n/ has become identical with the preceding /m/.
   c. In VL *debta the /b/ has assimilated to the /t/, becoming identical with it, producing Old French *dette*.
   d. The /t/ in VL *armata* is surrounded by vowels and therefore becomes voiced, resulting in *armada*.
   e. In VL *amta we have a bilabial /m/ next to an alveolar /t/. The /m/ becomes more like its neighbor by changing to the alveolar /n/.

f. Same as d. The voiceless /t/ between two vowels in *salata* becomes voiced, or /d/, because its neighbors are voiced.

g. The letter *c* in VL *securo* represents the sound /k/, which is voiceless. But because it is between two voiced sounds, vowels, it too becomes voiced as /g/.

h. The Old English *hæfde* was probably pronounced /hævdə/. The /v/ then assimilated to the /d/, becoming identical with it.

i. This is a case of palatalization. The /d/ is influenced by the following high front vowel and palatalizes to the alveopalatal /ǰ/.

All these assimilated forms, you will note, require less effort to say than their progenitors.

Exercise 2-7

1. Old English *brid,* young bird
2. Old English *thridda,* third
3. Old English *gærs* and *græs,* grass
4. Middle English *drit*

Exercise 2-8

1. Yes. The Middle English original of *glimpse* was *glimsen;* and the Old English original of *empty* was *æmtig,* which in Middle English became *emti* and *empti.* Old English and especially Middle English spellings were variable, so do not be disturbed at differences in etymologies in different dictionaries.
2. *Sampson* and *Thompson.* Both *p*'s are epenthetic.
3. These words are sometimes heard with an excrescent /p/: *comfort, warmth, Tomkins, dreamt.*

Exercise 2-9

1. *Lend.* Epithetic /d/. Middle English *lenen,* to lend.
2. *Bound.* Epithetic /d/. Middle English *boun,* ready, prepared.
3. *Against.* Epithetic /t/. Middle English *agenes* and *ageinst.*
4. *Midst.* Epithetic /t/. Middle English *middes.*
5. *Amongst.* Epithetic /t/. Middle English *amonges.*

Exercise 2-10

1. syncope
2. syncope
3. apocope

4. syncope

5. syncope

Exercise 3-1

a. 1. /s/   b. 6. /s/   c. 10. /i/

   2. /z/   7. /k/   11. /ɛ/

   3. /š/   8. /š/   12. /ɪ/

   4. /ž/   9. /č/   13. /ə/

   5. /Ø/ = none   14. /a/

Exercise 3-2 (other words are of course possible)

a. 1. shame

   2. machine

   3. ocean

   4. suspicious

   5. schist

   6. conscience (in some dialects)

   7. sure

   8. nausea (in some dialects)

   9. tension

  10. attention

  11. issue

  12. mission

  13. anxious

  14. luxury

b. 1. dote

   2. oh

   3. coat

   4. foe

   5. soul

   6. mow

   7. yeoman

   8. hautboy

   9. sew

  10. beau

  11. dough

  12. depot

Exercise 3-3

a. 1. /lit/

   2. /vek/

   3. /zayt/

   4. /nok/

   5. /fub, fyub/

   6. /θit/

   7. /nut/

   8. /dit/ or possibly /dɛt/

   9. /pot/

  10. /bo/ (cf. foe, doe, woe)

b. 1. dit

   2. tet

   3. jat

   4. zot

   5. chut

   6. zale, zail

   7. pobby

   8. bamthum,

      bamthem

   9. sile

  10. thoot

Exercise 3-4

/ɪn/		/æt/	
1. pɪn	pin	1. pæt	pat
2. bɪn	bin	2. bæt	bat

	/ɪn/			/æt/	
3.	tɪn	tin	3.	tæt	tat
4.	dɪn	din	4.	kæt	cat
5.	kɪn	kin	5.	gæt	gat
6.	fɪn	fin	6.	fæt	fat
7.	θɪn	thin	7.	væt	vat
8.	sɪn	sin	8.	ðæt	that
9.	šɪn	shin	9.	sæt	sat
10.	hɪn	hin	10.	hæt	hat
11.	čɪn	chin	11.	čæt	chat
12.	ǰɪn	gin	12.	mæt	mat
13.	wɪn	win	13.	næt	gnat
			14.	ræt	rat

In comparing the two lists of spelled words we find a high degree of correspondence between the consonant phonemes and the letters that represent them.

Exercise 3–5

a. In subset *a*, a one-syllable word ending in a silent *e* drops the *e* before a suffix beginning with a vowel.

b. In subset *b*, a one-syllable word ending in a single consonant preceded by a single vowel doubles the consonant before a suffix beginning with a vowel.

Exercise 3–6

When a suffix is added to words ending in a silent *e*, the *e* is retained before a suffix beginning with a consonant but is dropped before a suffix beginning with a vowel.

Exercise 3–7

1.	ænθəni	Tony	toni
2.	θiədɔr	Ted	tɛd
3.	dɔrθi	Dot (ty)	dat (i) or dadi
4.	arθər	Art	art
5.	əlɪzəbɛθ	Betty	bɛti or bɛdi
6.	mæθyu	Matt	mæt
7.	nəθæniəl	Nate	net

The /t/ of the nicknames has come down by oral tradition from the time when the *th* was pronounced /t/. The /θ/ of the full names is a spelling pronunciation.

Exercise 3–8

Answers cannot be given for this exercise because it is *your* pronunciation that you are investigating. But frequent spelling pronunciations are as follows:

1. bričɪz
2. blækgard

3. kəmptrolər, kamptrolər
4. almz

5. vɪkšuəl
6. kakswen
7. grinwɪč

8. fælkən
9. grayndston, graynston
10. fɔrhɛd

Exercise 3–9

1. kəm
   hom
2. muv
   šəv
3. frɛnd
   find
   sɪv
4. swɔr
   sɔrd
5. hɔrnɛt
   awər

6. haws
   kərawz
   feməs
7. kɔr
   aylənd
   dɛt
   savərn, savrən
   numædɪk
8. kərnəl

Exercise 4–1

1. defér
2. díffer
3. pervért (verb)
4. pérvert (noun)
5. conflíct (verb)
6. cónflict (noun)

7. évil
8. supérb
9. románce, or rómance
10. detáil, or détail
11. reséarch, or résearch
12. defénse, or défense

Exercise 4–2

1. díctionàry
2. sécretàry
3. sèparátion
4. íntellèct
5. fùndaméntal

6. àviátion
7. pèrpendícular
8. àcadémic
9. ùnivérsity
10. àbsolútely

Exercise 4–3

1. áccènt
2. aùstére
3. ámbùsh
4. hùmáne
5. bláckbìrd

6. fòrgíve
7. ìráte
8. páthòs
9. díphthòng
10. phónème

Exercise 4–4

1. ìntĕlléctŭăl
2. désĭgnàte
3. èdŭcátĭon

4. búsўbòdў
5. ìntĕrrúptĭon
6. hùmànĭtárĭăn

7. sócĭalìzed
8. cérĕmònў

9. mílĭtàrў
10. ùnĭnspíred

Exercise 4–5

1. remárkable
2. remârkable invéntion
3. tíresome
4. tîresome jób
5. cóntract (noun)
6. côntract brídge

7. práiseworthy
8. prâiseworthy remárk
9. académic
10. acadêmic procéssion
11. blóoming
12. blôoming plánt

Exercise 4–6

1. a wooden gáte
2. a gate of wóod
3. completely góne
4. gone complétely
5. run for the práctice
6. practice for the rún

7. Jack and Jíll
8. bread or wáter
9. not at áll
10. all at ónce
11. call the thief a líar
12. call the liar a thíef

Exercise 4–7

1. insíde
2. însìde jób
3. ôvernìght gúests   òverníght
4. cût-glàss bówl   cùt-gláss
5. înlàid tíles   ìnláid
6. âlmòst kílled   àlmóst (or álmòst)
7. òverséas   ôversèas jób
8. Chìnése   Chînèse ármy
9. fòurtéen   fôurtèen yéars
10. lêft-hànded pítcher   lèft-hánded

Exercise 4–8

1. bláckbòard
2. hótbèd
3. blúebèrry
4. máilmàn
5. shórtcàke

6. róundhòuse
7. páperbàck
8. rócking chàir
9. spínning whèel
10. flýing tèacher

Exercise 4–9

1. hôt hóuse
2. dârk róom
3. blâck bírd

4. tênder fóot
5. hându mán
6. swêet potáto

7. fûnny bóne
8. dâncing téacher

9. shôrt stóry
10. môving ván

Exercise 4–10

1a. a chair that is high
2a. a job involving snow
3a. a book that is blue
4a. a house that is green

5a. two u's
6a. a horse that is racing
7a. a room that is smoking
8a. a jump that is high

9a. any girl who is dancing
10a. a lotion that feels cool
11a. a teacher who is French
12a. a hand that is not short

1b. a special chair for babies
2b. a deception
3b. an examination booklet
4b. a glass-covered building where green things are raised
5b. the 23rd letter in the alphabet
6b. a horse for purposes of racing
7b. a room that is for smoking
8b. an athletic event that involves jumping over a designated mark
9b. a girl whose profession is dancing
10b. a lotion for cooling
11b. a teacher who teaches French
12b. writing by hand as opposed to typing

Exercise 4–11

1. Some people are running horses against one another.
2. They are horses for racing.
3. He likes to run or race greyhounds.
4. He raises greyhounds for racing.
5. On the stove they have apples that are being cooked.
6. These apples are for cooking.
7. Sally has a compulsive ambition to become a doctor.
8. Sally's ambition is to drive, so that she can use the family car.

Exercise 4–12

1. She abhors dogs that are scratching.
   She doesn't like to scratch dogs.
2. Books that are emotionally stirring always disturbed him.
   When anyone moved books, he was always disturbed.
3. We enjoy visitors who provide us entertainment.
   We like to entertain visitors.
4. Those reports encourage us.
   They encourage reports.
5. Oil that was burning frightened him.
   Whenever anyone burned oil, he became frightened.

Exercise 4–13

1. júmp ròpes
2. jûmp rópes

3. wâsh rágs
4. wáshràgs

5. mâp róutes
6. máp ròutes
7. flâsh líghts
8. fláshlìghts
9. wâtch dógs
10. wátchdògs

Exercise 4–14

1. cûtting úp
2. cútùp
3. hânded óut
4. hándòuts
5. hêld óver
6. hóldòver
7. côme dówn
8. cómedòwn

Exercise 4–15

1. ɪnstál, ɪnstɔ́l
2. ɪnstǝléšǝn
3. ár
4. ðe ǝr gán, ðe ǝr gɔ́n
5. dipóz
6. dɛpǝzíšǝn
7. hǽv
8. hi mǝstǝv léft
9. ór
10. wɪl ɪt bi wɪnd ǝr rén
11. hi kǽn bǝdi wónt
12. hí kǝn du ɪt
13. ǽz yu sí, ǽžu sí
14. jǝst ǝz gúd
15. mǽn
16. pósmǝn

Exercise 5–1

```
   2          3 1
```
1. He walked to the láb ↓
```
   2            3  1
```
2. Get out of my síght ↓
```
   2          3    1
```
3. Where is my néckťie ↓
```
   2                   3      3
```
4. She won't be home till twélve ↑
```
   2                    3   3
```
5. Are you going to the game éarly ↑
```
   2        3  3  2              3   1
```
6. To tell the trúth, ↑ I haven't learned to dánce ↓
```
   2             3  3  2      31
```
7. Unless you take the cár, ↑ I won't gó ↓

Exercise 5–2

```
   2          3 1
```
1. When do we éat ↓
```
   2       3  2     2       3  3
```
2. If you'll cóme, → (or If you'll cóme, ↑)
```
   2     3    2     2     3     3
```
3. For the móst part, → (or For the móst part, ↑)

 2   3   2
4. He's very hándsome, → (or ↑) (but)

  3 2   2   3
5. Géorge, ↓ (come home at once.) (or Géorge, ↑)

  2   3 1 2 3
6. We're going to eat in Chicágo ↓ Whére ↑ (= In what city did you say?)

  2   3 1 3 1
7. We're going to eat in Chicágo ↓ Whére ↓ (= In which restaurant?)

Exercise 5–3

  2   3   3 2 3 1
1. Will you have hot chócolate ↑ or mílk ↓ (one or the other)

  2   3   3 2 3 3
2. Will you have hot chócolate ↑ or mílk ↑ (or something different)

  2   2 3 2   3 2 3 2   3 1
3. I'm taking phýsics, ↑ chémistry, ↑ Gérman, ↑ and American hístory ↓

  2   3 1 1   2
4. "When are you driving hóme?" ↓ she ásked ↓

  2   3 1 1   2
5. Give me a líft, ↓ Gértrude ↑

Exercise 5–4

  2   3 3
1a. Did his sister make him a *cáke* ↑

  2   3   3
 b. Did his *síster* make him a cake ↑

  2   3   3
 c. Did his sister *máke* him a cake ↑

  2   3   3
 d. Did his sister make *hím* a cake ↑

  2   3 3
2a. Is the library in your college quite *lárge* ↑

  2   3   3
 b. Is the *líbrary* in your college quite large ↑

  2   3   3
 c. Is the library in *yóur* college quite large ↑

Exercise 5–5

1a. fâir crówd
 b. fáir cròwd
2a. wét sùit
 b. wêt súit

3a. a récord sàle
 b. a rêcord sále
4a. a sécondary ròad prògram
 b. a sêcondary róad prògram
5a. They're rúnning prògrams
 b. They're rûnning prógrams

Exercise 5–6

1a. Every dáy → passengers enjoy a meal like thís.
 b. Everyday pássengers → enjoy a meal like thís.
2a. The blue dréss → particularly ínterested her.
 b. The blue dress partícularly → ínterested her.
3a. French pláne → with twenty-four cráshes.
 b. French plane with twenty-fóur → cráshes.
4a. I consider thése → érrors.
 b. I consider these érrors.
5a. The sóns → raise méat.
 b. The sun's ráys → méet.

Exercise 5–7

1a. Students of cooking who belong to the Salvation Army.
 b. The Salvation Army is cooking up some students for a mission supper.
2a. I addressed or referred to Bill as a doctor (or I called a doctor to help Bill).
 b. I called Bill, who was a doctor.
3a. Haven't you anything better to do than to go around scratching someone else?
 b. Bess, why are you scratching yourself?
4a. Have some honey (on your waffle).
 b. Have some, honey.
5a. Candy, what are we going to have for a snack?
 b. Are we having candy for a snack?
6a. I am to leave instructions.
 b. I have been instructed to leave.
7a. I suspect that you were there on the spot.
 b. I suspect that you were right in that matter.
8a. People who eat Irish potatoes do so out of ignorance.
 b. People who eat Irish potatoes don't know any better potatoes.
9a. I believe man is idealistic.
 b. I believe that that particular man is idealistic.
10a. Body works that belong to George.
 b. George's body engages in work.
11a. He gave the books belonging to the library.
 b. He gave books to the library.
12a. More doctors and still more doctors are specializing.
 b. Doctors are specializing more and more.

1a. ay + skrim
  b. ays + krim

In *a* the /ay/ and the /s/ are both longer than in *b,* indicating that they are respectively prejunctural and postjunctural. In *a* the /k/ has only slight aspiration, indicating that it is a post-/s/ /k/. In *b* the /k/ has strong aspiration, showing that it is a postjunctural /k/.

2a. nayt + ret
  b. nay + tret

In *a* the /r/ is voiced, showing it is postjunctural. In *b* the /t/ has strong aspiration, showing that it is postjunctural. In *b* the /r/ may be devoiced, showing that it follows /t/ directly without an intervening juncture.

3a. ðæt + stəf
  b. ðæts + təf

In *a* the /s/ has the greater length of a postjunctural /s/, and the /t/ has the lack of aspiration of a post-/s/ /t/. The final /t/ of *a* is longer than the medial /t/ of *b.* In *b* the /s/ has the shortness of a prejunctural /s/, and the /t/ has the strong aspiration of a postjunctural /t/.

4a. sim + ebəl
  b. si + mebəl

The greater length of /m/ in *b* tells our ears that it is postjunctural. (We should expect the prejunctural /i/ of *see* to be longer than the /i/ of *seem,* but a laboratory experiment seems to show that the difference is not within the limits of human perception. Perhaps the /m/ following the /i/ serves to lengthen it. Compare for example the length of /i/ in *seat* and *seam.*)

5a. ɪts + lɪd
  b. ɪt + slɪd

In *b* the greater length of /s/ shows that it is postjunctural, and the /l/ may be partly or wholly voiceless, showing that it directly follows /s/ without intervening juncture. In *a* the /l/ with normal voicing indicates that it is postjunctural.

6a. nu + dart
  b. nud + art

In *a* the longer /u/ of /nu/ shows that it is prejunctural, and the longer /d/ of /dart/ shows that it is postjunctural.

7a. ɪt + sprez
  b. ɪts + prez

In *a* /sprez/ has the longer /s/ characteristic of postjunctural /s/ and also the unaspirated /p/ of the /sp/ combination. In *b* the /s/ is shorter and the /p/ is aspirated, indicating a prejunctural /s/ and a postjunctural /p/.

Exercise 6–2

ME form	Process
1. a naddre	became "an adder"
2. a napron	became "an apron"
3. a nauger	became "an auger"
4. an ekename	became "a nickname"
5. a noumpere	became "an umpire"

Exercise 6–3

1. fîne + jób
2. môst ŏf thĕ tíme
3. thĕ párty
4. thât + párty
5. tâlk + wísely
6. sòme ŏf thĕ + inspîred + ártìsts
7. Jâne + lôves + cándy
8. stône + fénce
9. bîrd ĭn thĕ búsh

Exercise 7–1

The answers are in the text.

Exercise 7–2 (Various answers are possible.)

1. splash	4. string	7. screech
2. spread	5. stupid	8. skewer
3. spew	6. sclerosis	9. squeak

Exercise 7–3 (Various answers are possible.)

a. 1. spider	3. pew	8. crazy	3. suit
2. stuff	4. trash	9. cute	d. 1. lute (Cf. loot)
3. skate	5. twig	10. quiet	
b. 1. please	6. Tuesday	c. 1. slam	
2. prey	7. clean	2. sweet	

Exercise 7–4 (Various answers are possible.)

1. snow	8. dwell	15. flame	22. view
2. smoke	9. gleam	16. fresh	23. whinny
3. bleed	10. grass	17. feud	24. huge
4. breeze	11. gules	18. thread	25. chew
5. beauty	12. sphere	19. thews	26. juice
6. dream	13. music	20. thwack	
7. dew	14. news	21. shred	

Exercise 7–5

OSV
1. t r ee

OSV
2. c l ass

OSV
3. s wig

O S V
4. c [y] ute

OSV
5. s mell

OSV
6. s n eeze

Exercise 7–6

VSO
1. clump

VSO
2. hi n t

VSO
3. he l p

VSO
4. ha r d

VSO
5. si n k

VSO
6. porch (the last sound /č/ is an obstruent.)

Exercise 7–7 (Various answers are possible.)

1. pueblo
2. Buena Vista
3. guava
4. moire
5. noir
6. svelte
7. spitz
8. shtick (schtick)
9. Schlesinger
10. schmaltz
11. schnitzel
12. schwa
13. tsetse
14. Vladivostok
15. Vries
16. zloty
17. Zwingli
18. joie

Exercise 7–8

1. /ŋ/   2. /ž/ (though many people now pronounce the word *genre* with an initial /ž/)

Exercise 7–9

1. s   1
2. sk   2
3. skt 3
4. lθ   2
(or 1tθ 3)
5. tθ   2
6. mpt 3
7. nts   3
8. nts   3
9. ŋkθ 3 (or nθ 2)
10. kst   3
11. rst   3
12. ksθ 3 (or kstθ 4)
13. lθ   2 (or 1fθ 3 or 1ftθ 4)
14. ksts 4
15. ksθs 4 (or kstθs 5)
16. lθs   3 (or 1fθs 4 or 1ftθs 5)

Exercise 7–10 (Various answers are possible.)

1. it
2. ɪt
3. et
4. ɛvri
5. æt
6. əbəv
7. ar
8. uz
9. ʊmlaut
10. ozon
11. ɔfəl

The final unstressed vowel in words such as *every, ready, forty* is usually pronounced with a tongue position between /i/ and /ɪ/. In this book we have arbitrarily assigned it to the /i/ phoneme.

Exercise 7–11

/u/	/ʊ/
uz	ʊmpf
udəlz	ʊrdu
ups	ʊmlaut
ulaŋ (ulɔŋ)	

Exercise 7–12 *(Various answers are possible.)*

1. sit
2. sɪt
3. set
4. sɛt
5. sæt
6. səb
7. sab
8. sup
9. sʊt
10. sop
11. sɔt

Exercise 7–13 *(Various answers are possible.)*

1. /mi/
2. /me/
3. /sofə/
4. /ma/
5. /glu/
6. /mo/
7. /sɔ/ (This might be pronounced as /sa/, depending on your dialect.)

Exercise 8–1

1. 1
2. 2
3. 1
4. 2
5. 1
6. 1
7. 2
8. 1
9. 2
10. 1
11. 2
12. 1
13. 2
14. 2
15. 1
16. 2
17. 1
18. 2
19. 2
20. 1

Exercise 8–2

1. before
2. again
3. like
4. one who
5. not
6. marked by
7. most
8. not
9. not
10. bad

Exercise 8–3

1. speak*er*
2. king*dom*
3. *petro*dollar
4. idol*ize*
5. selec*tive*
6. *bio*mass
7. *inter vene*
8. *re*make
9. dream*ed*
10. *un*do

Exercise 8–4

1. *woman*ly
2. en*dear*
3. *fail*ure
4. *fam*ous
5. in*fam*ous
6. *light*en

7. en*light*en
8. *friend*ship
9. be*friend*

10. *Boston*ian
11. un*likely*
12. pre*war*

13. sub*way*
14. *fals*ify
15. unen*live*ned

Exercise 8–5

1. hear
2. kill
3. mouth, speak
4. water

5. writing
6. body
7. one
8. hang

9. hand
10. throw

Exercise 8–6 (Your examples may vary.)

1. earth writing   geology
     oceanography
2. life study   biochemistry
     mythology
3. book lover   bibliography
     Francophile
4. come   convene
5. seize   apprehend
6. run   current
7. look   spectacles
8. place, put   depose

9. breathe   respire
10. gnaw   erode
11. carry   report
12. break   erupt
13. year   annuity
14. flesh   carnage
15. marriage   polygamy

Optional Exercise 8–7

1. day's eye
2. little mouse
3. eyebrow
4. wind eye
5. little donkey

6. the die (sg. of dice)
7. pebble
8. kick
9. goad
10. pond

Exercise 8–8 (Your examples may vary.)

1. against   antimissile
2. around   circumference
3. with   cocurricular
     collide
     comply
     convoke
     correlate
4. against   contravene
5. do the opposite of   deactivate
6. not   dishonest
7. not   incompetent

	impossible
	illegal
	irreplaceable
8. in, on	inscribe
	impale
9. between	intercede
10. within	intravenous
11. against, opposite	obstacle
	oppress
12. before	preconceive
13. after	postmortem
14. forward	progress
15. backward	retrogress
16. half	semisoft
17. under	substandard
18. over	superhuman
19. not	unattractive
20. do the opposite of	unfold

Exercise 8-9

1. 2	6. 3
2. 3	7. 2
3. 2	8. 2
4. 3	9. 2
5. 2	10. 3

Exercise 8-10

1. livened	6. workability
2. terminating	7. innermost
3. moralizers	8. marriageability
4. provincialisms	9. gangsterdom
5. gruesomely	10. affectionately

Exercise 8-11

1. {-D pt}	past tense
2. {-s pl}	noun plural
3. {-s 3d}	present third-person singular
4. {-s sg ps}	noun singular possessive
5. {-s pl ps}	noun plural possessive
6. {-ING vb}	present participle
7. {-ER cp}	comparative
8. {-D pt}	past tense
9. {-EST sp}	superlative

10. {-D pp}   past participle
11. {-D pt}   past tense
12. {-D pt}   past tense
13. {-ING vb}   present participle
14. {-s pl}   noun plural
15. {-s 3d}   present third-person singular

Exercise 8-12

1. happiness
2. friendship
3. boyhood
4. composure
5. shrinkage
6. activism
   activeness
   activation
   activity

7. supremacy
   supremeness
8. truism
   trueness
   truth
9. paganism
10. discovery

Exercise 8-13

1. V (N)	N	14. N (V)	Aj
2. V (N)	Aj	15. N (V)	N
3. V	N	16. N (Aj)	N
4. V	N	17. N	Aj (N or Av)
5. N (Aj)	V	18. V	Aj
6. Aj	V	19. V	Aj
7. Aj	Av	20. V	Aj
8. V (N)	Aj	21. N	Aj (N)
9. N (V)	N	22. N (V)	Aj
10. V (N)	N	23. Aj	V
11. V	N	24. Aj	N
12. N	Aj	25. V	N
13. N (V)	N		

Exercise 8-14 (Other words are possible.)

1. reasonableness
2. formality
3. organization
4. purification
5. realistic

Exercise 8-15 (Other words are possible.)

1. kindnesses
2. beautified

3. quarterlies
4. popularized

5. depths
6. pressures
7. arrivals

8. orientated
9. friendlier
10. funniest

No words can be formed by adding another inflectional suffix to the above words.

Exercise 8-16

You may have more than those given below.

1. sinful, sinfulness, sinless, sinlessness, sinner
2. kindly, kindliness, kindless, kindness, unkind, unkindly, unkindliness, unkindness
3. alive, aliveness, lively, liveliness, livelihood, liven, enliven, unenliven, unlively, unliveliness
4. transportable, transportability, transporter, transportation, transportational
5. audibility, auditory, auditive, audile, audio, audit, auditor, auditorium, audience, audition, audiophile

Exercise 8-17

1. {-ER cp}
2. {-ER rp}
3. {-ER n}
4. {-ER cp}
5. {-ER rp}

Exercise 8-18

1. Aj-al	6. V-al	11. Aj-al
2. N-al	7. V-al	12. Aj-al
3. V-al	8. Aj-al	13. V-al
4. Aj-al	9. V-al	14. Aj-al
5. N-al	10. N-al	15. Aj-al

Exercise 8-19

1. V-al	6. V-al
2. N-al	7. V-al
3. Aj-al	8. Aj-al
4. V-al	9. Aj-al
5. V-al	10. Aj-al

Exercise 8-20

1. a. He had a completed table.
   b. He had a polished table.
2. a. The animal was seen.
   b. The animal had spots.

Exercise 8–21

1. 1	5. 2	9. 2
2. 2	6. 2	10. 2
3. 2	7. 1	
4. 1	8. 2	

Exercise 8–22

1. IS	6. DS	11. DS	16. Amb
2. DS	7. Amb	12. DS	17. Amb
3. DS	8. DS	13. DS	18. DS
4. IS	9. DS	14. DS	19. DS
5. IS	10. DS	15. IS	20. DS

Exercise 8–23

1. Pauline	9. Caroline, Carolina
2. chanteuse	10. empress
3. protégée	11. laundress
4. czarina	12. executrix
5. songstress	13. proprietress
6. majorette	14. waitress
7. heiress	15. tragedienne
8. equestrienne	

Exercise 8–24

1. Bobby	6. lambkin	11. hatchling
2. gosling	7. packet	12. droplet
3. statuette	8. puppy	13. laddie
4. piglet or piggy	9. eaglet	14. diskette
5. dearie (or darling)	10. Annie	15. cigarette

Exercise 8–25

Unlawful is wrongly cut because the first cut leaves *unlaw,* which is not a free form.

Exercise 8–26

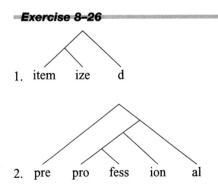

1. item   ize   d

2. pre   pro   fess   ion   al

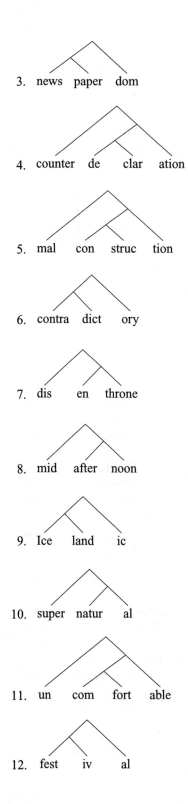

3. news paper dom

4. counter de clar ation

5. mal con struc tion

6. contra dict ory

7. dis en throne

8. mid after noon

9. Ice land ic

10. super natur al

11. un com fort able

12. fest iv al

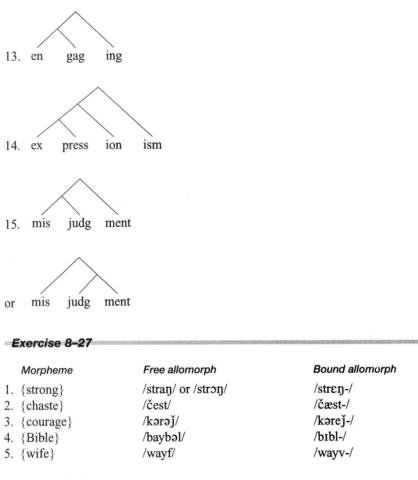

13. en gag ing

14. ex press ion ism

15. mis judg ment

or mis judg ment

Morpheme	Free allomorph	Bound allomorph
1. {strong}	/straŋ/ or /strɔŋ/	/strɛŋ-/
2. {chaste}	/čest/	/čæst-/
3. {courage}	/kərəǰ/	/kəreǰ-/
4. {Bible}	/baybəl/	/bɪbl-/
5. {wife}	/wayf/	/wayv-/

The two forms *a/an* have the same meaning and are in complementary distribution, *a* occurring before consonant sounds and *an* before vowel sounds.

1. {wide} = /wayd/ ~ /wɪd-/
2. {broad} = /brad/ or /brɔd/ ~ /brɛd-/
3. {wolf} = /wʊlf/ ~ /wʊlv-/
4. {able} = /ébəl/ ~ /əbíl-/
5. {supreme} = /səprim/ ~ /səprɛm-/
6. {divine} = /dəvayn/ ~ /dəvɪn-/
7. {fame} = /fém/ ~ /-fəm-/
8. {vise} = /víž-/ ~ /-vayz/
9. {sun} = /sən/
10. {atom} = /ǽtəm/ ~ /ətám-/

1. /sənz/
2. /næps/
3. /pæsəz/
4. /hagz/ or /hɔgz/
5. /sæks/
6. /fɪzəz/

7. /dɪšəz/   10. /stæfs/   13. /səmz/
8. /gəražəz/ or /gərajəz/   11. /čɔrčəz/   14. /hiθs/
9. /hoz/   12. /gɔrjəz/   15. /gaŋz/ or /gɔŋz/

Allomorphs: {-s pl} = /-s/   /-z/   /-əz/

Complementary distribution: /-əz/ after /s/, /z/, /š/, /ž/, /č/, and /ǰ/
                          /-s/ after other voiceless sounds
                          /-z/ after other voiced sounds

Exercise 8–31

{*be*} + {-D pt} = /wəz/ ∞ /wər/

Exercise 8–32

1. /sa/ = /si/ + /i > a/ or /sɔ/ = /si/ + /i > ɔ/
2. /bigæn/ = /bigɪn/ + /ɪ > æ/
3. /bɪt/ = /bayt/ + /ay > ɪ/
4. /gev/ = /gɪv/ + /ɪ > e/
5. /gru/ = /gro/ + /o > u/
6. /rod/ = /rayd/ + /ay > o/
7. /grawnd/ = /graynd/ + /ay > aw/
8. /tʊk/ = /tek/ + /e > ʊ/
9. /tɔr/ = /tɛr/ + /ɛ > ɔ/
10. /spok/ = /spik/ + /i > o/

Exercise 8–33

1. meat
   meet
   mete
2. might (noun)
   mite
   might (aux.)
3. you
   yew
   ewe
4. pear
   pare
   pair
5. pail
   pale
6. to
   two
   too (= also)
   too (= more than should be)

Exercise 8–34

1. point
2. moving light; smallness; repetition
3. light; smallness; repetition
4. smallness; repetition
5. undesirable
6. undesirable
7. abrupt stoppage of movement
8. unabrupt stoppage of movement
9. smallness
10. smallness
11. light
12. repetition

13. smallness
14. repetition
15. undesirable
16. smallness

17. abrupt stoppage of movement
18. smallness; repetition
19. smallness
20. repetition

Exercise 9-1

1. Ø, 8
2. 7, 7
3. 3, 5

4. 6 7 8, 6
5. Ø, 7
6. 6, 7

Exercise 9-2

1. knave	S	8. pur│ist	Cx	15. en│able	Cx
2. knav│ish	Cx	9. oyster	S	16. mete	S
3. graph	S	10. mis│anthrope	Cx	17. met│er	Cx
4. tele│graph	Cx	11. philo│sophy	Cx	18. hydro│meter	Cx
5. aqua│naut	Cx	12. cannibal	S	19. disco│graphy	Cx
6. bi│cycle	Cx	13. refus│al	Cx	20. shin│y	Cx
7. pure	S	14. dent│al	Cx		

Exercise 9-3

1. 1
2. 7
3. 2
4. 4
5. 3
6. 8

7. 8
8. 3
9. 3
10. 5
11. 3
12. 9

Exercise 9-4

1. Cd
2. Gs
3. Cd
4. Gs
5. Cd, Gs
6. Cd
7. Gs

8. Cd
9. Cd
10. Gs
11. Cd
12. Gs
13. Cd
14. Gs

Exercise 9-5

1. shárp│shòoter	Cd	6. pass│book	Cd
2. shârp shóoter	Gs	7. apparatus	S
3. act	S	8. glow│worm	Cd
4. re│act	Cx	9. im│port	Cx
5. rattle│snake	Cd	10. rip│cord	Cd

11. un|earth	Cx	16. búlls| èye (of target)	Cd
12. rat-|a-|tat	Cd	17. bûlls| éye (of bull)	Gs
13. beauty	S	18. out|last	Cd
14. beauti| fy	Cx	19. bio| chemical	Cx
15. geo| metry	Cx	20. in|accessible	Cx

Exercise 10–1

1. C
2. D
3. E
4. I
5. I

6. E
7. C
8. E
9. D
10. D

Exercise 10–2

1. advertisement
2. discothèque
3. taxicab
4. cabriolet
5. delicatessen
6. vibrations
7. zoological (gardens)
8. fanatic

9. curiosity
10. memorandum
11. Frederick
12. Albert, Alfred, Alvin
13. Thomas
14. Joseph
15. Philip, Philbert

Exercise 10–3

1. alligator
2. turnpike
3. omnibus
4. caravan
5. parachute

6. periwig
7. acute
8. Eugene
9. Elizabeth
10. Anthony or Antonio

Exercise 10–4

1. American Indian
2. maître d'hôtel
3. condensation trail
4. taximeter cab(riolet)
5. motor + pedal
6. communications satellite
7. agriculture business

Exercise 10–5

1. recreational vehicle
2. National Organization of Women, negotiable order of withdrawal (bank term meaning check)

3. Mothers Against Drunk Driving
4. Old Kinderhook
5. self-contained underwater breathing apparatus
6. Organization of Petroleum Exporting Countries
7. White, Anglo-Saxon Protestant
8. Intercontinental Ballistic Missile
9. light amplification by stimulated emission of radiation
10. Federal Deposit Insurance Corporation
11. Internal Revenue Service

Exercise 10–6

1. breakfast + lunch
2. happen + circumstance
3. stagnation + inflation
4. simultaneous + broadcast
5. motor + hotel
6. smoke + fog
7. dumb + confound
8. tele- + broadcast
9. fluster + frustrated
10. splash + spatter

Exercise 10–7

1. transistor
2. autobus
3. escalator
4. blurt
5. squawk

Exercise 10–8

1. need   needy
   speed   speedy
   seed   seedy
   bead   beady
2. televise
3. donate
   orate

Exercise 10–9

1. housekeeper
2. typewriter
3. administrator or administration
4. resurrection
5. baby-sitter
6. enthusiasm
7. lazy
8. laser
9. sideling
10. escalator
11. reminiscence
12. deficit-spending
13. emotion
14. burglar
15. party-pooper

Exercise 10–10

1. femelle
2. Fr. carriole (cariole)
3. Sp. cucaracha
4. agnail, angnail (*ag-, ang-* meant painful.)
5. Welsh rabbit (*Welsh rabbit* was probably a jocular term, like *prairie oysters* for eggs and *Cape Cod turkey* for codfish.)
6. Dutch *kool* (cabbage) + sla (salad) became English coleslaw.
7. bridegome (When *-gome* [man] became obsolete, the nearest similar term for a human male was *groom*.)
8. helpmeet (*Helpmeet* was formed by a misunderstanding of Genesis 2:18 and 20, ". . . an help meet [= fitting] for him.")
9. otchock (From a Native American language)

Exercise 10–11

1. From the fourth Earl of Sandwich "who once spent twenty-four hours at the gaming table with no other refreshment than some slices of cold beef between slices of toast." OED
2. Frankfurter (= of Frankfurt, Germany)
3. Bologna, Italy
4. French, serge de Nîmes (= serge of Nîmes, France)
5. Kashmir, India
6. Short for *jean fustian,* a tough cloth. The *jean* is from French Gênes (Genoa, Italy), where it was made.
7. Jules Léotard, an aerial gymnast
8. Guy Fawkes, an English conspirator of the seventeenth century. In England on Guy Fawkes Day his effigy, clad in grotesque and ill-fitting garments, was carried about the streets and then burnt in the evening amid fireworks. It was accompanied by other effigies of unpopular persons which were called "guys."
9. Named for William Lynch, whose approach to punishing criminals in the absence of authorized law enforcement officers has caused his name to be associated with vigilante activity, particularly hangings.
10. Named for Charles C. Boycott, a land agent with whom many in the local community refused to interact or do business.

Exercise 10–12

1. wiggle
2. patter
3. wit
4. super
5. silly
6. (both)

Exercise 10–13

1. 3
2. 3
3. 3
4. 1

5. 2		8. 3
6. 2		9. 2
7. 2		10. 2

Exercise 11–1

		Plural
Plural	*Possessive*	*+ Possessive*
1. carpenters	carpenter's	carpenters'
2. women	woman's	women's
3. brothers	brother's	brothers'
brethren		brethren's
4. clouds	cloud's	clouds'
5. cattle	_____	cattle's
6. ducks	duck's	ducks'
duck		
7. Japanese	_____	_____
8. means	_____	_____
9. athletics	athletics'	_____
10. scissors	scissors'	scissors

(There are differences of usage among the noun forms, particularly with the possessive.)

Exercise 11–2
---

1. them	Pl		7. it	Sg
2. it	Sg		8. it or them	Sg or Pl
3. it	Sg		9. it	Sg
4. them	Pl		10. it	Sg
5. them	Pl		11. they	Pl
6. them	Pl			

Exercise 11–3
---

1. few
2. that
3. its
4. their
5. both

Exercise 11–4
---

1. was
2. were
3. is

4. are
5. has

Exercise 11–5

1. Sg	4. Sg	7. Pl
2. Pl	5. Sg	8. Sg
3. Pl	6. Pl	9. Sg
		10. Pl

Exercise 11–6

1. child, children
   /čıldrən/ = /čayld/ + /ay > ı/ + /-rən/
2. moose, moose
   /mus/ = /mus/ + /Ø/
3. foot, feet
   /fit/ = /fʊt/ + /ʊ > i/
4. leaf, leaves
   /livz/ = /lif/ + /f > v/ + /-z/
5. wolf, wolves
   /wʊlvz/ = /wʊlf/ + /f > v/ + /-z/
6. path, paths
   /pæðz/ = /pæθ/ + /θ > ð/ + /-z/ or perhaps /pæθs/ = /pæθ/ + /-s/

Exercise 11–7

One allomorph	Two allomorphs
grief	scarf
chief	truth
belief	wharf
waif	sheath
	wreath
	staff

Exercise 11–8

1. /-ə > -e/
2. /-z/ or /-ə > -e/
3. /-əz/ or /-s > -rə/
4. /-əz/ or /-ıks > -əsiz/
5. /-z/ or /-əm > -ə/
6. /-ıs > -iz/
7. /-ım/ or /-im/
8. /Ø/ or /-əz/
9. /-z/ or /-əm > -ə/

10. /-əs > -ay/
11. /-z/ or /-əm > -ə/
12. /-o > -i/
13. /-əz/ or /-əs > -ay/
14. /-əs > -iz/
15. /-n/

Exercise 11-9

1. 4	5. 5	9. 1
2. 3, 5	6. 3	10. 5
3. 2	7. 5	
4. 6	8. 4	

Exercise 11-10

1. 5, 6
2. 1, 3, 5, 6
3. 1, 2
4. 1, 3, 5, 6
5. 5, 6

Exercise 11-11

There are no *right* answers, as this is an investigation of the usage of the class.

Exercise 11-12

1. N	6. N	11. —
2. —	7. N	12. N
3. N	8. N	13. N
4. —	9. —	14. N
5. —	10. N	15. —

Exercise 11-13

Pres. 3rd Sg.	Pres. P.	Past T.	Past Part.	
1. walks	walking	walked	walked	4
2. bites	biting	bit	bit, bitten	4 or 5
3. keeps	keeping	kept	kept	4
4. freezes	freezing	froze	frozen	5
5. sets	setting	set	set	3
6. sells	selling	sold	sold	4
7. puts	putting	put	put	3
8. rises	rising	rose	risen	5
9. teases	teasing	teased	teased	4
10. sleeps	sleeping	slept	slept	4

Exercise 11–14

Past T.	Past P.		Past T.	Past P.
1. stəŋ	stəŋ	8. rɛŋ (or) ræŋ	rəŋ
2. krɛpt	krɛpt	9. kɛpt	kɛpt
3. drov	drɪvən	10. dɛlt	dɛlt
4. sɛŋ (or) sæŋ	səŋ	11. swæm	swəm
5. rod	rɪdən	12. spən	spən
6. rot	rɪtən	13. wən	wən
7. kləŋ	kləŋ		

Class 1: sting, cling, spin, win   {-D pt} = /ɪ > ə/
                                      {-D pp} = /ɪ > ə/

Class 2: creep, keep, deal   {-D pt} = /i > ɛ/ + /t/
                                      {-D pp} = /i > ɛ/ + /t/

Class 3: drive, ride, write   {-D pt} = /ay > o/
                                      {-D pp} = /ay > ɪ/
                                                   + /ən/

Class 4: sing, ring, swim   {-D pt} = /ɪ > e/ or /ɪ > æ/
                                      {-D pp} = /ɪ > ə/

Exercise 11–15

1. N	5. N	9. N	13. NV	17. N
2. NV	6. V	10. NV	14. N	18. NV
3. V	7. NV	11. N	15. N	19. NV
4. N	8. V	12. V	16. NV	20. V

Exercise 11–16

1. I have practiced my piano lesson <u>yesterday afternoon.</u>
2. I practiced my piano lesson yesterday afternoon.
3. Her roommate received an award last Wednesday.
4. Her roommate has received an award <u>last Wednesday.</u>
5. <u>Two years ago</u> I have visited Spain.
6. She stayed in the hospital fifteen days.
7. She has stayed in the hospital fifteen days.
8. It has rained since one o'clock.
9. She has played tennis <u>last night.</u>
10. I have worked in the garden for three days.

Exercise 11–17

1. progressive	4. progressive	7. progressive
2. perfective	5. perfective-progressive	8. perfective-progressive
3. perfective-progressive	6. perfective	

Exercise 11-18

1. <u>were</u>	6. <u>write</u>
2. <u>were</u>	7. <u>were</u>
3. <u>save</u>	8. <u>be</u>
4. <u>stand</u>	9. <u>were</u>
5. <u>be</u>	10. <u>answer</u>

Exercise 11-19

1. imperative
2. indicative
3. imperative
4. subjunctive
5. indicative
6. subjunctive
7. imperative
8. indicative
9. imperative
10. indicative

Exercise 11-20

With some of these forms there is variation in usage both among different speakers and in the speech of a single individual. Your answers may vary from what is listed below.

1. angrier	angriest	
2. healthier	healthiest	
3.	bitterest	
4. commoner	commonest	
5.	cruelest	
6.		
7.	handsomest	
8.		
9. mellower	mellowest	
10.		
11. quieter	quietest	
12. remoter	remotest	
13.	severest	
14. solider	solidest	
15.	stupidest	
16. nobler	noblest	
17. dustier	dustiest	
18. dirtier	dirtiest	
19. livelier	liveliest	
20. gentler	gentlest	

Exercise 11–21

1.	oftener	oftenest
2. No		
3. No		
4. No (But cf. Tennyson's		

      Music that gentlier on the spirit lies
      Than tired eyelids upon tired eyes.)

5.	later	latest
6. No		
7. No		
8. No		
9. No		
10.	slower	slowest
11. No		
12.	nearer	nearest
13. No		
14.	farther	farthest
	further	furthest
15.	quicker	quickest
16. No		
17.	louder	loudest
18. No		
19.	higher	highest
20.	lower	lowest

Exercise 11–22

1. better	best		4. littler	littlest
2. worse	worst		less	least
3. older	oldest		5. more	most
elder	eldest		6. fewer	fewest

Exercise 11–23

1. Aj		6. NA	
2. NA		7. Aj	
3. Aj		8. Aj	
4. NA		9. Aj	
5. NA		10. Aj	

Exercise 12–1

1. <u>president</u> . . . <u>plan.</u>	3, 3
2. <u>janitors</u> . . . <u>umbrella.</u>	2, 3
3. <u>counselor</u> . . . <u>approach.</u>	3, 3
4. <u>aunt</u> . . . <u>son.</u>	3, 3

5. Mother's <u>cake</u>   1, 3
6. <u>chef's sisters</u>   1, 2

[Exercise 12–2 omitted]

Exercise 12–3

1. <u>failure</u>	fail	-ure	11. <u>sickness</u>	sick	-ness
2. <u>payment</u>	pay	-ment	12. <u>refusal</u>	refuse	-al
3. <u>assistant</u>	assist	-ant	13. <u>width</u>	wide	-th
4. <u>sailor</u>	sail	-or	14. <u>sincerity</u>	sincere	-ity
5. <u>catcher</u>	catch	-er	15. <u>freedom</u>	free	-dom
6. <u>collision</u>	collide	-ion	16. <u>Childhood</u>	child	-hood
7. <u>leakage</u>	leak	-age	17. <u>lawyer</u>	law	-yer
8. <u>Reformation</u>	reform	-ation	18. <u>scholarship</u>	scholar	-ship
9. <u>discovery</u>	discover	-y	19. <u>fragrance</u>	fragrant	-ce
10. <u>amusement</u>	amuse	-ment	20. <u>intimacy</u>	intimate	-cy

Exercise 12–4

1. met	4	past tense	6. eats	5	pres. 3rd sg.
2. swept	4	past part.	7. set	3	past tense
3. leave	4	stem	8. lying	5	pres. part.
4. spreading	3	pres. part.	9. bought	4	past part.
5. eaten	5	past part.	10. sank	5	past tense

Exercise 12–5

1. <u>amplified</u>	ample	-ify
2. <u>personifies</u>	person	-ify
3. <u>prove</u>	proof	-ve
4. <u>weaken</u>	weak	-en
5. <u>liberalized</u>	liberal	-ize
6. <u>strengthen</u>	strength	-en
7. <u>idolize</u>	idol	-ize
8. <u>terrorized</u>	terror	-ize
9. <u>soften</u>	soft	-en
10. <u>frightened</u>	fright	-en

Exercise 12–6

-er	*-est*	*-ly*	*-ness*
1. closer	closest	closely	closeness
2. icier	iciest	icily	iciness
3. sweeter	sweetest	sweetly	sweetness
4. sadder	saddest	sadly	sadness
5. higher	highest	highly	highness

6. sunnier	sunniest	sunnily	sunniness
7. gentler	gentlest	gently	gentleness
8. smaller	smallest	—	smallness
9. littler	littlest	—	littleness
10. faster	fastest	—	fastness
11. friendlier	friendliest	friendlily	friendliness
12. —	—	naturally	naturalness

The word *natural* is an adjective but does not fit the test explained above.

(Note that the use of a word such as *friendlily* is a matter of dialect or idiolect.)

Exercise 12–7

1. gold   -en
2. help   -less
3. love   -ly
4. mess   -y
5. peace   -ful
6. insul-   -ar
7. nerve   -ous
8. fragment   -ary
9. repent   -ant
10. affection   -ate
11. fool   -ish
12. rhythm   -ic
13. region   -al
14. tire   -ed
15. separate   /et/   /ət/
16. recur   -ent
17. instruct   -ive
18. perish   -able
19. meddle   -some
20. congratulate   -ory
21. please   -ant
22. good   -ly
23. live   -ly

Exercise 12–8

1. Aj	9. Aj
2. Av	10. Aj
3. Av	11. Av
4. Aj	12. Av
5. Av	13. Av
6. Av	14. Av
7. Av	15. Av
8. Av	

Exercise 12–9

1. NS	6. Aj
2. N	7. NS
3. N	8. Av
4. V	9. Aj
5. N	10. NS

Exercise 13–1

1.	very	Aj
2.	too	Aj
3.	quite	Av
4.	somewhat	Aj
5.	rather	Aj

Exercise 13–2

1. NS	7. NS
2. Av	8. NS
3. V	9. Aj
4. N	10. Av
5. V	11. N
6. Av	

Exercise 13–3

1. a bit, a good deal, a great deal, almost, a lot, lots, much, no, kind of, any (in questions and negatives), a whole lot, even, indeed, somewhat, sort of, still
2. enough
3. indeed, still
4. right, just, even

Exercise 13–4

1. The car stopped <u>at</u> the <u>station.</u>
2. We walked <u>under</u> the <u>tree.</u>
3. He came <u>from</u> the <u>farm.</u>
4. Did the party advance <u>into</u> the <u>jungle?</u>
5. This is the farm he came <u>from.</u>   <u>No</u>
6. These roses are <u>for</u> <u>you.</u>
7. The chimpanzee <u>in</u> the <u>cage</u> was yawning.
8. The boy stood <u>on</u> a <u>barrel.</u>
9. We know <u>what</u> you are looking <u>for.</u>
10. The plumber washed <u>in</u> the <u>basin.</u>
11. Our train passed <u>beneath</u> <u>them.</u>

12. The rose <u>by</u> the <u>window</u> was wilted.
13. He walked <u>to</u> the last <u>platform.</u>
14. <u>What</u> is it <u>for</u>?
15. We invested <u>despite</u> the <u>risk</u>.

Exercise 13–5

1. <u>below</u>
2. <u>below</u>
3. <u>near</u>
4. <u>near</u>
5. <u>off</u>
6. <u>off</u>
7. <u>after</u>
8. <u>after</u>
9. <u>since</u>
10. <u>since</u>

Exercise 13–6

1. <u>Barring</u>
2. <u>following</u>
3. <u>following</u>
4. <u>regarding</u>
5. <u>regarding</u>
6. <u>Considering</u>
7. <u>including</u>
8. <u>including</u>
9. <u>beginning</u>
10. <u>concerning</u>

Exercise 13–7

1. <u>ahead of</u>
2. <u>on account of</u>
3. <u>up at</u>
4. <u>Contrary to</u>
5. <u>by way of</u>
6. <u>on behalf of</u>
7. <u>instead of</u>
8. <u>in lieu of</u>
9. <u>In spite of</u>
10. <u>In case of</u>

Exercise 13–8

1. D
2. NS
3. D
4. D
5. NS
6. D
7. D
8. D
9. D
10. D
11. NS
12. D
13. D
14. D
15. D
16. NS

Exercise 13–9

1. Police raid a gathering
2. Complete the faculty at State

A complete faculty at State
3. Rule the book not obscene
   The rule book not obscene
4. A clean model house
   Clean the model house
5. A girl shows top baby beef
   Girl shows top the baby beef

Exercise 13-10

1. 2
2. 2
3. 3
4. 0
5. 2
6. 1

Exercise 13-11

1. PA
2. MA
3. PAD
4. MA
5. PA

Exercise 13-12

   MA be
1. <u>must be</u>
   MA   have
2. <u>ought to have</u>
   MA be
3. <u>could be</u>
   MA have be
4. <u>could have been</u>
   MA have
5. <u>might have</u>

None differs from the sequence described.

Exercise 13-13

1. Neg. He was not eating.   Aux
   Q.   Was he eating?
2. Neg. He did not quit eating.   V
   Q.   Did he quit eating?

3. Neg. The worker was not killed.   Aux
    Q.   Was the worker killed?
4. Neg. The worker has not gone.   Aux
    Q.   Has the worker gone?
5. Neg. We should not hurry.   Aux
    Q.   Should we hurry?
6. Neg. We cannot hurry.   Aux
    Q.   Can we hurry?
7. Neg. They are not going.   Aux
    Q.   Are they going?
8. Neg. They did not keep going.   V
    Q.   Did they keep going?
9. Neg. He could not have been sleeping.   Aux
    Q.   Could he have been sleeping?
10. Neg. He will not play.   Aux
    Q.   Will he play?

Exercise 13–14

1. whom
2. whom
3. who
4. whom
5. whom

Exercise 13–15

1. who   Hum
2. who   Hum
3. which   Nhum
4. which   Nhum
5. which   Nhum

Exercise 13–16

1. PP		6. SbP
2. SbP		7. PP
3. PP		8. PP
4. SbP		9. SbP
5. SbP		10. PP

Exercise 14–1

1. <u>fence</u>		4. <u>fence</u>
2. <u>fence</u>		5. <u>fence</u>
3. <u>fence</u>		6. <u>fence</u>

7. <u>putter</u>

8. <u>putter</u>

9. <u>car</u>

10. <u>swings</u>

Exercise 14-2

1. the small study <u>table</u>
2. any great European <u>opera</u>
3. that somber evening <u>sky</u>
4. my roommate's tennis <u>shoes</u>
5. all the other white linen <u>handkerchiefs</u>
6. a soft <u>pat</u> on the head
7. a hard <u>blow</u> which staggered him
8. that broken <u>ski</u> lying in the basement
9. a <u>junior</u> with a lame leg who was walking on crutches
10. the <u>girl</u> in the front row whose books he was carrying

Exercise 14-3

Here are a few samples of the kinds of modifiers you might use.

1. <u>The sailboats on the bay</u> are beautiful to watch.
2. They sailed under <u>the wooden bridge near the lighthouse.</u>
3. He makes <u>exquisite jewelry which is bought by collectors.</u>

Exercise 14-4

1. count
2. mass
3. mass
4. mass
5. count
6. mass
7. count
8. mass
9. mass
10. count

Exercise 14-5

1. count   proper
2. mass   count
3. count   proper
4. mass   mass
5. proper   count
6. mass   count
7. count   count
8. mass   count
9. proper   count
10. proper proper

Exercise 14-6

1. <u>stepped</u>
2. <u>stepped</u>
3. <u>stepped</u>
4. <u>stepped</u>
5. <u>shouted</u>
6. <u>shouted</u>
7. <u>watching</u>
8. <u>eaten</u>
9. <u>driven</u>
10. <u>spoke</u>

Exercise 14–7

1. <u>sold</u>
2. <u>sold</u>
3. <u>appeared</u>
4. <u>chose</u>
5. <u>remained</u>

6. <u>gave</u>
7. <u>paid</u>
8. <u>called</u>
9. <u>was</u>
10. <u>returned</u>

Exercise 14–8

1. <u>pony</u> . . . | <u>galloped</u>
2. <u>students</u> | <u>attended</u>
3. <u>senior</u> . . . | will be <u>honored</u>
4. <u>pipes</u> . . . | <u>pounded</u>
5. <u>choir</u> . . . | <u>sang</u>

Exercise 14–9

Here are samples of what you might do.

1. The tiny leak in the hose soon became enlarged.
2. The canoe that he wanted was a narrow, aluminum model.
3. The pie fell.
4. The steaming apple pie made her mouth water.
5. The passenger in the front seat who was watching the speedometer became nervous.

Exercise 14–10

Here are samples of what you might do.

1. Emil later regretted his decision.
2. The lad with the freckled nose came after his dog when school was over.
3. The summer vacationers will soon return to college.
4. That gloomy student always seemed to have a complaint to make.
5. The mountaineer merrily swung the heavy pack on his back to begin the long hike.

Exercise 14–11

1. linking
2. transitive
3. linking
4. intransitive
5. transitive
6. transitive
7. intransitive
8. linking
9. intransitive
10. linking

Exercise 14-12

1. to	8. -ing
2. -ing	9. both
3. both	10. both
4. to	11. to
5. -ing	12. -ing
6. both	13. both
7. to	14. -ing

Exercise 14-13

1. indirect object
2. object of a preposition
3. subject
4. direct object
5. objective complement
6. subjective complement
7. verb
8. subjective complement
9. direct object
10. subject

Exercise 14-14

1. The cat purrs.
2. The student studies.
3. The house deteriorates.
4. The vase breaks.
5. The visitor departs.

Exercise 14-15

1. The cats prowl.
2. The musicians play.
3. The professors teach.
4. The buses wait.
5. The comedians laugh.

Exercise 14-16

1. purposes   make
2. leader   selects
3. one   maintains
4. difference   appears
5. troublemakers   were

Exercise 14–17

1. The patients <u>are</u> being watched.
2. The janitors <u>have</u> waxed the floor.
3. The wrestlers <u>do</u> not smoke.
4. The cars <u>have</u> been stolen.
5. The ships <u>were</u> disappearing beyond the horizon.

Exercise 14–18

1. slept
   sleeps   cat
   sleep   cats
2. called
   calls   schoolboy
   call   schoolboys
3. went
   goes   paper
   go   papers
4. chased
   chases   she
   chase   they
5. refuses
   refuses   junior
   refuse   juniors
6. do
   does   soldier
   do   soldiers
7. join
   joins   acrobat
   join   acrobats
8. have
   has   rose
   have   roses

Exercise 14–19

1. Was <u>the boy who mows the lawn</u> ill?
2. Did <u>her youngest brother</u> break his bicycle?
3. Should <u>the students on the debate squad</u> be excused?
4. Are <u>the monkeys playing on the swings</u> from India?
5. Will <u>the old gymnasium, which was built in 1907,</u> be replaced?

Exercise 15–1

1. InV
2. InV
3. InV
4. —

5. InV
6. —
7. InV
8. —
9. InV
10. —

11. InV
12. InV
13. InV
14. —
15. InV

Exercise 15–2

1. 2A
2. —
3. 2A
4. —
5. 2A

6. —
7. 2A
8. 2A
9. —
10. 2A

Exercise 15–3

1. 2A
2. other
3. other
4. 2A
5. 2A

6. other
7. other
8. 2A
9. 2A
10. other

11. 2A
12. 2A
13. other
14. other

Exercise 15–4

1. other
2. 2A
3. 2A
4. other
5. 2A

6. 2A
7. 2A
8. other
9. 2A
10. 2A

Exercise 15–5

1. 2B
2. 2B
3. other
4. other
5. 2B
6. other
7. 2B
8. other

9. 2B
10. 2B
11. other
12. 2B
13. other
14. 2B
15. 2B

Exercise 15–6

1. No
2. No

3. Yes
4. Yes
5. Yes
6. Yes
7. No

Exercise 15–7

1. 3		6. 3
2. 2A		7. 3
3. 2A		8. 3
4. 3		9. 2A
5. 3		10. 3

Exercise 15–8

1. it	5. it	9. them
2. him or her	6. it	10. each other (or one another)
3. them	7. her	11. himself
4. her or him	8. it, him, or her	12. each other (or one another)

Exercise 15–9

1. TV	4		9. TV	4
2. LV	3		10. LV	2
3. LV	2		11. LV	2
4. LV	2		12. TV	4
5. TV	4		13. LV	2
6. LV	2		14. InT	1
7. InT	1		15. TV	4
8. LV	2		16. LV	2

Exercise 15–10

Note: When forming the passive from a sentence containing a prepositional phrase, the "by-phrase" may be placed either before or after the prepositional phrase.

1. The window was opened (by the servant).
2. The dice were rolled (by him).
3. Dancing is enjoyed (by most adolescents).
4. The mountains were chosen (by us) for our vacation.
5. *King Lear* has never been read (by Jim).
6. Wood was burned in the fireplace (by the tourists).
7. The sheep were counted (by the shepherd).
8. The game was begun (by us) at four o'clock.
9. A new house on the river was built (by the Smiths).
10. A pileated woodpecker was spotted (by the nature club).

Exercise 15-11

The subject may vary in sentences 3, 4, 5, 8, and 10.

1. was <u>killed</u>
   The terrier killed the rat.
2. were <u>turned</u>
   The cook turned the pancakes.
3. is <u>raised</u>
   Farmers raise much corn in Iowa.
4. was <u>heard</u>
   We heard an early folk tune.
5. been <u>washed</u>
   Mavis has washed the dishes.
6. was <u>had</u>
   All had a good time.
7. was <u>teased</u>
   Allison's boyfriend teased Jane.
8. been <u>lowered</u>
   The sergeant had lowered the flag.
9. were <u>stopped</u>
   The traffic officer stopped the motorcycles.
10. is <u>played</u>
    A carillonneur plays a carillon concert at 7:45 in the morning.

Exercise 15-12

1. The librarian found the pamphlet for me.
2. He assigned the toughest job to Jack.
3. The spaniel brought the stick to his master.
4. Susie fed some juicy worms to the baby robins.
5. Her mother sent a new sweater to her.

Exercise 15-13

1. He was given a dirty look (by her).
   A dirty look was given (to) him (by her).
2. The manager was made a fine offer (by the company).
   A fine offer was made to the manager (by the company).
3. I was dealt a bad hand (by the dealer).
   A bad hand was dealt (to) me (by the dealer).
4. His roommate was offered the car (by him).
   The car was offered to his roommate (by him).
5. She was asked a question (by the instructor).
   A question was asked (of) her (by the instructor).

Exercise 15–14

1. The committee declared Isabelle to be the winner.
   The committee declared that Isabelle was the winner.
2. She believed George to be honest.
   She believed that George was honest.
3. I imagined her to be capable.
   I imagined that she was capable.
4. We thought him to be a great scholar.
   We thought that he was a great scholar.
5. The owner of the newspaper appointed Marcos to be editor-in-chief.
6. The inspector found the premises to be clean.
   The inspector found that the premises were clean.

Exercise 15–15

1.	She taught a trick.	5
2.	We appointed Evelyn.	6
3.	You threw a curve.	5
4.	The student body selected Arabella.	6
5.	The faculty chose Sieverson.	6
6.	We found a sandwich.	5
7.	The dealer sold an air mattress.	5
8.	She gave a toy.	5
9.	The city elected Mouchy.	6
10.	He named his new boat.	6

Exercise 15–16

1. 2	7. 2	13. 4	18. 2
2. 3	8. 4	14. 3	19. 3
3. 5	9. 6	15. 6	20. 2
4. 2	10. 5	16. 7	21. 6
5. 1	11. 2	17. 2	22. 7
6. 6	12. 6		

Exercise 15–17

1. 5, 6	8. 1, 4
2. 1, 2A	9. 4, 6
3. 2B, 4	10. 5, 6
4. 4, 5	11. 2B, 4
5. 4, 5	12. 4, 6
6. 2A, 2B	13. 1, 2A
7. 1, 4	14. 4, 6

Exercise 15-18

1. There is a rabbit in your garden.
2. There were some squirrels cracking nuts.
3. There was a moon craft pictured by *Life.*
4. There was some idiot chosen commissioner.
5. There have been five men working on the rules.

Exercise 15-19

1. that the tree fell in that direction
2. that the road might be impassable
3. to see the difference
4. whether she wears the green or the yellow suit
5. that you write a tactful letter.

Exercise 15-20

1. to revise all her papers
2. to set out in this storm
3. that we postpone the game
4. to deny their petition
5. his leaving so suddenly

Exercise 15-21

1. Exp
2. Imp
3. Exp
4. Imp
5. Imp

Exercise 16-1

1.	Aj	Subj
2.	N	Subj
3.	N	Subj
4.	V	DO
5.	NS	OP
6.	N	SC
7.	N	SC
8.	N	OC
9.	Av	SC
10.	NS	IO
11.	NS	Subj
12.	NS	DO

Exercise 16-2

1. DO
2. SC
3. OC
4. IO

5. OP
6. Subj
7. Subj

Exercise 16-3

1. that or it	Subj
2. your seat	OP
3. her	OP
4. that or it	IO
5. that or it	Subj
6. that	SC
7. that or it	DO
8. that or it	DO
9. that, it, or her beauty	Subj
10. that	OC
11. them or those	DO

Exercise 16-4

1. what we said	DO
2. What you do	Subj
3. what I thought	SC
4. what you have	OP
5. whoever came there	IO
6. whatever his grandfather wishes	DO
7. the car	OP
8. whichever is the most durable	DO
9. to bring the notes	DO
10. mailing the letter	DO
11. To speak of her contributions	Subj

Exercise 16-5

1. making
2. made
3. left
4. stolen
5. sung

Exercise 16-6

1. 4
2. 5

3. 1
4. 2

5. 1
6. 2
7. 3
8. 2
9. 6

10. 2
11. 4
12. 4
13. 4
14. 7

Exercise 16–7

1. having sprinkled the lawn	4
2. seeing the play before	4
3. to be there	3
4. the guests to remain for dinner	1
5. being a member of the band	2
6. the teacher to give him an A	5
7. After having been cheerful for weeks	2
8. Keeping quiet	2
9. his brother repay the loan	4
10. Calling Josephine an artist	6
11. his becoming a Marine	2

Exercise 16–8

1a. Subj
 b. Subj
2a. OP
 b. OP
3a. DO
 b. DO

4a. OP
 b. OP
5a. DO
 b. DO
6a. SC
 b. SC

Exercise 16–9

1. to miss the party		DO
2. to remain calm		SC
3. Shooting quail		DO
4. you to be truthful	Subj	SC
5. Finding the trail again		DO
6. washing dishes		DO
7. Being a golf champion		SC
8. them break the window	Subj	DO
9. him to stop smoking	Subj	DO
10. Electing Betty president	DO	OC
11. to give Harold a bicycle	IO	DO
12. visiting museums		DO

Exercise 16–10

1. Aj
2. N

3. N
4. N
5. Aj
6. NS
7. N
8. Aj
9. N
10. V
11. V
12. NS
13. N
14. N
15. N
16. NS
17. Aj
18. Aj
19. V
20. N

Exercise 16–11

1.	<u>old</u>	1st	7.	<u>tall</u>	2nd
2.	<u>dark</u>	2nd	8.	<u>angry</u>	2nd
3.	<u>afraid</u>	2nd	9.	<u>becoming</u>	2nd
4.	<u>asleep</u>	2nd	10.	<u>history</u>	1st
5.	<u>alive</u>	2nd	11.	<u>dirty</u>	2nd
6.	<u>student</u>	1st	12.	<u>hostile</u>	2nd

Exercise 16–12

1. <u>alone</u>   NS
2. <u>there</u>   NS
3. <u>black</u> and <u>smooth</u>   Aj, Aj
4. <u>today</u>   NS
5. <u>homeward</u>   Av
6. <u>speaking</u>   V
7. <u>grim</u>   Aj
8. <u>abroad</u>   NS
9. <u>particularly</u>   Av
10. <u>ajar</u>   NS

Exercise 16–13

(Word-group adjectivals are underlined; words they modify are set in italics.)

1. *day* <u>to remember</u>
2. *chap* <u>sitting in that cubicle</u>
3. *size* <u>I ordered</u>

4. *drugstore* <u>on the corner</u>
5. *week* <u>when I was housecleaning</u>
6. *girl* <u>spoiled by her mother</u>
7. *time* <u>convenient to yourself</u>
8. *head* <u>of this club</u>
9. *book* <u>I lent you</u>
10. *sight* <u>to behold</u>

Exercise 16–14

1. <u>sweet</u>
2. <u>desirable</u>
3. <u>exciting</u>
4. <u>interested</u>
5. <u>concerned</u>

Exercise 16–15

recently   1, 2, 4
everywhere   1, 4 ⟶ (Though position 2 may sound all right, it is excluded
gradually   1, 2, 3, 4   because it is modifying *leaves* rather than *turned* and is
                               thus not an adverbial.)

Exercise 16–16

1. definite time
2. frequency
3. 1, 4

Exercise 16–17

1. loud	4	Aj
2. Indeed	1	NS
3. madly	5	Av
4. certainly	2	Av
5. singing	4	V
6. frequently	2	Av
7. below	4	NS
8. inside	5	NS
9. eventually	3	Av
10. usually	2	Av
11. around	4	NS
12. here	5	NS
13. still	4	NS
14. already	3	NS
15. rapidly	4	Av

16. seldom	3	NS
17. Meanwhile	1	NS
18. also	4	NS
19. Saturday	4	N
20. everywhere	4	NS

Exercise 16–18

1. 4	5. 1	9. 1
2. 1	6. 4	10. 4
3. 3	7. 1	11. 5
4. 5	8. 1	12. 2

Exercise 16–19

1. N-al	8. N-al	15. N-al
2. Aj-al	9. V-al	16. Av-al
3. Av-al	10. Aj-al	17. Av-al
4. Av-al	11. N-al	18. Av-al
5. N-al	12. Av-al	19. Av-al
6. Av-al	13. Av-al	20. N-al or Aj-al
7. Aj-al	14. Aj-al	

Exercise 16–20

1. N	7. Av	13. Aj
2. V	8. N	14. N
3. N	9. N	15. NS
4. N	10. Aj	
5. NS	11. V	
6. NS	12. NS	

Exercise 16–21

1. VAC	6. VAC
2. V + A	7. VAC
3. VAC	8. V + A
4. V + A	9. VAC
5. VAC	10. VAC

Exercise 16–22

1. VAC + O
2. V + PP
3. VAC + O
4. V + PP

5. VAC + O
6. V + PP

1. V + PP
2. VAC + O
3. VAC + O
4. V + PP
5. VAC + O
6. V + PP

1. VAC + O
2. The pasture in which the horses ran. V + PP
3. VAC + O
4. The moonlight in which the teacher stood drinking. V + PP
5. VAC + O
6. Ambiguous.
   a. VAC + O Looked over = examined.
   b. Her painting over which Keith looked. V + PP
7. The dean on whom we prevailed. V + PP
8. VAC + O
9. The chair over which he stepped. V + PP
10. VAC + O

1. A, B, C
2. A, B, C
3. A, B, C
4. A, B, C
5. A, B, C

6. A, B, C
7. A, B, C
8. A, B, C
9. A, B, C
10. A, B, C

1. On whom did she look down?
2. With whom did McBride make off?
3. With whom did we make up?
4. With whom won't they put up?
5. On whom should we look in?

[The other form of these questions, e.g., "Whom did she look down òn," also suggests that the words in question, *on* and *with,* are prepositions because these words have weak or third stress, and this stress is characteristic of prepositions, not of the adverbials of VACs.]

Exercise 17–1

1. His laughter was loud.
2. The jar is filled with dates.
3. McPherson was a man.
4. The two strolled.
5. The constable laughed.
6. We heard the clank.
7. The squirrel scolded the blue jays.
8. The contract had paragraphs of fine print.
9. The searchers found the car.
10. Claribel jumped.

Exercise 17–2

1. motorcycle
2. sputtered
3. motorcycle
4. stopped
5. stopped
6. nice
7. often
8. stopped
9. fellow
10. whip

Exercise 17–3

1. I knew how to swim, luckily.
2. We climbed in the back window, since the door was closed.
3. The contract is, in fact, invalid. OR The contract, in fact, is invalid.
4. We resumed the normal household routine, the guests having departed.
5. You should be provided with a fly, to keep dry in a tent.
6. He was lucky, considering the circumstances, to escape alive. OR He was lucky to escape alive, considering the circumstances.
7. I will find her, wherever she is.

Exercise 17–4

1. _____
2. Happily
3. _____
4. to tell the truth
5. Hopefully
6. _____
7. Honestly
8. _____
9. Frankly
10. _____

Exercise 17–5

1. a narrow village street
2. this large college dormitory
3. those tall sophomore players
4. that photogenic girl swimmer

5. this enthusiastic senior counselor
6. George's blue wool necktie
7. her old leather shoes
8. his large hardwood desk
9. these cheap ballpoint pens
10. my portable laptop computer

Exercise 17–6

1. a. An arms factory that is small
   b. A factory for small arms
2. a. That stuff for greasy kids
   b. That kid stuff which is greasy
3. a. The service for basic books
   b. The book service that is basic
4. a. A language teacher who is foreign
   b. A teacher of a foreign language
5. a. A car enthusiast who is old
   b. An enthusiast about old cars

Exercise 17–7

1. half your new cement blocks
2. all the long copper wires
3. both her lovely engagement rings
4. all those fresh prairie flowers
5. both my young baby rabbits

Exercise 17–8

1. a. A girl's bicycle that is old
   b. A bicycle for an old girl
2. a. The congress of world women
   b. The women's congress of the world
3. a. A woman's fur coat that is nice
   b. A fur coat of a nice woman
4. a. A garment of a large woman
   b. A woman's garment that is large
5. a. A dictionary for advanced learners
   b. An advanced dictionary for learners

Exercise 17–9

      IVb   II   I
1. Another huge glass ornament
      IVb   II
2. Each rural púmpkin pàtch

    IVb   II   I
3. Some long winter vacations
    V IVa   II   I
4. All our friendly neighborhood dogs
    IVb   II   I
5. Either short cotton dress
     IVb   I
6. Enough college friends
     V   IVa   II
7. Both my studious roommates
    IVb II   I
8. No cold cheese sandwich
     IVb   I
9. Much evening enjoyment
      IVb   II
10. Neither tall Chrístmas trèe

Exercise 17–10

    IVa III   III
1. The last three pickles
    IVa III
2. His every wish
    III   II   I
3. Many fine university seniors
    IVb III   II
4. Some other bad bóok repòrts
    IVb III   II
5. Much more white sand

    IVa III   II
6. Those same hungry ants
    V   IVa III   II
7. Both those two aimless fellows
    IVb III   II
8. Any such childish pranks
     IVa   III
9. Harry's few acquaintances
    IVb III   II
10. What other foolish ideas

Exercise 17–11

    III   II   I
1. Several pink summer flowers
    V IVa II   I
2. Both his old garden hoes
    V IVa   III   II
3. All these three terminal junctures

    IVb   II
4. Another bad examinátion schèdule
    IVa III   II   I
5. My two pretty silk dresses

Exercise 17–12

    IVb   II
1. Any large delívery trùck
    IVb   II
    Any large trúck delìvery

    IVa   II   I
2. That heavy steel construction
    IVa   II
    That heavy constrúction stèel

    IVb   II
3. Some excellent párts fàctory
    IVb   II
Some excellent fáctory pàrts
  IVa   III   II   I
4. The student's long summer vacation
  IVa   III   II
The student's long vacátion sùmmer

    IVa III   II
5. Her first good hóuse dòg
    IVa III   II
Her first good dóg hòuse

(Possessive common nouns, such as *student's* may, as we have seen, occur in different positions. Here we have labeled *student's* a class III.)

Exercise 17-13

    VI   V IVa
1. Especially all our guests
    VI   IVa   I
2. Particularly her photography skills
    VI IVa   II
3. Even the expensive gift
    VI IVb   II
4. Just some white athlétic sòcks
    VI III   II
5. Only ten short minutes

Exercise 17-14

1. 8
2. 3
3. 11
4. 9
5. 7
6. 2
7. 10
8. 6
9. 6
10. 5
11. 10
12. 1
13. 4

Exercise 17-15

1. scarlet . . . exotic
2. expensive
3. stalwart . . . proud
4. new . . . glossy
5. complicated

Exercise 17-16

1. The paragraph abóve → is too lóng.
2. The students hére → are a cóurteous group.

3. This <u>matter</u> <u>tóo</u> → must be discússed.
4. The <u>party</u> <u>yésterday</u> → had a large atténdance.
5. The <u>weather</u> <u>outsíde</u> → is fóul.

Exercise 17–17

1. My older bróther →
2. The discússion →
3. Her fiancé →
4. The rábbits →
5. The mémbers →

Exercise 17–18

1. <u>that time</u>
2. <u>this morning</u>
3. <u>the next time</u>
4. <u>last fall</u>
5. <u>the third hour</u>

Exercise 17–19

1. <u>of the voters</u>	6	7. <u>gliding across the bay</u>	7
2. <u>licking his ice-cream cone</u>	7	8. <u>covered with mud</u>	8
3. <u>to eat</u>	9	9. <u>of the garage</u>	6
4. <u>with the white trim</u>	6	10. <u>tugging at the rope</u>	7
5. <u>urged on by the crowd</u>	8	11. <u>living</u>	7
6. <u>to do</u>	9	12. <u>obtained</u>	8

Exercise 17–20

1. <u>whom</u> he studied with	OP
2. <u>who</u> performed the operation	Subj
3. <u>I ordered</u>	Ø
4. <u>that</u> Jack used	DO
5. <u>whose</u> mother is president of the PTA	Md
6. <u>which</u> had long been our meeting place	Subj
7. <u>that</u> her mother was	SC
8. <u>who</u> immediately won our hearts	Subj
9. <u>who</u> helps me	Subj
10. <u>whom</u> I met at the play	DO

Exercise 17–21 (Your answers need not include intonation numbers.)

1. The blouse that she preferred was made of sea island cotton.   R

         3   1

2. She wore an old blue blóuse ↓ which had always been her favorite.   NR

       3   2

3. The hóuse → which he had long admired, was built of bricks.   NR
4. The house that he built was of steel.   R

       3 2

5. Jáne → who is fond of dictionaries, bought the new *Webster's Third*.   NR
6. The man whom I marry must have curly hair.   R
7. I'll take a man who respects me.   R
8. The car I want is a BMW.   R
9. The student whose purse he returned offered Dick a generous reward.   R

            3   1

10. Thomas bought a silk, red-and-gray-striped nécktie ↓ which his
    roommate admired.   NR

Exercise 17–22

1. <u>why she deserted him</u>   why
2. <u>where we camp</u>   where
3. <u>after he enlisted</u>   after
4. <u>when he comes in</u>   when
5. <u>where I lost it</u>   where

Exercise 17–23

(Relatives are set in regular type; subordinating conjunctions are set in italics)

1. *that*
2. that   DO
3. *that*
4. *that*
5. that   Subj

Exercise 17–24

1. <u>when</u>
2. <u>where</u>
3. <u>after</u>
4. <u>before</u>
5. <u>why</u>

Exercise 17–25

1. <u>the debating club</u>
2. <u>a graduate in journalism</u>
3. <u>offspring of registered parents</u>
4. <u>A Republican from Olga Valley</u>
5. <u>a sluggish, slowly winding stream</u>

Exercise 17–26

	3 1	
1.	*Hámlet* ↓ <u>a play by Shakespeare</u>	NR
2.	*Hamlet*	R
3.	<u>Keith</u>	R
	3 2	
4.	Kéith → <u>my oldest brother</u>	NR
5.	<u>Shelley</u>	R
6.	<u>Severn</u>	R
7.	<u>the Conqueror</u>	R
	3 1	
8.	Býron ↓ <u>a fiery, Romantic poet</u>	NR

Exercise 17–27

1.	angrily	M		11.	happily	M
2.	often	F		12.	anywhere	P
3.	rarely	F		13.	cautiously	M
	carelessly	M			sidewise	P, M
4.	fearfully	M		14.	aloud	M
5.	never	F		15.	timidly	M
	long	D		16.	nights	DT
6.	ahead	P		17.	sleeping	DT
7.	even	O		18.	seated	M
8.	always	F		19.	cleaner	M
	there	P		20.	prepared	M
9.	inside	P				
10.	still	O				

You may have noticed how hard it is in some cases to fit an adverbial into a semantic pigeonhole. For example, do *ahead* (6) and *sidewise* (13) show place, or is it direction? Does *sleeping* (17) indicate time or manner or something else? Are *seated* (18) and *prepared* (20) really adverbials of manner; do they seem to belong in the same class with *angrily* and *carelessly?* Such difficulties often occur with semantic classifications.

Exercise 17–28

1.	Amb			6.	V	
2.	N	V		7.	V	V
3.	V	V		8.	N	
4.	Amb			9.	Amb	
5.	Amb			10.	V	V

Exercise 17–29

1. . . . <u>this Friday</u>
2. . . . <u>the following day</u>
3. . . . <u>the whole way</u>

4. . . . <u>a little while</u>
5. . . . <u>another time</u>

Exercise 17–30

1. D   Aux
2. D   SCj
3. SCj   P

4. SCj   Aux
5. Q   SCj

Exercise 17–31

1. C
2. Md
3. C
4. Md
5. C

6. C
7. C
8. C
9. Md
10. C

Exercise 17–32

1. CAv
2. NP
3. CAv
4. NP
5. PP
6. CAv
7. PP
8. CAv

9. NP   NP
10. CAv
11. NP
12. CAv
13. NP
14. CAv
15. CAv

Exercise 17–33

1. DO
2. AM
3. DO

4. AM
5. AM

Exercise 17–34

1. VM
2. VM
3. VM or NM
4. NM
5. VM

6. VM
7. VM or NM
8. NM
9. VM
10. VM or NM

Exercise 17–35

1. 1

2. 4

3. 2		7. 3
4. 6		8. 1
5. 3		9. 2
6. 5		10. 5

Exercise 17–36

1. Nom	9. Aj
2. Av	10. Nom
3. Aj	11. Aj
4. Aj	12. Av
5. Av	13. Aj
6. Aj	14. Nom
7. Aj	15. Aj
8. Aj	

Exercise 17–37

1. <u>that women are poor drivers</u>
2. <u>that Mink had been cheating</u>
3. <u>that water runs only downhill</u>
4. <u>that leaked badly</u>
5. <u>that the stars influence our lives</u>
6. <u>that the stars influence our lives</u>

Exercise 17–38

1. <u>to buy the whole lot</u>
2. <u>to raise money for the needy</u>
3. <u>to love</u>
4. <u>to register late</u>
5. <u>to watch</u>
6. <u>to win</u>
7. <u>to practice daily</u>
8. <u>to admire</u>
9. <u>to stay away from the telephone</u>
10. <u>to live within her budget</u>

Exercise 17–39

1. DO	6. CAj	11. CAj
2. CAj	7. DO	12. Av-al
3. CAj	8. CAj	13. CAj
4. CAj	9. Av-al	14. CAj
5. DO	10. CAj	15. CAj

Exercise 17–40

1. <u>and</u>
   personal pronouns
2. <u>yet</u>
   adverbs
3. <u>or</u>
   nominal clauses
4. <u>for</u>
   sentences
5. <u>not</u>
   prepositional phrases

6. <u>so</u>
   sentences
7. <u>but</u>
   verb phrases
8. <u>nor</u>
   sentences
9. <u>or</u>
   infinitives
10. <u>and</u>   <u>and</u>
    present participles   verbs

Exercise 17–41

1. <u>Either</u> . . . <u>or</u>
   sentences
2. <u>both</u> . . . <u>and</u>
   prepositional phrases
3. <u>neither</u> . . . <u>nor</u>
   noun phrases

4. <u>not only</u> . . . <u>but</u>
   adjectives
5. <u>not</u> . . . <u>but</u>
   noun phrases
6. <u>whether</u> . . . <u>or</u>
   infinitives

Exercise 18–1

(The answers to this exercise will vary depending on the usage dictionaries that you consult. But we will briefly indicate what issues are at stake with each of the three items.)

1. *Disinterested* vs. *uninterested.* Many speakers use *disinterested* and *uninterested* as synonyms to describe someone who is bored or has no desire to pay attention to something. The tendency to use these words interchangeably is understandable, given the similar use of the prefixes *dis-* and *un-*. Some speakers, however, maintain a careful distinction between the two words. For these speakers, *uninterested* conveys the meaning of being bored, whereas *disinterested* conveys the idea of not having a special self-serving bias in how something turns out. Along these lines we would, for example, hope that anyone judging a matter would be disinterested. The distinction between the two terms has largely been lost.
2. Some prescriptive grammarians object to the use of *hopefully* as a sentence modifier. The objection to this is perhaps based, at least in part, on the fear that the use of the word as a sentence modifier could then create an ambiguity with its use as a modifier of a verb. Such a confusion, however, would be rare. The intended meaning of *hopefully* when it is used as a sentence modifier is very clear.
3. The use of *appreciate* to mean "thanks" has been criticized by some prescriptivists as an attempt to stop short of saying "thank you" and thus an undesirable form. But its use is now widespread enough that there should no longer be a problem with using the expression.

Exercise 18–2

1. every day
2. everyday
3. every day
4. of
5. have
6. have
7. too
8. too
9. to
10. too
11. to

Exercise 18–3

1. [no change]
2. cost-effective
3. no-nonsense
4. [no change]
5. changing-tables
6. [no change]
7. free-loading
8. [no change]
9. [no change]
10. big-wig
11. [no change]
12. The book, which . . . days, ...
13. [no change]
14. The thief, who . . . careless, ...
15. [no change]
16. His animosity, which . . . unexplainable, ...

Exercise 18–4

1. Back-formation
2. The foreign plural form was not used.
3. No problem (the double *e* merely resembles but is not related to the suffix *-ee* we have been discussing).
4. This acronym should be capitalized.
5. The adverb is missing an *-ly.*
6. The foreign plural was not used.
7. Overuse of the suffix *-ize*
8. Overuse of the suffix *-ly*
9. Unnecessary capitalization of an acronym
10. No problem

11. Informal clipping
12. Overuse of the suffix *-ee*
13. No problem

Exercise 18–5

1. No
2. Yes
3. No
4. Yes
5. No
6. No
7. Yes (Despite a superficial resemblance, this sentence does not involve a split infinitive.)
8. No
9. Yes
10. Yes
11. No
12. Yes
13. No
14. Yes

Exercise 18–6

1. is
2. is
3. helps
4. are
5. are
6. is
7. was (But it might be better to reorder the subject.)
8. were
9. is
10. is
11. is (*Is* would be the prescribed form, even though *are* is commonly used, particularly in speech.)
12. was
13. is
14. is (Some prescriptivists might allow for *are* in this sentence.)
15. drive
16. appears

Exercise 18–7

1. me
2. Jessica's
3. Whom

 4. myself
 5. who
 6. whom
 7. your
 8. bad
 9. Ted
10. protestors
11. badly
12. me
13. I
14. Who

Exercise 18–8

 1. lying
 2. laid
 3. laid
 4. lay
 5. lain
 6. lie
 7. lies
 8. laid
 9. laying
10. lay
11. Lie

Exercise 18–9

1. Yes
2. No
3. Yes
4. Yes
5. No
6. No
7. No
8. Yes

Exercise 18–10

1. OK
2. Not OK, fragment
3. OK
4. Not OK, fragment
5. Not OK, comma splice
6. OK
7. OK (Imperatives have an implied subject.)
8. Not OK, fused sentence

9. Not OK, fragment
10. Not OK, fragment
11. OK
12. Not OK, fragment (The addition of the extra word has turned this into a subordinate clause.)
13. Not OK, comma splice
14. OK
15. Not OK, fragment
16. Not OK, comma splice
17. OK

Exercise 18–11

1. Yes
2. Yes
3. No
4. Yes
5. No
6. No
7. No

Exercise 18–12 (Your rewritten sentences may vary.)

1. Dangling modifier
   While I was sleeping in bed, the smoke detector started buzzing.
2. Dangling modifier
   The final straw for the man, already tired and angry, occurred when the dishwasher broke.
3. Misplaced modifier
   The money a person needs to purchase a car is phenomenal.
4. Misplaced modifier
   We took to the veterinarian the dogs that had fleas.
5. Misplaced modifier
   The children avoided the car that was leaking gas dangerously.
6. Dangling modifier
   The professor having taught the class, the chalk and eraser were no longer needed.
7. Misplaced modifier
   The attorney brought the jury a case without a leg to stand on.

Exercise 19–1

1. p
2. c (but actually the /k/ sound)
3. p
4. c (/k/)

5. p
6. t
7. p
8. t
9. c (/k/)
10. t
11. c (/k/)

Exercise 19–2

1. p
2. t
3. k
4. f
5. θ ("th")
6. h

Exercise 19–3

1. tree
2. fishy
3. eat
4. know
5. lip
6. foot
7. fatherly
8. head
9. kind

Exercise 19–4

1. *-s*
2. gone
3. *-'s* (The apostrophe indicates that the vowel *-e* has been removed.)
4. gone
5. gone
6. gone (But the form *-eth* survived as late as the seventeenth century in England and even longer in particular religious contexts.)
7. gone (Like 6 above, the form *-est* survived for a while and even continues in some very specialized contexts.)
8. *-ed*

Exercise 19–5

1. [e]
2. [e]

3. [i]
4. [ay]
5. [o]
6. [u]
7. [aw]

Exercise 19–6

In Modern English the first auxiliary verb within the main clause of the sentence is moved to the front for questions. In the case of negative statements, the word *not* must be placed after the first auxiliary verb. If no auxiliary verb is present for a question or negative statement, an appropriate form of the auxiliary *do* must be used. In the Early Modern English of Shakespeare's time, questions and negatives did not need to locate or move an auxiliary. Questions could begin with the main verb, which was moved to the front, and negative statements could place the negative word *not* after the main verb, or in the case of a transitive verb, after the direct object, which followed the verb.

Exercise 19–7

1. Attorney
2. Baby buggy/carriage
3. Billboard
4. Checkers
5. Diaper
6. Drug store
7. Flashlight
8. Hood
9. Potato chips
10. Sneakers
11. Thumbtack
12. Trashcan
13. Truck
14. Trunk
15. Vest
16. Windshield
17. Wrench

Exercise 19–8

1. relative
2. modal(s)
3. auxiliary
4. *more*
5. lax, tense
6. *-in'*
7. *seen*

8. object
9. glide (semivowel)

Exercise 19–9

1. No
2. Yes
3. No
4. No
5. No
6. Yes
7. No
8. Yes
9. No
10. Yes

Exercise 19–10

1. The use of *learn* to mean *teach.*
2. The use of *right* as an adverbial to modify an adjective.
3. Double superlative.
4. Multiple negation.
5. The lack of *-ly* on an adverb of manner.
6. Subject-verb agreement problem.
7. Nonstandard past-tense form.
8. Nonstandard use of the prefix *a-* with a present participle.
9. Nonstandard past-tense form.
10. The use of *which* rather than *who* as a relative pronoun for people.

Exercise 19–11

1. You can't teach an old dog new tricks.
2. Beauty is only skin deep.
3. All's fair in love and war.
4. Birds of a feather flock together.
5. Don't cry over spilled milk.
6. Beauty is in the eye of the beholder.
7. Where there's smoke, there's fire.
8. Pride goes before a fall.
9. United we stand; divided we fall.
10. A bird in the hand is worth two in the bush.
11. People who live in glass houses shouldn't throw stones.
12. Sticks and stones may break my bones, but names will never hurt me.
13. The love of money is the root of all evil.
14. You can't judge a book by its cover.
15. You can lead a horse to water, but you can't make it drink.

1. The angry man left.

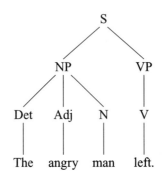

2. Our sister watched the man.

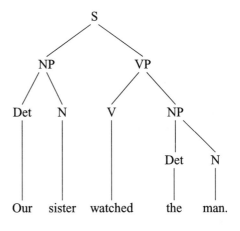

3. Marleen saw gray cats.

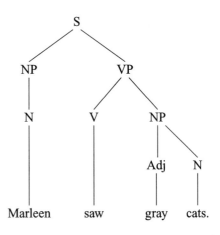

4. The answer to the question
   surprised Jim.

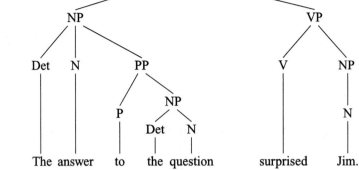

5. John sneezed.

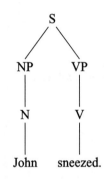

6. The student wrote her paper with the computer.

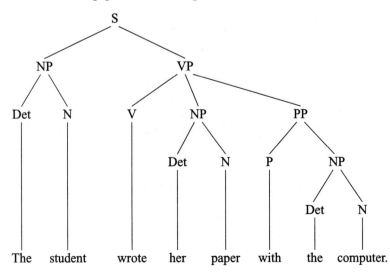

7. Large deficits lead to problems.

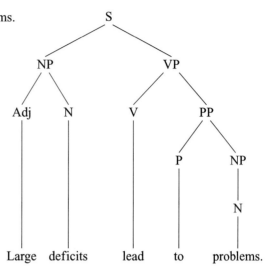

8. My sympathy for her problems diminished.

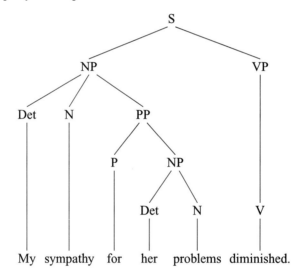

Index

Credits

The introductory quotation at the beginning of Chapter 11 on page 137 is reprinted with permission of Pocket Books, a Division of Simon & Schuster, Inc., from *Crazy English* by Richard Lederer. Copyright © 1989 by Richard Lederer.

The Old English version of "The Lord's Prayer" on page 347 is from *A History of the English Language* 4th ed. by Albert C. Baugh & Thomas Cable, © 1993. Reprinted by permission of Prentice-Hall, Inc., Upper Saddle River, NJ.

The words for exercise 19-7 on pages 356–57 as well as the answers on page 462 are excerpted from *The English Language* by David Crystal. London: Penguin Books, 1988. Pages 249–50. Copyright © David Crystal, 1988. All rights reserved. Reproduced by permission of Penguin Books Ltd.

The proverb selections in exercise 19-11 on pages 364–65 as well as the answers on page 463 are excerpted with permission of Pocket Books, a Division of Simon & Schuster, Inc., from *The Play of Words* by Richard Lederer. Copyright © 1990 by Richard Lederer.